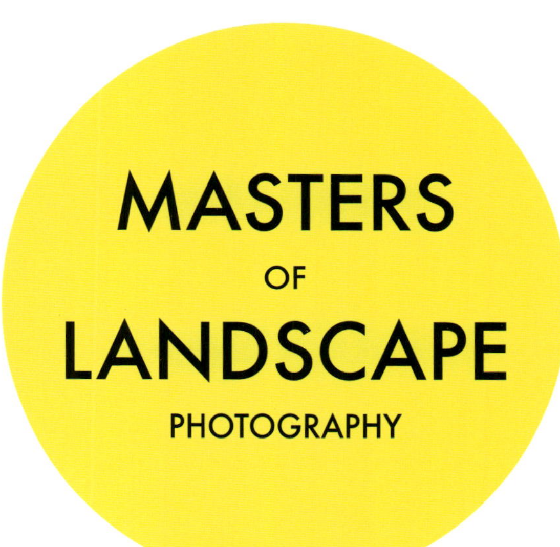

MASTERS
OF
LANDSCAPE
PHOTOGRAPHY

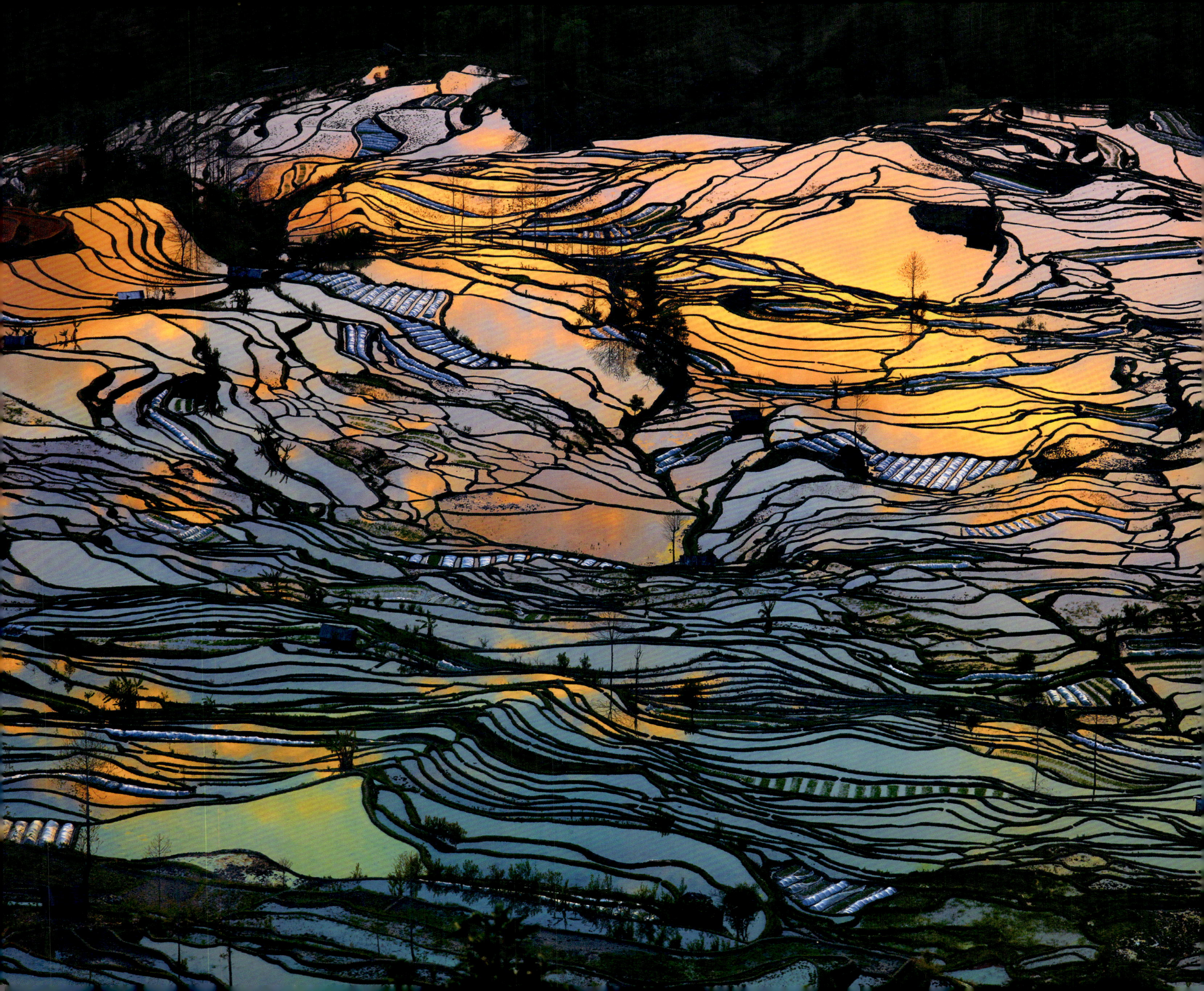

MASTERS

OF

LANDSCAPE

PHOTOGRAPHY

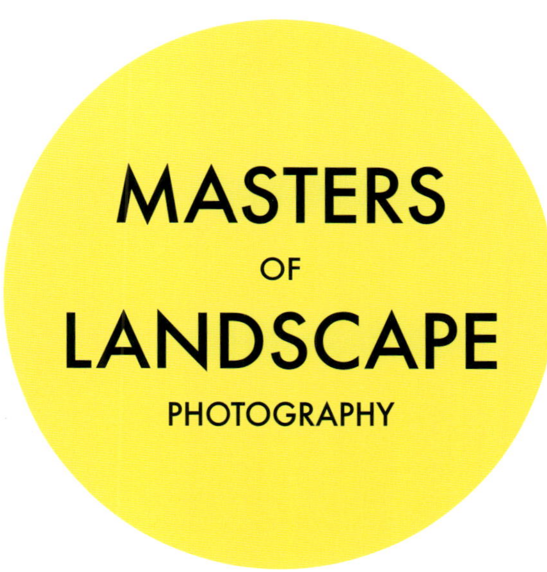

CONSULTANT EDITOR: ROSS HODDINOTT
FOREWORD: ROBERT MACFARLANE
EDITOR: ROB YARHAM

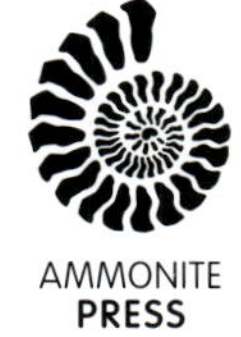

AMMONITE
PRESS

First published 2017 by
Ammonite Press
an imprint of Guild of Master Craftsman Publications Ltd
Castle Place, 166 High Street, Lewes, East Sussex, BN7 1XU,
United Kingdom
www.ammonitepress.com

Reprinted 2022

ISBN 978 1 78145 320 9

Publisher: Jason Hook
Designer: Robin Shields
Editor: Rob Yarham

Color reproduction by GMC Reprographics
Printed and bound in China

Front cover image: © Ross Hoddinott
Title page image: © Thierry Bornier

CONTENTS

FOREWORD

We live in a golden age of landscape pornography. Never before in the history of representation has landscape been so ubiquitously pictured and so lustfully consumed in the form of image. Instagram, Twitter and Tumblr teem with hundreds of millions of hyper-saturated sunsets and immaculate reflections.

That this profusion should coincide with catastrophic habitat loss, the sixth great extinction pulse, and the near-abolition at the planetary level of the possibility of wilderness, is of course no accident. We use these images to deceive ourselves: that all is well with the world and all will be well; that nature remains imperishably available for our remote gratification. We circulate such photographs between ourselves by the billion each year, passing these counters of consolation from screen to screen. The cumulative effect is one of anaesthetised passivity: a dulled knowledge that something is drastically wrong with our environment, combined with a dulled willingness to mend it for the good.

One might reasonably have expected this flood of imagery to have annihilated landscape photography as an art. Yet as this extraordinary book proves, we also live—against the odds, and thrillingly—in a golden age of landscape photography. Every image in the pages that follow possesses a power to grip the heart, gasp the lungs, or unsettle the conscience. Every image provokes a response categorically more committal than the finger-tap of a social-media "like". The work of these 'masters of landscape' changes one's sense of the world: leaves it somehow brighter around the edges, darker in its currents, or more lively in its energies.

Joe Cornish quotes Ansel Adams on the camera's role as, at its best, "an instrument of love and revelation", and that phrase could stand as epigraph to the collection as a whole. There is a striking humility to the way these photographers characterize and practice their work: a deliberate move away from a (neo-colonial) 'taking' of images and 'shooting' of the landscape, towards something much more like pilgrimage—in which process and journey supersede destination. Photographers, as Colin Prior memorably puts it, must learn to place themselves "in the way of a situation that has yet to develop". Throughout this book, appealingly to me, mystery replaces mastery and ecocentricism is preferred to egocentricism.

The contributors here are all, unmistakably, artists. Most have passed briefly at some point in their careers through a 'realist' phase of photography, and then moved beyond that—by means of technique and technology, certainly, but also by shifts of vision—into art. Thus the repeated references to painters as inspirations upon general atmospheres or specific compositions: Edvard Munch, Georges Braque, Albert Bierstadt, the Pointillists . . . All of the painters named are men, and it would be remiss of me not to mention the maleness of this book: evident not only in the gender imbalance of the contributors, but also in the roster of tutelary names invoked, from Adams through Rowell, Bierstadt to Braque. That there are only two women among these sixteen 'masters' is both cause for regret and cause for hope. The regret is obvious; the hope is that the example of this book and the work it contains may inspire more diversity of all kinds among landscape photographers of the future.

For too long now we have been content with an understanding of "landscape" as a passive backdrop to human life: an aesthetic surface that we are 'on' but not 'in'. This sense is, fascinatingly, already present at the moment of the word's arrival into English in the early 1600s. 'Landscape' comes from the Dutch 'landschap', a technical term from painting that means 'a picture representing natural inland scenery'. These connotations of 'landscape' as painterly, inert and submissive to the gaze are strongly with us still. The standard synonyms for 'landscape' offered by the Microsoft Word thesaurus are "scenery", "scene", "setting", "background", "backcloth" and "backdrop". For some years now I have argued that we need a vastly more dynamic understanding of "landscape" as a force that shapes us and scapes us, a presence that infiltrates our minds and our bodies, a medium with which we are reciprocal and on which we depend.

The astonishing photographs that follow here all catch at this dynamism of landscape, and all perform its vibrancy. They help us—to borrow the title of one of Marc Adamus's images—to look through 'the eye of ice' (or the eye of stone, or the eye of water, or the eye of wood, or the eye of cloud) and in this way briefly to see the planet as it might see itself.

Robert Macfarlane, 2017

INTRODUCTION

master v. to acquire complete knowledge or skill in a subject, technique, or art.

Is it actually possible to master photography—or any other art form, for that matter? Landscape photography is as subjective as it is varied and popular. And that means it is surely impossible to say one photograph—or photographer—is better than another, as so much is down to personal taste. While this is undoubtedly true, the skill, mastery, innovation, and vision of some photographers simply stand out for all to see.

Of course, they themselves would never dare suggest that they are masters of their art. They remain humble in the knowledge that there is always so much to learn: skills to hone, a style to develop, and a philosophy that will continue to evolve. They fully understand that there is no such thing as the perfect photograph, and yet they continue to strive for perfection. Their desire to capture and highlight the beauty and diversity of our planet in their own unique style is their drive and motivation, while their understanding of light and visual balance, and their ability to convey mood enable them to produce extraordinary images that leave viewers breathless. Even if it is true that you cannot fully master photography, photographers such as these have surely earned the privilege of being considered masters of their profession.

Much has changed since the days when the pioneering landscape photographer Ansel Adams captured his large-format images of the American West. Surely, no genre of photography is more popular today than landscape, while the innovation of digital imaging has made creating such photographs more accessible than ever before. And there are so many modern landscape photographers who stand out

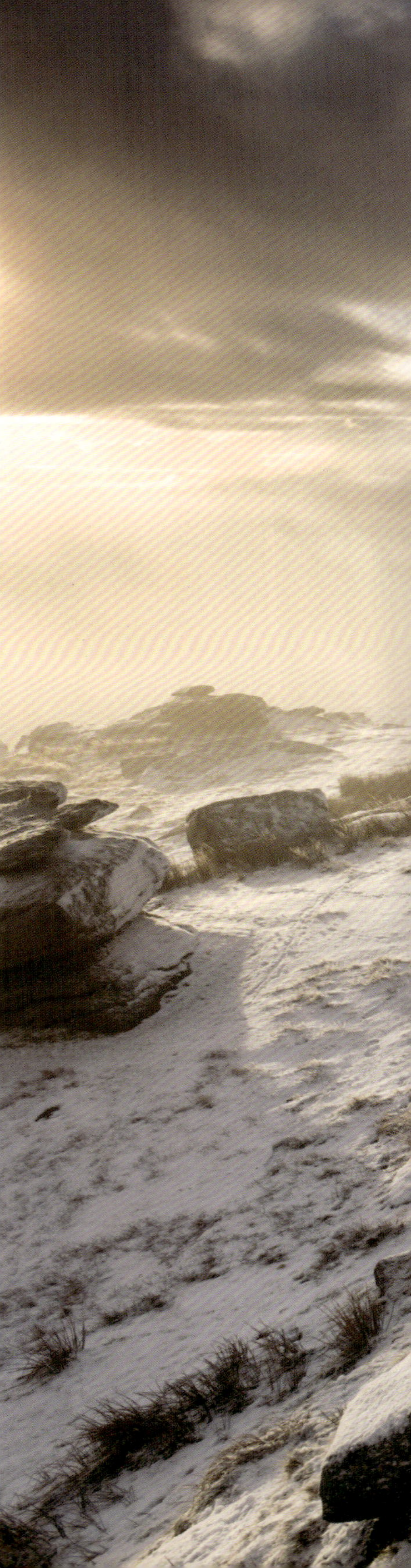

GREAT MIS TOR

For landscape photographers, there is an exceptionally fine line between success and failure. Magical conditions are rare and light is transient. Moments before this image was taken, the fog was still thick. I had waited for hours, was cold, frustrated and ready to give up. My persistence was rewarded, though, as the cloud briefly cleared to produce a few moments of magic. These are the moments photographers live for.

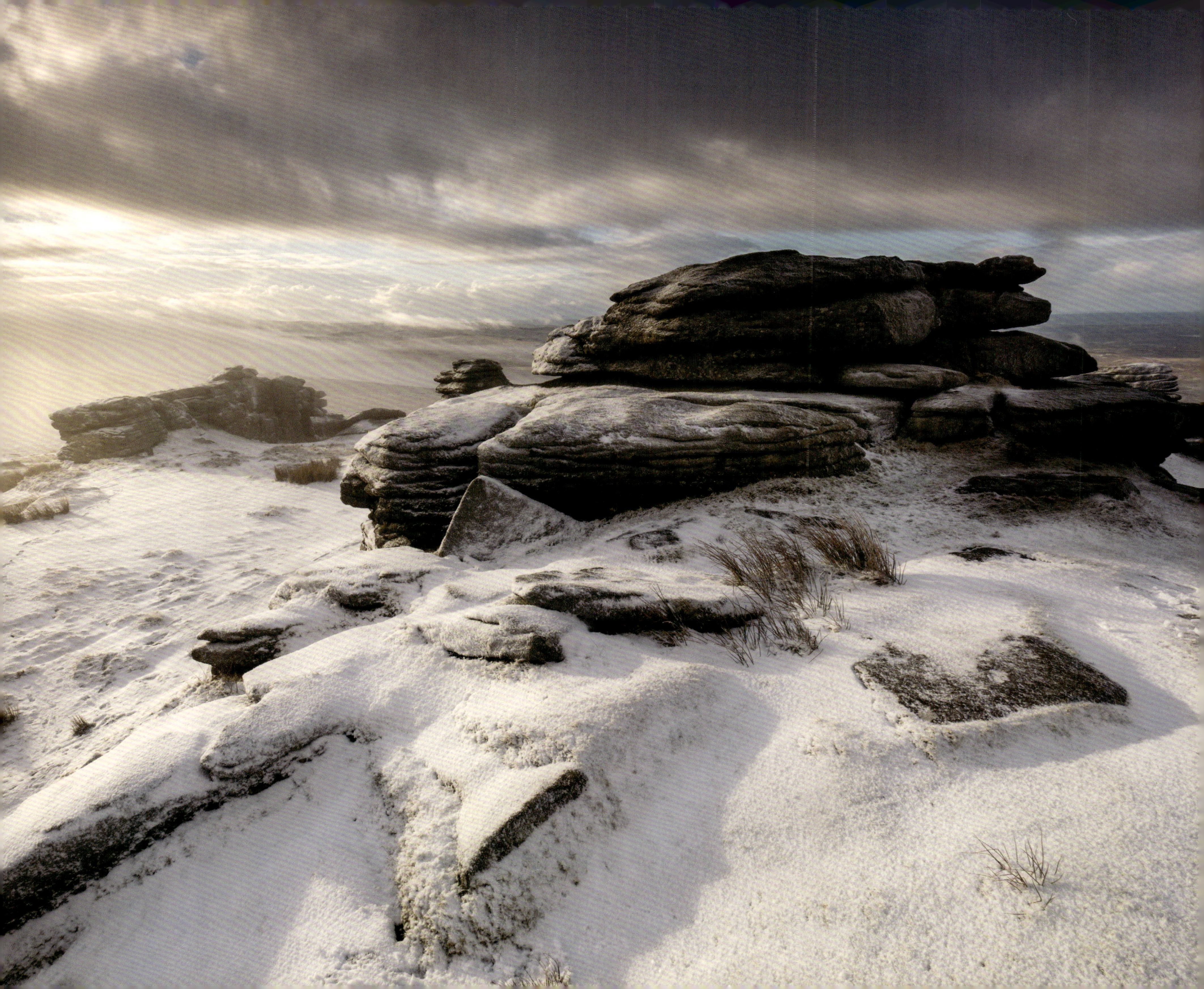

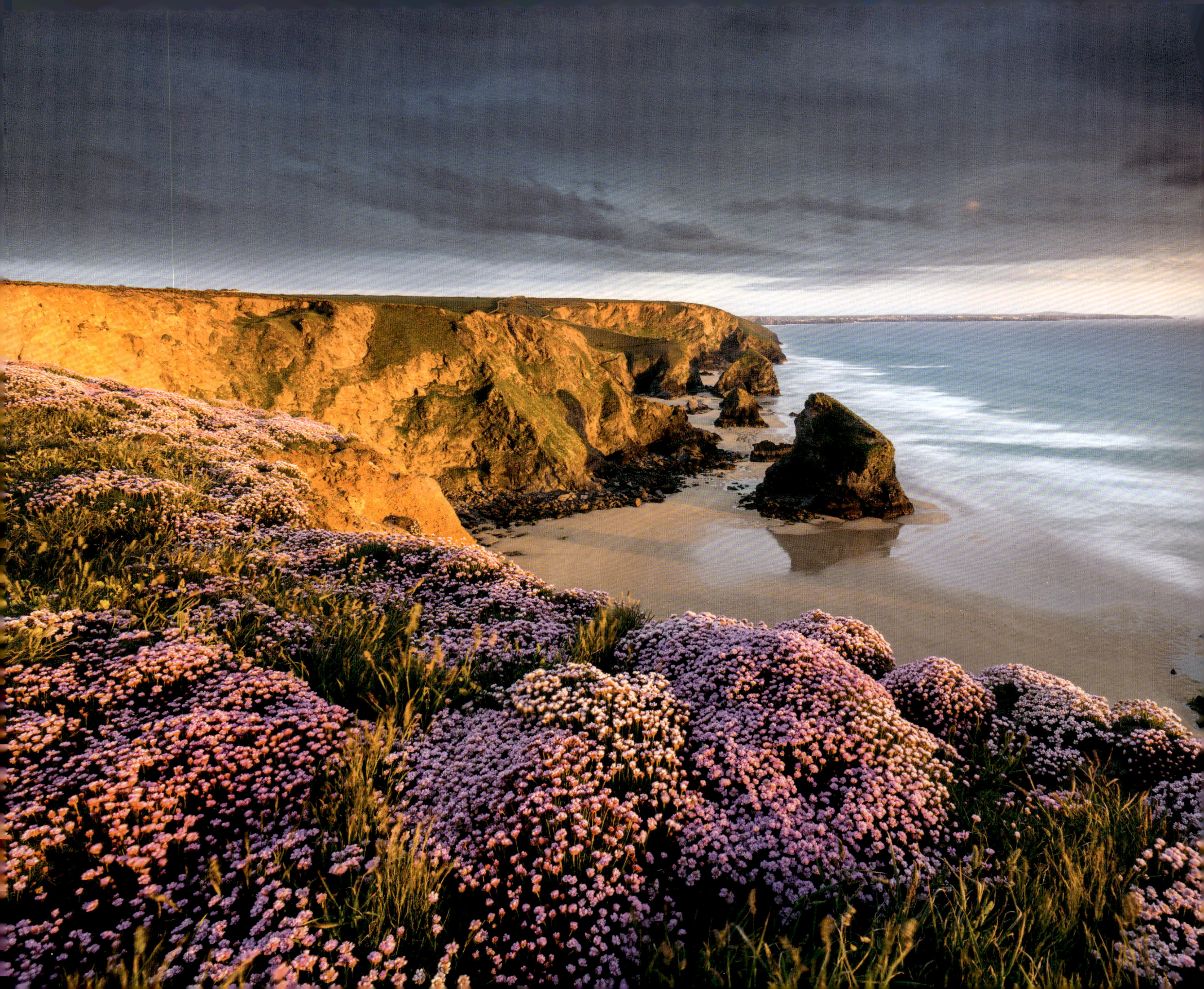

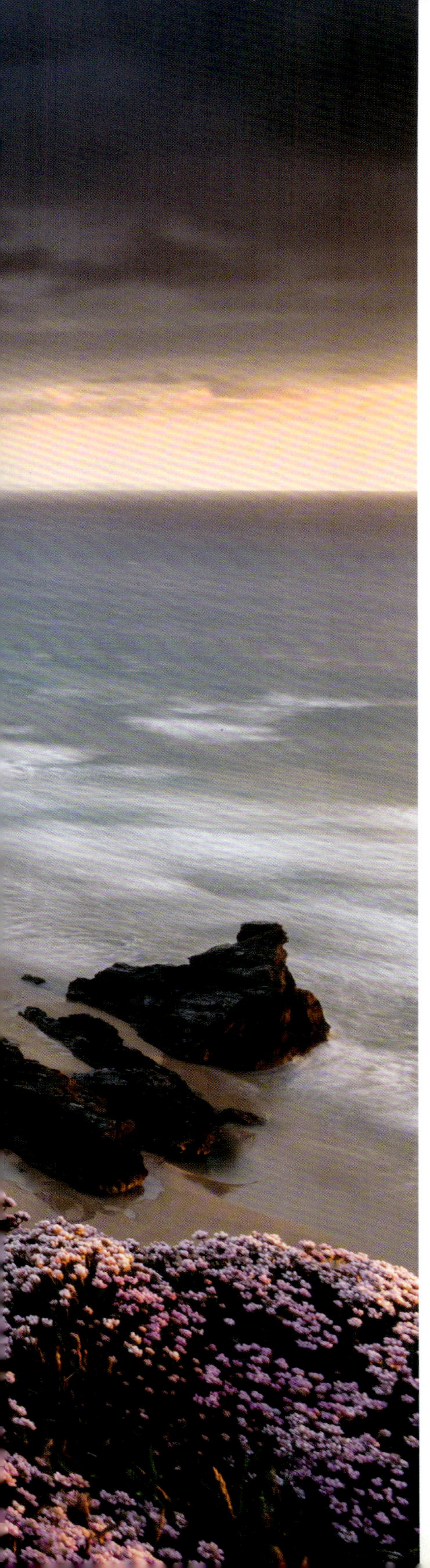

for a wide variety of reasons. Yet, there is only room in this book to feature just a handful. How can you possibly differentiate or choose between them? Of course, it is impossible to say one photographer is better than another, and that is certainly not the aim of this book. Instead, in the lavishly illustrated pages that follow, we celebrate our planet's beauty, as well as the skill and dedication of just some of the talented photographers who set out to capture it.

Each photographer has been carefully chosen because of their pedigree and reputation in what is becoming an increasingly competitive and crowded field. You don't reach the very top of any creative profession without being versatile or multi-skilled, and all our featured photographers have mastered many different techniques and genres, as a look at the website galleries and published work listed at the back of the book demonstrates. But here, each photographer has agreed to select for us just a few of their creations in a particular field, to better illustrate the wide range of skills and specializations in landscape photography—such as a certain landscape type, a style, an approach, or a perspective. The result is a publication with an irresistible blend of spectacular landscape images, showcasing how the landscape can be interpreted in different, sometimes contrasting, ways.

We have also asked each photographer to share the stories behind their chosen images, to give us a better understanding of their thought processes and outlook at the moment they triggered the shutter. Each chapter features Question and Answer sections, too, to provide the reader with a real insight into the techniques and equipment they employ, as well as their creative philosophies. So, sit back and enjoy this wonderful visual celebration. We hope this unique look into the lives of some of the world's master landscape photographers will inspire you, and may even set you on your own path to success . . .

Ross Hoddinott, 2017

BEDRUTHAN STEPS

Careful research, planning, preparation, and timing still offer no guarantee you will be rewarded with a great shot. Often, the most important ingredient is out of our control—the drama and light created by weather. All a landscape photographer can do is to place themselves in the right place, and just hope it is the right time.

MASTER OF CONSERVATION
ART WOLFE

Art Wolfe is one of the world's leading nature and landscape photographers. The son of commercial artists, he was born in 1951 in Seattle, Washington, where he still lives. He graduated from the University of Washington with degrees in fine art and art education. Since then, his photography career has spanned five decades, a remarkable testament to the durability and demand for his images, his expertise, and his passionate advocacy for the environment and indigenous culture. During that time he has worked on every continent, and on a dazzling array of projects.

Art's unique approach to photography is based on his training in the arts and his love of the environment, and promotes conservation issues by "focusing on what's beautiful on the Earth." He is a pioneer in the field of conservation photography, creating one of the world's first conservation-themed photography competitions. Art has taken an estimated two million images in his lifetime, and travels nearly nine months out of the year photographing for new projects, leading photographic tours and seminars, and giving inspirational presentations to corporate, educational, conservation, and spiritual groups. Art's photographs have appeared in hundreds of magazines and books, and have been exhibited in museums and galleries worldwide.

ALSEK LAKE

This is a great example of how a single salient photo can capture the spirit of a place, touch people on an emotional level, and rally support. You look at the photo and cannot but think, "Of course, this must be saved, especially for generations to come." Over the decades, it has been driven home to me time and time again that, yes, a single photo can be an exceptionally important conservation tool, connecting with people on a visceral level. I captured this image while on a rafting trip to photograph the Tatshenshini River in the Yukon, which was threatened by the development of a massive copper mine. Everything downstream of this mine would be affected; environmental calamity knows no borders. Not only would it affect waters and lands on the Canadian side of the border, but the mine drainage would flow downstream into Glacier Bay and affect the rich fisheries and wildlife in the Gulf of Alaska. This became the image that was used to convince lawmakers in Canada and the US to oppose the mine and instead create the Tatshenshini-Alsek Park, now a UNESCO World Heritage Site.

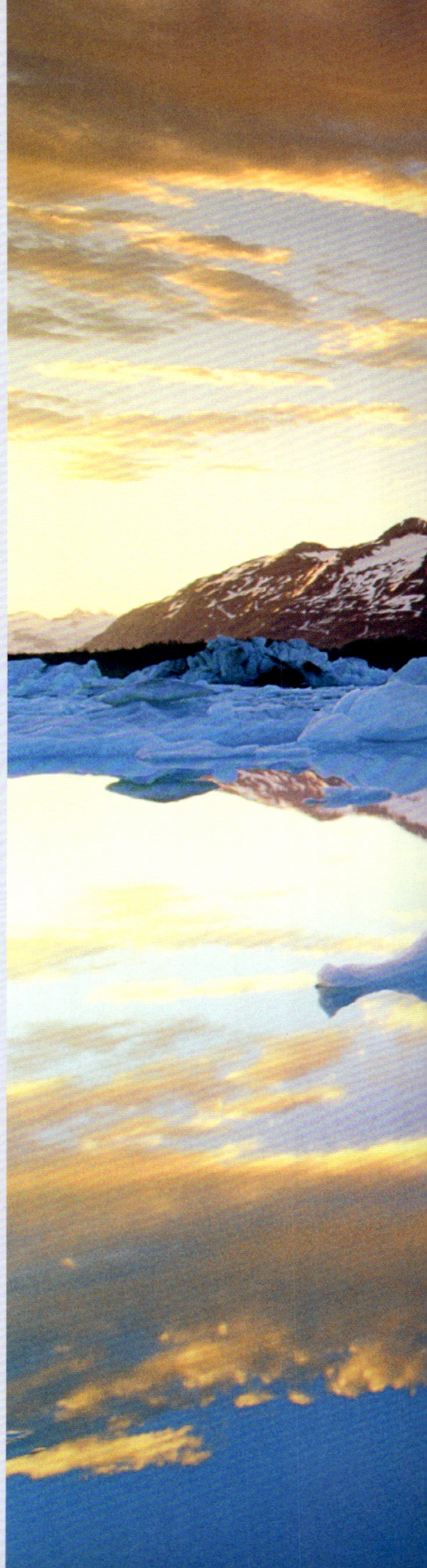

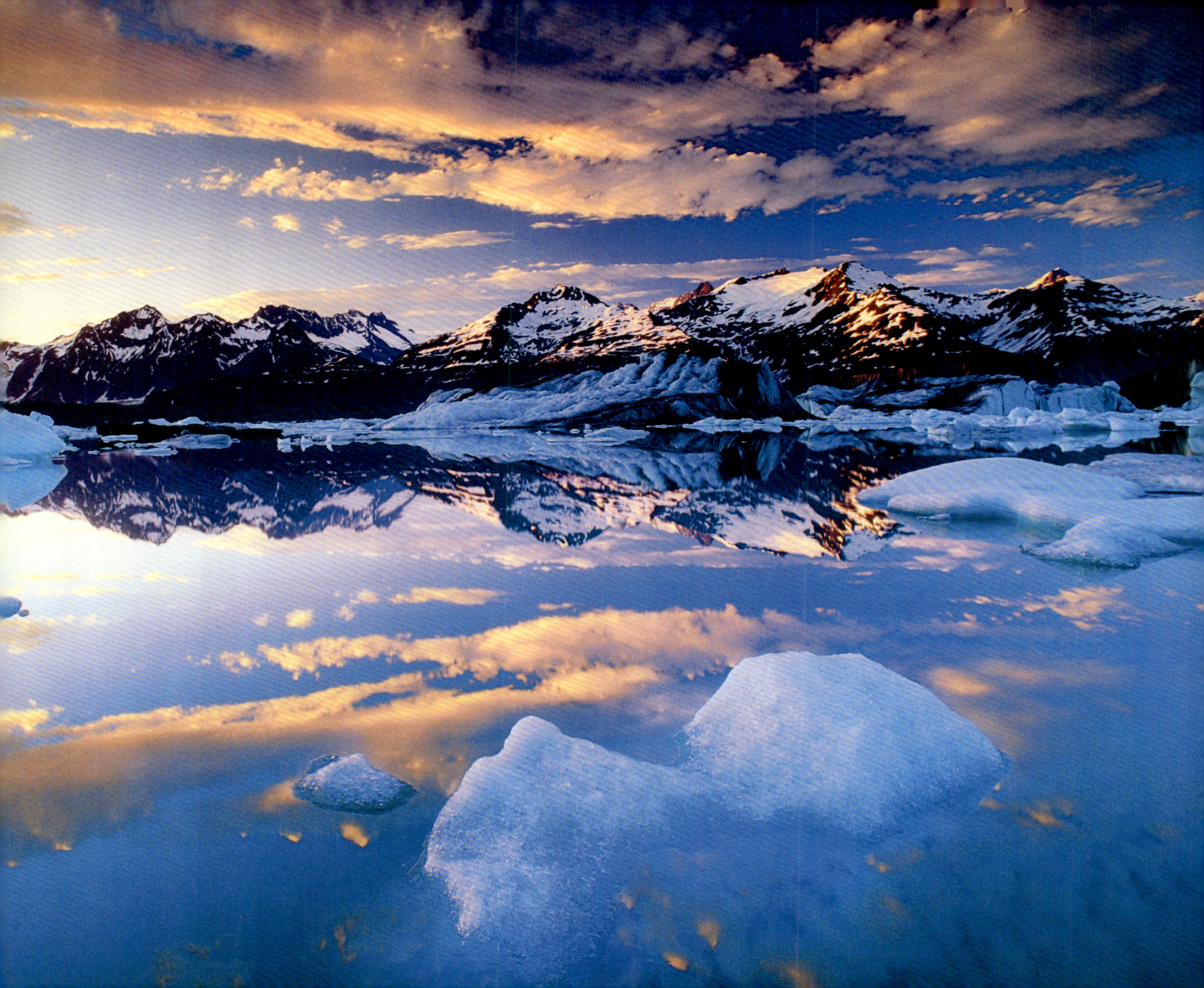

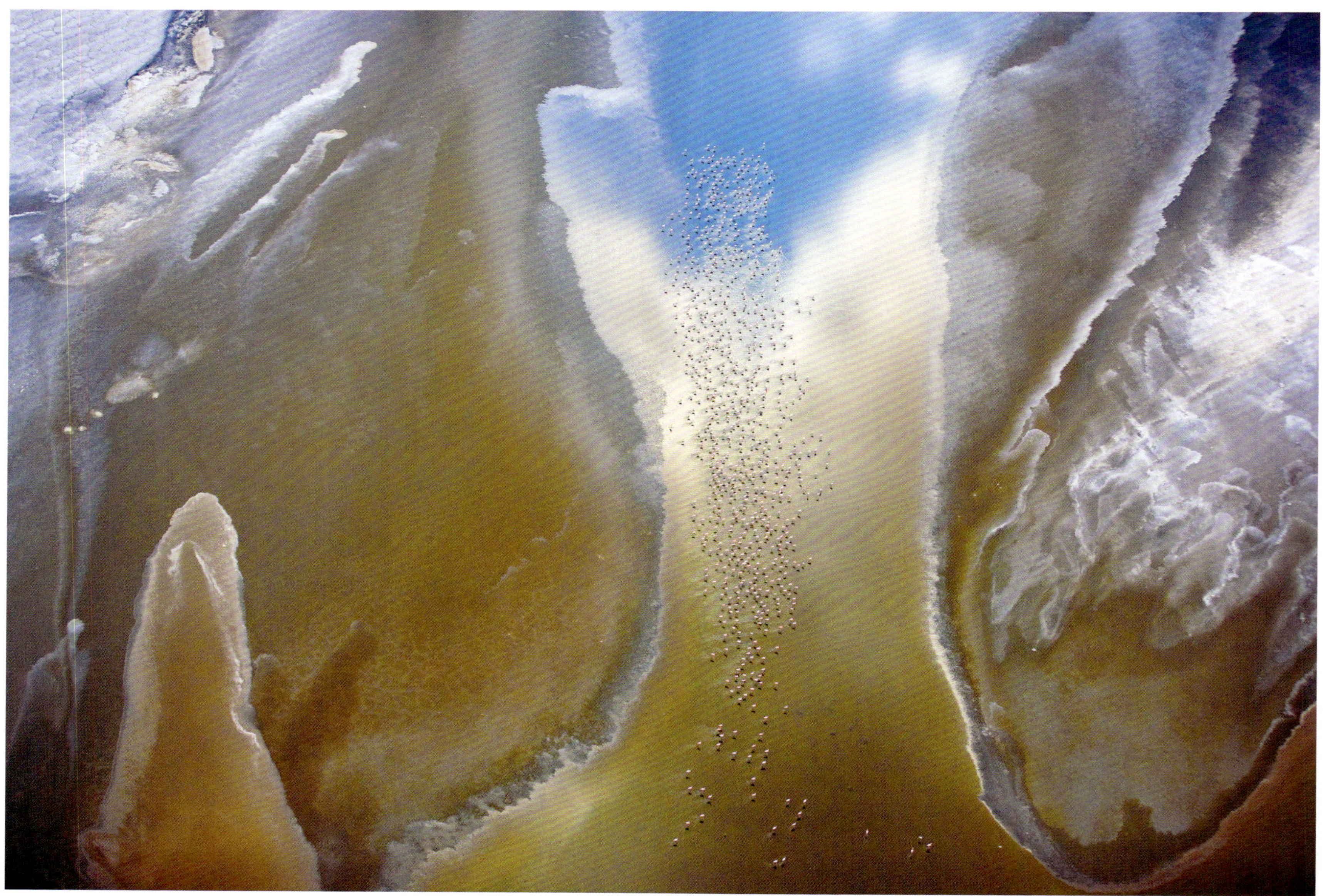

AERIAL, LAKE NATRON

Natron is an endless joy to photograph. It is constantly changing and alive with flocks of birds, especially flamingos. The first time I photographed the soda lakes of East Africa from an ultralight, I thought I was going to die, because the reflections of the clouds and light were so disorienting. The multi-hued water gets its colors from algae, salts, and minerals.

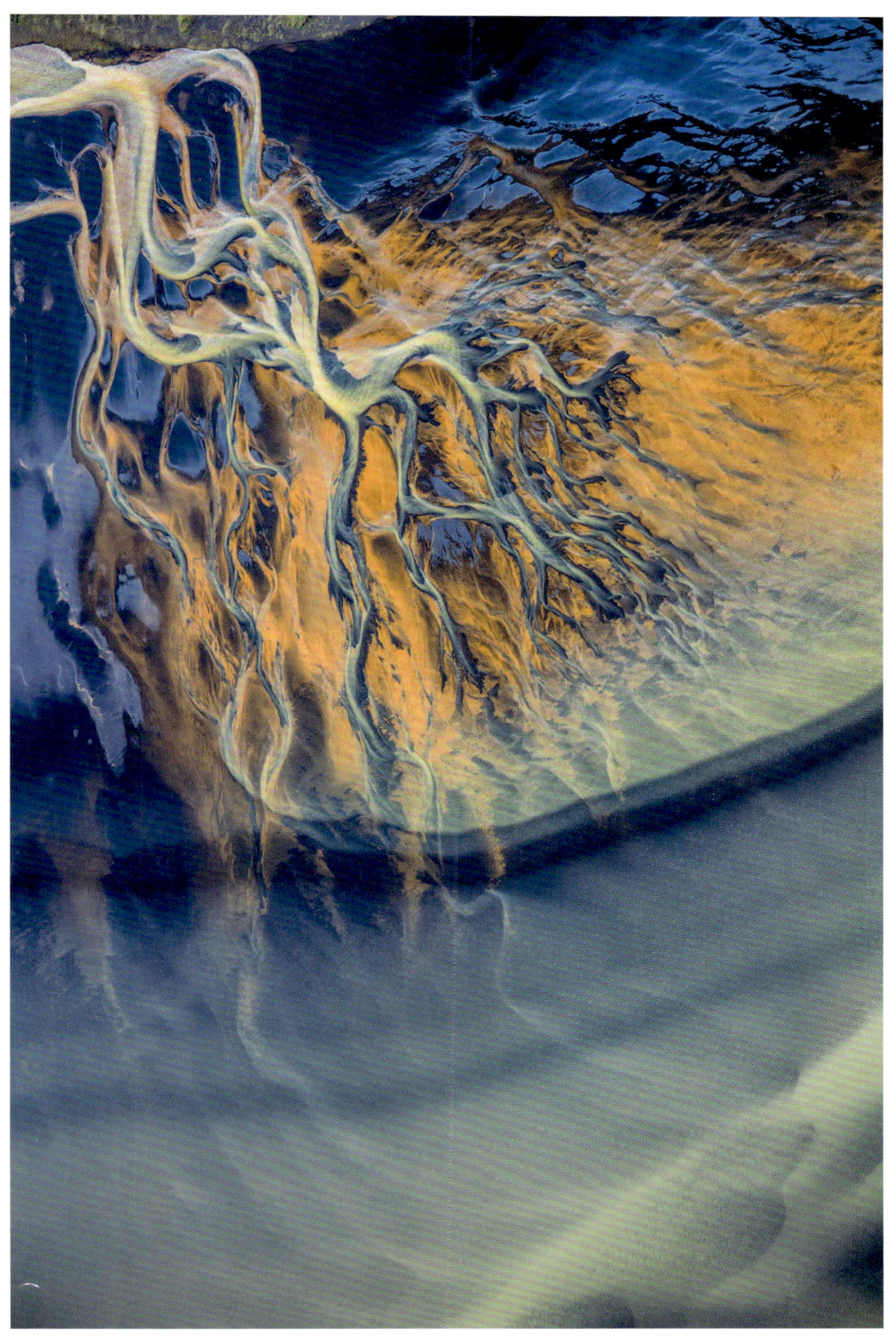

RIVER DELTA AERIAL

Geologically young, Iceland formed only 10 million years ago, when oceanic volcanoes erupted along the Earth's tectonic plates, resulting in this rapidly changing landscape. These aerial views display the exquisite beauty of erosion patterns on floodplains left by jökulhlaups—the glacier bursts that occur when geothermal heat melts subglacial ice and water bursts through in a catastrophic flood.

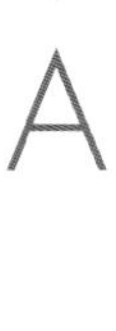

Q + A

How much planning and research go into a typical Art Wolfe shoot?

This is such a critical part of the business as my schedule is planned out years in advance, yet it has to be flexible enough to allow for last-minute changes. Yes, there is serendipity involved with photography, but you also create your own luck. I get a lot of recommendations, warnings, and tips from other travelers, friends, and associates. I bring these ideas back to the office and, together with my small staff, we sift and research to find what is best for my current projects. The web is an amazing resource, but it is only one aspect. Getting on the phone and talking to people on the ground is still extremely relevant. I first try to anticipate the photographs I hope to take. I then get organized by acquiring the necessary maps and travel books, in addition to the web—I like both analog and digital sources. Any special permits or visas for a particular location are researched beforehand. I also rely on guides and fixers during my visit. Then I plan all the travel connections, from the massive jetliner, to the smallest prop plane, to the boat, and finally to the trail leading into the place I have been thinking about for the previous months. There are certainly peak times when photographers will flock to a location, but I won't write off other times of the year. It is an ever-changing landscape, and, rather than simply rely on what others have shot before, I like to look for beauty wherever I may be.

How do you set about visualizing your shots?

I'll storyboard what I intend to shoot, sketch out what I aim to get, and plan and organize for any extra equipment I may need, such as scaffolding or ladders for a high vantage point. I guess you could say I "daydream" about a future shoot. Once on location, I'll follow my visualizations, while always remaining open to the moment and what may unfold serendipitously. I always have several projects ongoing in various states, from contracted to pie-in-the-sky, and I am an assiduous planner. These projects are drilled down to specific lists, and then further to sketches.

What are the key ingredients that make a great composition?

Never stop looking. Period. I take those words to heart to their fullest extent, and wherever I am I will find a subject. If the subject is obvious, I never stop looking for another angle. How would a wide-angle lens tell a different story? What about the compression of a telephoto? Getting stuck or being overwhelmed is not an option when I am out on a shoot. Especially when I think I've nailed it, I never stop looking. The grand scenic—a landscape that includes distant vistas and the sky—can be one of the most difficult images to capture. I try getting low to the ground and incorporating some interesting foreground elements that contribute to the story, such as flowers, rocks, or a stream. These will dominate the foreground and capture the viewer's eye, and then lead them through the image to the middle ground—a pond, reflections, trees—and then to the mountains in the distance that originally caught my eye. I use leading lines to guide the viewer through the composition. Using a tripod, a small aperture, and mirror lock-up are critical to capturing the scene in sharp focus from the closest elements in the photo through to infinity. I wouldn't say I favor any one design structure—you can certainly find circles and triangles in my photographs, leading lines, S-curves, diagonal lines, intersecting lines. A great deal of attention is paid to the negative space as well as the positive.

What or who has been the biggest influence on your work?

I studied Fine Art and Art Education at the University of Washington in Seattle, where I developed a deep appreciation for the great masters. There are very sound reasons why certain works and artists have remained significant over the centuries—principles applied on their canvases serve as inspiration for photographers today. When I am out in the field, I am often inspired by a specific artist's work and I will "see" a pointillist painting in the soft colors of fall with falling snow, or an M.C. Escher in the repeating patterns of wildlife huddled or moving together. Most artists, including me, began their careers as realists, painting precise replications of what they saw with their own eyes, and as they progressed through their lives, nearly every one became more and more abstract in their work. I have followed that path myself. These days I find more and more inspiration from abstract painters, looking for what I call "found art" in everyday scenes of a weathered surface, the build-up of detritus on a wall, or tight compositions in nature that may resemble the controlled mayhem of a Jackson Pollock.

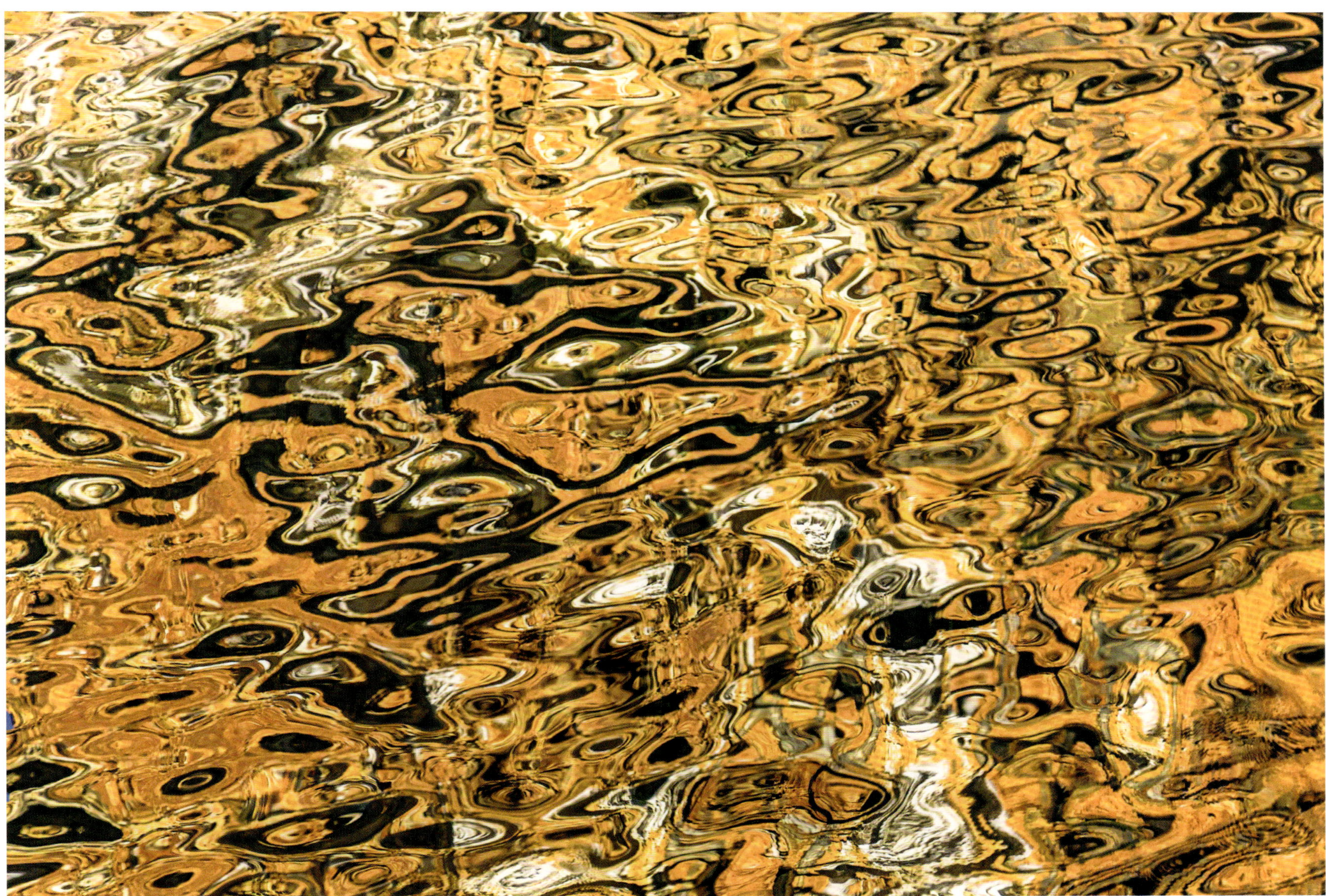

CANYON REFLECTIONS

Jackson Pollock said his paintings ended where your imagination began—images of water reflections take me to this same place. I can get lost looking at the details of this image, which also is reminiscent of works by Gustav Klimt. In the Kimberley, in Western Australia, blue rivers flow through deeply cut canyons of ocher sandstone. In this image, the cliffs become a rhythmic disruption of shape and pattern, gilded under the bright blue sky.

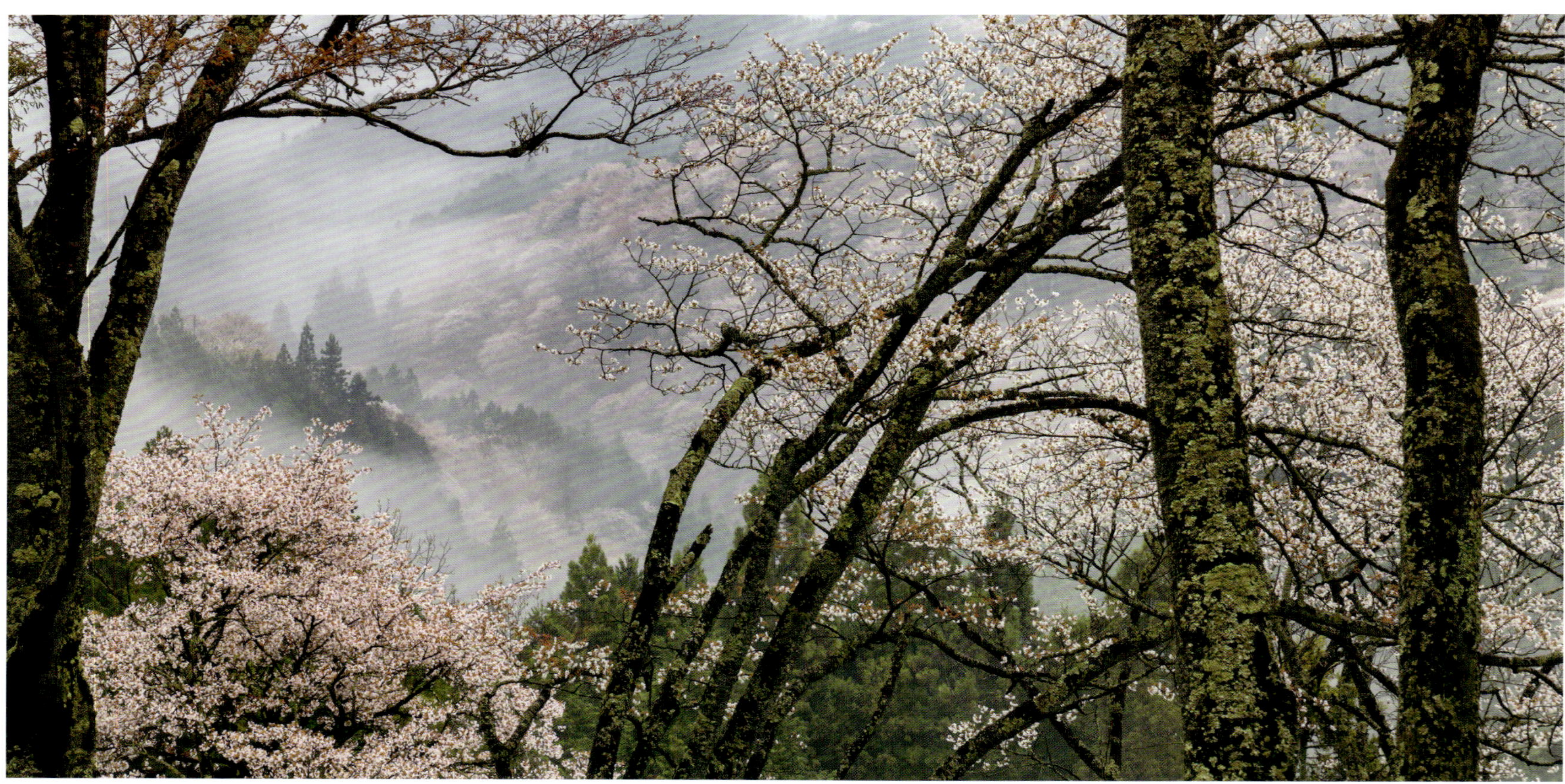

CHERRY BLOSSOMS

Photographing the cherries in peak bloom is "combat photography," and for good reason. The beauty is unparalleled, but the actual blossoms last only a week or so. This particular trip was exhausting; I was up at 4am to photograph in the subdued morning light, so the pale pinks would stand out. Also, the wind was calm and the crowds hadn't arrived yet. This image was taken after fresh rain—the fog is still settled in the valley beyond and softens the mountain ridges.

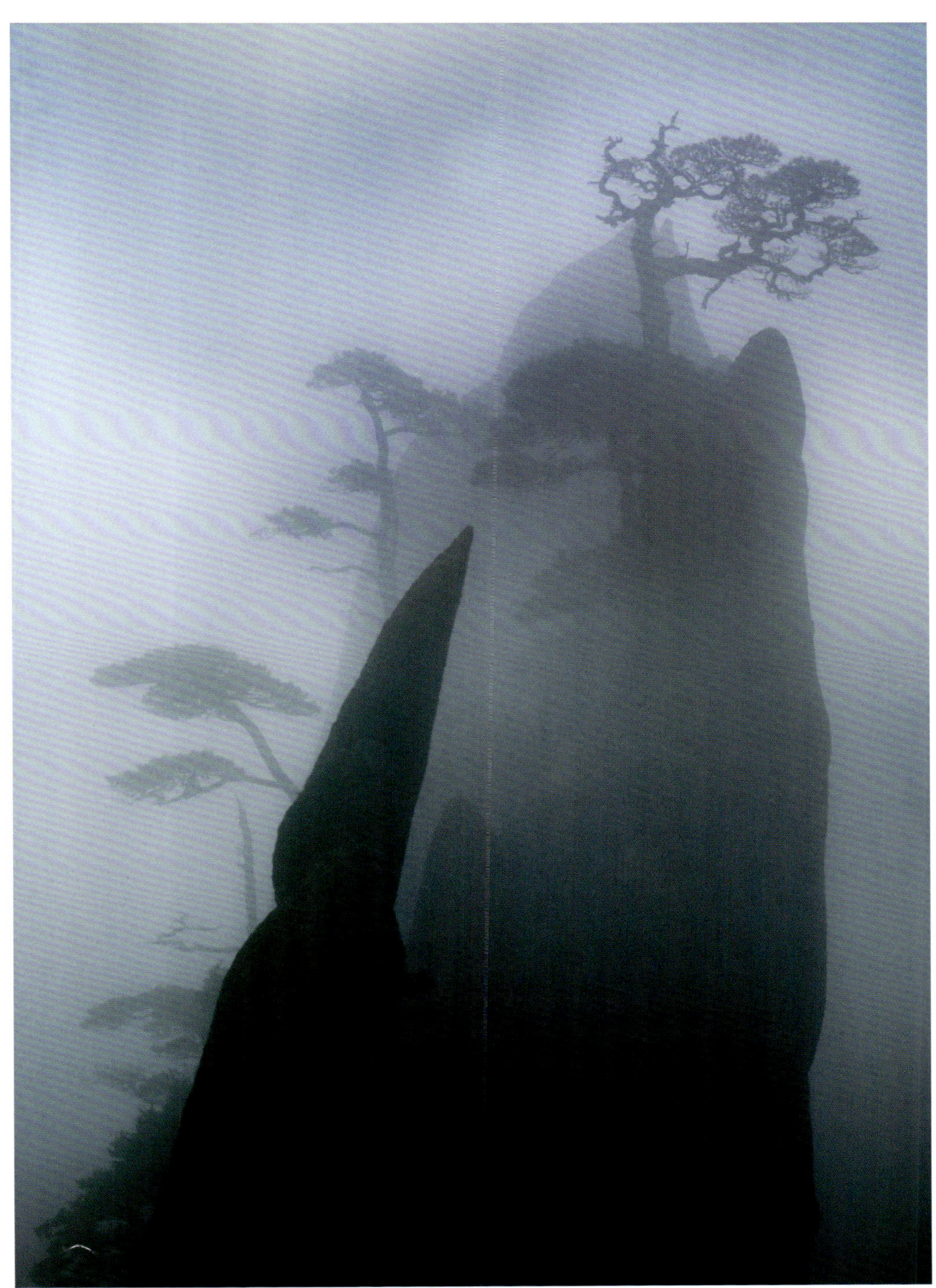

ROCK SPIRES AND PINE TREES IN MIST

I always believed that Chinese master landscape painters had creative imaginations, until I visited Huangshan, which resembled a sumi-e painting more than a real place. This mountainous region of jagged pinnacles, sheer walls, and twisted pine trees became an endless source of inspiration to me, from photography to gardening. Long a favorite theme of mine is the use of a mist or fog to make a solid mass seem somewhat translucent. Using a long lens, I zoomed in on these two pinnacles to make the simple shapes and lines dominant in the frame.

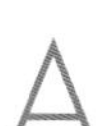

Q + A

How do you manage to capture the environment in such an intimate and beautiful way?

I have been an artist all my life, and I would have to credit my roots as a painter for my eye for composition today, going back to junior high school. A successful painting relies on the artist not just to copy what they see, but their personal interpretation of the situation of angles and light. Just as in photography, you can choose to paint with a wide-angle perspective or a compressed telephoto point of view. There is more crossover between the disciplines than you might at first imagine. A photograph is not simply taken, it's created. It's not an exact replica of what you saw (how boring would that be)—like a successful painting, it's a successful application of discipline, principles, and creativity. I am always learning, striving to evolve my work and make it better. With digital photography, I evaluate every image I shot during the day before I go to bed that night. If I am not making mistakes I'm not pushing myself. I push the boundaries of my style, to try and photograph the familiar in new ways. I won't be successful the first time out, I look at what I've captured (immediately and later), apply the principles of design and story, and shoot it again. I continually push myself to reinvent myself and evolve with the intention of learning and improving along the way.

How does your passion for the landscape and environment influence your photography?

I simply love nature. I love getting out and into the forest, the mountains, and the ocean. At the beginning of my career, photography was a way to spend time in nature, and I created a livelihood that allowed me to stay there. Whether I am taking a picture or painting a picture, I feel complete and satisfied. When I'm not holding a camera, taking a photograph, the chances are I'm thinking about the next time I will be. If a week goes by without shooting, I get very anxious. I am at peace and happy, and giddy even at times, working a subject or a landscape—art is what I live for. I think many of our problems— environmental, social, and behavioral— come from the sad fact that people have become so separated from nature. As mammals, we need green spaces, flowing water, and quiet, otherwise we lose empathy, patience, and wisdom. I will answer this with one of my own quotes: "It is in the wild places, where the edge of the Earth meets the corners of the sky, the human spirit is fed."

How do you achieve commercial success with your images while conveying an environmental and conservation message at the same time?

Photography and conservation go hand-in-hand. The relationship got a big boost when the photo of Earth from the Apollo spacecraft was published in the early 1970s. This view of the planet, called "The Blue Marble," became a rallying cry for environmentalism. My photos have been used to protect the Alaskan Arctic, Canadian rivers, and a myriad of other areas. As a fellow of the International League of Conservation Photographers (iLCP), one of my goals of photography is to show the beauty of Earth and the need for conservation. With a particular niche in the photography world, nature photographers draw from the natural world and the natural environment. It becomes a moral obligation, then, to return it. At least, this is my perspective; and, in fact, this is reflected in the themes of all the books and other projects I've completed over the years.

As a master of landscape photography, what is your motivation to continue making photographs?

The motivation comes naturally to me—I simply love to take pictures. I always have. My mother and father were both professional commercial photographers, so you could say it's in my DNA. I am open to almost any subject; I don't limit myself, and I always have a dozen different projects in my mind at any one time. Motivation is a challenge for any artist—photography and travel are my stimulants of choice, along with the coffee! I get a huge charge out of being on the move, seeing new things, and meeting new people. As an artist, I feel inspired when I am inspiring other people. It's a simple but extraordinary task to share this passion, which I do by teaching, whether in the classroom or in the field. One thing art school drilled into me is never to be complacent—I have always put the carrot out there for myself. The day photography gets stale for me is the day I die.

TECHNICAL INFORMATION

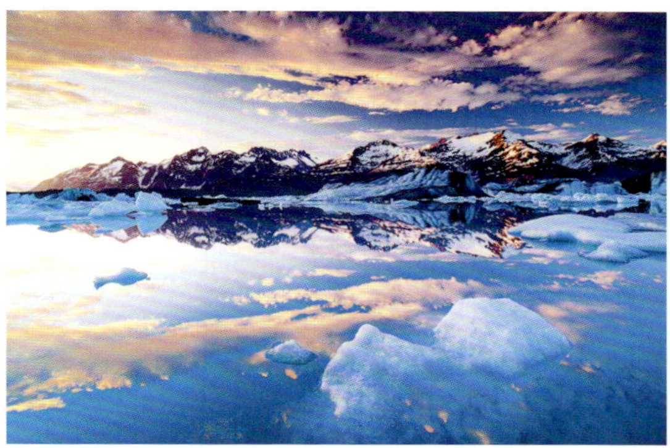

ALSEK LAKE
GLACIER NATIONAL PARK, ALASKA, USA

Camera: Nikon F4
Lens/Focal length: Nikkor 20mm f/2.8
Aperture: f/11
Shutter speed: 1/60 sec.
ISO: 50
Film type: Fujichrome Velvia 50

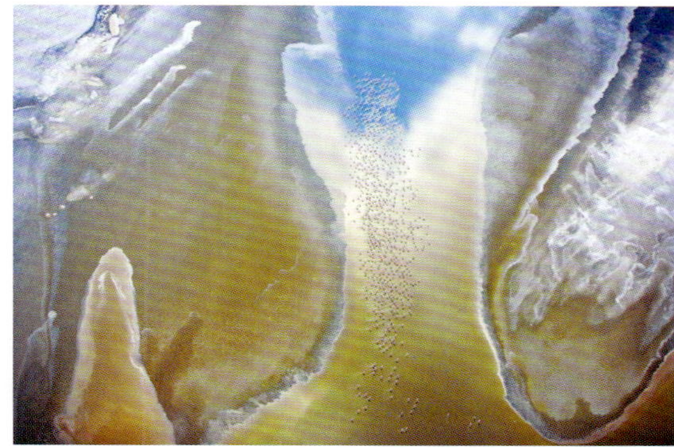

AERIAL, LAKE NATRON
TANZANIA

Camera: Canon EOS-1Ds Mark II
Lens/Focal length: Canon EF 70-200mm f/2.8
Aperture: f/3.2
Shutter speed: 1/1250 sec.
ISO: 400

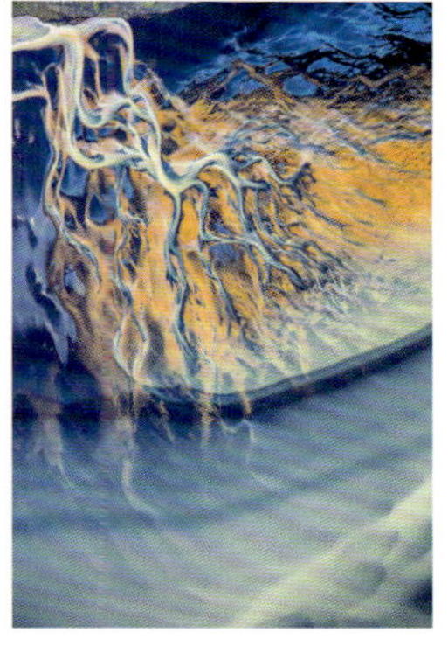

RIVER DELTA AERIAL
ICELAND

Camera: Canon EOS 5DS R
Lens/Focal length: Canon 24-70mm f/4
Aperture: f/4.5
Shutter speed: 1/1000 sec.
ISO: 800

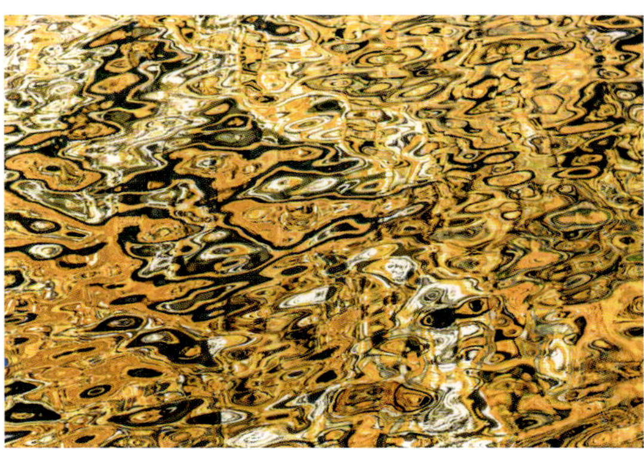

CANYON REFLECTIONS
KING GEORGE RIVER, KIMBERLEY,
WESTERN AUSTRALIA

Camera: Canon EOS 5D Mark III
Lens/Focal length: Canon 24-105mm f/4
Aperture: f/4
Shutter speed: 1/800 sec.
ISO: 2000

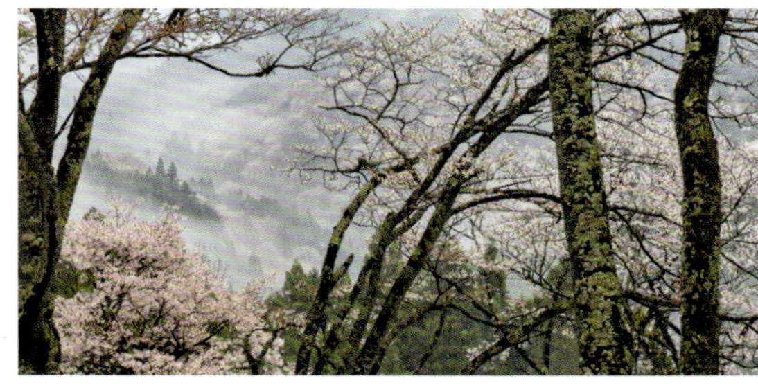

CHERRY BLOSSOMS
YOSHINO,
JAPAN

Camera: Leica S (Typ 006)
Lens/Focal length: Leica Vario-Elmar-S 30-90mm f/3.5-5.6
Aperture: f/19
Shutter speed: 1/4 sec.
ISO: 100

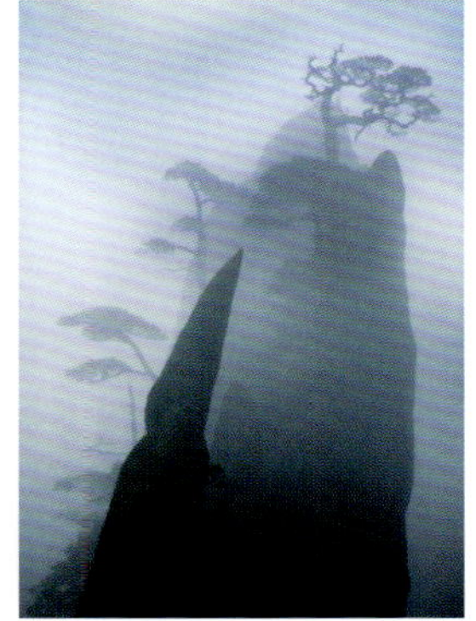

ROCK SPIRES AND PINE TREES IN MIST
HUANGSHAN, ANHUI,
CHINA

Camera: Nikon F3
Lens/Focal length: Nikkor 300mm f/2.8
Aperture: f/8
Shutter speed: 1/25 sec.
ISO: 64
Film type: Kodachrome 64

COLIN PRIOR

Colin Prior has gained recognition as a photographer, naturalist, and conservationist. His career path into photography began underwater when, in 1981, he won best newcomer to underwater photography; and he soon began working in the North Sea as a photo-technician with a commercial diving company. He spent the next 10 years working as a commercial photographer for advertising and design agencies and in the exhibition industry.

It wasn't until 1989, when Colin purchased a Linhof Technorama 617S camera, that he began to develop his personal work—the panoramic format's 3:1 ratio fascinated him in a way like no other. His photographs capture sublime moments of light and land, which are the result of meticulous planning and preparation and often take years to achieve. Colin is a photographer who seeks out patterns in the landscape and the hidden links between reality and the imagination.

In a career spanning 35 years, he has traveled to over 40 countries and lived alone for extended periods of time to pursue his subjects. He has produced seven books, including the internationally published *The World's Wild Places* and *Living Tribes*, and recently completed a four-year project in Pakistan's Karakoram Mountains. His current project, *Fragile*, explores the habitats of wild birds and their vulnerability to change. Colin was recently the subject of two BBC documentaries entitled *Mountain Man*.

TRANGO TOWERS

There's nothing in this world that can prepare you for the sheer scale and magnitude of the Trango Towers in Pakistan. It is perceived often as surreal and appears to rise from a computer-generated scene. This image was the result of a third early morning attempt, when I literally had around 30 seconds to capture the towers as the clouds parted simultaneously in the east and west, allowing me to capture the drama.

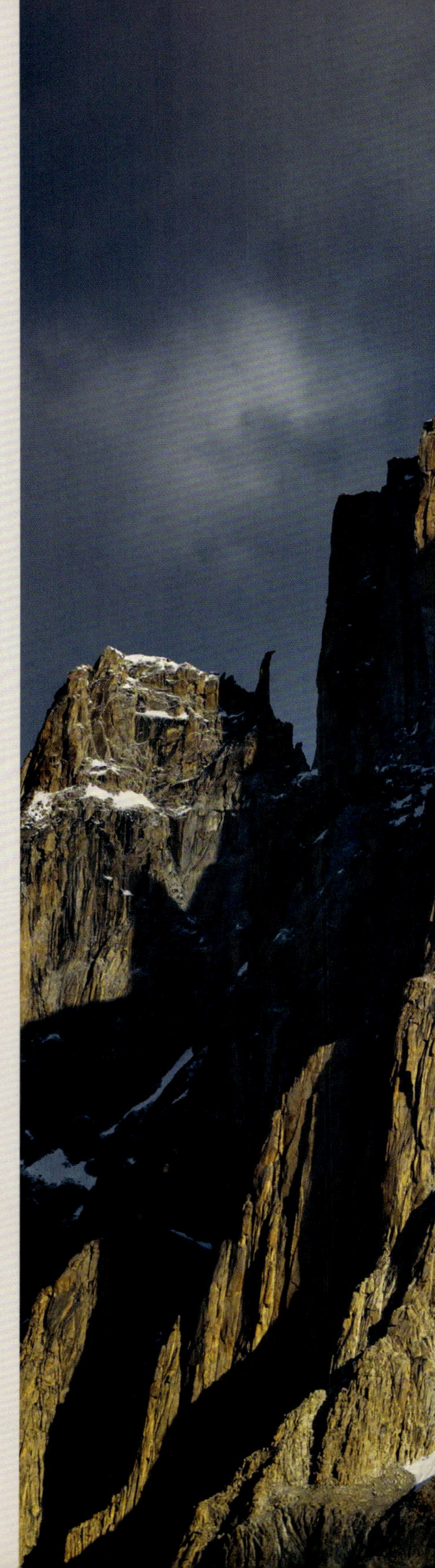

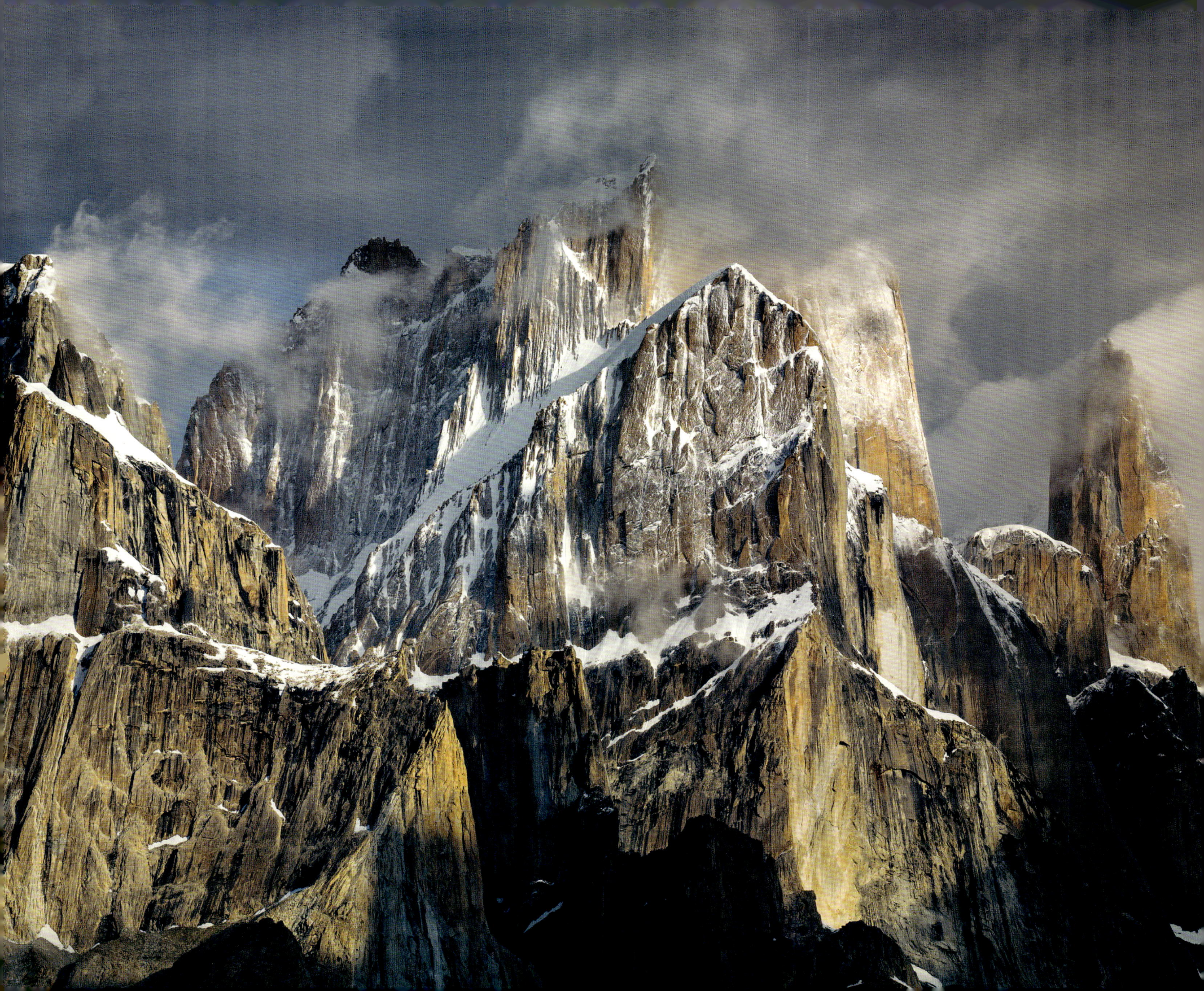

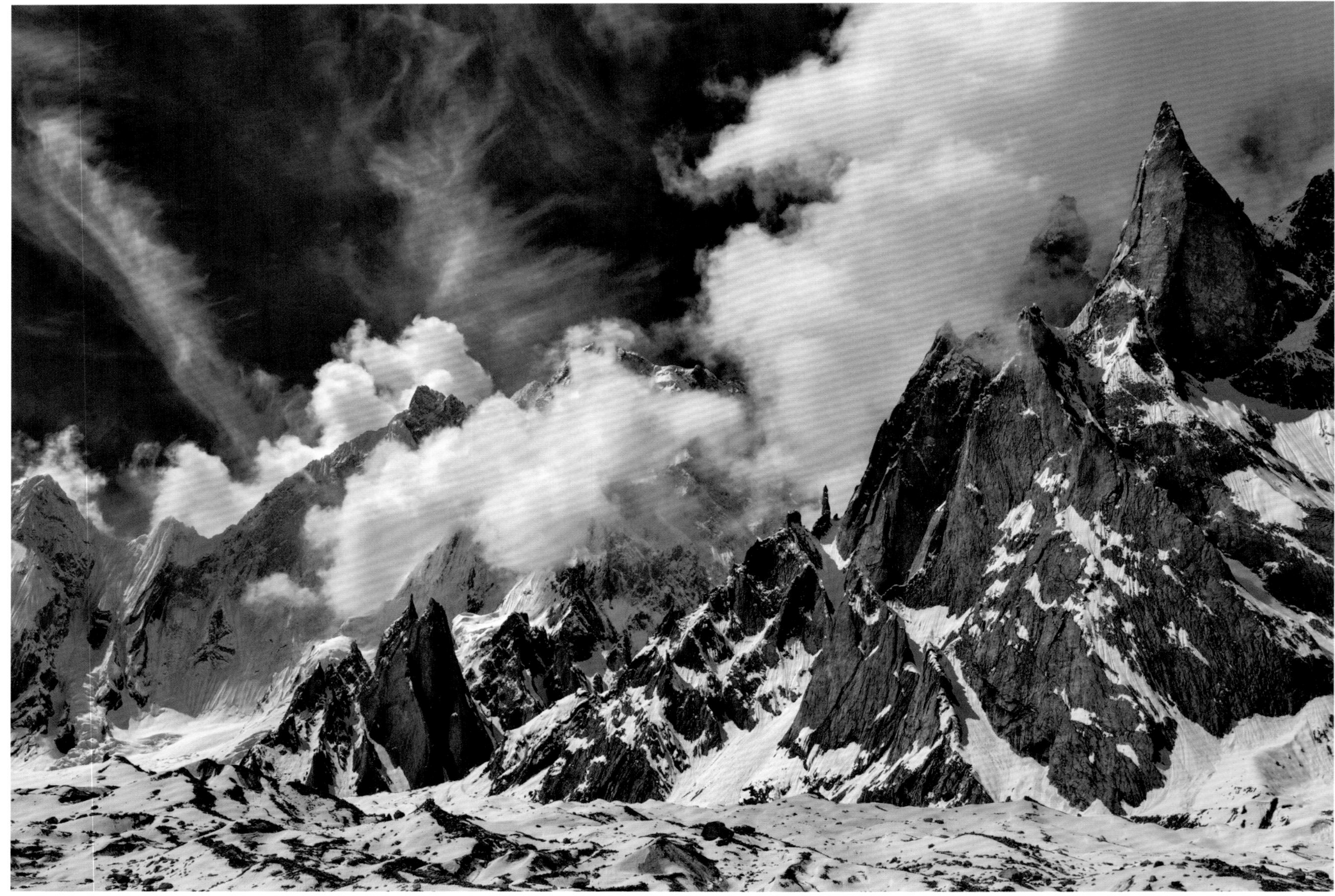

K6 AND FATHI BRAKK TOWERS

As we approached K7 basecamp at the head of the Charakusa Glacier, low cloud suddenly gave way to clear skies striped with cirrus streamers and revealed Link Sar, K6, and the Fathi Brakk Towers. For me, this image sums up the character of the Karakoram Mountains—a vast mountain range of desert and crumbling rock, bereft of any vegetation—and is indicative of how much they differ from most other great ranges and, in particular, the Himalayas.

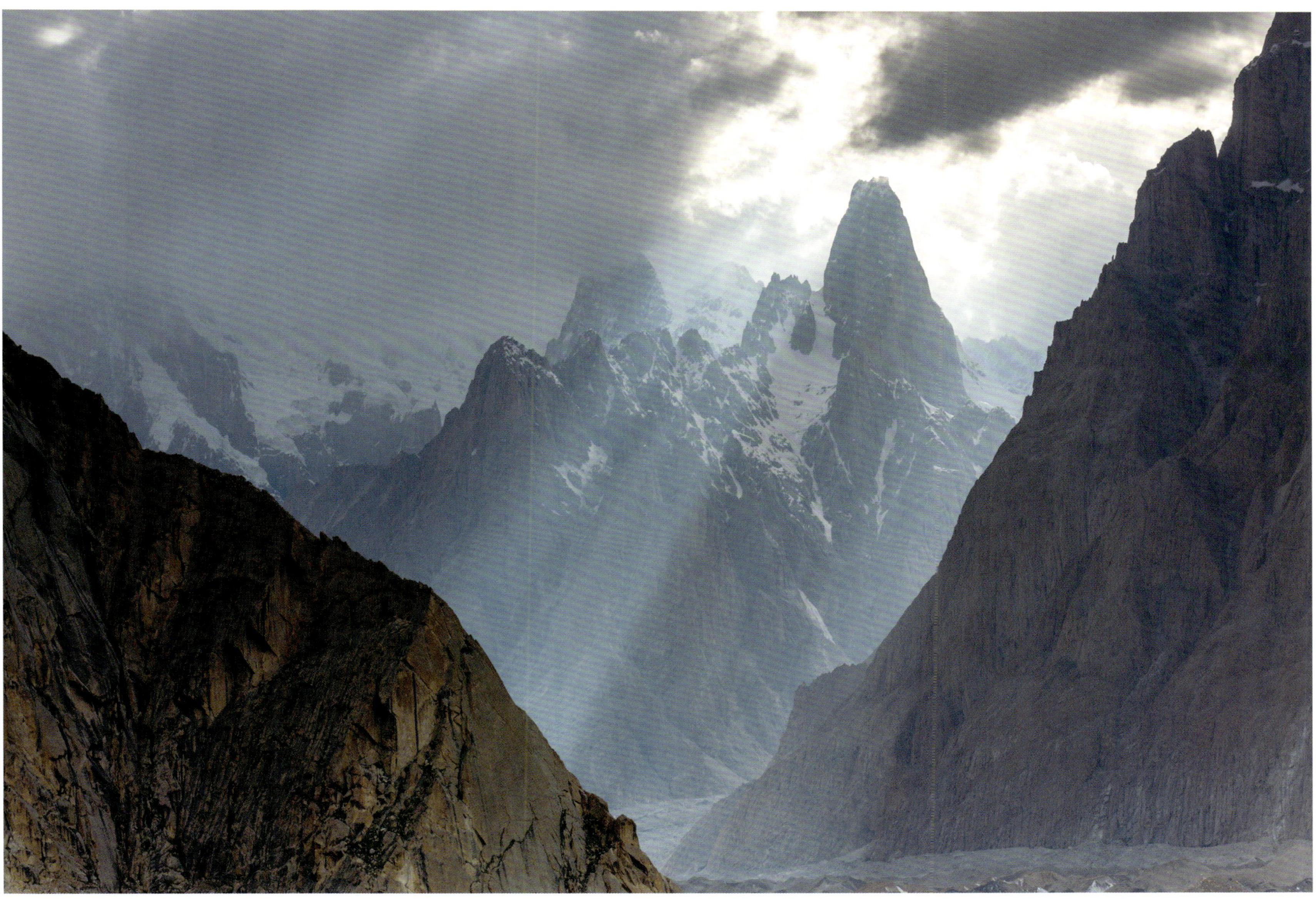

ULI BIAHO TOWER

Rising above the Trango Glacier to 6,109m (20,042ft), the Uli Biaho Tower, together with the Trango and Cathedral Towers, forms what is arguably the most dramatic region of the Greater Karakoram. Photographed high above the Baltoro, the sudden appearance of crepuscular rays helped the mood of the photograph.

Q
+
A

You are world-renowned for your spectacular, far-reaching mountain vistas—what draws you to photograph high places?

My desire to photograph from high places is driven by two reasons. Firstly, when photographing from an elevated position the character of the landscape is revealed in a way not possible from ground level. Secondly, being on or around the summit of a mountain at dusk or dawn allows the photographer to work with that warm low light at their feet, often as much as an hour after the light has been lost from the glens. This helps to create three-dimensionality in the resulting images.

What technical and practical issues do you encounter when photographing such remote, hard-to-reach landscapes?

The formula I have developed for high-altitude photography is analogous with the concept of a military strike. Reconnaissance is crucial and involves walking the ground, perhaps more than once, to establish the "firing point." The second part is straightforward in that it simply requires checking and rechecking that everything required to spend a night on a mountain top is packed, and that all necessary photographic equipment is checked and rechecked. The final part of the equation is the "strike" which is triggered by a favorable weather forecast at the designated time of the year. If all these factors converge at the optimum moment, then success may result. Great landscape photographs are the result of personal observation over a long period in which a photographer must immerse themselves to understand the land's patterns and cycles. Like a hunter, they must place themselves in a location that will allow them to take advantage of a situation that has yet to develop.

What do you look for in a landscape when composing a shot—what makes you press the shutter?

I am fascinated by the relationship between the elements of the natural world. At the moment in which light and land converge, I consider myself the third layer, capturing and recording the moment for posterity, not as an observer but as an integral part of the experience—essentially baked into the image. We must never forget that the camera looks both ways—outwardly into the landscape and, importantly, inwardly to the mind of the photographer.

Do you still set yourself creative challenges?

As a creative artist, I continually evolve my work and explore new and innovative ways of visual expression. I spent much of my career working with the panoramic format but latterly I have found that it had become a creative straitjacket and it was time to hunt new game. I've gone back to my roots and am enjoying exploring subjects with a fresh vision.

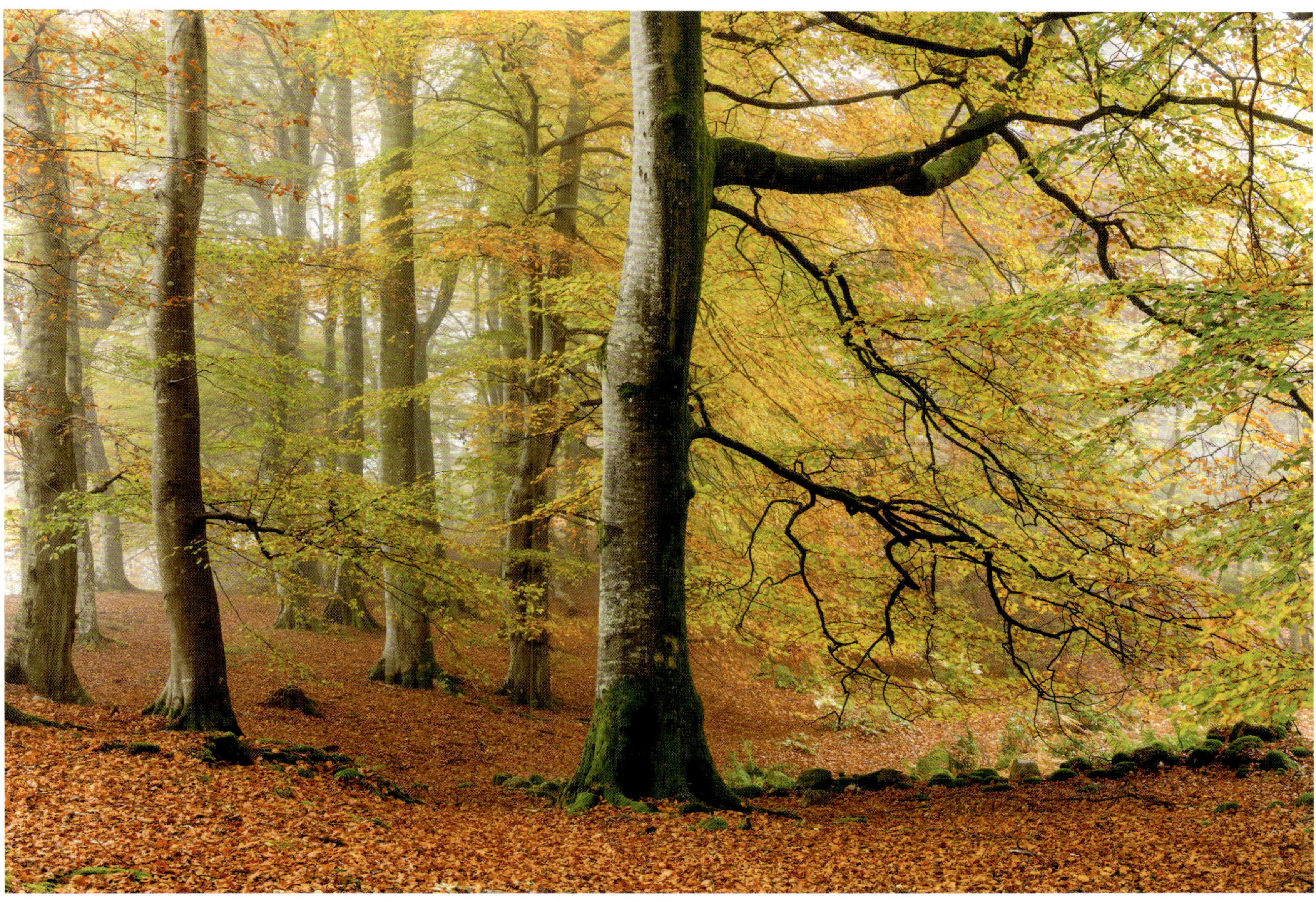

BEECH FOREST

After a decade of photographing this wood in fall, I finally arrived on a day when the conditions were perfect—optimal colors, no wind, and thick mist conducting a soft luminosity deep into the wood, like a giant diffuser. It's no different from photographing mountains—it's simply about being in the right place at the right time, and that seldom happens by accident.

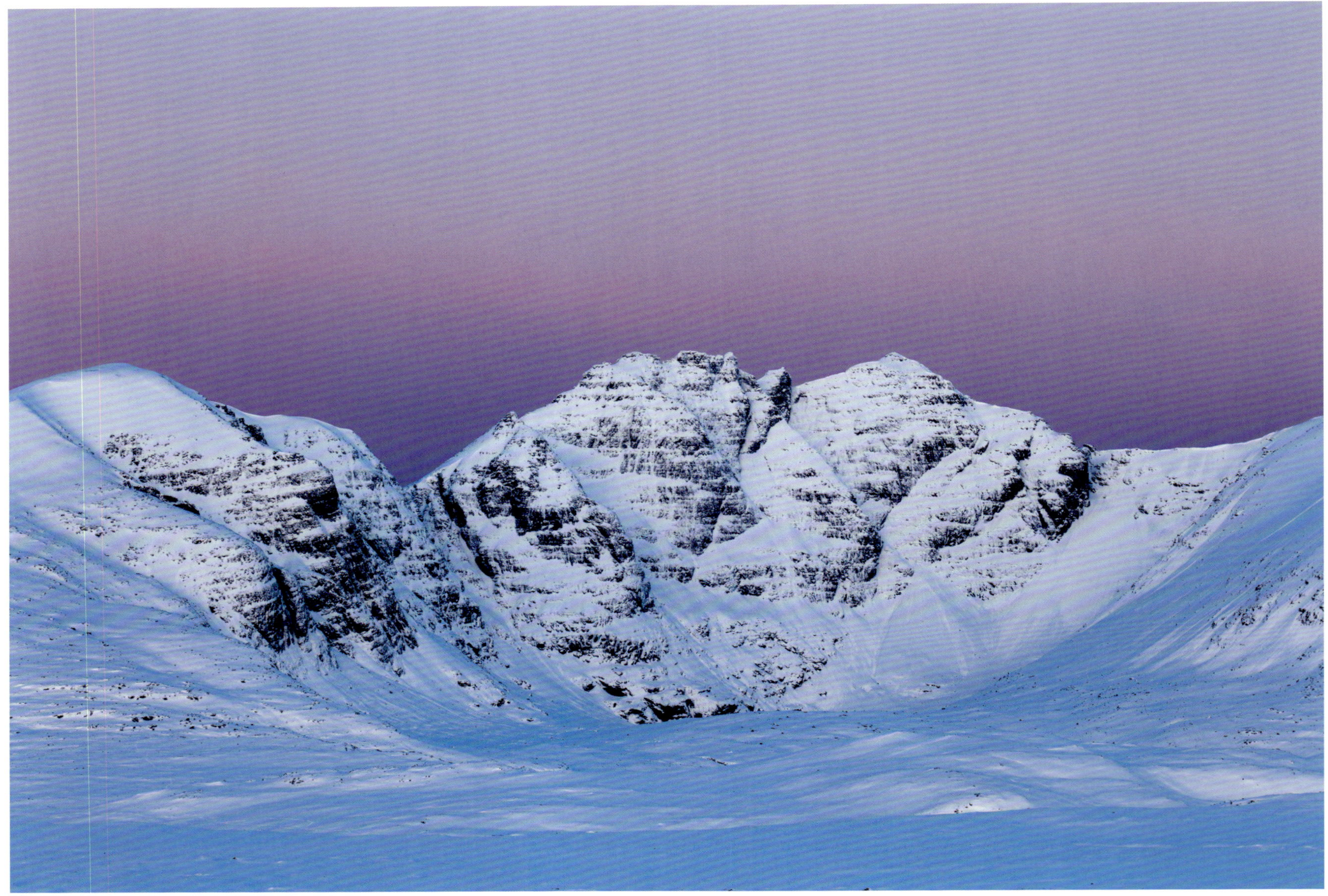

AN TEALLACH

Following several days of heavy snow, An Teallach emerges into the Belt of Venus (or anti-twilight arch), a reddish band seen above the antisolar horizon. This is underlain by the Earth's shadow—a mauve band often referred to as the twilight wedge, which is cast on the atmosphere and is best seen from points of elevation, such as mountain summits.

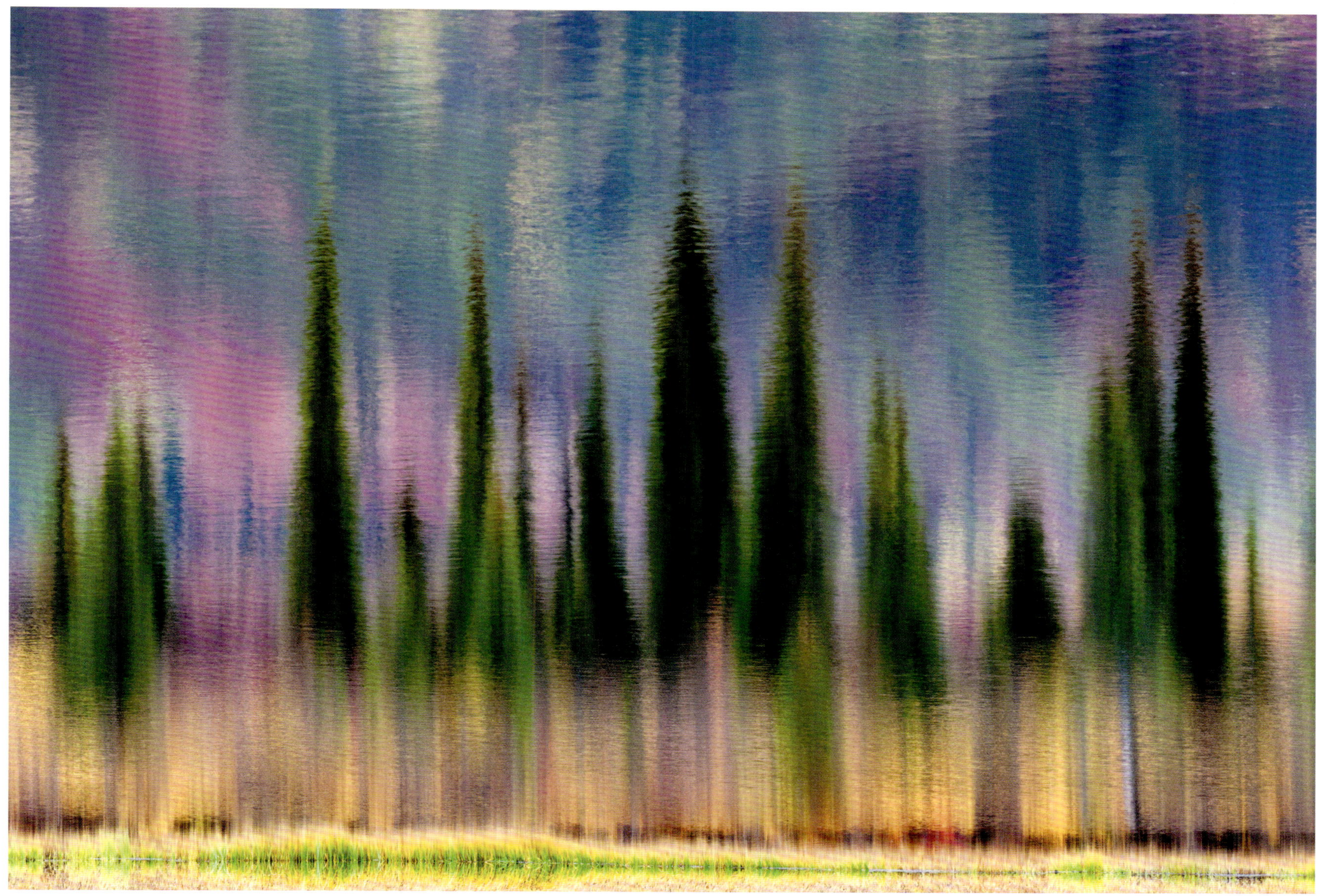

MIRROR LAKE

I spent some time one morning around the shores of Mirror Lake, and, while most of its surface was agitated
by wind, one small corner lay sheltered and projected the most amazing reflection. Although the trees appear
upside-down in the water, I visualized the image inverted so that the trees looked the way they appear to us in
reality. I also recognized the similarity of colors to those in Monet's palette in his series of water lilies at his home
in Giverny, France.

Q + A

How do you achieve such a wonderful feeling of depth in your images—is depth of field the key?

Depth of field is an illusion. Remember, we are looking at pixels on a page or screen and one of the challenges to becoming an authoritative photographer is in being able to create the illusion of three-dimensionality. It goes beyond small apertures and being able to move the plane of focus and depth of field with a tilt and shift lens. It is fundamentally the ability to read the three-dimensional world in which we live and understand how it will translate into the two-dimensional world of photography.

How have developments in digital technology affected or influenced your photography?

Digital technology has democratized photography and has liberated photographers in a way that would have been unimaginable 15 years ago. Having come from a large-format film background, the biggest change for me is to have no film, processing, and scanning costs associated with capture. Also, the precision of current digital cameras means that when I leave a location, I now know unequivocally that I've got the shot. Gone are the uncertainties of returning home from the other side of the world with a bag of unprocessed film and hoping that you'd got everything right.

What are the biggest commercial challenges—and opportunities— for professional landscape photographers today?

Whether we like it or not, the currency of photography has been devalued. Few outdoor photographers, myself included, now make any money from selling photographs and we have entered an era where images are now in the same place as music—free and for sharing. Like musicians, who no longer make their living by selling music but by live performances at concerts and from selling merchandise, photographers have been forced to adopt a similar business model, albeit on a smaller scale. Having once been dependent on retail, my business is now a mixture of corporate, workshops, and publishing, and my personal time behind the camera is always compromised by the need to make a living. Photography has been democratized and it has affected every photographer's ability to make a living.

What single piece of kit is most useful in your work?

Throughout my working career, I have used Gitzo tripods. I currently use a Systematic model which eradicates camera shake, which has as much to do with image sharpness as lens design.

TECHNICAL INFORMATION

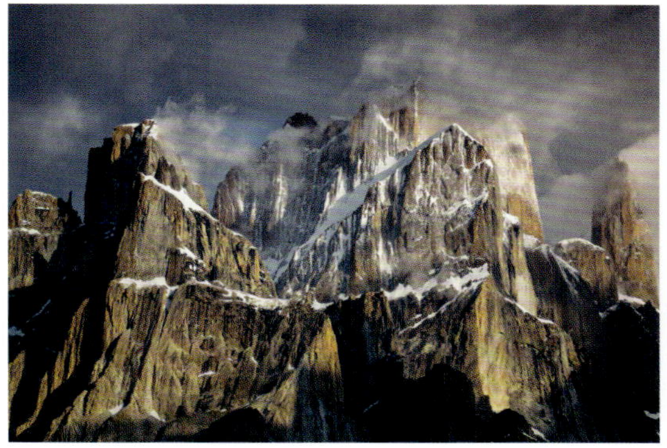

TRANGO TOWERS
KARAKORAM MOUNTAINS,
PAKISTAN

Camera: Canon EOS 5D Mark III
Lens/Focal length: Canon 70–200mm f/2.8 at 125mm
Aperture: f/10
Shutter speed: 1/100 sec.
ISO: 100
Kit: Tripod

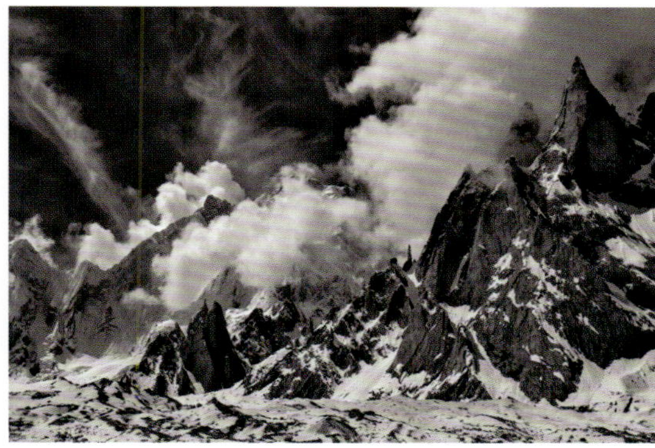

K6 AND FATHI BRAKK TOWERS
CHARAKUSA GLACIER,
PAKISTAN

Camera: Leica S
Lens/Focal length: Leica Elmarit-S 45mm f/2.8
Aperture: f/8
Shutter speed: 1/750 sec.
ISO: 100
Kit: Tripod

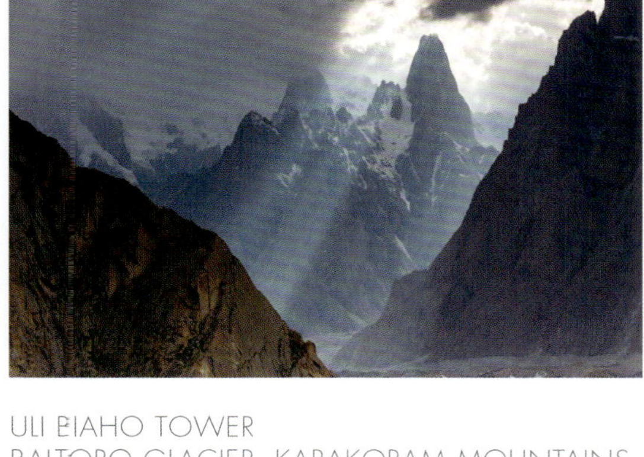

ULI BIAHO TOWER
BALTORO GLACIER, KARAKORAM MOUNTAINS,
PAKISTAN

Camera: Canon EOS 5D Mark III
Lens/Focal length: Canon 70–200mm f/2.8 at 90mm
Aperture: f/10
Shutter speed: 1/60 sec.
ISO: 100
Kit: Tripod

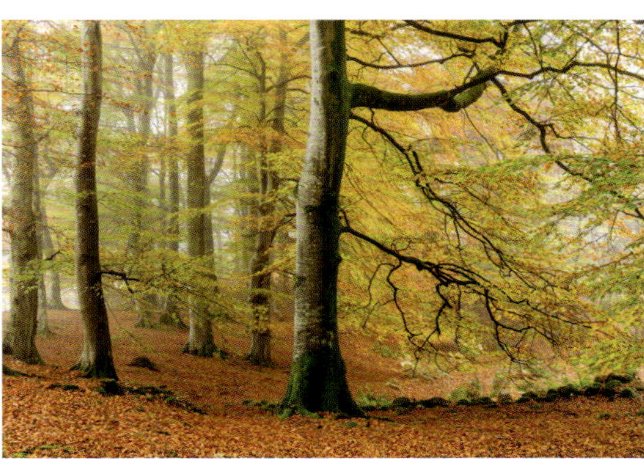

BEECH FOREST
GANNOCHY ESTATE, GLEN ESK,
SCOTLAND

Camera: Canon EOS 5DS R
Lens/Focal length: Canon 24–70mm f/2.8 at 42mm
Aperture: f/11
Shutter speed: 1 sec.
ISO: 100
Kit: Tripod

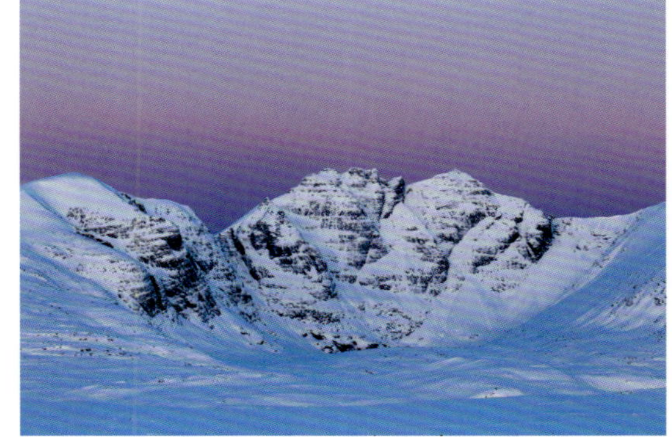

AN TEALLACH
FISHERFIELD FOREST, DUNDONNELL,
SCOTLAND

Camera: Canon EOS 5DS R
Lens/Focal length: Canon 100–400mm f/4.5–5.6 at 148mm
Aperture: f/9
Shutter speed: 1/5 sec.
ISO: 100
Kit: Tripod

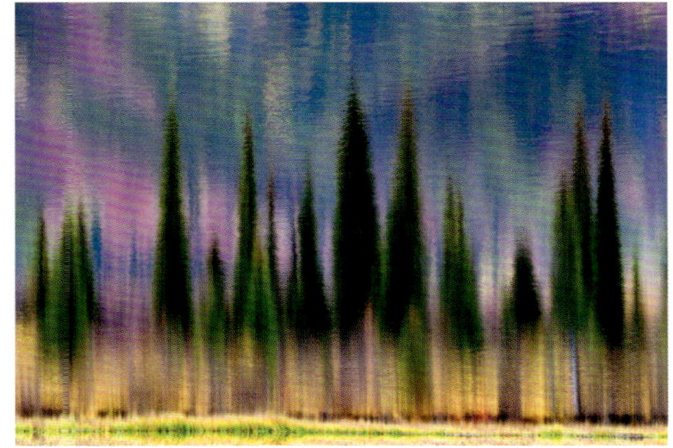

MIRROR LAKE
CANTWELL, ALASKA,
USA

Camera: Canon EOS-1DS Mark II
Lens/Focal length: Canon 300mm f/2.8
Aperture: f/18
Shutter speed: 1/30 sec.
ISO: 400
Kit: Tripod

DANIEL KORDAN

Daniel Kordan has been fascinated by the possibilities of photography since his early childhood. He grew up in a beautiful lake region near Moscow, exploring the wild and spending most of his free time around nature, and went on to graduate from art school. Mix art, nature, and being constantly active, and Daniel seemed destined to be a landscape photographer. Even while at university, working on a quantum physics thesis, and enjoying time off with family and friends, he has always found pleasure in the pathless woods: places he always returned to and always admired.

Nature is Daniel's inspiration, with all its beauty and variety of colors and compositions. During his study at the Institute of Physics and Technology, he gained experience, not only in physics, but also in mountain-climbing and hiking—guiding tourist groups in winter and summer. He became a guide for photography workshops and chief editor of *Continent Expedition* magazine, writing about travel and adventure all over the world. Today, Daniel continues to travel all around the world, but spends the most time in Tuscany and the Lofoten Islands, guiding photography groups from Europe, the USA, and Asia. He has won many awards, including a Golden Turtle Nature nomination and the *National Geographic* Russia contest, and has many corporate clients—including Apple, Gazprom Neft, and RedBull.

GOLDEN ARCH

I took this photograph during my sailing expedition in 2016. It took us two months to reach the eastern side of Greenland from Saint Petersburg. The steel yacht, "Peter the First," was specially prepared for the journey through the ice fields of Greenland. During our sailings in early August, we scouted for the best locations, and biggest icebergs. We had a Zodiac boat, so we could easily change our position, and we asked the navigation team to position the yacht in this arch, to create the sense of scale. Water dripping from the melting iceberg was lit from behind by the golden light of the setting sun.

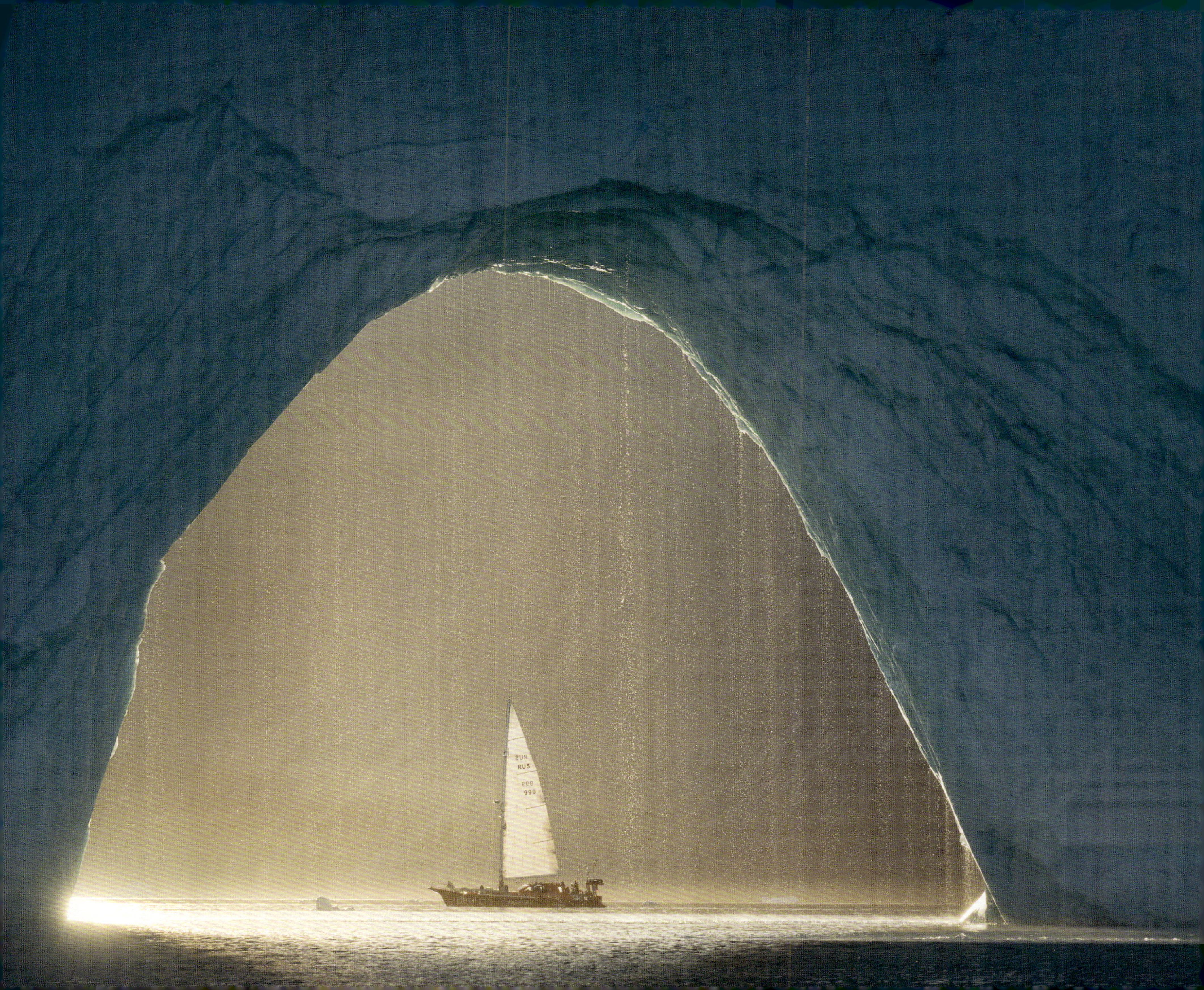
RUS
999

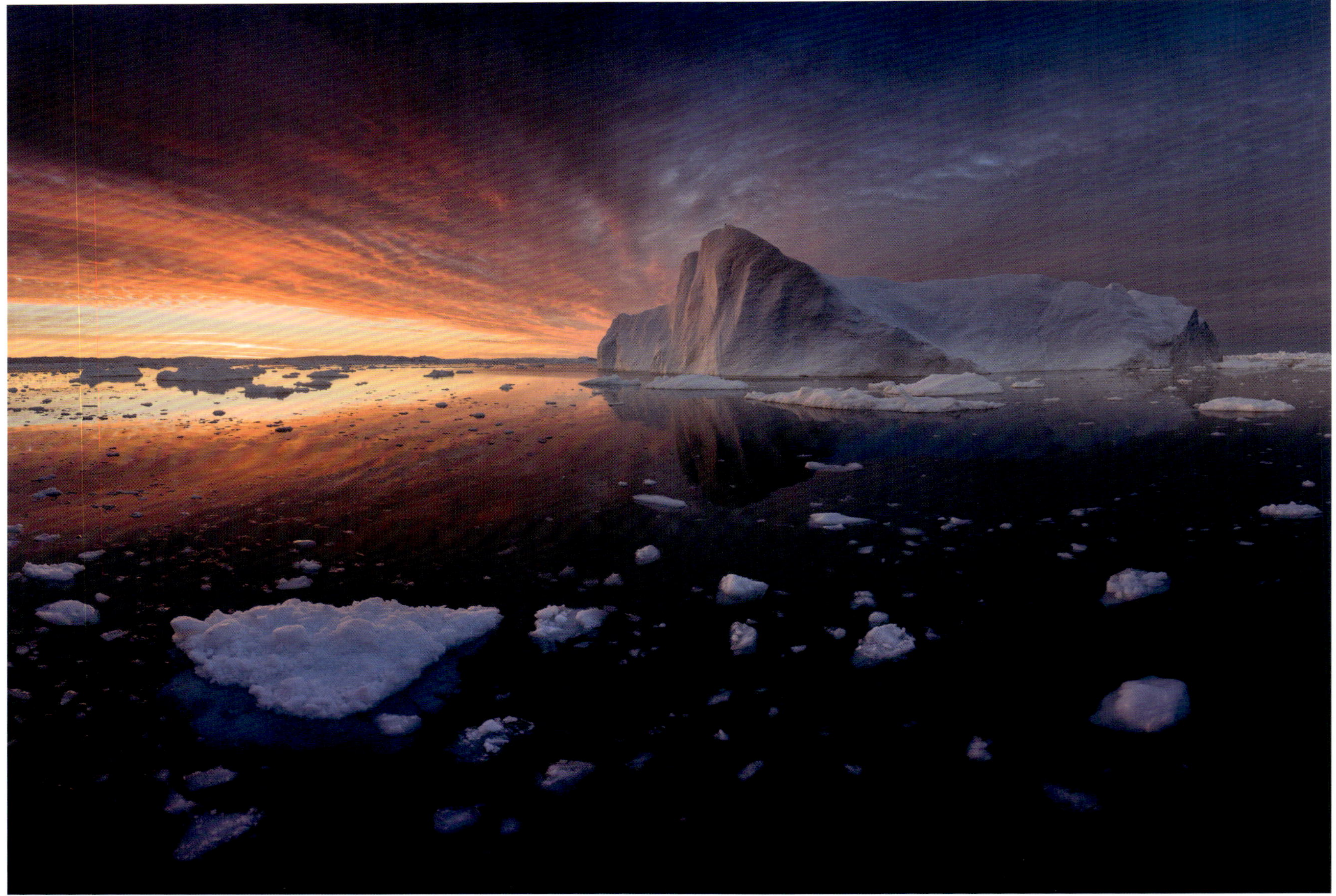

DISKO BAY

During the midnight sun period at the end of July, the sun sets just for a few minutes, giving the opportunity to shoot all night long. Disko Bay is a sheltered place, which means we had reflections almost every night. The icebergs calve from the Kanger glacier, and the icescapes are changing every day! This panorama is created from four vertical images.

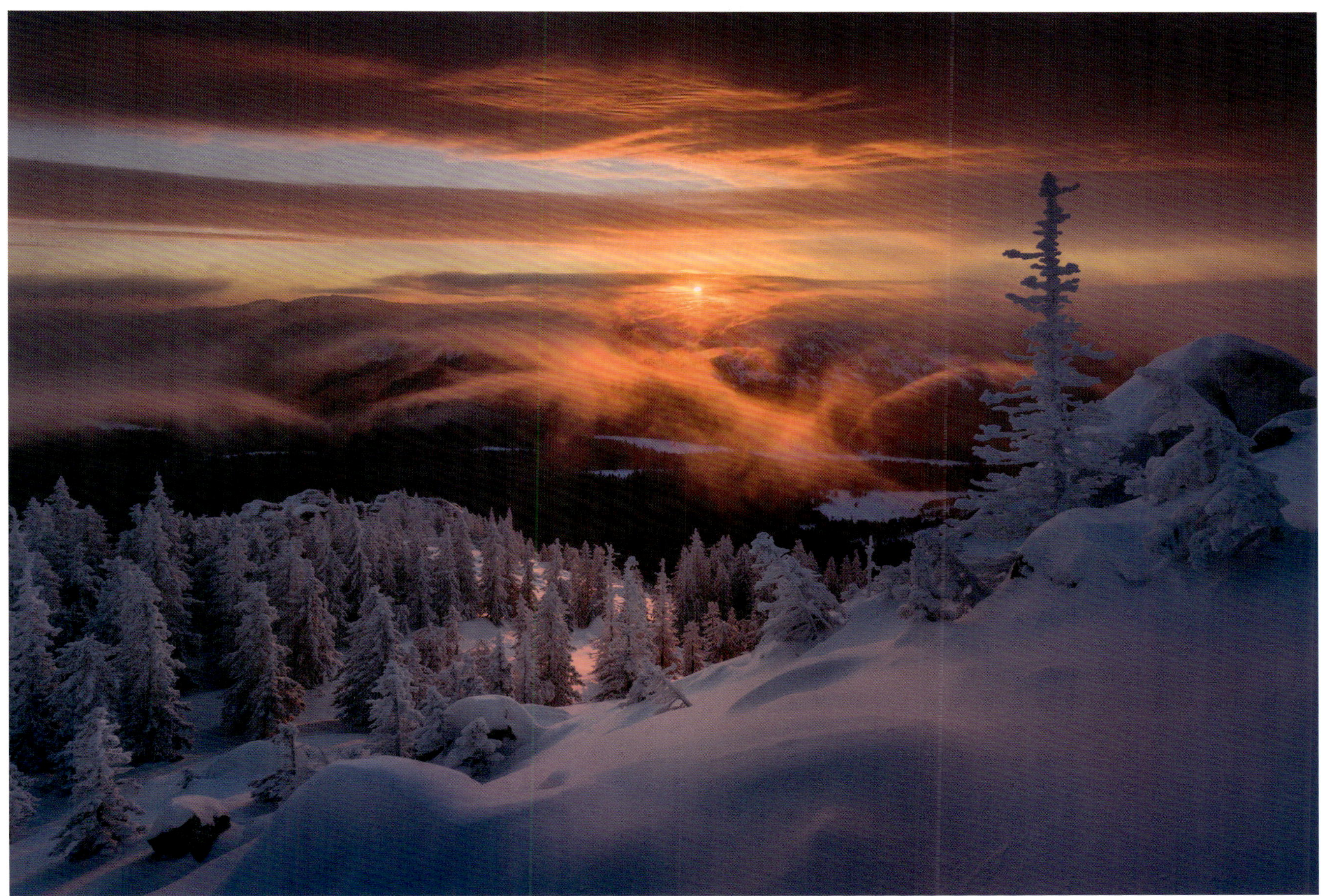

TAGANAY

Taganay is a National Park in Russia, in the Ural mountains. This sunrise was one of the most incredible in my life. The light changed every second, and veils of mist were floating in the air, shining with the first rays of the sun. It's quite a small territory, but it's a paradise for hiking in winter. I climbed to the top of the mountain in the middle of the night, long before sunrise, to make this image. I bracketed the shot at 1/200 sec., then blended the photographs together in an HDR RAW file using Adobe Lightroom, to capture the detail throughout the image.

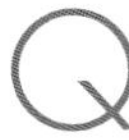

Q + A

Were you attracted to the outdoors before outdoor photography?

I started as a mountain and climbing guide in my university mountain club. We hiked and traveled a lot, watching sunrises above the clouds. It would be hard not to start sharing the beauty with others, wouldn't it? I never thought that photography could be my work or profession. I enjoyed my scientific work at university, and photography was always a passion. I still do not consider my workshops as work, really. It is an essential part of my life. Besides, I grew up in a beautiful region in Russia, by a lake, and from my early childhood spent lots of time around nature— camping, cycling, and swimming. I bought my first small camera when I was 16 and my first photograph, of course, was of my beautiful lake.

How has your background shaped your photography style and philosophy?

My background is physics. It is quite funny to say this, but quantum physics, in particular, has influenced my photography—I got used to solving complicated problems. In travel and photography, you always need to solve logistical and compositional problems, so it's good training for the brain. My childhood bond with nature synthesized with university technical studies into my love for photography. It was hard to choose between science and photography, but I've made the decision and I doubt I'll return to science. Photography opens new horizons and helps me make amazing friends all over the world. It offers motivation to travel, seek, and explore. There are no white spaces left on maps, but there are lots of white spaces left for photography. My style has developed over the years, first in the way I see and seek compositions, and secondly in my color representation—the way I see and feel the color. Besides, a landscape photographer's style is not just in the processing, but first of all in the planning. The way I plan my year reflects my style. So the ideas of my trips, realized in a particular project, make my style. Currently, I prefer to mix photography workshops with expeditions to remote locations.

What is it about remote locations that inspires you so much?

Our planet was given to us to explore. We are here not to produce money, but we are here to feel, listen, and explore our beautiful world. When I see the first rays of the sun, the beautiful colors in the sky, they inspire me to move forward. The photographer's world is saturated with copies of the same locations. But there are still plenty of places to explore in the world. Most of them require hard planning and truly tough expeditions, like my Greenland sailings. Many locations in Russia are hard to reach, but you can get unique stuff from them. I like the feeling of being an explorer when I approach the remote shores of Svalbard or Greenland on our yacht, or stand on the snowy peaks of the Tien-Shan mountains. My current favorite location is Greenland. This land of ice has everything: icebergs, mountains, northern lights, fjords. It is a beautiful country barely explored by photographers. I was born in Russia and really admire the country's nature, especially in regions such as Kamchatka and Lake Baikal, in northern Russia.

How important is it to plan trips in advance, and how many of your images are spur of the moment?

Planning takes you half the way to a good picture. I plan each of my expeditions very precisely. If we speak about "civilization," I try to read a lot about the place I intend to visit. There are plenty of useful tools for analyzing a location: I use services like Panoramio (Google Earth), TPE, PhotoPills, Flickr, and 500px, and look at photographs from locations. But, for many of the places I visit (such as Greenland), there aren't yet any photographs, so we plan the expedition to the region to explore it, while saving enough time for photography. In Greenland, we communicate with local fishermen, helicopter pilots, and geologists. Some trips might result in zero outcome in terms of photographs, because of bad weather, for example, but it's always a great adventure in the company of great people.

AURORA TORNADO

I guide tours to the Lofoten Islands each winter. The landscape is very diverse, and offers many opportunities to photograph the northern lights. The temperature jumps above zero from time to time, breaking and melting the ice. I arranged this composition around the foreground from a more messy original breakage. This is a "vertorama," or vertical panorama, which consists of two horizontal shots both using a 14mm focal length. The lower frame consists of two horizontal photographs taken with different focus points—one on the ice and the other on middle ground—for focus-stacking.

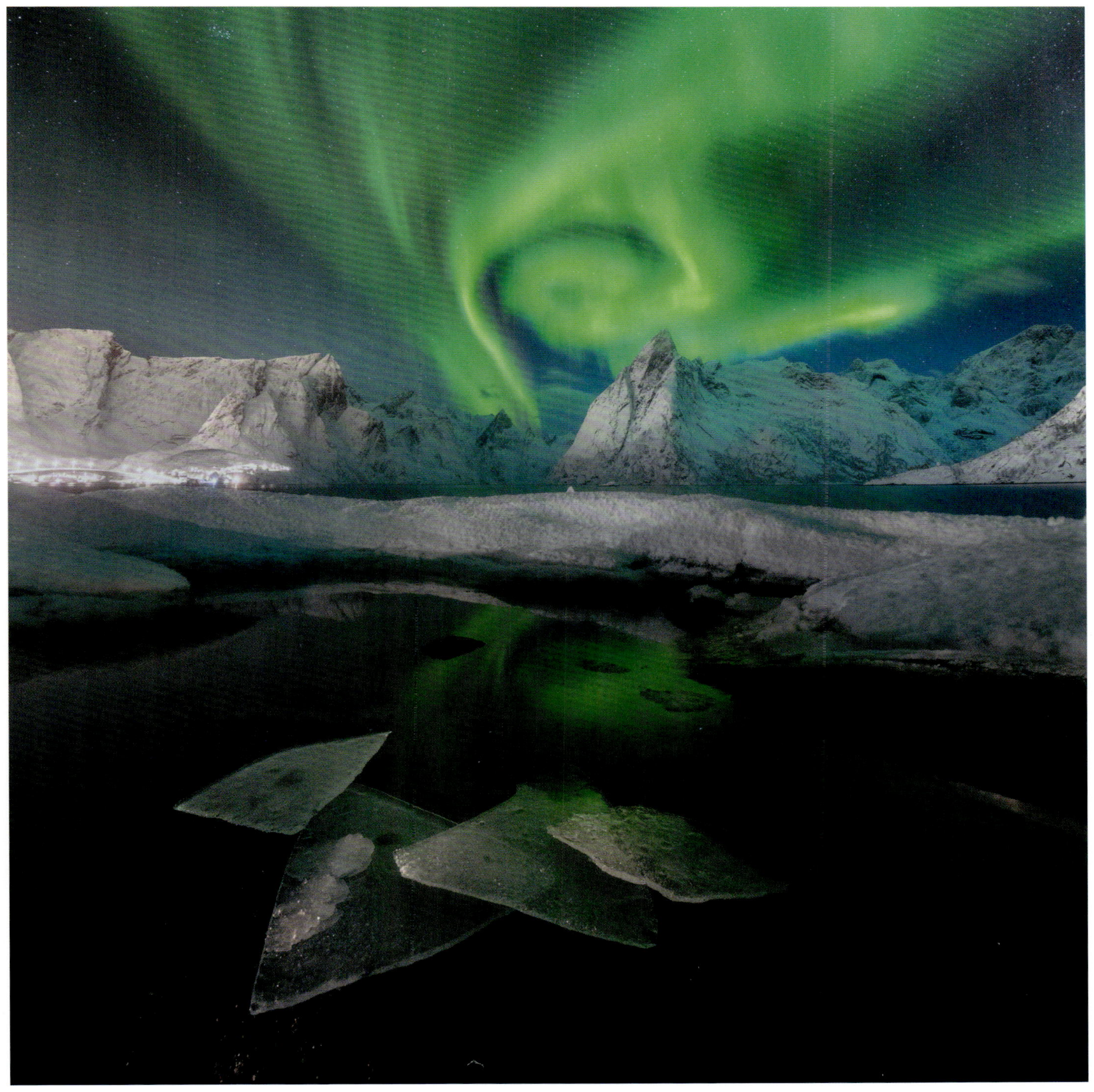

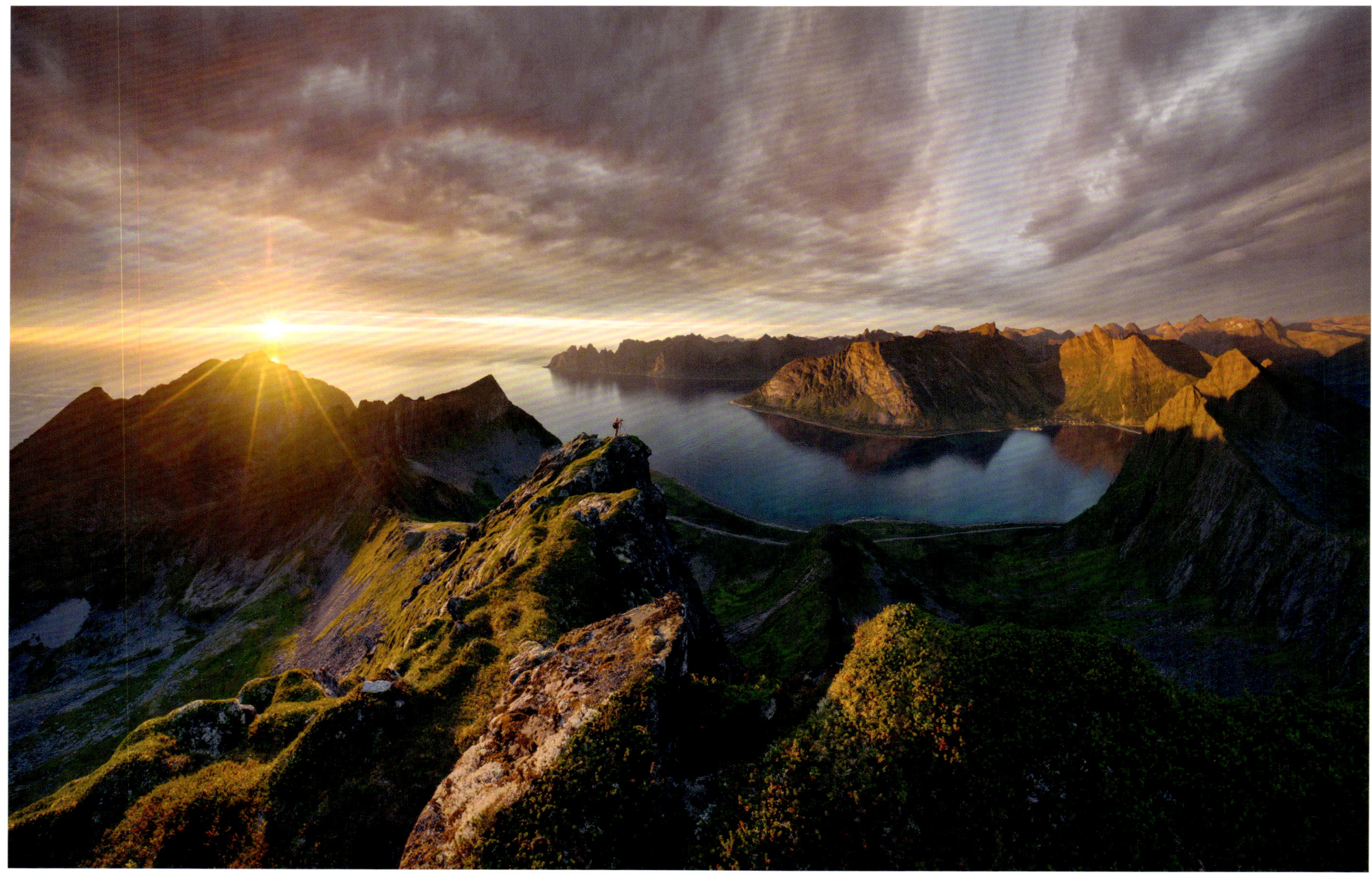

MIDNIGHT SUN

We had a wonderful three-hour hike to reach the top of the Husfjellet mountain on Senja Island, in northern Norway, in the midnight sun season of mid-August, when the sun never sets. We were lucky with the light the night that I took this photograph. This is actually a high-dynamic-range image, from five photographs, made in Photoshop using masks. I photographed the sky at 1/60 sec. exposure for each of the five frames, then I stitched them together to make this panorama.

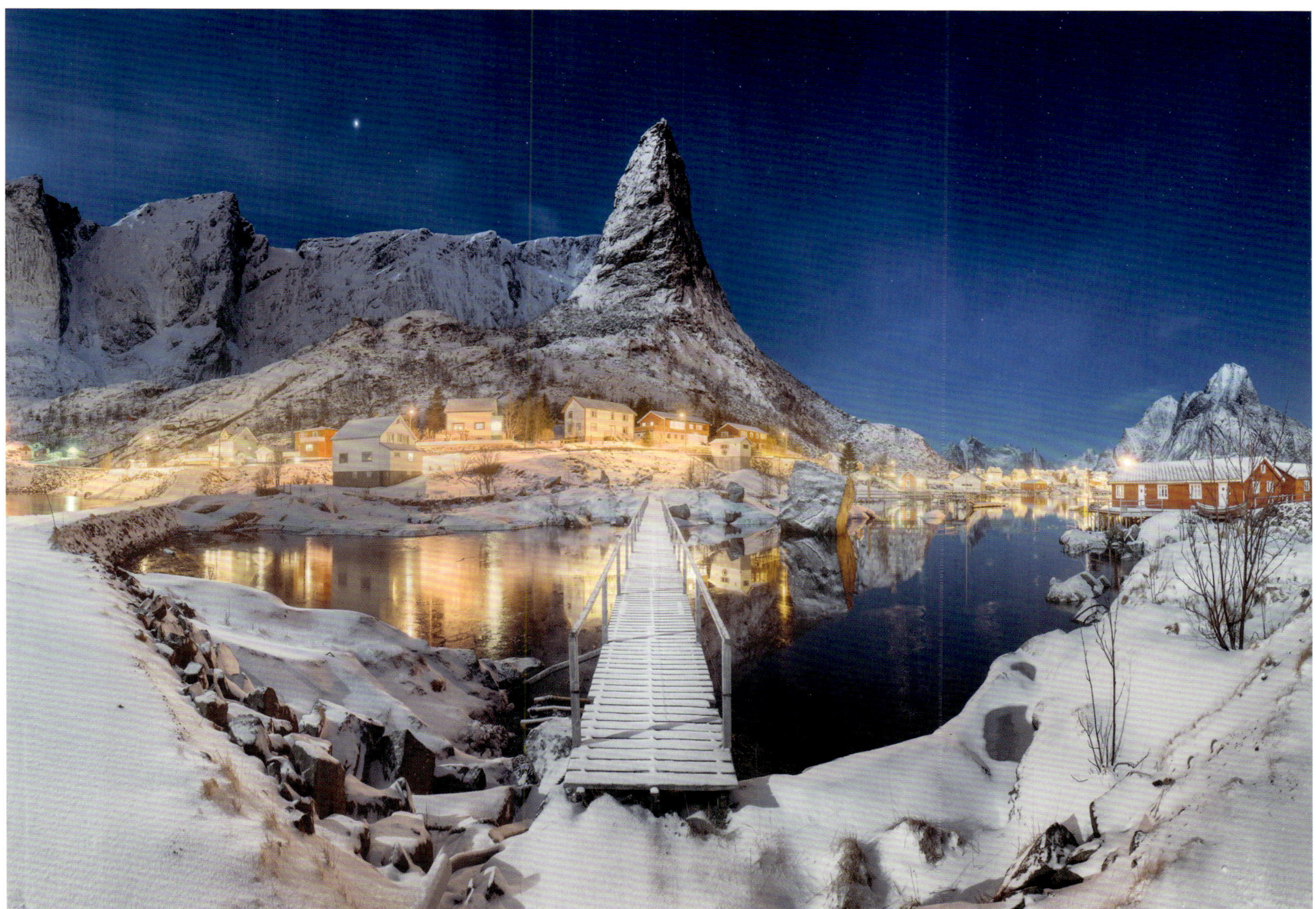

NORTHERN MATTERHORN

I love the Lofoten Islands in northern Norway, with their remarkable atmosphere, and I return here often. This is the small fishing village of Reine in February. Usually in winter, you can see the northern lights above the mountains, but even without them the village looks like a Christmas paradise, with its small fishing boats and a charming seaside ambience. This is another panoramic photograph, constructed from five vertical images.

Q + A

Just how do you create the sense of drama and awe that is such a feature of your landscape images?

I'm in constant search of light and strong compositions. On the one hand, the idea for a composition should be clear and simple, and on the other I prefer to have complicated three-dimensional scenes with a distinctive foreground, which is balanced with the other elements in the image. I use strong perspective, rhythmical perspective, and visual paths in my photographs, all while trying not to lose the sense of scale.

How much equipment do you take with you on a hike or climb—have you refined your kit over the years to travel light?

I use a Nikon D810 and D810A, as well as Nikkor 14–24, 24–70, and 70–200mm lenses, and the 400mm f/2.8 for animal photography. I also carry Lucroit filters (165mm), a Really Right Stuff tripod, and an F-stop backpack. I do not take the 70–200mm or 400mm lenses, or the filters for the 14–24mm lens on my hikes, because they're too bulky. But I do use an L-plate and nodal slide rail (or a panoramic head) for my panoramic images. I also carry Gitzo Traveler tripods for light hikes and the more sturdy mountain series for my seascapes. I prefer to use the Nikon D810 instead of mirrorless cameras because of its reliability and battery life.

What practical problems do you face when traveling to remote places for landscape photography— is it necessary to restrict the photographic equipment you take, for instance?

When we travel to Greenland or Antarctica on the yacht, we do not limit ourselves in terms of gear weight. These trips are technical, but mostly in terms of planning and enduring everything the sea throws at you. On my hikes, though, I'm very precise in choosing equipment—I limit myself to only one body, and I carry the 14-24mm and 24-70mm lenses, as well as a light tripod. When I traveled in Russia, I even cut down the straps on my backpack to save weight, but I still carried a heavy Nikon D810 and a set of four to five batteries. Durability and reliability are the top requirements on expeditions to remote places.

What single piece of kit is the most useful in your work?

The Nikkor 14–24mm is my favorite lens—it is wide, crisply sharp, and very well built. I've taken 90 percent of my shots with this lens.

TECHNICAL INFORMATION

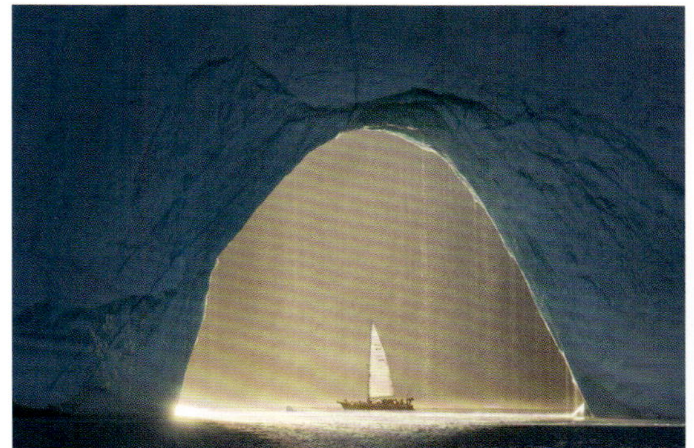

GOLDEN ARCH
SCORESBY SOUND, GREENLAND

Camera: Nikon D810
Lens/Focal length: Nikkor 80–200mm f/2.8 at 155mm
Aperture: f/16
Shutter speed: 1/1000 sec.
ISO: 400

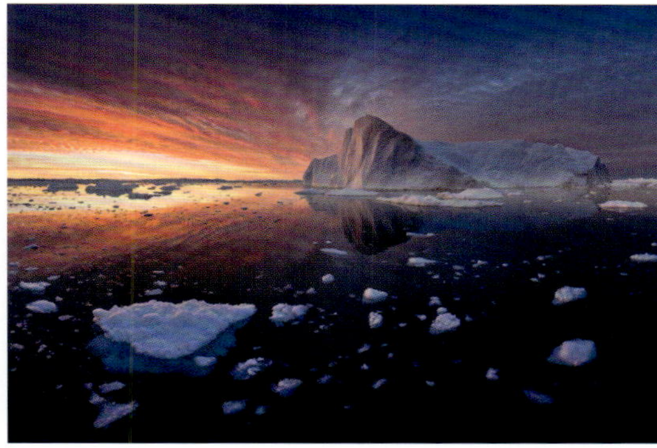

DISKO BAY
DISKO BAY, GREENLAND

Camera: Nikon D810
Lens/Focal length: Nikkor 14–24mm f/2.8 at 14mm
Aperture: f/5.6
Shutter speed: Bracketed frames at 1/60 sec.
ISO: 400
Other: Four frames

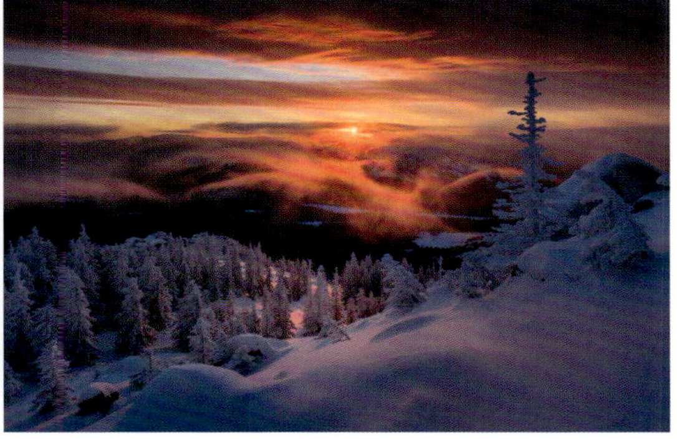

TAGANAY
TAGANAY NATIONAL PARK, ZLATOUST, RUSSIA

Camera: Nikon D810
Lens/Focal length: Nikkor 14–24mm f/2.8 at 19mm
Aperture: f/16
Shutter speed: 1/13 sec.
ISO: 160
Other: Bracketed frames at 1/200 sec.

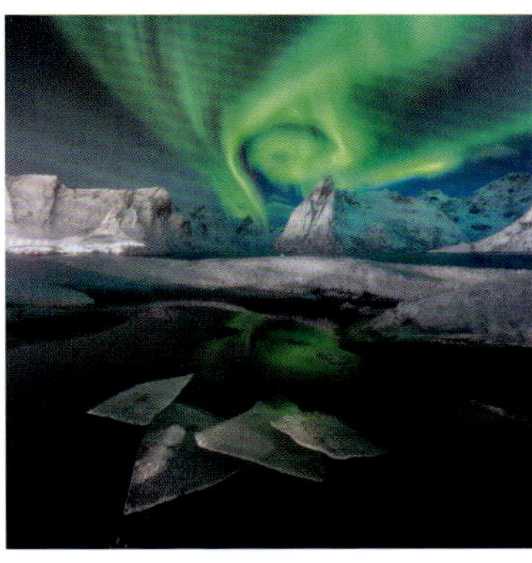

AURORA TORNADO
REINE,
NORWAY

Camera: Nikon D810
Lens/Focal length: Nikkor 14–24mm f/2.8 at 14mm
Other: Two frames:
  Upper frame at f/2.8, 6 sec., ISO 3200
  Lower frame of two horizontal shots at f/6.3, 30 sec., ISO 2500

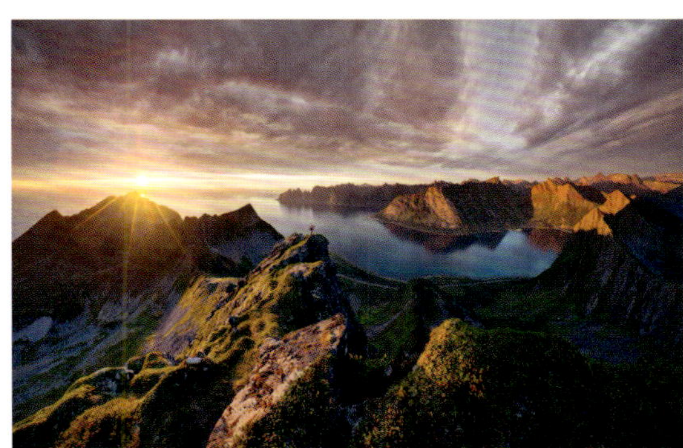

MIDNIGHT SUN
HUSFJELLET MOUNTAIN, SENJA ISLAND,
NORWAY

Camera: Nikon D800
Lens/Focal length: Nikkor 14–24mm f/2.8 at 14mm
Aperture: f/16
Shutter speed: 1/4 sec.
ISO: 100
Other: Bracketed frames at 1/60 sec.

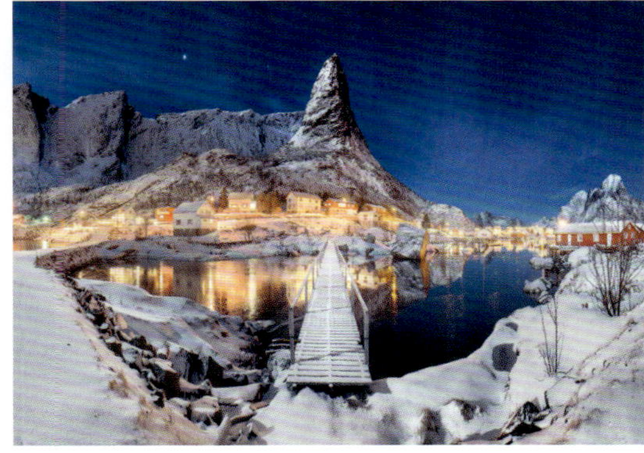

NORTHERN MATTERHORN
LOFOTEN ISLANDS,
NORWAY

Camera: Nikon D810
Lens/Focal length: Nikkor 14–24mm f/2.8 at 14mm
Aperture: f/4
Shutter speed: 20 sec.
ISO: 800

DAVID NOTON

With 32 years' experience as a wandering professional, David Noton is recognized as a leading landscape and travel photographer. His passion for photography, travel, and the world's beautiful places is the defining influence that has shaped his life, work, and creative approach. David's images sell all over the world, both as fine art photography and commercially in advertising and publishing. He is a multiple award winner in the BBC Wildlife Photographer of the Year competition.

After an upbringing in Canada and a stint in the Merchant Navy, David returned to college to study photography. Graduating in 1985, he embarked on a career as a commercial and stock photographer specializing in landscape and travel work. In 2008, David's first book *Waiting for the Light* was published, followed by his groundbreaking film *Chasing the Light*, the foundation for the innovative *Chasing the Light Road Show* that now tours Europe. David's other books are *Full Frame* (2010), published alongside the film *Photography in the RAW*, and *The Vision* (2013); and in 2012 he launched the innovative *f11 Photography Magazine*. David has been a Canon Ambassador since 2012, given the title Official Canon Explorer, and has been inducted into the Manfrotto Ambassador Program.

EMERALD LAKE

South of Whitehorse, the scenery changes as big mountains rear up. Dropping down toward Carcross, we see below the startling sight of Emerald Lake. There are a few emerald lakes in Canada—we know the one in Yoho well—but this one certainly deserves its name; the colors of the water are beyond belief. We stop to log the location for a return shoot, but immediately I'm struck by how perfect the reflections are here and now, in the late afternoon. Such conditions cannot be taken for granted—it's best to make the most of it while I can. As I frame up the simple composition, I'm wondering if anyone will believe these colors are real. Of course, I know because I Googled it that the intense color derives from light reflecting off white deposits of clay and calcium carbonate called marl, which lie at the bottom of the shallow waters and come from limestone gravels eroded from the nearby mountains, deposited here 14,000 years ago by the glaciers of the last ice age. But I fear some will think I've just got a bit carried away with the vibrance slider in Lightroom.

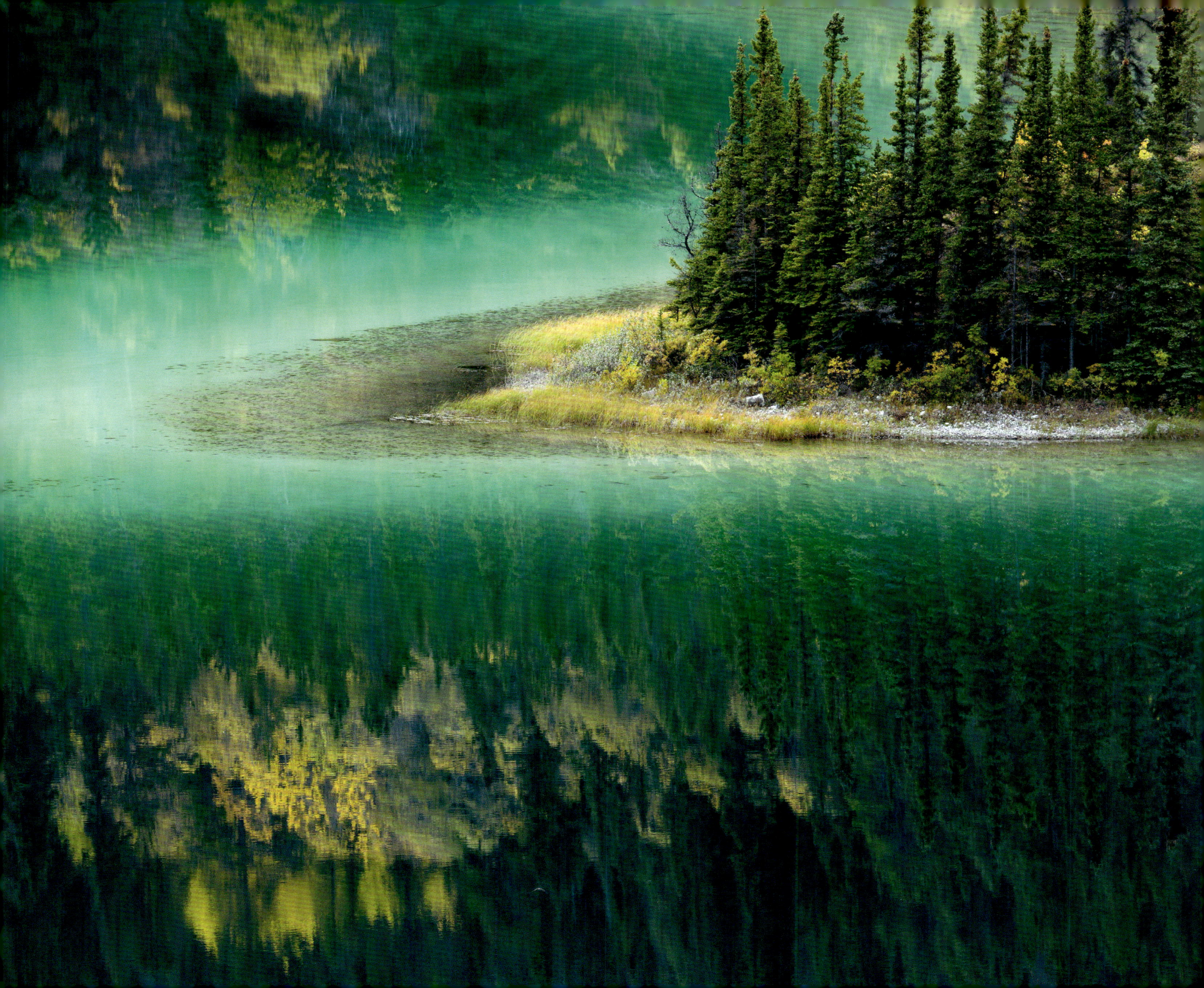

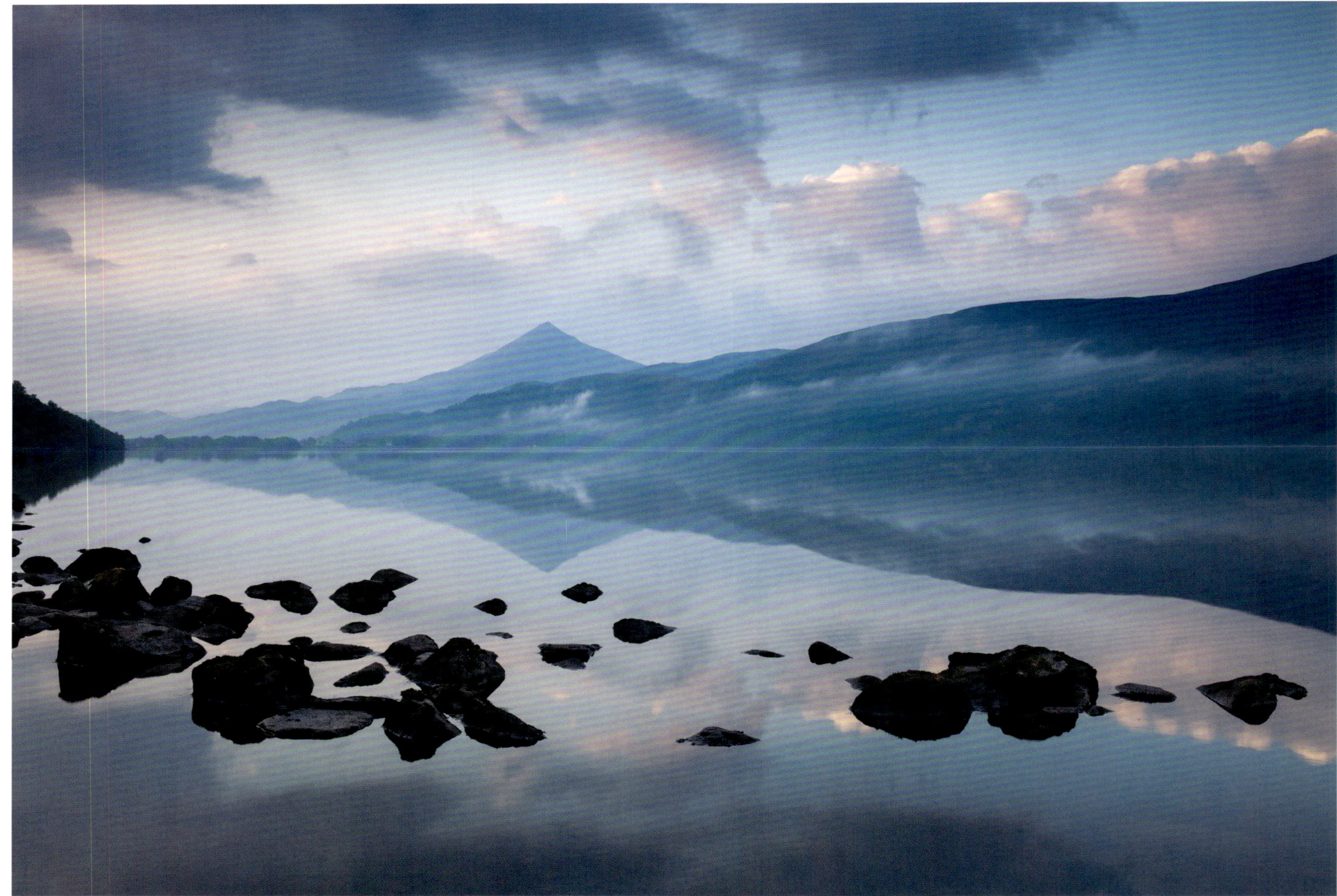

SCHIEHALLION REFLECTED IN LOCH RANNOCH AT DAWN

Symmetry is what this composition will all be about. That, and the light, the peace, the tranquility, and the resonance of being here behind the lens on such an achingly atmospheric morning all these years after my first attempt in 1980. I fine-tune my composition, wait for my self-induced ripples to subside, and shoot. It is a different scene from my first visit—such experiences can never be re-created—but this is a very special moment, and one I know I'll remember for the rest of my days. I'm in awe of the sublime, ethereal beauty. Two hours standing in a loch pass in what feels like minutes. Since that dawn 37 years ago, I have been lucky to have witnessed the light painting this Earth at dawn and dusk in magical places all over the world more times than I care to mention, and yet I can remember them all with startling clarity. They are the experiences that make me a wealthy soul, and it all started here.

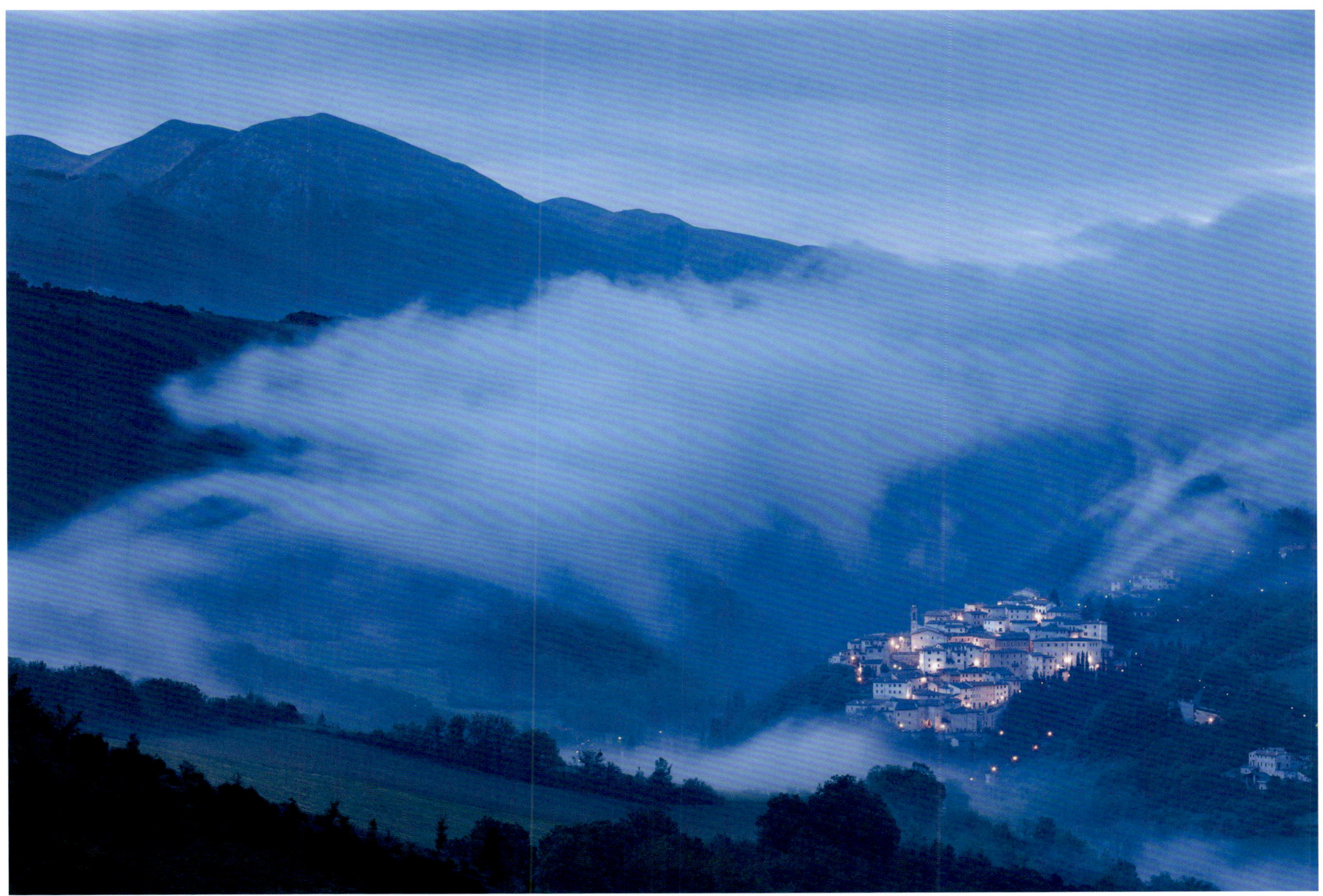

PRECI SURROUNDED BY MIST AT DAWN

This is a scene I have photographed maybe 20 times or more, but every single time was different. Being there as dawn breaks, watching the light paint the landscape, was a special experience—it always is—and the shot that worked best that particular morning came particularly early, as the mist swirled and the lights of Preci clinging precariously to the slopes of the Valnerina still glowed. As usual I chose to shoot the image with daylight white balance set, capturing the cool blue light of pre-dawn without any alteration either in-camera or during post-production. I hardly ever adjust the color balance of Mother Nature's benevolence. This is now an image given extra significance as the scene will never be the same again, due to the devastating earthquakes that shook the region in 2016. Preci is now in ruins.

Q

+

A

How much research and preparation go into a typical David Noton shoot?

Quite a bit. It would be very rare for me to visit a location that I haven't eyeballed beforehand. Normally, I spend more time on location-searching and planning than I actually do behind the camera, and I think that's probably true for most photographers. I find that the actual preparation and finding the location are the hardest bits really. Originality is the key. Approaching each location with a new eye is the challenge, and I believe that even with somewhere as popular as the Eiffel Tower, say, I think there's always scope for doing something different. And that, in a nutshell, is what the game's about—bringing to bear your different photographic vision. It's not easy, but creating something original is so much more satisfying. Developing a style comes with time—it can't be forced. It's a process of investigation and inspiration, and it gradually comes. The danger is, of course, that you evolve a look and a style and never deviate from it, but it should be something that is permanently evolving, as you're trying new things. There's nothing wrong with being inspired by other photographers' or artists' work—that's all part of the process. There's a thin line between being inspired by something and copying it, of course, but artists throughout the generations have been inspired by each other.

Why is light such an important ingredient in a landscape image?

I sometimes think that I'm photographing the light as much as the subject itself, and so if you take a landscape—such as a field of barley as it turns gold—then really the light itself will be so critical. That barley, particularly during the middle part of the day, when the sun has parched it, can look yellow and unappealing. But when it is lit by the first or last light of the day, it will absolutely glow golden. I think sometimes the light is the most important aspect of photography—you could make a lump of coal look visually interesting with the right light.

What do you find yourself doing more—"chasing the light" or "waiting for the light"?

Definitely waiting. I hardly ever chase light. I think it's really just a case of when I've found a good idea, and when I've found a good location, then I'll wait . . . and wait, and wait . . . and whether that wait is going to be a few minutes, a few hours, or maybe months, sometimes years, then I will wait. That's the difference between a cracking shot and just an average shot. When I'm out location-searching, or just going for a walk, I'll see a location, and I might determine it's not the right time for that shoot, and I'll go back in the fall or winter. And if it's a good enough idea, it'll often warrant several attempts, to extract the best from that idea. I first got into landscape photography following a visit to Loch Rannoch in the Scottish Highlands, way back in 1980, when I just bought my first proper SLR. I experienced this fantastic morning on the banks of the loch, with this beautiful mist and flat-calm reflections of the perfect pyramidal peak of Schiehallion, rising up, and, in my naive inexperience, I just shot two frames. Now I've been going back to that same place fairly regularly for the last 37 years, and just last May I got conditions again that were as good, if slightly different, as that original shoot way back then—so that's how long a good photograph can take to make!

The "golden hours" at dawn and dusk are renowned for being the best times of day to take landscapes—are these the only times when good landscapes are possible?

There is no denying that the light at that time of the day is appealing and inspiring and can transform a landscape—but I think it's a mistake to restrict yourself just to that kind of light. I was up in Scotland photographing the dappled light on the landscape in the middle of the day, with those fantastic Caledonian pine trees set against a majestic backdrop. Normally, I wouldn't think of shooting in that light, but every rule is there to be broken, and, even after 32 years as a professional, I'm still learning about light, still trying new things, still challenging accepted norms. I also think that the cameras we're using now, which have increasing dynamic range, can cope with the contrast of the light in the middle of the day much better.

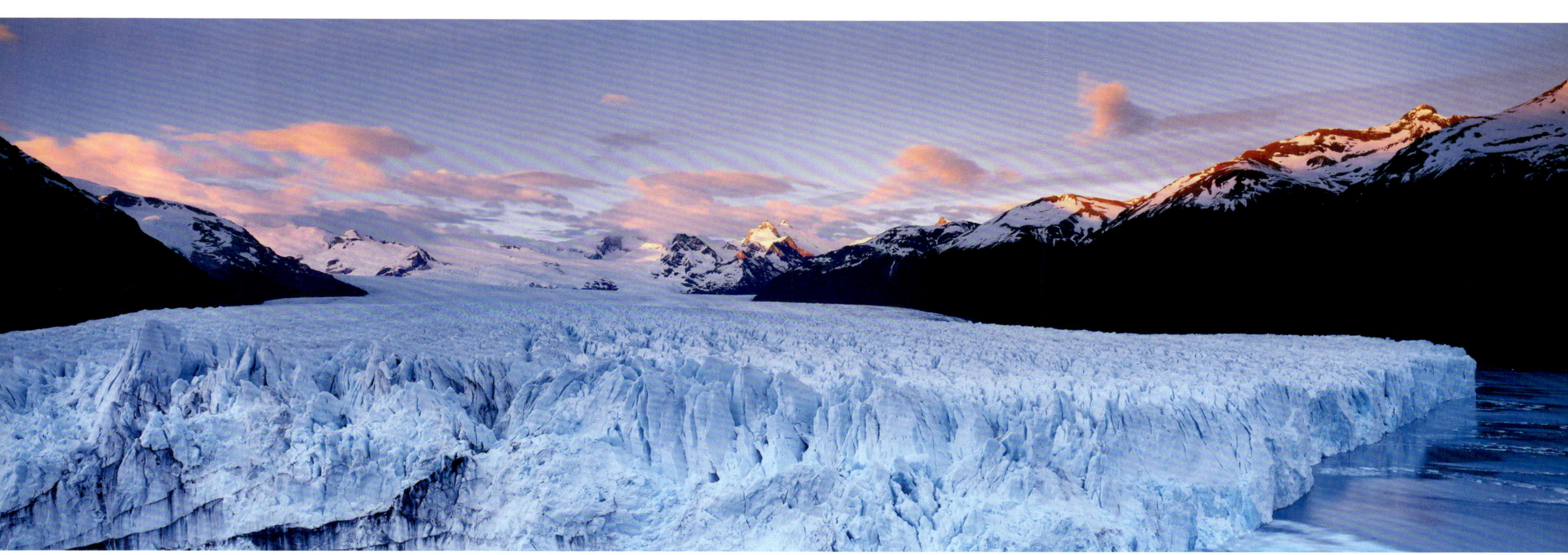

PERITO MORENO GLACIER

During my time as a professional photographer, the whole world of photography has changed massively, both in how we capture images and what we do with them subsequently. This image of the Perito Moreno Glacier, in Argentine Patagonia, was shot before the digital revolution on an old behemoth of a camera, using that horrid, environmentally damaging stuff commonly called film. Compared to the cameras and lenses I'm using now it all seems hopelessly antiquated, and yet the fundamentals of what makes a successful photograph haven't changed an iota—it's still all about the light, the subject, the composition, and being there for the decisive moment. I have no nostalgia for the technology of that era. Traveling the world packing hundreds of rolls of light-sensitive silver halide emulsion, and two completely incompatible camera systems, is something I'm glad to leave behind. I love the flexibility of modern digital cameras, but that doesn't mean the old images from the film era are in any way diminished—at the end of the day, it's all about the picture, not how it was produced.

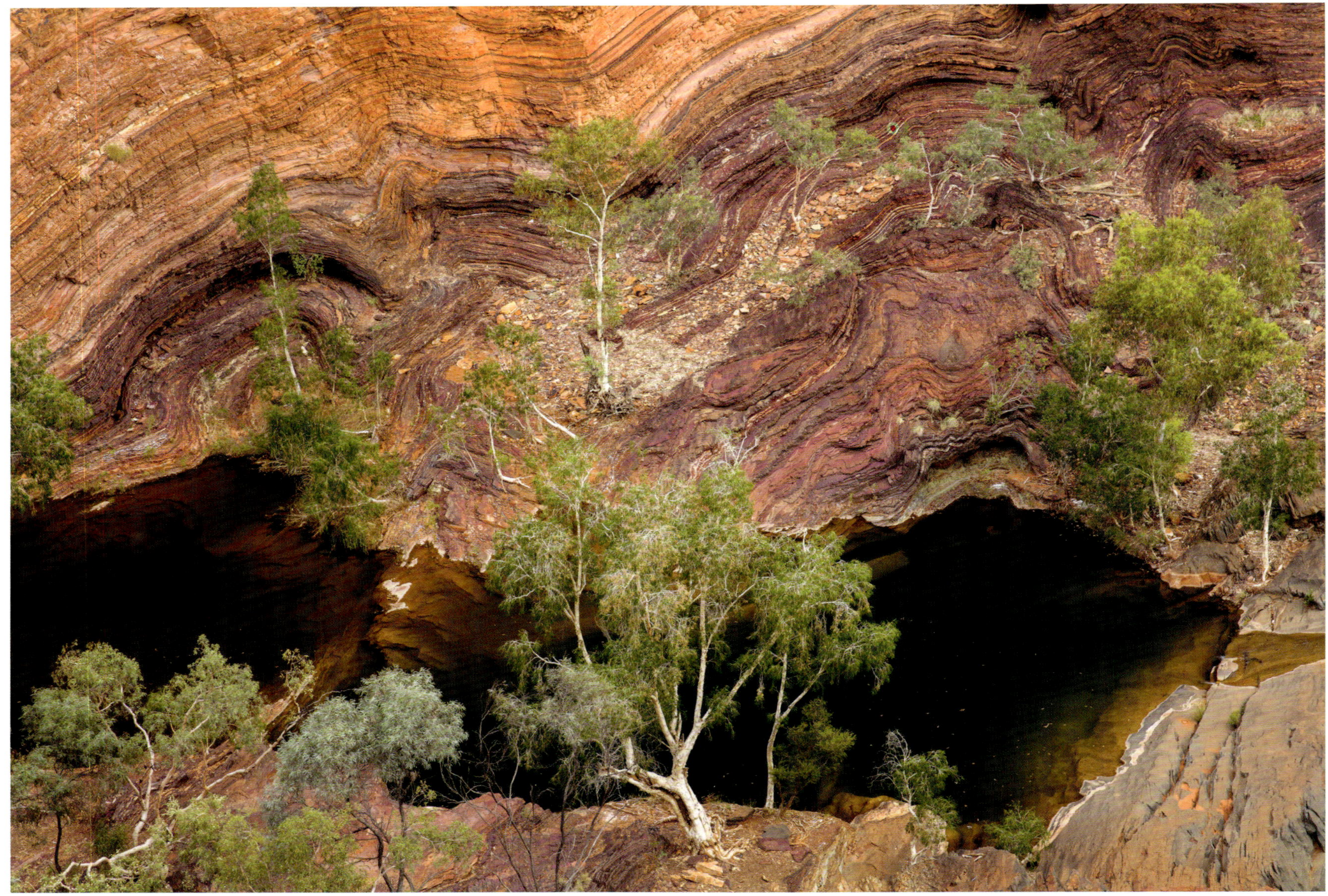

HAMERSLEY GORGE

Hamersley Gorge is at the end of a long dirt road with the worst corrugations we've experienced. It feels like the "Troopy" is being shaken apart, but I suppose it's built for this—we're not. The drive into the twilight gathering in the sky to the east takes 90 minutes, as predicted, but feels much longer. I'm looking down into the gorge, working on a green tree against a backdrop of twisted rock layers. The contortions of the layers below belie their age—some are 2,500 million years old. The image in my frame of color and texture is unique enough purely from a visual sense, and so typical of this part of Australia, but the knowledge that I am photographing one of the oldest landscapes in the world gives this shoot special significance.

FOX IN A FIELD

It's 4.50am, and I'm setting up with the big 200–400mm 1.4x lens on the tripod. From here on a roadside embankment, I can see the village through a narrow gap in the trees. If I move either up or down, right or left, the tight cluster of honey-colored buildings is lost. In the field below are some freshly rolled hay bales. With a bit of careful maneuvering, I can just about include them in my frame. A long focal length allows me to isolate all else from the image area, concentrating just on the village with the foreshortened perspective of the ultra-long lens working to my advantage. The soft early light is just starting to paint the paysage from the northeast, sidelighting the scene as I perceived it would when we stumbled across this view on last week's hike. I switch on Live View, check all my settings, and make my first exposure. What's that speck in the field? It's a fox. "Basil" scampers across the field, and then stops just in the right place, as if posing for my lens. The shutter clicks. Cue euphoria: it could be the shot that encapsulates the trip in a nutshell.

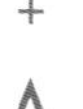

You achieve wonderful depth in your shots—how do you maintain sharpness throughout a landscape photograph?

That is an entirely technical process which involves calculating the hyperfocal distance that determines where my focus point will be, and what aperture I need to use to get that depth from foreground to background. That's the theory, which is all well and good, but that's just the starting point—you can't beat trial and error, doing test shots, and zooming in on the screen to check critical sharpness to ensure clarity. But I think another aspect is the lighting, which can give that sense of depth and sharpness, and, in particular, side lighting, which I suppose is my favorite form of lighting for my landscape work. That really reveals that extra form in the foreground and background, and gives that sense of depth and clarity.

Do you have a favored post-processing workflow—is there anything you always do with your images to enhance them?

I try to get the image as perfect as I can in-camera, so the image needs as little attention as possible. Sometimes, in certain situations, particularly with a high-contrast image, then it might require a bit more work. For most images, I will just pay attention to the black and white points in Lightroom, then make tonal and contrast adjustments, possibly to selected areas, to darken some and brighten others. That's all fairly straightforward, and most images pass through my workflow in just a few minutes. I am a great believer in keeping things simple! Occasionally, though, there will be a situation in which I need to give the image more attention, and I'll resort to exposure merging, if I have to, in order to tame the contrast. But, increasingly, I'm finding that less and less necessary, because of the dynamic range of today's camera sensors.

How important is it to a photographer—both commercially and creatively—to work on projects, developing a body of work instead of individual shots?

Most of what I do is project-based, rather than individual shots, even if the projects are self-imposed. It just gives direction and purpose to my photography—I find it useful to force myself to look in certain ways. I think it's actually very difficult to just walk out of the door and say, "Well, I'm going to take a picture now"—you question what it's for, really. On the other hand, a project has definite structure to it, and I quite like the notion of photo essays, for example. When I go on a trip abroad, I want to come back with a selection of images, which, if you put the best 10 or 20 together, they're going to tell a story—they're going to be far more powerful than they would be individually. They will relate the experience of what it's actually like to be in that place for the viewer. Most of my photography now is driven by my online *f11 Photography Magazine*, so I set out with the intention of bringing back a set of pictures that is going to make a feature in that magazine.

As a master of landscape photography, what is your motivation to continue making photographs?

My lifetime in photography has introduced me to experiences around the world in some of the most beautiful, incredible places, which I would never have had or witnessed if it hadn't been for the photography. The photography is the prompt that makes me go out and stand by a glacial lake in the middle of the Yukon territories in the middle of the night—I don't think I'd do that if it weren't for photography! The picture aside, doing that is really, quite frankly, a life-enhancing experience. I can think back to so many times like that. And that really is the motivation to keep doing it.

TECHNICAL INFORMATION

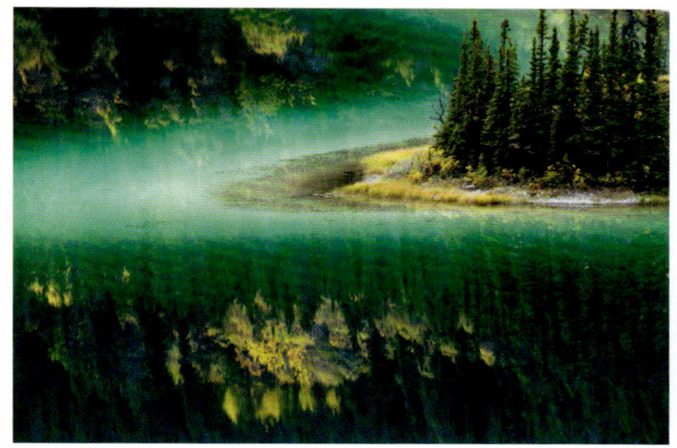

EMERALD LAKE
NEAR CARCROSS, YUKON TERRITORIES,
CANADA

Camera: Canon EOS-1D X
Lens/Focal length: Canon 200–400mm f/4 at 329mm
Aperture: f/7.1
Shutter speed: 1/200 sec.
ISO: 100

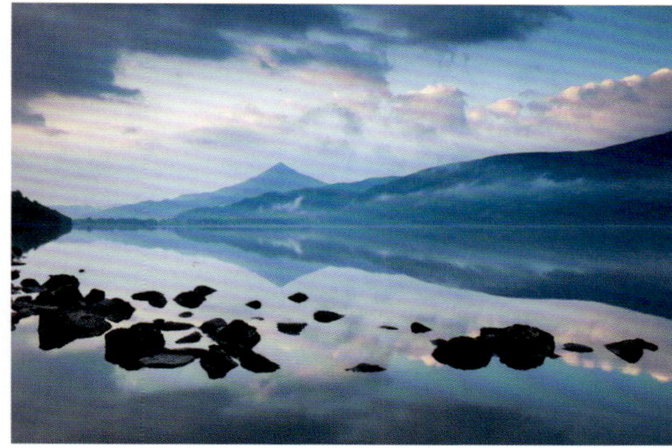

SCHIEHALLION REFLECTED IN LOCH
RANNOCH AT DAWN
PERTHSHIRE, SCOTLAND

Camera: Canon EOS 5DS R
Lens/Focal length: Canon 24–70mm f/2.8 at 35mm
Aperture: f/16
Shutter speed: 0.4 sec.
ISO: 100
Kit: 0.6 ND grad medium filter

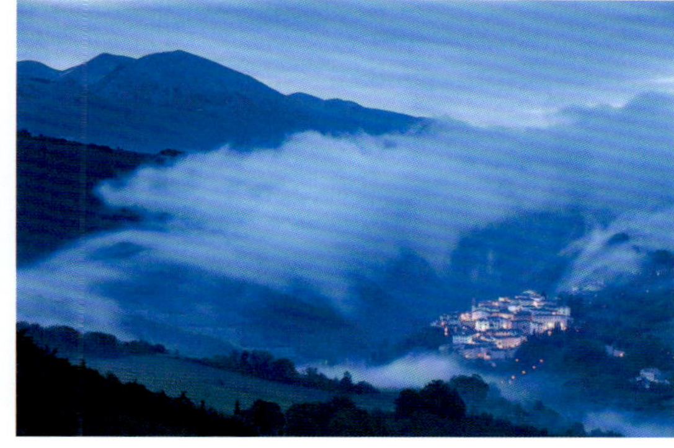

PRECI SURROUNDED BY MIST AT DAWN
VALNERINA, MONTI SIBILLINI NATIONAL PARK,
UMERIA, ITALY

Camera: Canon EOS-1D Mark III
Lens/Focal length: Canon 70–200mm f/2.8 at 110mm
Aperture: f/8
Shutter speed: 4 sec.
ISO: 100

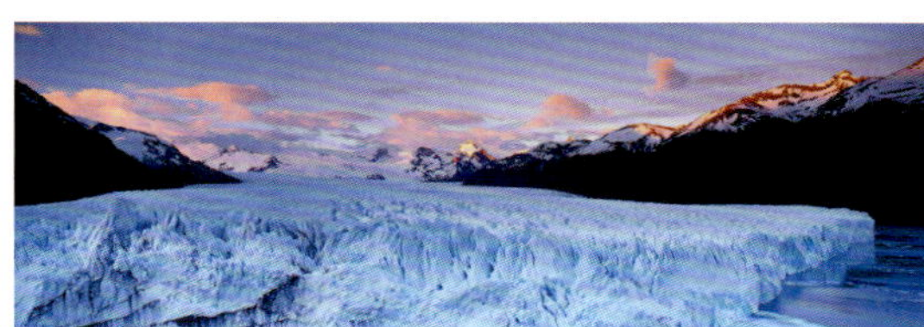

PERITO MORENO GLACIER
PATAGONIA,
ARGENTINA

Camera: Fuji GX617 panoramic film
Lens/Focal length: 90mm
Other information: Unrecorded

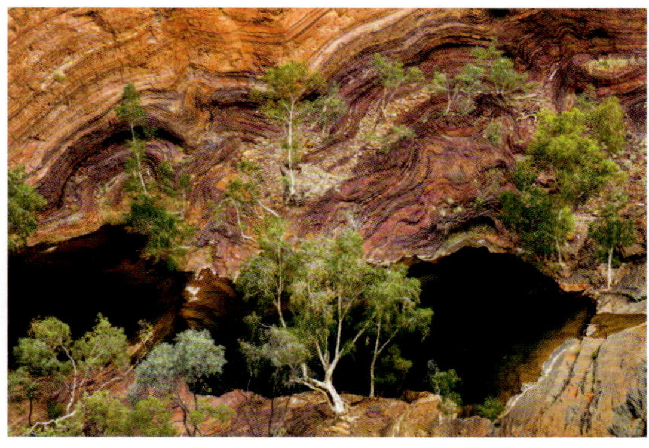

HAMERSLEY GORGE
KARIJINI NATIONAL PARK, PILBARA, WESTERN
AUSTRALIA

Camera: Canon EOS 5DS R
Lens/Focal length: Canon 24–70mm f/2.8 at 67mm
Aperture: f/11
Shutter speed: 0.5 sec.
ISO: 100
Kit: Polarizing filter

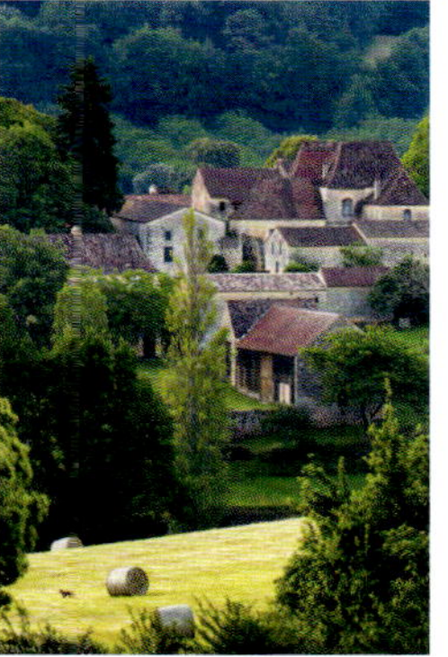

FOX IN A FIELD
NEAR MOLIÈRES, PAYS DE BERGERAC,
PÉR GORD, DORDOGNE, AQUITAINE, FRANCE

Camera: Canon EOS 5D Mark III
Lens/Focal length: Canon 200–400mm f/4 at 400mm
Aperture: f/22
Shutter speed: 1.6 sec.
ISO: 400

HANS STRAND

Hans Strand was born in 1955, in Marmaverken, Sweden. After a nine-year career in mechanical engineering, he decided to make a dramatic change and devote his life to landscape photography, which had been his long-held hobby and great passion. It is a change he has never regretted. Hans has always been drawn to the untamed and uncontrolled that he finds in nature. As he says, "The wilderness is the mother of all living things. It is always true and never trivial." Over the years, Hans has had the entire world as his workplace, photographing everything from the vast expanses of the Arctic and Antarctic, to steaming rainforests and parched deserts.

His work has been displayed in numerous exhibitions and published in many international photography magazines. He has also received several awards for his photography, including the Hasselblad Master Award in 2008 and as winner in the Land category in Wildlife Photographer of the Year. He has published seven books with landscape photographs, most recently *Iceland Above & Below* and *Intimate I.*

Hans lives in Hägersten, a southern suburb of Stockholm, Sweden, with his wife Carina and his daughter Johanna.

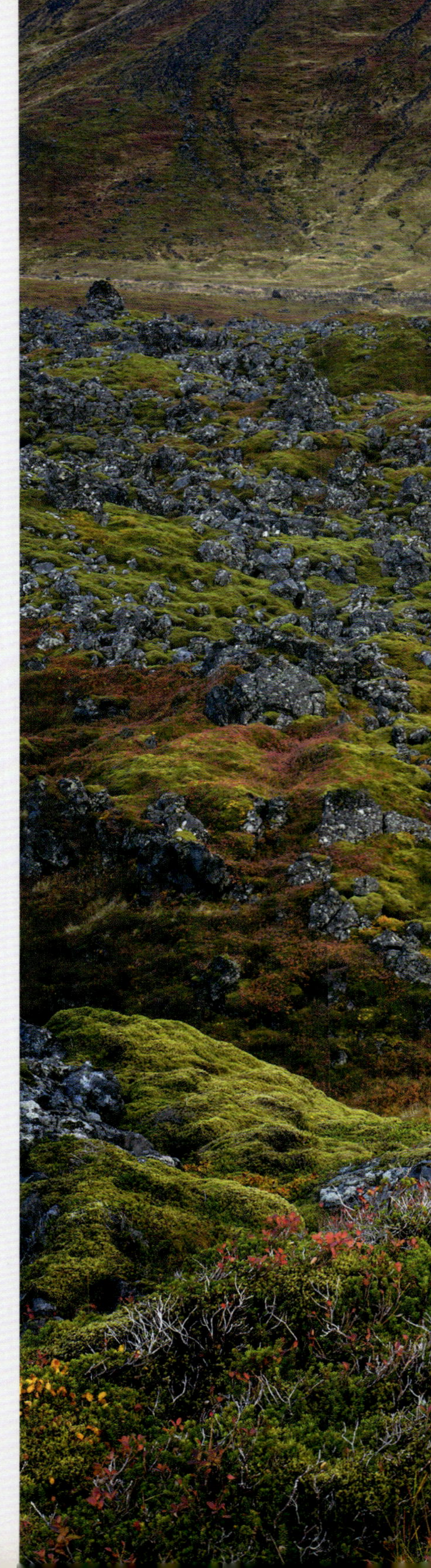

LAVA FIELD

One might think that a place like Iceland, with almost no trees, would not show a great amount of fall colors, but that is wrong. The ground vegetation of red berry plants and green mosses contrast perfectly against each other. I gave the lava monolith a central position in this composition. This is to provide a dominant character and some extra dynamism in the image. I quite often break away from using the "rule of thirds" for this reason.

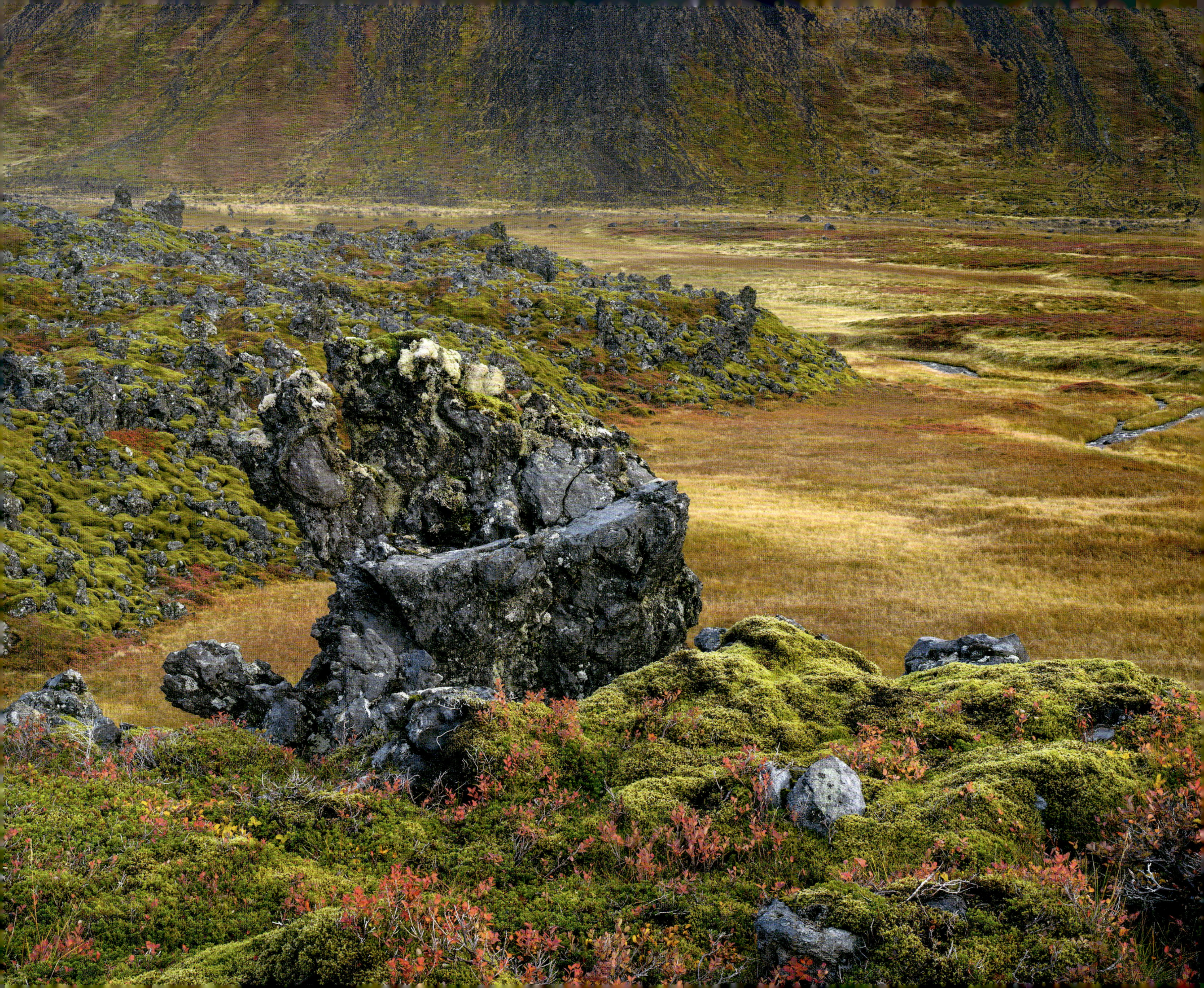

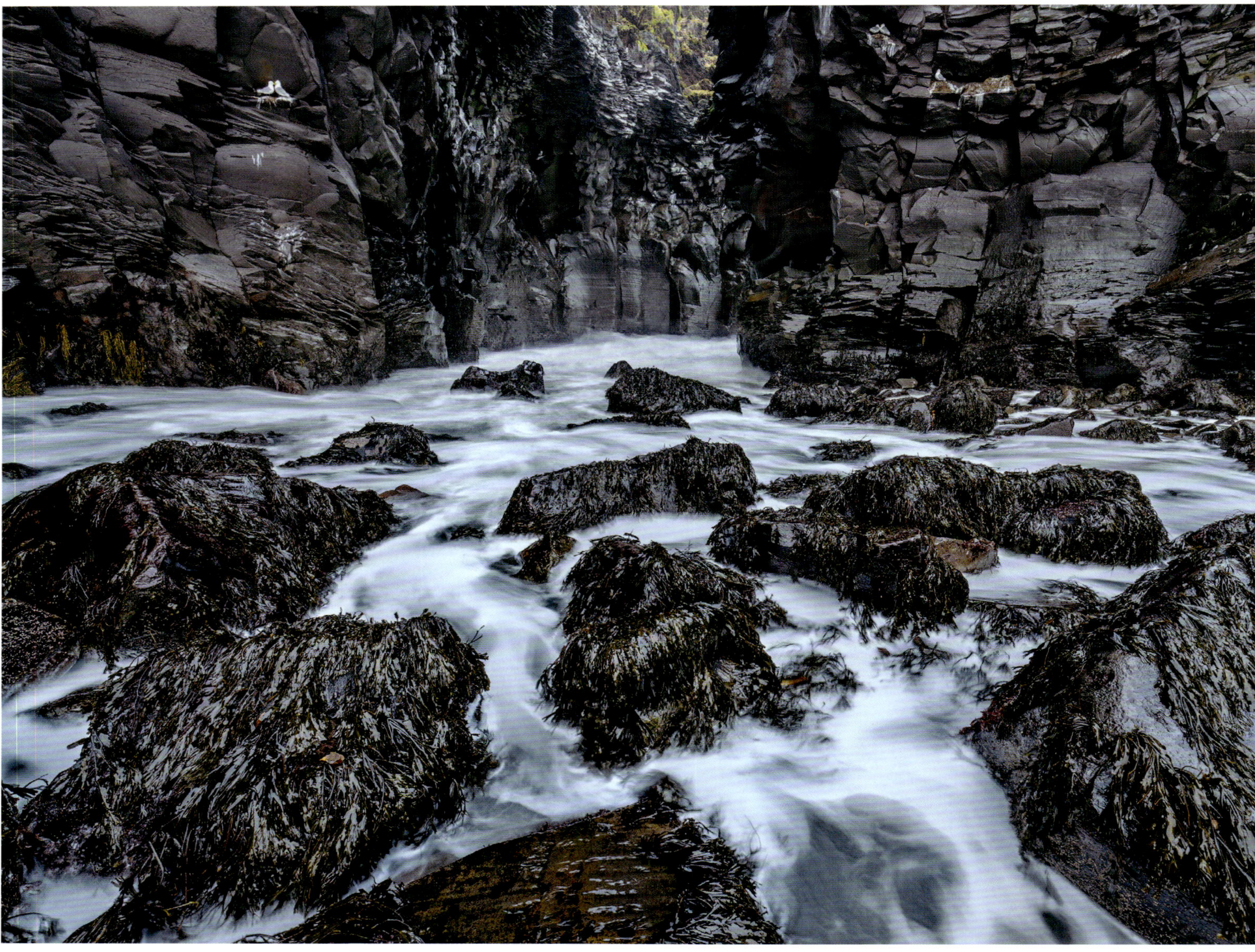

TIDE COMING IN

I shot this image just when the tide was coming in between the cliffs. The scene with dark rock and white water in motion attracted me. To get as much volume in the frame as possible, I used a 15mm super-wide-angle lens. I positioned myself carefully to make a composition with the kelp-covered boulders in the foreground. To keep the life in the scene, I wanted the incoming water to show some motion blur. The shutter speed was 2 seconds which showed enough of the motion without losing the texture in the water.

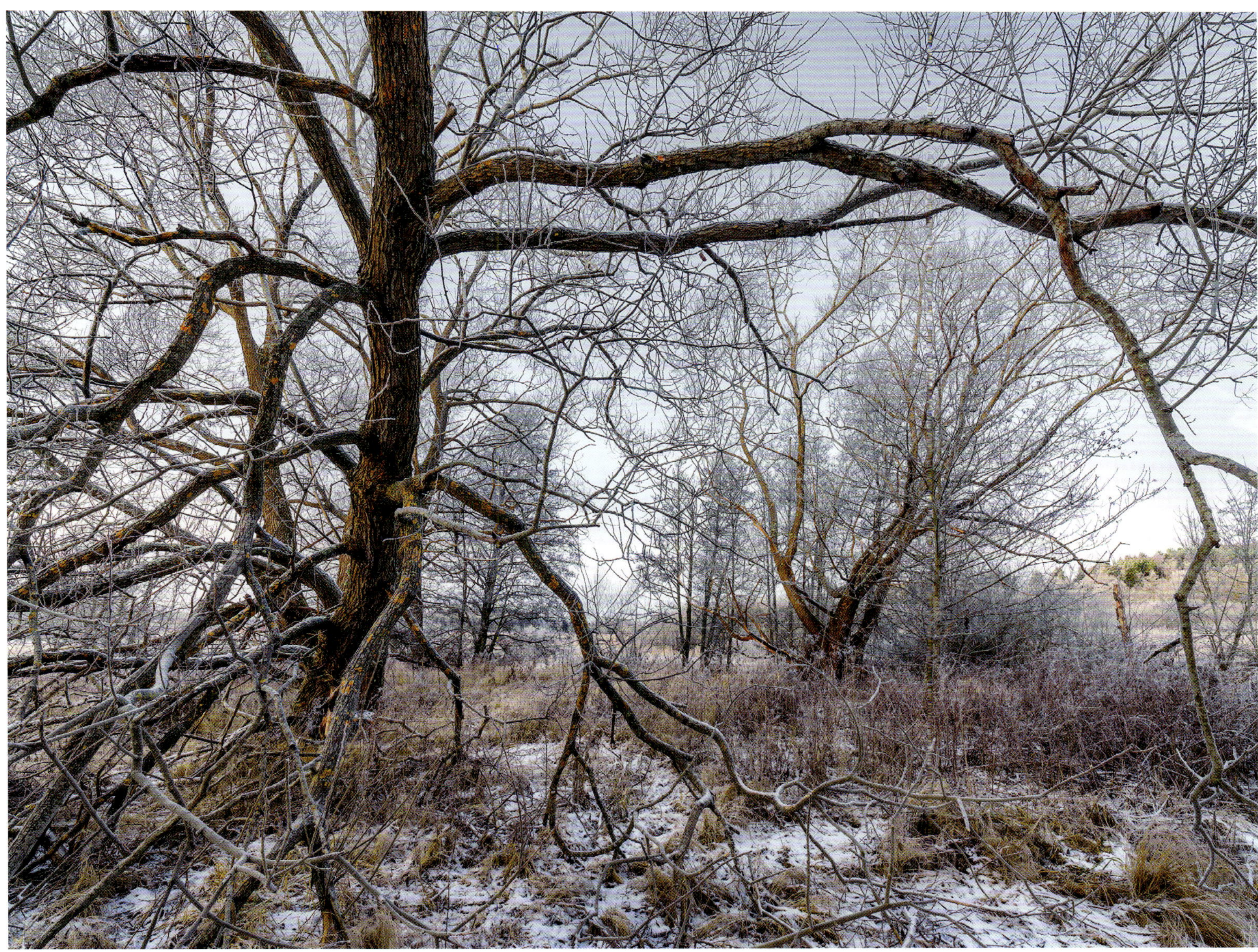

WINTER TREES

Taming the chaos of nature is the most demanding challenge in landscape photography. It demands your full attention and concentration. I saw the potential in this location, but it took me quite some time to find a position where the branches were forming a frame around the distant tree. I used a 15mm super-wide-angle lens, which made the positioning even more critical, since every single inch up or down, and left or right, makes a significant difference in the composition with such a wide lens. Finally, I ended up with this composition, with lots of geometry and fairly organized chaos.

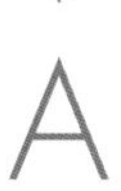

How did you start out in professional photography?

I didn't grow up with a camera in my hands. I was 25 years old when I bought my first camera, which happened on a school trip to California with my class from the Institute of Engineering in Stockholm. I took my first rolls of film in Yosemite National Park in the United States, and I immediately felt a connection with the landscape in front of me. That feeling is still there after 36 years. After the California trip, I worked as an engineer and was an amateur photographer for nine years, using all my weekends and vacations for photography. It took nine years of boring engineering before I had the guts to quit my work and to become a full-time landscape photographer. That happened in 1990.

Your work spans such a wide variety of subjects—is that for commercial or creative reasons?

In the field of landscape photography there are many subjects. I love trees, water, coastline, mountains, aerials, and also, more and more, the landscapes affected by humans. It has always been for creative reasons. The commercial spin-off is something I try to make come through after I have got my images. I seldom do assignments.

You are well known for your intimate landscape photographs—what do you look for when taking this style of image?

I find the best connection with nature in the intimate landscape. The complexity of nature's chaos is a tough subject and it takes a lot of brain power to organize it into an image. That process is what I find the most rewarding in photography. In the beginning of my career, I was more into drama and sensation, but as I get older, I like a more poetic expression in my work. I very rarely shoot sunsets and sunrises for that reason. I think this is too romantic an approach, and more about showing the power of nature—rather than its naked, subtle, and nuanced sides, which interest me most.

Are there any particular technical challenges involved in shooting a close-up landscape?

The main challenge is to make something quiet and subtly interesting. When you speak with small letters you are always balancing on a thin line. If the content and composition are too simple, the image comes out as banal. The technical quality is also very important to me. It is easier to communicate with your intimate work if there is great tonality and detail.

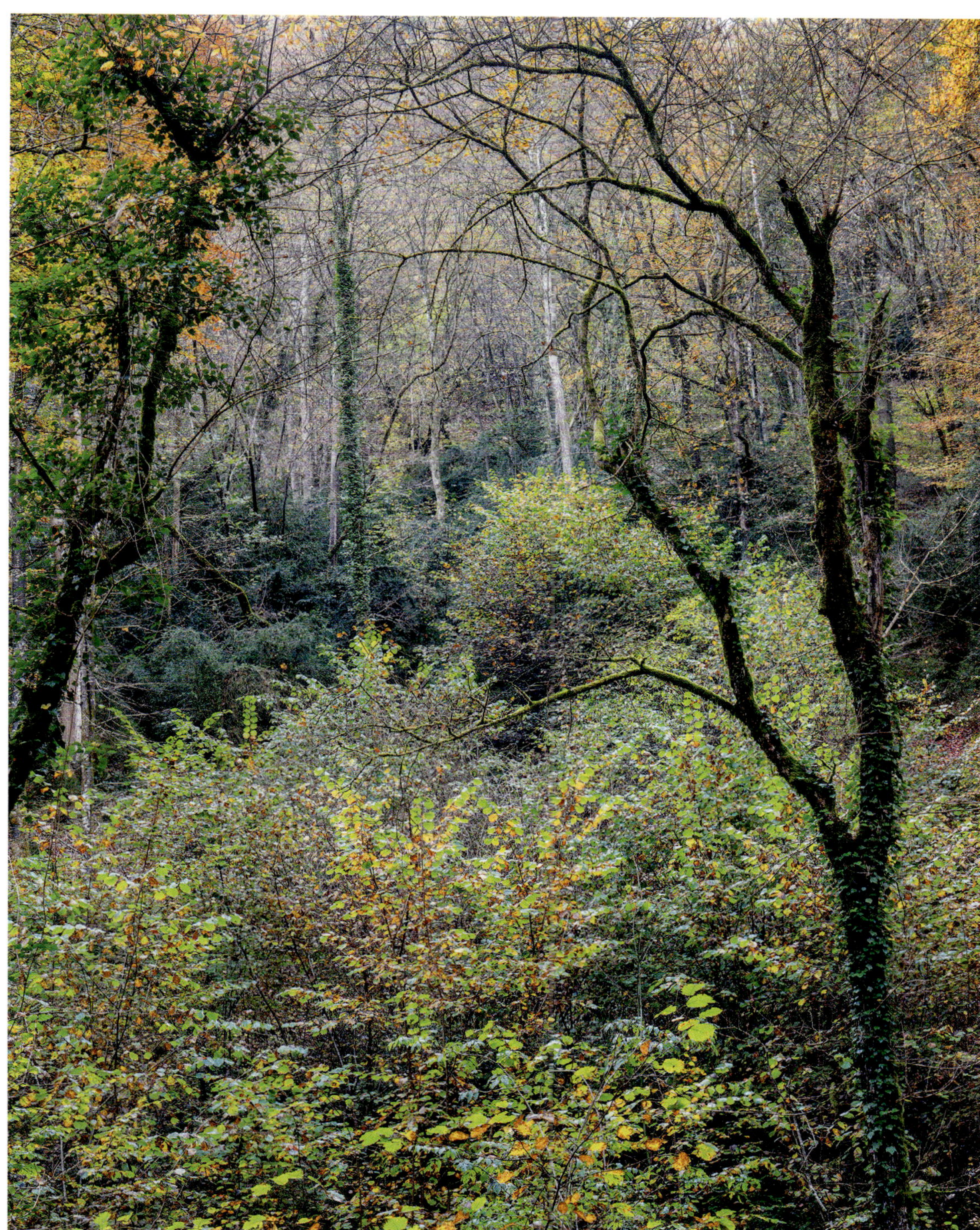

COMBE LAVAUX

This is another chaotic forest shot, this time with lots of colors. The complexity of this image comes from the interaction between the frame of naked trees and the interior of multi-colored leaves, which look almost pointillistic in their expression. An image like this one has enough color by itself, so adding any further saturation in post-processing would be a disaster. This is actually my general approach in post-processing—I think too much color makes an image look silly.

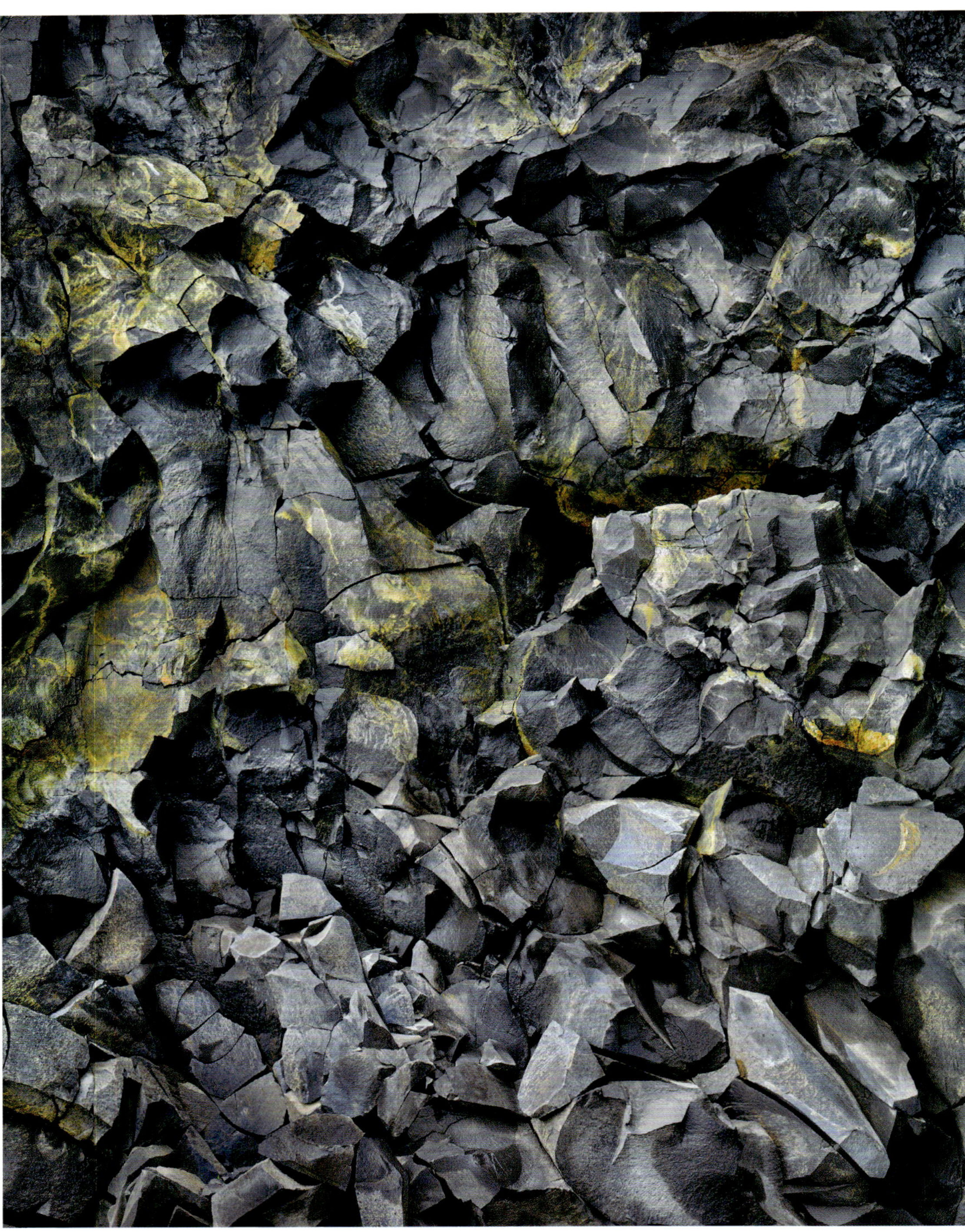

CUBISMO

My thoughts went to Cubism and the French painter Georges Braque when I saw this cliff. As always, the task was to find a functioning composition. In this case, I found a vertical composition more interesting than a horizontal one. I tried to get each corner in harmony to make a nice framing. In the post-processing, I did some local dodge and burning to optimize the balance. I also added a bit of vignetting to concentrate the image.

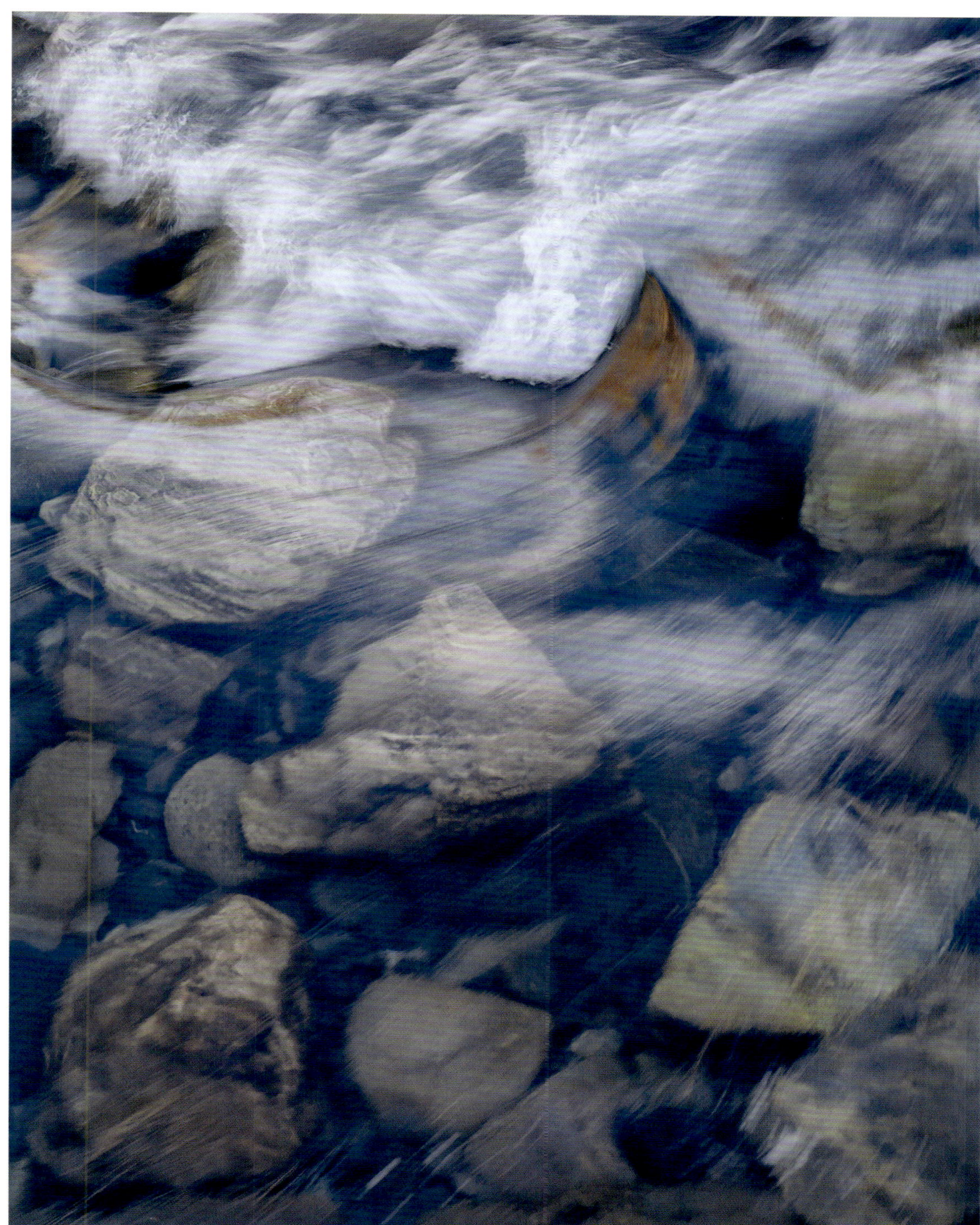

RAPIDS

Water in motion is one of my favorite subjects. Ever since I started photography, in 1981, I have had a continuous love affair with water. To interpret the way it moves and reflects its surroundings is a lifelong creative process. Even though I like to show its motion, I always try to keep the texture in the water. I therefore often check the difference in texture by trying several different shutter speeds. Too long an exposure and the texture is lost. In this case, I found 1/8 sec. the one I liked the best.

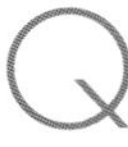

Q + A

Do you have a favorite lens or preferred focal range for your landscape abstracts?

Normally, I would use a moderate wide-angle lens like a 35mm on a DSLR, or a 50mm on a medium-format camera. I make exceptions, of course. When the positioning is limited, and I cannot come close enough to a subject, I tend to use longer lenses, and when the place is tight I use wider lenses. In the selection of images for this book, for instance, I have used everything from 15mm to 200mm lenses.

How long would a typical Hans Strand image take to process?

The shooting normally takes a few minutes. I have a good eye for positioning, and I usually find where to place my tripod quickly. Then I work out a framing and start taking the pictures. I often work myself into the optimal composition bit by bit. I especially check the harmony in the corners. I consider the corners of an image to be the backbone of a good composition. My post-processing is always cautious. I ask myself if this was the way I saw it, and this is what I try to reproduce. I would rather under-process than over-process. For me the post-processing is about balancing the light in an image. To accomplish that, I darken highlights and brighten shadows, and try to get an even light over the frame. I also often add a little vignetting to concentrate the image. The right color temperature is also very important—out of balance, too cold or too warm, and you lose the color dynamics. Both warm and cold colors must be able to exist together. I very seldom add any color saturation. Too much color is taking the authenticity away from a landscape photograph, and makes it look "kitsch." This is also true with extensive use of high dynamic range (HDR). I know that lots of color and drama are liked on the internet and in social media, but listening to the voices of crowds is dangerous for your personal development as a photographer. Remember, "Only dead fish float with the stream."

How do you maintain the high quality in your work across such a diverse range of subjects?

I try to find the best camera-lens combination for each subject. When I shoot aerials, I often use my Hasselblad medium-format camera, and when I hike I prefer lighter equipment, which is a Nikon D800E and some Zeiss prime lenses. Most of the time, I use prime lenses to get the maximum quality out of my images. The only zoom I have is a 70–200mm lens, which I seldom use.

What single piece of equipment or software is most useful in your work?

I personally think that focus-stacking has become the most powerful tool in my work. I use it very often to get the maximum depth of field. This is a procedure that improves the technical quality dramatically. In the old days, we had no such possibilities. Now we can even shoot in forests right through branches and get perfect depth of field, by using f/8 or f/11, and not having to deal with the diffraction from smaller apertures—simply amazing! This is something I practice in almost all of my photography. I also never use filters nowadays. If a sky is too bright in relation to the landscape, I simply make an extra minus 2–3-stop exposure, and blend it in with the exposure of the landscape in post-processing. This way, I get seamless and natural-looking transitions between the land and the sky in a way you never get by using graduated filters.

TECHNICAL INFORMATION

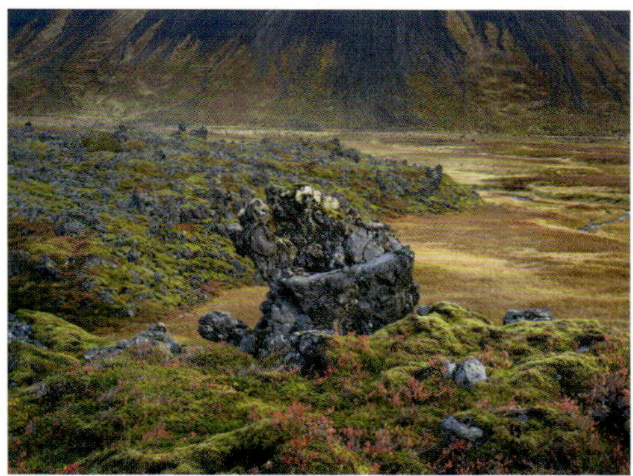

LAVA FIELD
SNAEFELLSNES, ICELAND

Camera: Nikon D800E
Lens/Focal length: Zeiss Otus 55mm f/1.4
Aperture: f/16
Shutter speed: 1/10 sec.
ISO: 100

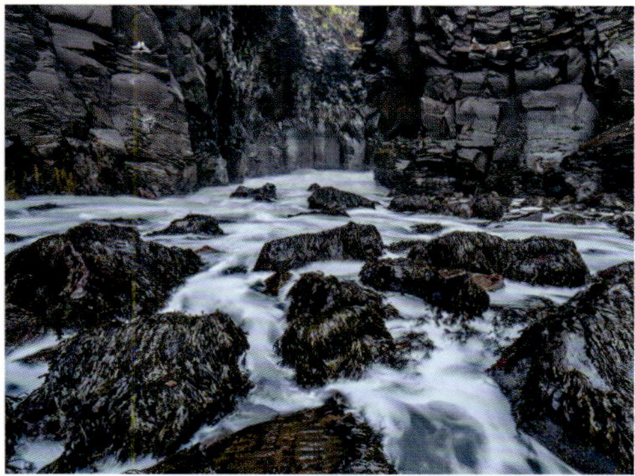

TIDE COMING IN
SNAEFELLSNES, ICELAND

Camera: Nikon D800E
Lens/Focal length: Zeiss Distagon T* 15mm f/2.8
Aperture: f/14
Shutter speed: 2 sec.
ISO: 100

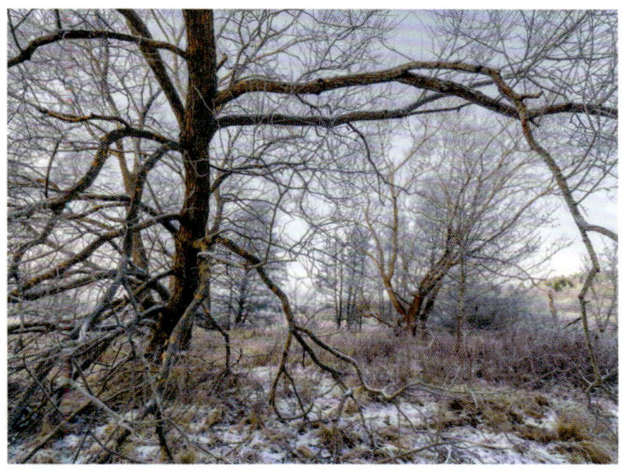

WINTER TREES
MÄRSTA, UPPLAND, SWEDEN

Camera: Nikon D800E
Lens/Focal length: Zeiss Distagon T* 15mm f/2.8
Aperture: f/14
Shutter speed: 1/20 sec.
ISO: 100

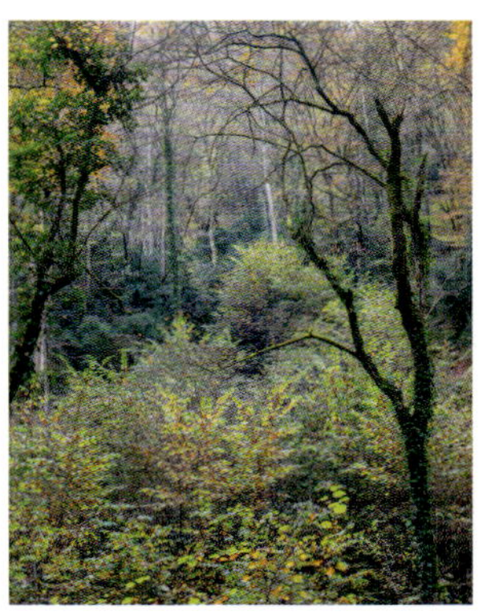

COMBE LAVAUX
BURGUNDY, FRANCE

Camera: Nikon D800E
Lens/Focal length: Zeiss Makro-Planar T* 50mm f/2
Aperture: f/13
Shutter speed: 1/5 sec.
ISO: 100

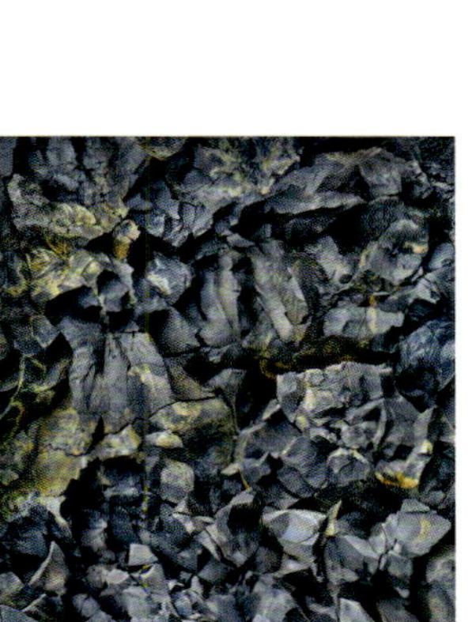

CUBISMO
REYNISFJARA, ICELAND

Camera: Hasselblad H3DII-50
Lens/Focal length: Hasselblad HC 210mm f/4
Aperture: f/16
Shutter speed: 1 sec.
ISO: 50

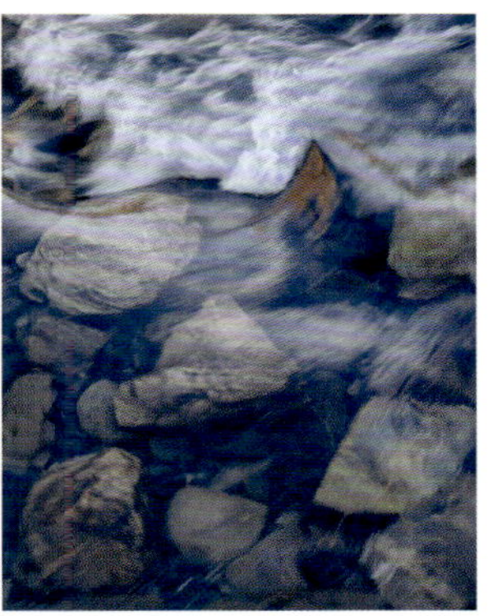

RAPIDS
ABISKO RIVER, LAPLAND, SWEDEN

Camera: Hasselblad H3DII-50
Lens/Focal length: Hasselblad HC 80mm f/2.8
Aperture: f/16
Shutter speed: 1/8 sec.
ISO: 50

JOE CORNISH

Joe Cornish studied fine art at Reading University, assisted professional photographers in Washington, D.C., and London, and started to freelance in 1984. Shooting travel books was the training ground for a career devoted to landscape photography. Early inspiration ranges from war and documentary photographers (especially W. Eugene Smith) to iconic American photographers Edward Weston and Ansel Adams, and color landscape master Charlie Waite. Later influences include Galen Rowell, David Muench, Paul Wakefield, and Peter Dombrovskis.

Just as important to Joe has been the thinking and style of painters from 18th- and 19th-century landscape traditions to 20th-century abstract expressionism. From 1997 to 2008, Joe worked mostly with a large-format Ebony field camera, a choice that characterizes his craft-based and reflective style. Having changed to digital, he now uses a broader and more experimental method, but the fascination remains with fine detail, depth, balance, and connection—core characteristics that emerged from shooting large format.

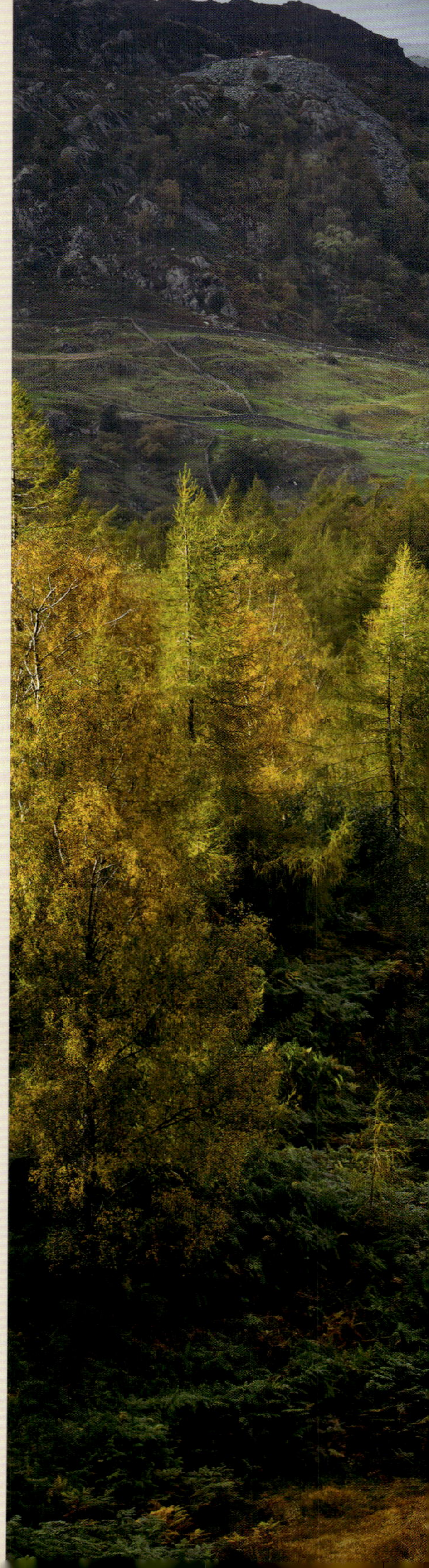

HODGE CLOSE AND LANGDALE PIKES FROM HOLME FELL

The Lake District is rightly regarded as a picturesque highlight of the British Isles; but what, at first glance, appears a bucolic pastoral paradise is in fact a recovering industrial landscape. The massive quarry at Hodge Close is typical, and here an entire valley has been hacked to pieces by the slate industry. Much has been hauled away but, even so, vast heaps of tailings remain, and these can be seen in the middle distance. There are also huge excavations in evidence. But since the decline of industry, nature has made a striking return, softening the scars. In the distance, the Langdale Pikes stand as a symbol of the enduring and apparently immutable beauty of the fells.

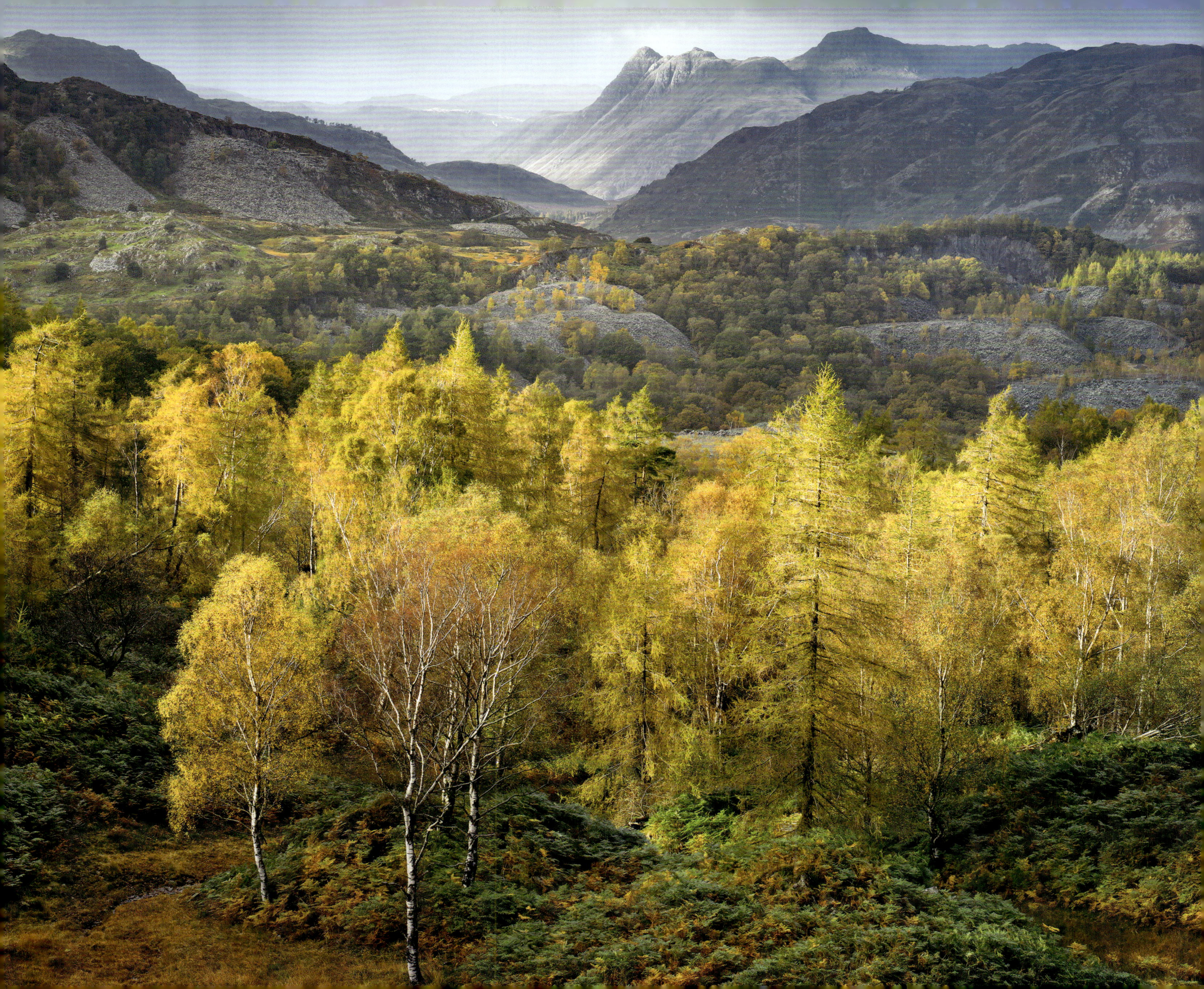

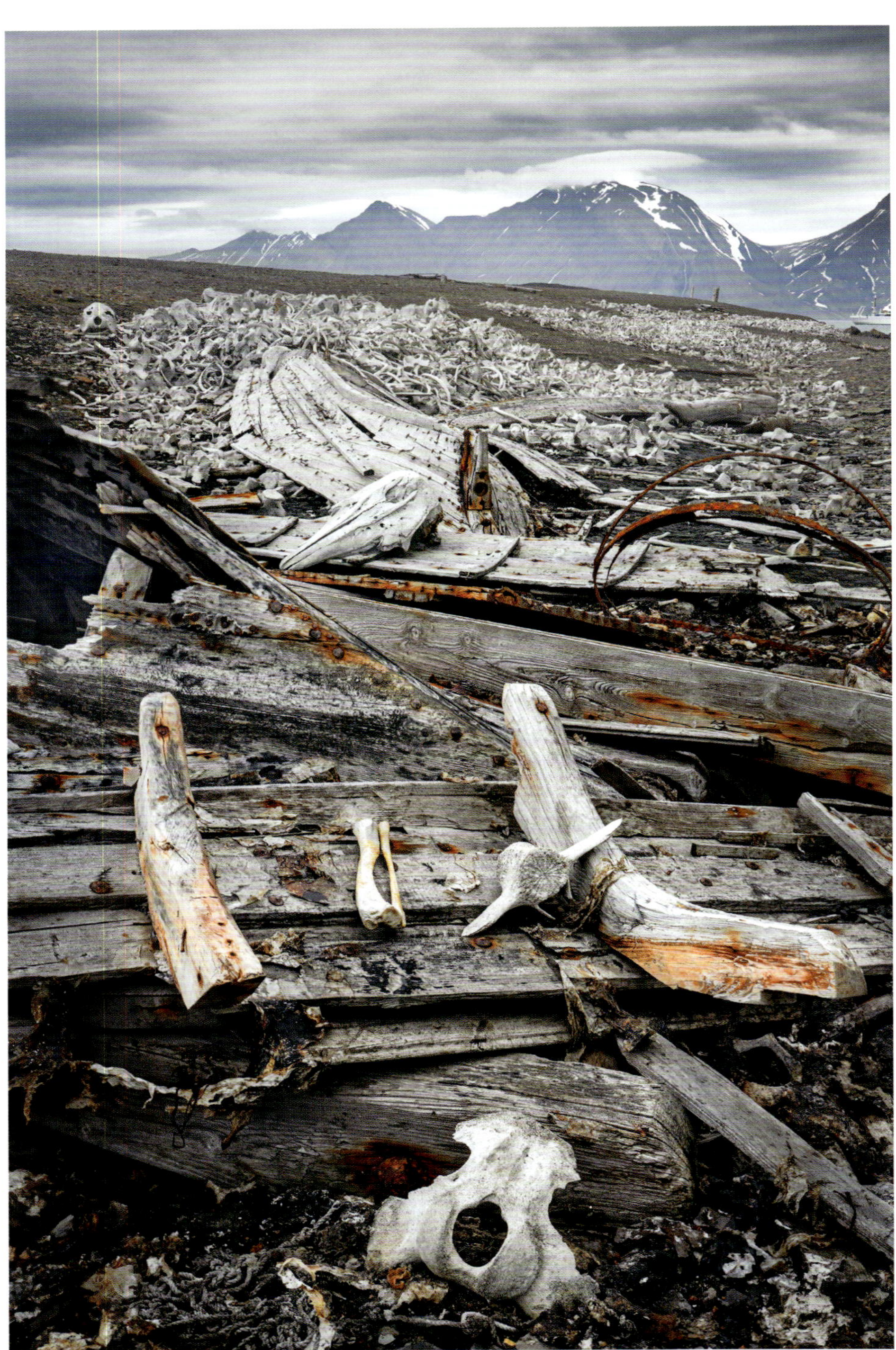

BELUGA CHARNEL

The bones of countless beluga whales lie scattered above the high tide line in the Svalbard archipelago. Corralled into a small bay, their exit was blocked by a metal mesh raised across its mouth, and they were then slaughtered in situ. This was just one seasonal act in a holocaust that has made these remarkable white whales effectively extinct in this part of the Arctic. Self-referential, our expedition ship is visible in the distance. The composition is an (admittedly distant) homage to Edvard Munch's *The Scream*. On the last day of our voyage, belugas swam near to our ship . . . it was a moment of redemption.

STILL STANDING

Like so many northern landscapes in the UK, this one is full of contemporary clues to its recent past, including forestry, agriculture, and heavy industry. Recent felling has cleared part of the plantation, opening a stand of impossibly slender Scots pines. Old mining cottages, now desirable country residences, occupy a middle distance that was once noisy with the excavation of minerals, including iron ore. A light fall of snow transforms the patterns of a landscape that I have been out in countless times, with my camera, and walking the dog.

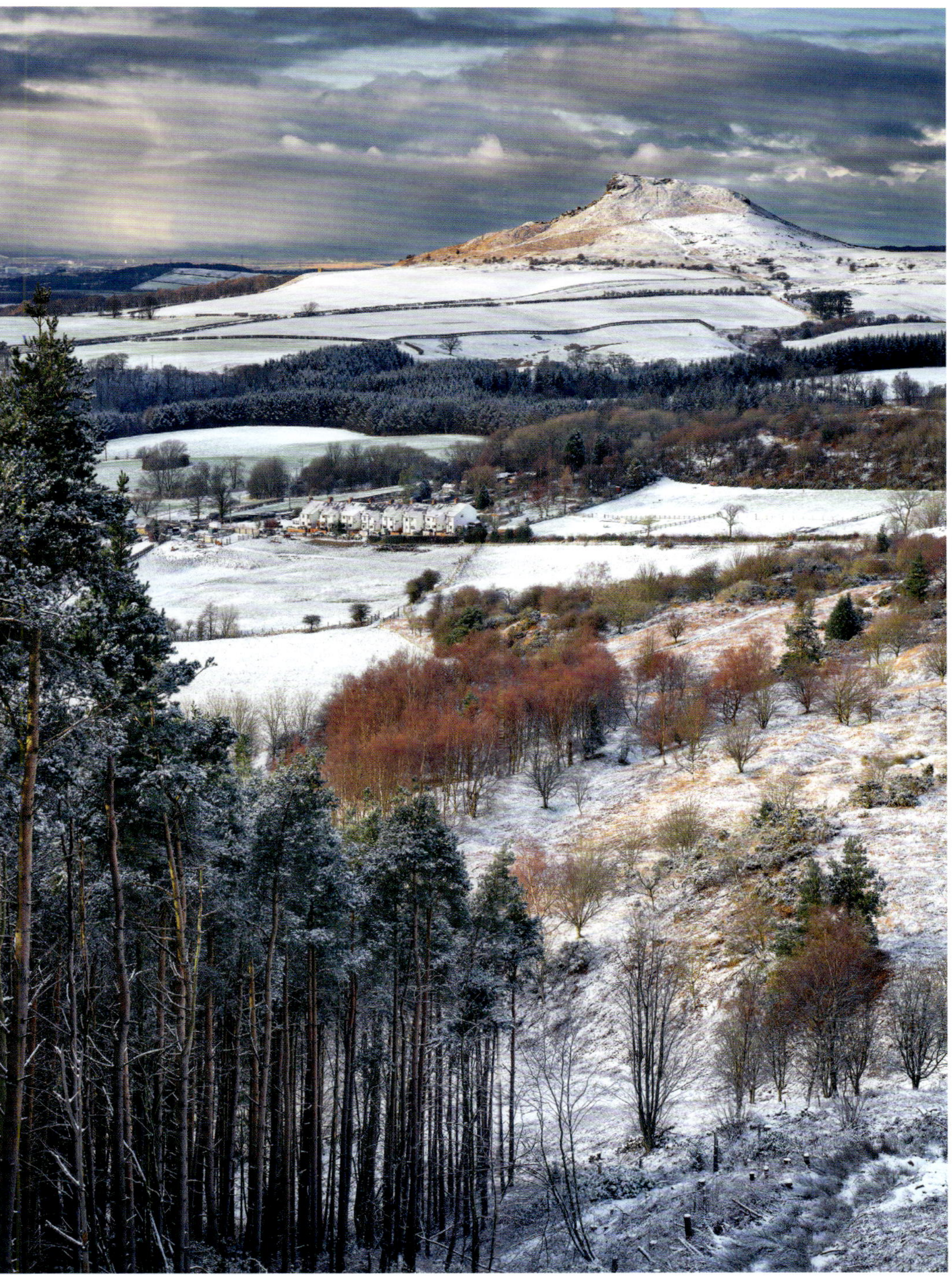

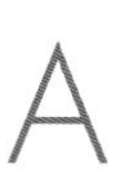

Q + A

How do you avoid cliché in your work?

It is important to make the distinction: no place is a photographic cliché. The only clichés are the overused, mindless, and derivative approaches used in making pictures of these places. Every generation must discover the world for themselves; yet, in a time when a proliferation of image-making and the internet has made exotic landscapes familiar before they are witnessed first-hand, the pressure to discover a fresh way of seeing grows. Art embodies the idea of expression and interpretation, whatever the medium. Photography's problem is that it is both descriptive and easy, and apparently sophisticated appearances can be achieved effortlessly, especially with a phone camera and the myriad of apps that create stylish gimmicks out of dull ideas. I believe in individual seeing, the possibility of a relationship with the subject (the landscape), and the unique circumstances and conditions of each encounter. However familiar a place, it is possible to retain a certain innocence, so that each time we see anew. If there is a genuine feeling of enchantment in what is being seen, from the microscopic to the mighty, we should strive to translate that enchantment with hope, energy, and perhaps a sense of wonder.

What steps do you take to create an image with impact?

I have no idea. I do not set out to "create impact." It's true that when I go out with my camera I'd like to make a picture, maybe more than one. Sometimes I might carry an idea, an agenda, and aspiration for what that picture might be. But the lighting opportunities that arise and the eyewitness experience determine the outcome. Others might consider that the resulting image has impact, but that is not something I seek. Rather, I want the voice of the image to reflect something about the moment, the place, a state of mind, perhaps ... which might be quiet, reflective, even meditative. Perhaps I seek to create atmosphere, or emotion, a feeling. But not impact. One of my favorite Ansel Adams quotes is: "Some photographers take reality ... and impose the domination of their own thought and spirit. Others come before reality more tenderly, and a photograph to them is an instrument of love and revelation." My goal is to be in the latter category.

How much of a role does spontaneity play in creating a shot?

Spontaneity is a fundamental creative "skill," in that it suggests a photographer is responsive to the place, situation, conditions, and is aware enough to make good use of opportunities and new thoughts as they arise. It's actually a very difficult skill to nurture when using large-format and technical cameras, which are cumbersome and demand rigorous technique to fulfill their potential. Yet, spontaneity remains important. Managing technical distractions and responding quickly to changing conditions, new opportunities, and fresh ideas require regular practice ... practice that never ends. This is the craft of photography. And since I think language plays a part in everything we do as humans I never think of a considered photograph as a "shot"—too immediate, too aggressive, too alcoholic, too fatal.

Of course, you're well known for your large foregrounds—what do you look for when creating such an image?

In a word, relationship. Philosophically, I try to make images where every element within the frame has a role, however minor; and compositions that convey depth and space, intimacy and connection, all at the same time. The foreground/background relationship is critical if the image is to be evocative, and to express my view of life. Which fundamentally is that everything counts and is, on some level, connected: every dewdrop, flower, leaf, blade of grass, stone, tree, fence post, road, river, mountain, cloud. It is the poetry of light and form linking and separating these discrete elements that brings the image to life. Paying close and devoted attention to all the relationships within the frame is technically, aesthetically, and philosophically essential. It might be worth pointing out that this foreground/background approach is a fundamentally "photographic" way of seeing, dating back to the 19th century, and was developed by photographers, not painters. Wide-angle lenses have certainly fostered its adoption as a style in photography. I believe it remains just as relevant today. Nevertheless, it is also slightly frustrating to be saddled with the reputation, "Large Foreground", as this suggests I only have one idea—without wishing to be defensive, this seems like an unjustified observation!

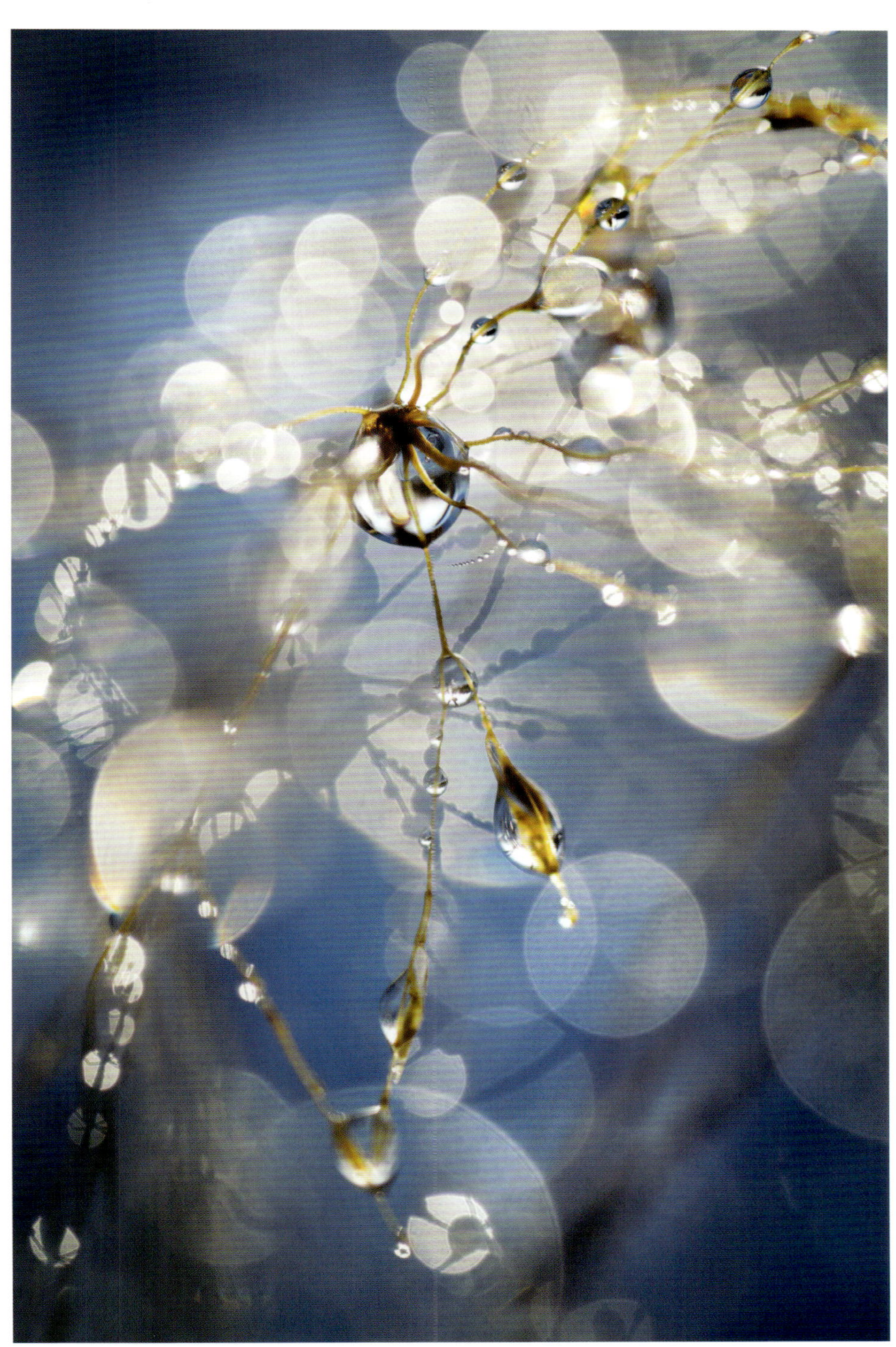

DEWDROP GALAXY

"Galaxy?" Or possibly "Nucleus" for the way that the droplets have captured light, appearing to illustrate the fizzing energy of atomic structures. The idea began with the simple realization that sunlight melting the frost was a good incentive to test a new macro lens. Abandoning the tripod and using the camera really low and close to the subject was liberating. The exposures made were simply a joyful intersection of optical physics and visual fun.

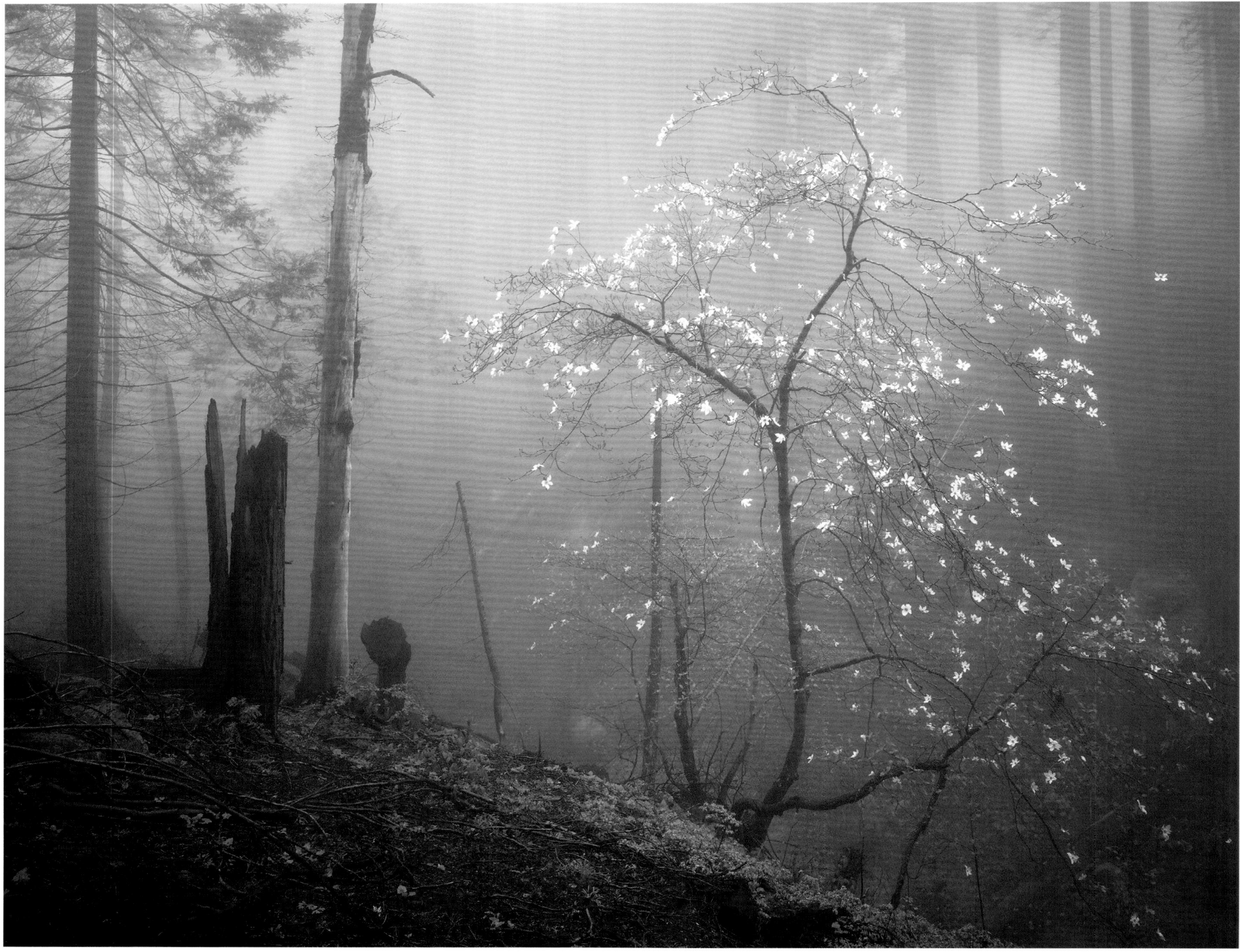

DEFIANCE

(Left) It seems almost unfair that, in an area with some of the most spectacular landscapes in the world, Yosemite has its share of intimate beauty, too. The simplifying influence of mist is wonderful for emphasizing form. Although the delicacy of the white roses floating on the air was a tempting close-up theme, the contrast between the defiant gesture of the dogwood with its life-affirming flowers, and the somber tree stump on the left, was compelling.

ASPENS

(Right) A day of overcast gray only enhances the luminous beauty of aspens. Shot from an embankment, the high viewpoint emphasizes the perspective, with its multiple vanishing points. A few dead or dying trees provide a necessary darker note to contrast with the three-dimensional luminosity of the grove. Returning there three years later, I found that, although the foreground tree was recognizable, the entire scene had been transformed by subsequent growth. A good example of how in landscape photography every idea and moment, however subtle, is in some way unique.

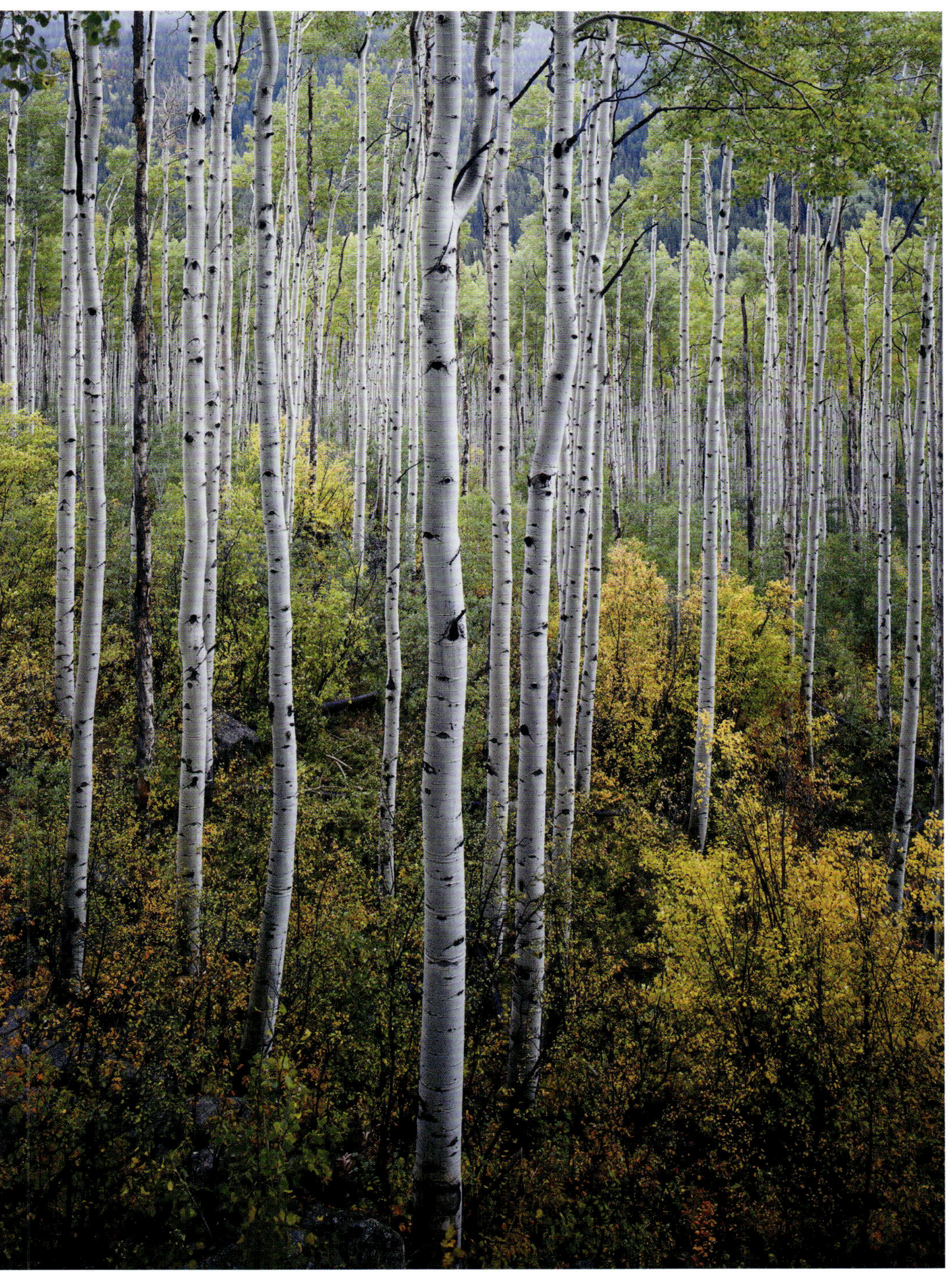

Q + A

How do you achieve such wonderful "balance"? Is it a conscious or instinctive process?

It's certainly not an accident! It is consciously sought, but often instinctively realized. Among my favorite landscape photographers and influences, many are large-format practitioners. A distinguishing characteristic of their work is a special quality, not just of extra detail or superior tonal gradation (although these certainly contribute), but rather a quality of seeing. I adopted the large format myself in 1997, and fell in love with it. Working with an inverted image projected onto a (fairly dim) ground glass screen under the darkcloth is difficult but immersive. It encourages a thorough exploration of, and a deep commitment to, each picture. If the composition isn't balanced, it is much more obvious upside down. And if it isn't balanced, the picture isn't made. Years of working this way made me see balance as the non-negotiable characteristic of good composition. However, balance is much more complicated than it sounds . . . and it also has to accommodate deliberate imbalance. Once balance of tone, line, form, texture, color, tension, harmony, proportion, light, and shade have all been accounted for, there are still the moderating and skewing effects of energy and flow to take into account. These sound like woolly concepts, impossible to analyze, but they are essential in understanding balance.

Your recent work has shown a move toward a less conventional portrayal of grand landscapes—how has your photographic philosophy changed?

It is common for artists to experience creative arcs, during which some ideas or approaches are brought to fulfillment and developed until something changes, and a process of retreat, reinvention, and renewal follows. These arcs may be punctuated by a time of crisis, even a loss of self-belief. That is certainly true for me. Fortunately, having studied the experience of others, I know this to be the price of renewal. My core ideas about life have evolved, and my attitude to using the camera has as well. In addition, my desire for personal expression has increased, while my need to problem-solve for others (as in commissioned work) has diminished. To put it another way, I am increasingly selfish in my photography. The photographs and the process of making them are primarily for my own pleasure. Although I still love the authority of perfectly focused images, I am now less dogmatic in my search for this quality at all costs. I have become open to the out-of-focus in photographs, and also to more experimental ideas, such as stitching, assemblages, and collage. I hope my intention has shifted more to the evocative, of the idea of the soul of a landscape, or of a photograph. Balance is part of life, and the human condition a struggle between light and dark, growth and decay, ebb and flow . . . life and death. Landscape pictures can on some level reflect those contrasts and that tension.

What inspired the move to digital from large-format film cameras, and how has it changed your approach?

"Inspired" isn't how I would describe it, since I was definitely reluctant to switch. However, aware of the change coming throughout the industry, the need to learn, and impressed by the print quality and potential for experimentation that digital seemed to offer, there seemed no alternative. Perhaps foolishly, I tried to preserve as many of the large-format principles as I could (continuing to use a technical camera, tripod, filters) in my digital workflow. As I struggled to rediscover my confidence during those early years, I did learn a lot about the process and the potential of digital. It fast-tracked my understanding of post-production editing, and encouraged me to become a fully fledged printer. These changes, especially the printing, encouraged me to reconsider my photography deeply. Printing adds to a photographer's expressive skills, as post-production is so critical in interpretation. Now I am totally responsible for how to interpret the recorded image, whereas previously I relied on the "signature" color and tone of the film stock itself to determine the outcome. This realization has also encouraged me to "remaster" many of my old (scanned) film images, using recently acquired post-production skills. Deep down I still believe in the post-production principle: "Do as little as possible; do as much as is necessary." The critical issue is: the judgment and sensitivity applied to the adjustments made.

As a master of landscape photography, what is your motivation to continue making photographs?

There must come a point in your artistic life when you know that what you do is probably what you will always do. I never understood how Henri Cartier-Bresson could abandon photography and take up painting, except perhaps out of pure snobbery (painting is a "proper" art, after all). Landscape photography is my identity, it's what I do, even who I am. If I stopped, I'd be stopping part of me. Anyone who studies nature is privileged, be that study scientific or artistic; after all, this is "Life, the Universe, and Everything," and everything is connected to everything else through it. If those studies also involve regular encounters with the outdoors, the weather, the cycles of the seasons, wildlife, and even fellow outdoor artists and enthusiasts, well, why would you want to stop doing it? On a more serious note, I would like to do another book or two, and find ways of encouraging greater awareness of, and engagement with, the environmental challenges that we face as a human family. However, I hope I am not arrogant enough to think I should be telling other people what they should do. Most of my interest in the environment is simply because I love being in the woods, on the beach, by a river, up a mountain. Photography gives me the incentive, and the excuse, to keep going.

TECHNICAL INFORMATION

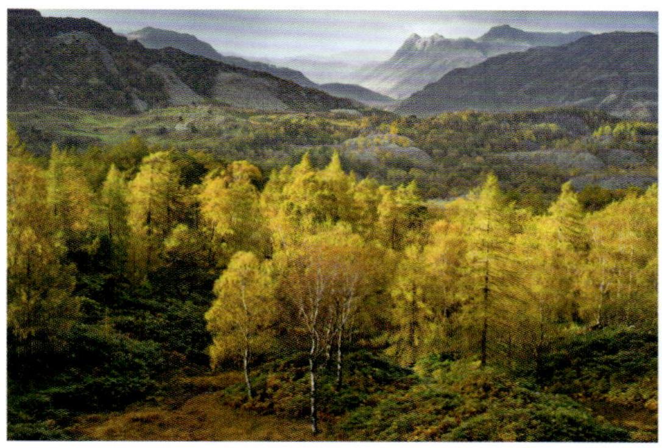

HODGE CLOSE AND LANGDALE PIKES
FROM HOLME FELL
CUMBRIA, ENGLAND

Camera: Sony a7R
Lens/Focal length: Zeiss Sonnar 55mm f/1.8
Aperture: f/10
Shutter speed: 1/25 sec.
ISO: 100
Kit: Tripod, 0.6 ND filter

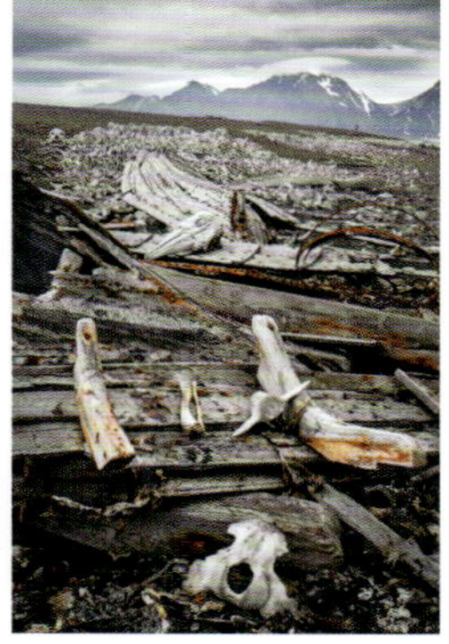

BELUGA CHARNEL
BOURBONHAMNA, SVALBARD,
NORWAY

Nikon D800
Lens/Focal length: Hasselblad Zeiss Distagon T* 40mm f/4
Aperture: f/8.5
Shutter speed: 1/15 sec.
ISO: 100
Kit: Tripod, 0.9 ND grad filter

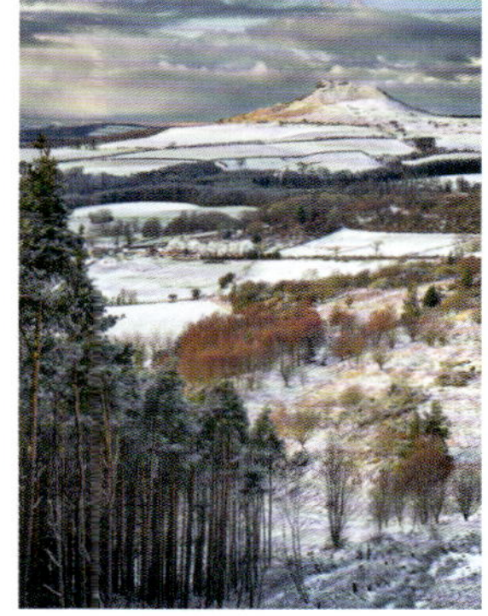

STILL STANDING
GRIBDALE, ROSEBERRY TOPPING,
NORTH YORKSHIRE, ENGLAND

Camera: Sony a7R
Lens/Focal length: Zeiss Sonnar 55mm f/1.8
Aperture: f/11
Shutter speed: 1/20 sec.
ISO: 100
Kit: Tripod, 0.6 ND grad filter

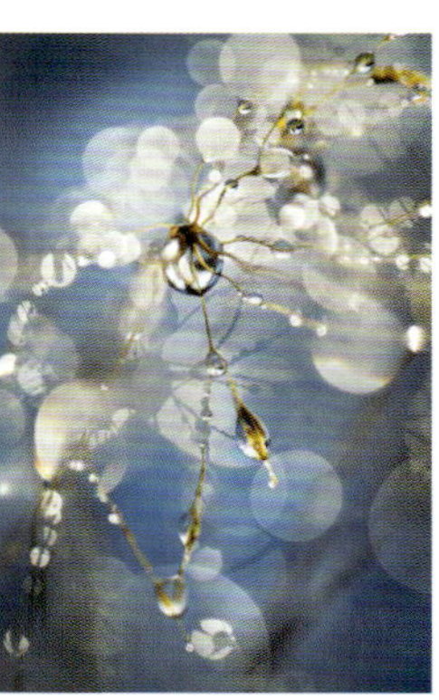

DEWDROP GALAXY

Camera: Sony a7R II
Lens/Focal length: Sony 90mm f/2.8
Aperture: f/2.8
Shutter speed: 1/500 sec.
ISO: 100
Kit: Handheld, no filter

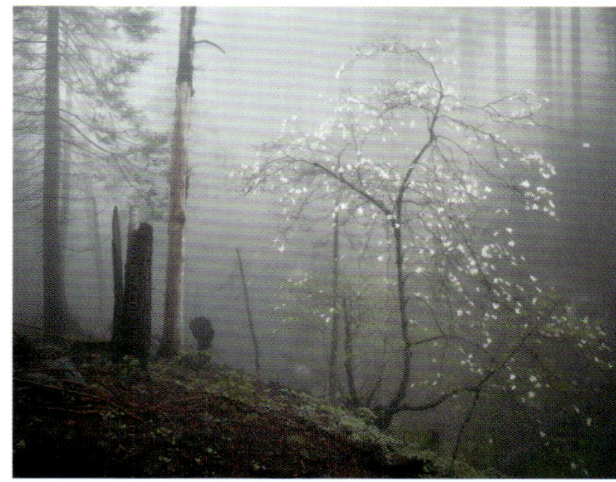

DEFIANCE
DOGWOOD, YOSEMITE NATIONAL PARK,
CALIFORNIA, USA

Camera: Cambo Actus, Phase One IQ-280
Lens/Focal length: Rodenstock 40mm f/4
Aperture: f/11
Shutter speed: 1 sec.
ISO: 35
Kit: Tripod, no filter

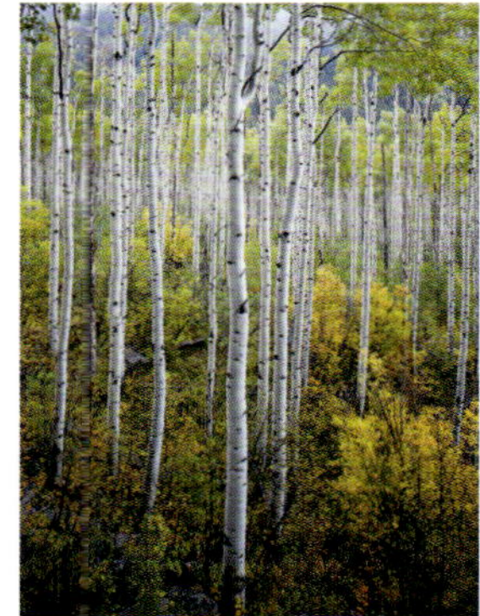

ASPENS
INDEPENDENCE PASS, COLORADO,
USA

Camera: Linhof Techno, Phase One IQ-180
Lens/Focal length: Rodenstock 50mm f/2.8
Aperture: f/11.5
Shutter speed: 1/4 sec.
ISO: 35
Kit: Tripod, no filter

JONATHAN CHRITCHLEY

Jonathan Chritchley is one of the foremost fine art photographers in the world today. His instantly recognizable work is seen all around the world in exhibitions, galleries, magazines, and books, and forms part of many international fine art collections. His regular clients include Ralph Lauren, Hilton International, Fortuny, and P&O Luxury Cruises. Jonathan also speaks about and presents his work at photography and sailing events worldwide, and is the founder and owner of Capture Earth and Ocean Capture, two companies specializing in luxury photography workshops and tours.

Born in London, England, Jonathan became infatuated with the sea after moving to the famous sailing town of Lymington on the country's south coast at the age of 14. Years later, having moved to the South of France, he gave up a successful career as a marketing and brand director in order to return to his true passion—a combination of the sea and fine art photography. He has now worked in over 35 countries, including Japan, China, South America, Greenland, and South Africa.

BOAT AND POSTS

I was on my way to working on a project photographing horses in the Camargue, and I just happened to pass this scene. It was very early in the morning, and there was a very strange, misty light. I stopped and I just shot for about 10 minutes. The posts almost jump out at you from the water, and I liked that, as well as the impressionistic form of the boat. I'm very fond of this picture—it has a lot of what I look for in this sort of image, with a painterly feel to it.

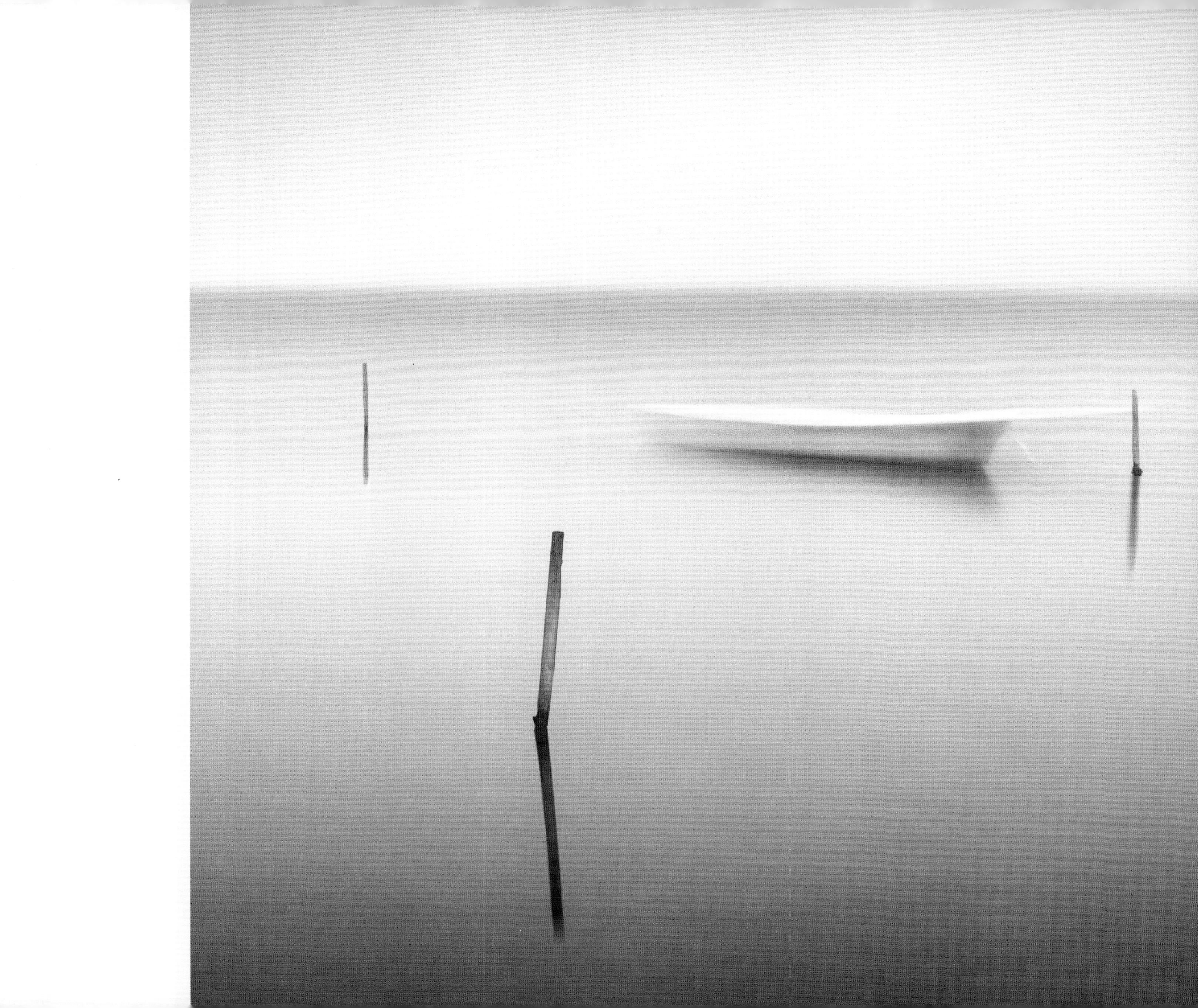

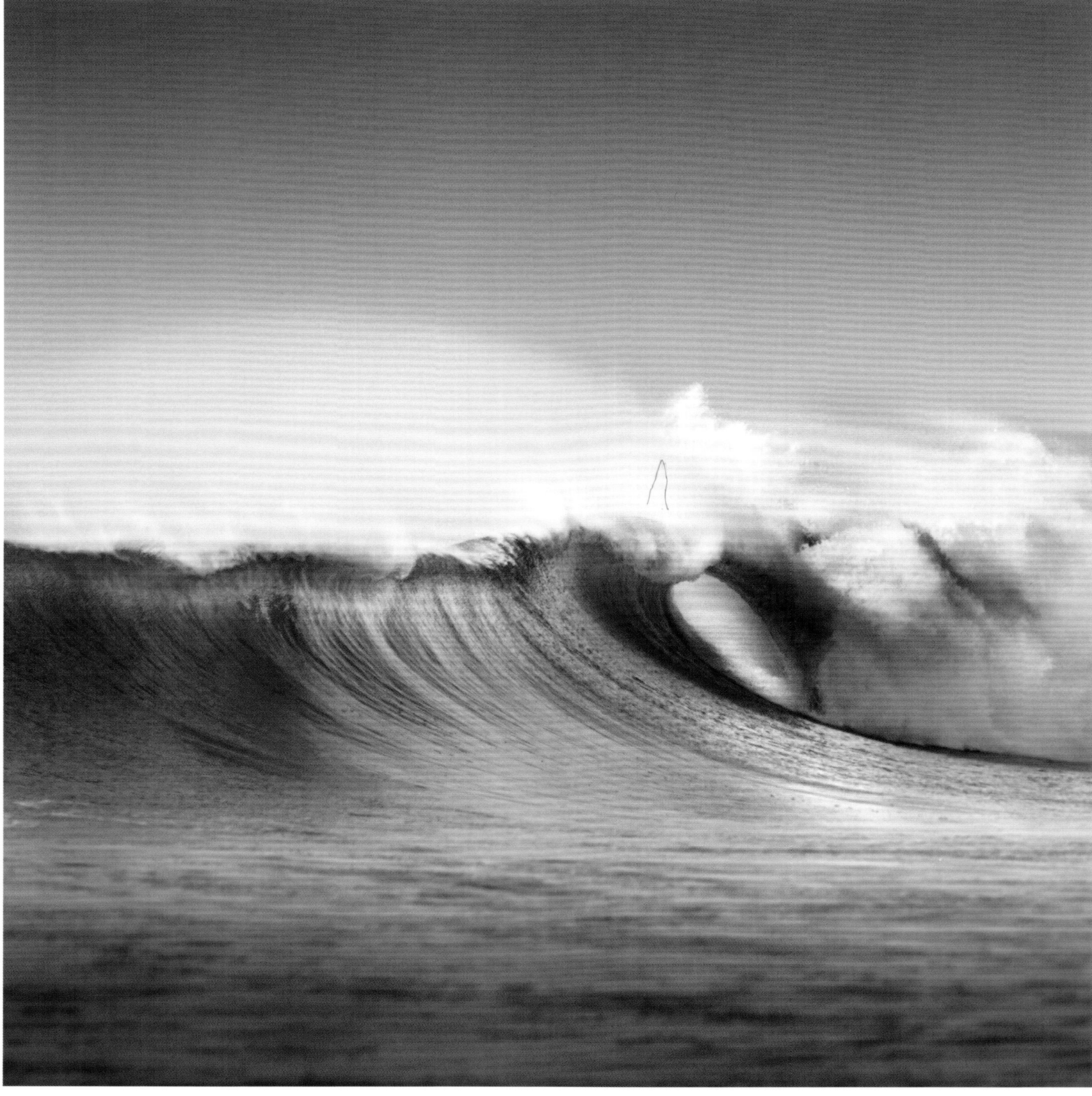

LA NORD

(Left) I do a lot of work with waves, living in
an area in France which is very well known for
them—it's a world-renowned surfing break. I
shot this particular image in the morning with a
600mm lens, in an area that probably has the
best waves. This one was probably about 60 or
80m (200ft) out, and as you can see by the plume
on top of the wave, this was created by a light,
offshore wind—and those always create the best
waves—it just holds the wave up. The light was
stunning—there were no clouds, but there was a
slight sea mist diffusing the light, and it caused
this lovely, silvery light on the water that I always
love. This was one of about 20 shots, and I just
happened to get the wave in the right place, with
a nice balance of light.

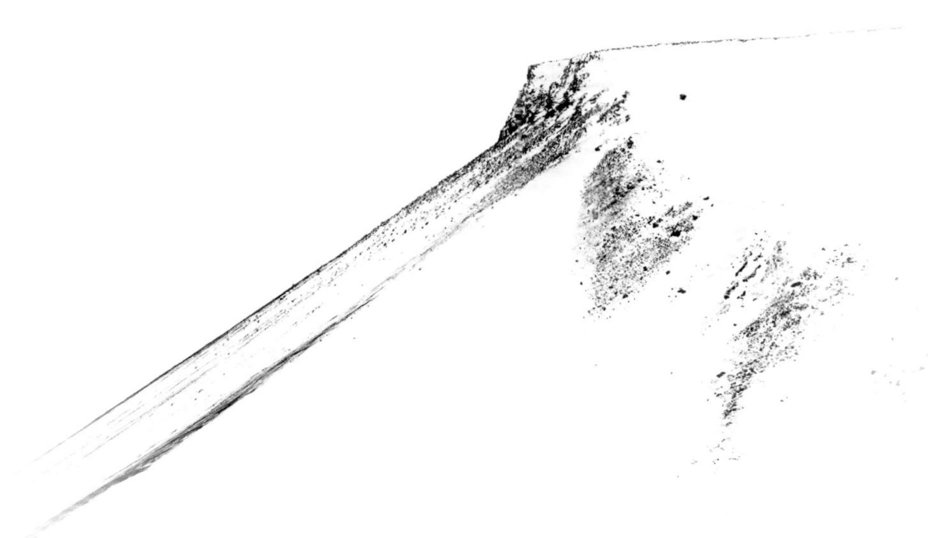

EMERGE

(Right) As fundamentally a water photographer, I
generally find the thought of mountains, and not being
able to see the horizon, rather claustrophobic. In this
case, however, driven by a need to push myself out of
my comfort zone I ventured into the stunningly beautiful
interior of Iceland. Here I discovered the new snow
on the volcanic hillsides had created these wonderful
shapes, which reminded me of charcoal sketches.

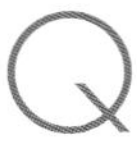

Q + A

Your work spans a range of subjects and locations—what initially draws you to a subject?

My greatest passion, above minimalist photography, is water. I'm a sea person through and through, and I feel most comfortable shooting in and around the ocean, or on the sea, or on a lake, or in a puddle! I just need water to make it work—that's the ingredient that makes it come together for me, that inspires me, so what draws me is anything that's to do with water in some way. And the minimalism really came from that—realizing that I could use space and how I felt when I was by the sea, with its huge skies and great sense of space—so, one thing led to another. Beyond photography, the water is just a place where I feel relaxed. If I don't have a camera, and just want to feel completely relaxed, it's where I go. I live by the sea, and I don't feel comfortable anywhere else. I've been asked the question a lot, and one looks for answers to questions one doesn't necessarily ask oneself. I am quite claustrophobic, I don't like to be in small spaces, and I think that when you're by or on the sea, there's not much danger of that, so it's somewhere where I can breathe. It's beyond photography—it goes deeper than that. I always believe that you take the best pictures where you feel the most comfortable, or with a subject you feel most comfortable with, and for me, that's a no-brainer—it has to be the sea.

What ingredients make a minimalist image that works?

I look for space, and I do love negative space, which is something I use quite a lot. This has never been a conscious process, it's just what comes naturally. It's what I found myself doing, completely subconsciously. I still don't know why that happened, I tend often to use just a third of a frame, and the rest of it is negative space, and I don't know why I do that—I just like the notion that it has that space around it. It's probably something to do with how I feel in that environment; that I can breathe when I have all that space around me. It's difficult to actually notate the ingredients that make a minimalist picture that works, but what I look for are the possibilities of creating space around a subject matter that appeals to me very strongly. I never really go out with preconceptions when I'm going to a shoot—I have my camera and everything I need, and I just see what happens. It is very instinctive, and I don't have a formula as such— it's just the way I like it. If someone was to look at all my photographs side by side, they'd probably come up with a formula, but that's not how they're conceived.

Why use the square format to express yourself?

This is probably the question I've been asked the most about my work, and, as usual, I didn't have an answer! So, I had to dig deep to come up with three possible reasons that led to the square. Firstly, as a child, I had a very small black-and-white TV from the '70s, which I nabbed from my dad's office, and I used to watch everything on it, and the picture was cropped into this funny square. The second was that I was a lifeguard in southern England for some time, and we used to keep our boats—fast, rigid inflatables—by the water. Every morning I used to sit in the boathouse and look out and watch the sun come up, and I could see the sea, horizon, and sky through this dark, perfect square of the open boathouse doors, which left its mark. And the third reason was that I originally got into photography at art college. The students were able to use whatever they had to hand, and I saw this Hasselblad and just fell in love with everything about it, and I really learned a lot on that camera. Of course, that was a square-format camera, and everything I was trying, taking it down to the beaches, was with that format, and that definitely made an impression.

How important is in-camera filtration in this age of Photoshop—are physical filters still relevant?

I'm very old school in my methods of post-processing, which takes five minutes. I'm a great believer in getting it right in-camera, which some people may scoff at, but that's just the way I like it—it works for me. I'm not someone who likes sitting in front of a computer, stuck indoors. I'd much rather be out on the water taking pictures, and, of course, if I can reduce the amount of time that I have to sit in front of the blasted computer, then I'll do it; I'll do all I can to shorten that as much as possible! Filters are in my bag, along with everything else, but, again, I don't go out with a preconception, and say, "Right, today I'm going to shoot a long-exposure photograph." If the moment arrives when I think I need to simplify an image, because it's too complex, because the sea is too choppy, for instance, then I will pull out a filter. I don't consider myself to be a long-exposure photographer—it's just another method of getting space and simplicity into one of my photographs.

FIR LAKE

I'd been shooting all day, and was on my way to a restaurant—I had the camera, with a 50mm lens, slung over my shoulder—when I saw these branches overhanging the water as I walked past. I shot it for just about a minute, taking about six or seven photographs of the branches. I was very much inspired by oriental sumi-e paintings—these branches looked ust like Chinese pen and ink strokes to me. It's an image with next to nothing in it, but it's one of my favorites—I find it very peaceful.

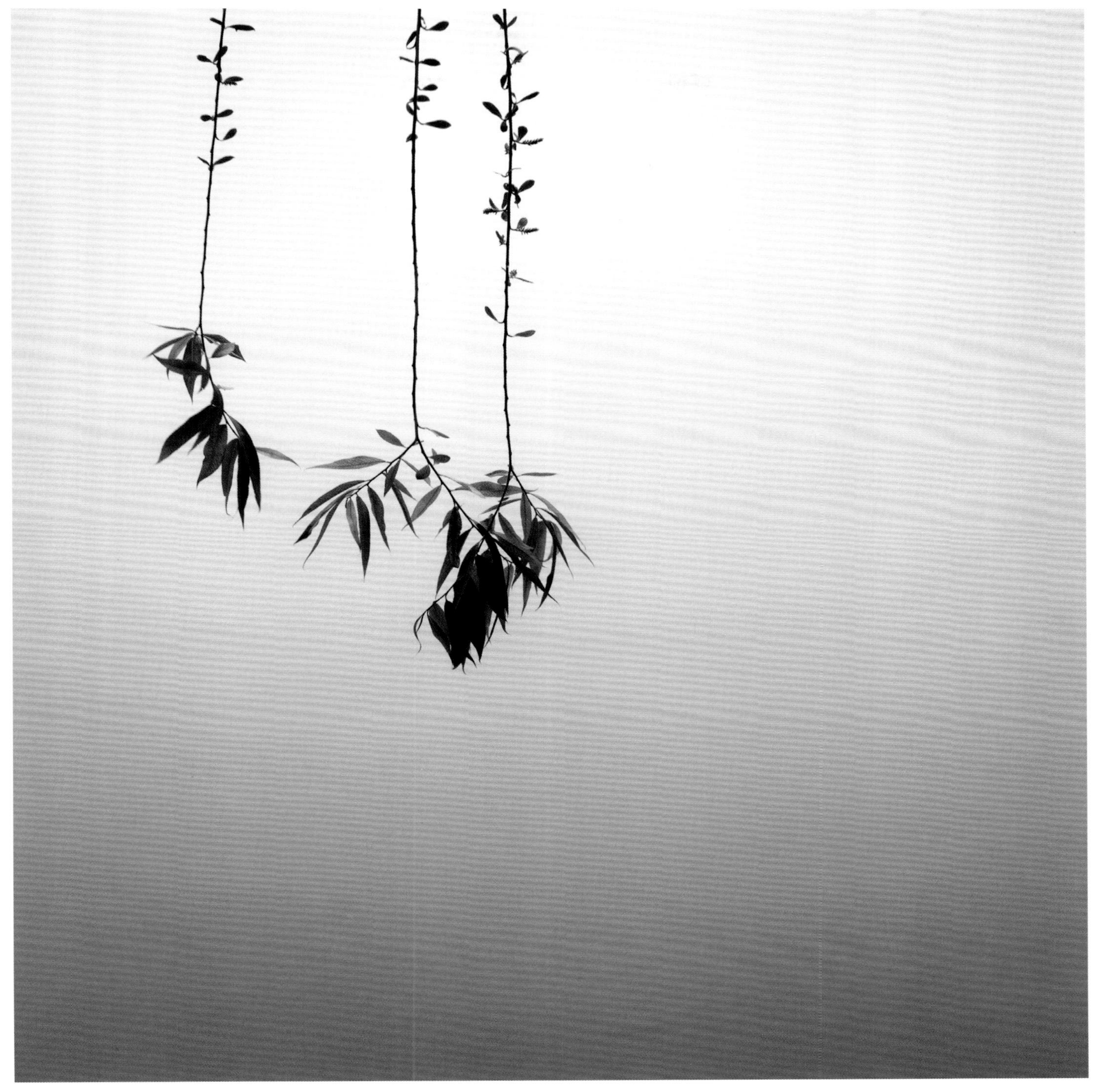

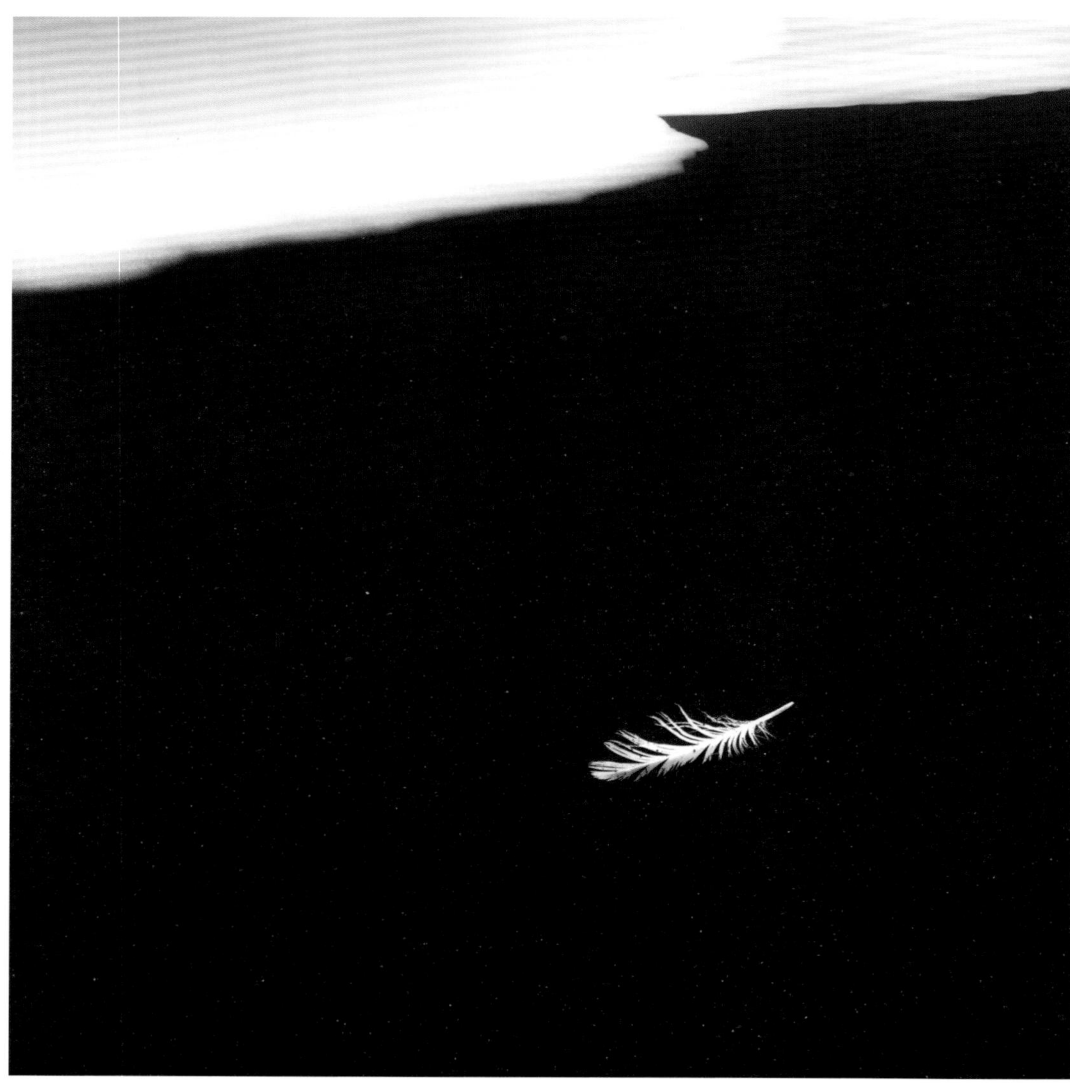

FEATHER

(Left) This was the outcome of incredibly bad weather in Iceland—I'd gone to shoot something else entirely on the coast, but the wind and rain were so bad. I thought, "I'm just not going to go back to the hotel with a grumpy expression," so I looked for something to shoot. And the only place I could point without the camera getting soaking wet was down. I just happened to be walking along the shore, with my head down, and I saw this feather, lying just as it is in the photograph, and its relationship with the white surf coming in on the black volcanic-sand beach, so the idea for the picture just came into my head. I quickly set up the tripod and pointed everything down, and took a series of six pictures. I used an exposure of about 2 seconds, so I could get just a little bit of movement in the water—it wasn't necessary to use filters because there wasn't enough light anyway. As I was taking it, this photograph just felt right—the balance of the feather and the little "V" shape in the water at the top of the picture—and it all just came together. But what I'm most pleased about with this photograph is that I got it just because the weather was so bad!

TEMPLE

(Right) This is a temple by a lake on the island of Honshu, in Japan. It was three in the afternoon, on one of those murky, misty days I like so much. It was very still, and there was no wind. I originally tried to find a shot with just the temple, but although that was nice, it was just not interesting enough—it wasn't really "doing it" for me. But further along the coast of the lake, I spotted these trees overhanging the water, and I shot a bit wider, and managed to find a branch that was pointing in exactly the right direction. I wanted to bring out the reflection of the hut, and I found that 10 seconds was just enough to keep that reflection.

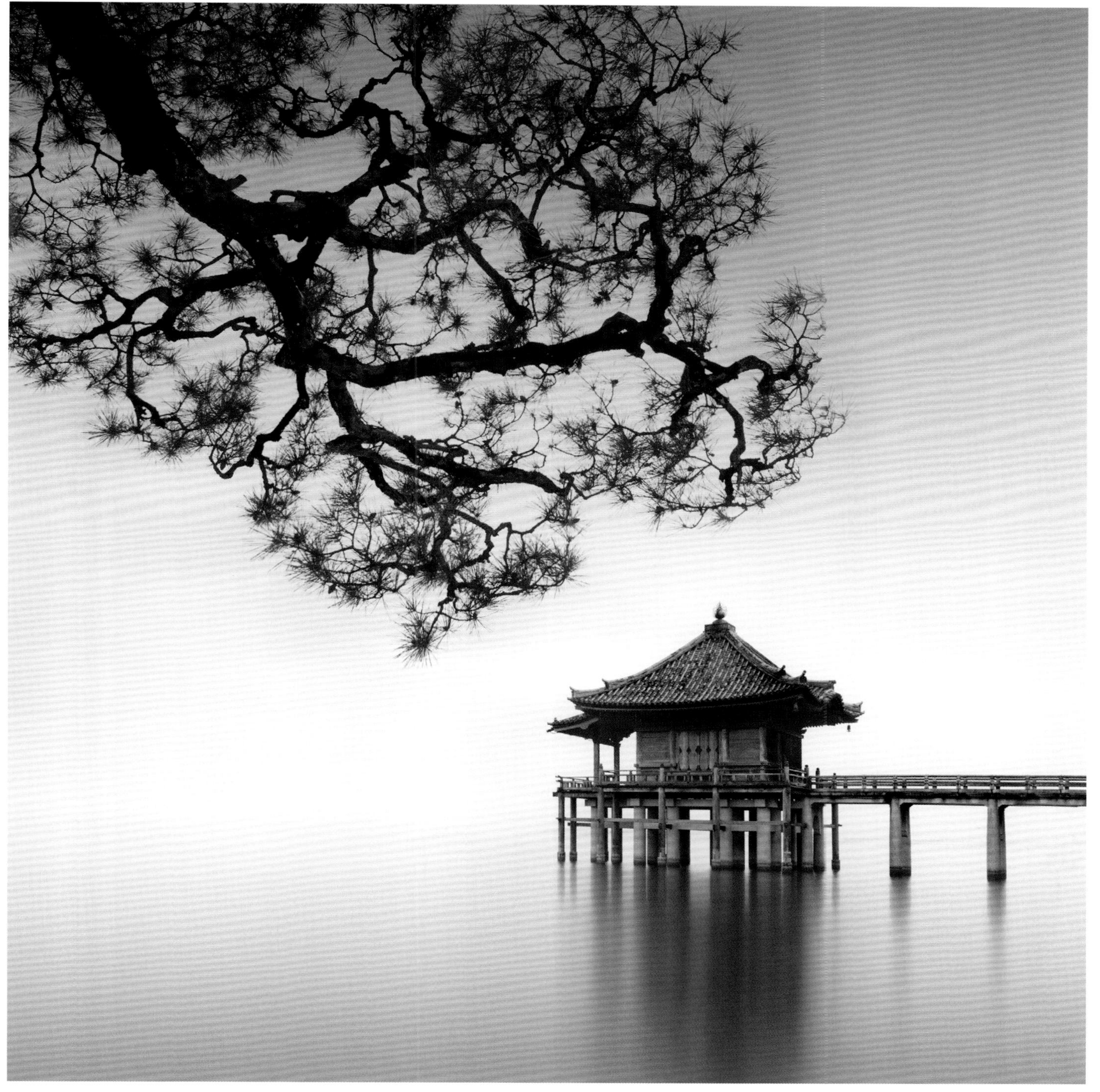

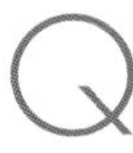

What techniques do you use to simplify an image and isolate a subject?

I use Lee filters—I have done for years—and I keep their 6-stop, 10-stop, 15-stop filters in my bag. I do use grads occasionally, but only in very bright circumstances, but working on the water so much I don't have the need to use them often—it's not as if I'm working with a dark foreground and bright sky. The filter I tend to use the most to simplify an image is the 10-stopper. But I really like working in very murky, misty, rainy conditions, because I like the very flat light that you get. I come from a darkroom background, so I like flat light, because it enables me to bring out the contrast, and not fight against any light. When you're working as I do, with one single subject, I'm generally isolating one thing and working with that; when you do that, you're committed to making sure that everything is in the right place. You need to make sure that the light is not going to be in a place that's going to distract you from looking at that one object. I'm used to employing light and contrast, and dodging and burning, to lead the viewer to the point of the picture I want them to look at. I don't use traditional foreground interest or leading lines at all. The mist or murk simplifies things so that the subject is isolated, whereas before it might have had a background of trees behind it— that way, the viewer is just seeing the thing you want them to look at.

What practical challenges do you face shooting near or on the water?

It depends on what I'm doing. If I'm on a fast-moving yacht, hanging off the bow, photographing the sails, then I'm usually getting covered in saltwater, and so the camera is, too. I tend not to protect it, though; I just wipe it down with warm water and a cloth afterward. But I do get through camera bodies— they do tend to rust up a little bit—but this is my office, as it were, so I just get on with it. Sometimes, when I'm working in the water, creating wave abstracts, I use a waterproof housing. It's a big cumbersome thing, weighing 9kg (20lb) and looking like a large pistol with a trigger—and that keeps everything dry. Also, I use Nikon equipment, and I'm very happy with the way that it responds in the conditions I work in, because I do push things beyond what they're supposed to cope with.

Why are black-and-white images still regarded as so important in fine art photography?

I've never been a color photographer myself—and, when I do shoot in color, the colors are pretty muted and desaturated. But black and white has always had an element of mystery about it, leading the viewer in a different direction to color photography. For instance, if I were to show you a picture taken in Greece of a bright blue door against a white wall, you would be overwhelmed by the color of the beautiful, vivid blue door. But if I was to convert it to black and white, and add some contrast, you'd look at the wonderful texture in the old door. So, it pushes you in a different direction. And one of the reasons it still has such an important place in fine art photography is that it leaves things to the imagination—it makes the viewer think, and leaves a question mark, not telling you the whole story, leaving it to you to ask questions and answer them yourself. And that's what I like about black and white photography— you're involving the viewer in your discussion of a subject by not telling them everything.

As a master of landscape photography, what is your motivation to continue making photographs?

I'm one of the people lucky enough to be able to earn a living from my two passions—photography and the sea. While I still have a story to tell about the sea, and while I still feel so passionate about the water, I'll continue making photographs. It's been there for me for such a long time, I'll still be making photographs until they put me in a box. It's become part of me. I swim, I sail, and I take photographs, and it's too much a part of my life to mean that I'll ever stop.

TECHNICAL INFORMATION

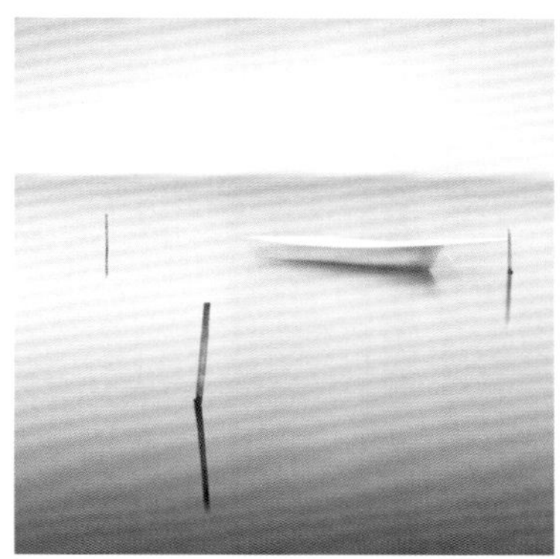

BOAT AND POSTS
CAMARGUE, FRANCE

Camera: Nikon D3X
Lens/Focal length: Zeiss Planar T* 50mm f/1.4
Aperture: f/16
Shutter speed: 30 sec.
ISO: 100
Kit: Tripod, 6-stop ND filter

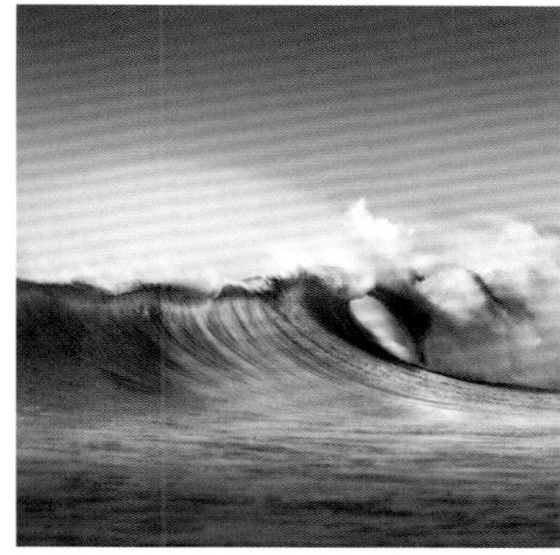

LA NORD
HOSSEGOR, FRANCE

Camera: Nikon D810
Lens/Focal length: Nikkor 600mm f/4
Aperture: f/6.3
Shutter speed: 1/1,250 sec.
ISO: 250

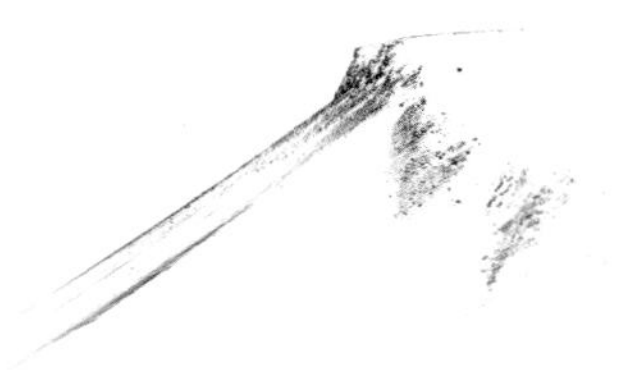

EMERGE
ICELAND 2015

Camera: Nikon D800
Lens/Focal length: Nikon 200-400mm f/4 at 240mm
Aperture: f/8
Shutter speed: 1/320 sec.
ISO: 100

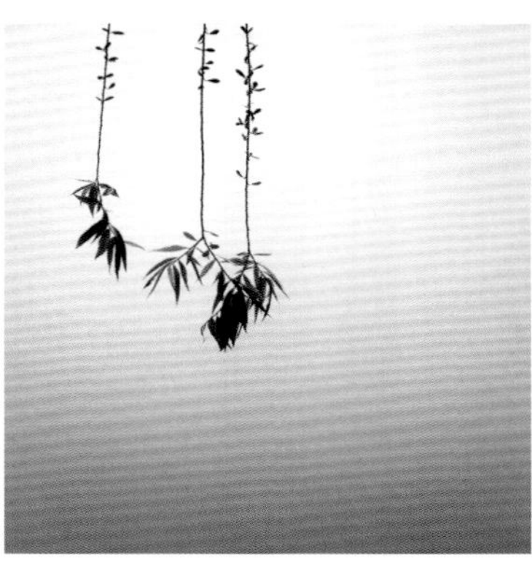

FIR LAKE
GUILIN, CHINA

Camera: Nikon D3X
Lens/Focal length: Zeiss Planar T* 50mm f/1.4
Aperture: f/8
Shutter speed: 1/160 sec.
ISO: 400

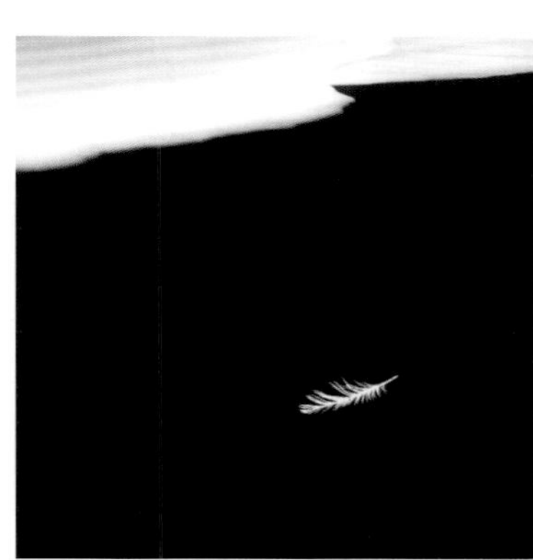

FEATHER
ICELAND

Camera: Nikon D3X
Lens/Focal length: Zeiss Distagon T* 35mm f/1.4
Aperture: f/20
Shutter speed: 2 sec.
ISO: 100

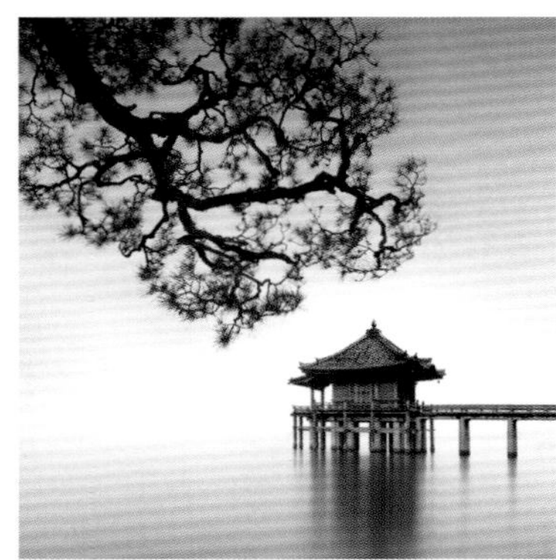

TEMPLE
HONSHU, JAPAN

Camera: Nikon D810
Lens/Focal length: Zeiss Distagon T* 28mm f/2
Aperture: f/11
Shutter speed: 10 sec.
ISO: 100
Kit: Tripod, 10-stop ND filter

LARS VAN DE GOOR

Dutch photographer Lars van de Goor was born in 1964 on a houseboat in the middle of lush farmland, and here he grew up being virtually part of the nature that surrounded him. At the time he first picked up a camera, Lars was living near Amsterdam, and he would go out on his bicycle to explore his local area looking for pictures. Near his house was a long, tree-lined canal, and he began to look for interesting compositions along its banks. After posting the images online he received a positive response, and this encouraged him to become more involved. The fact that he has no formal training is something he's pleased about, because he doesn't feel limited by any rules.

Lars won the Landscape section of the 2016 Hasselblad Masters Awards. Lars also took first prize in the "Season and Weather" and a Gold Medal in the "Streets and Paths" categories of the prestigious Trierenberg Super Circuit, the world's largest photo salon. While being influenced by romantic landscape painters—including the Dutch Masters, such as Barend Cornelis Koekkoek, and the work of other photographers—Lars's prime source of inspiration comes from the mysterious encounter of nature and light, and the main theme of his work is the trees of his native Gelderland.

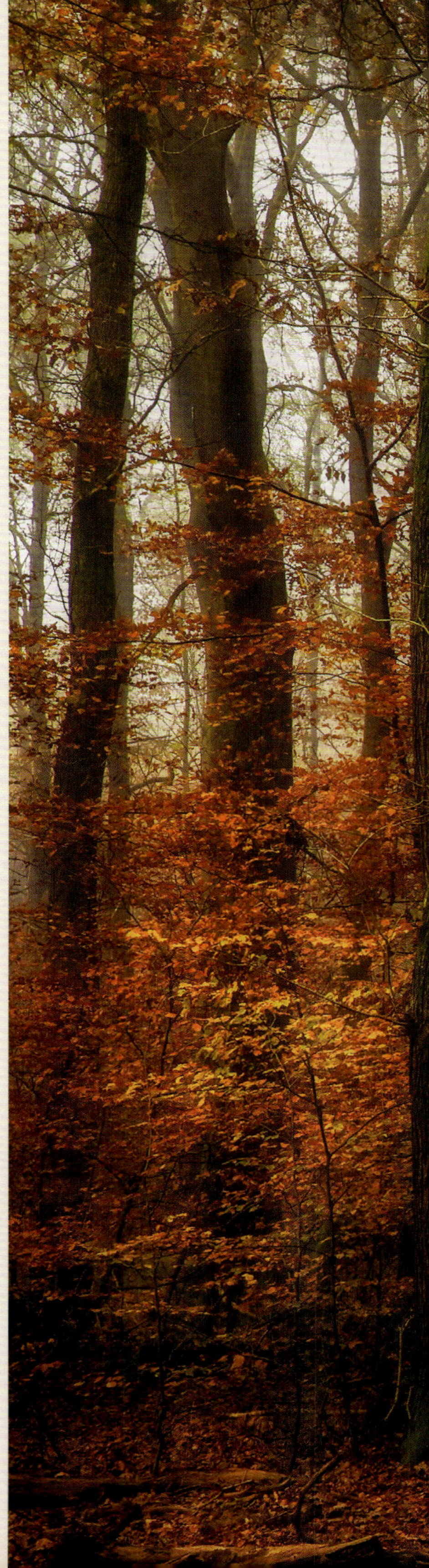

CLASSIC WOODS

This is one of many beautiful forest paths in Speulder Forest in the Netherlands. Fog in combination with fall colors creates my favorite conditions, because in this way they really stand out. When I am in the woods, I feel like I am walking in a painting sometimes. To translate this feeling to the viewer I will edit my images with the Old Masters in mind.

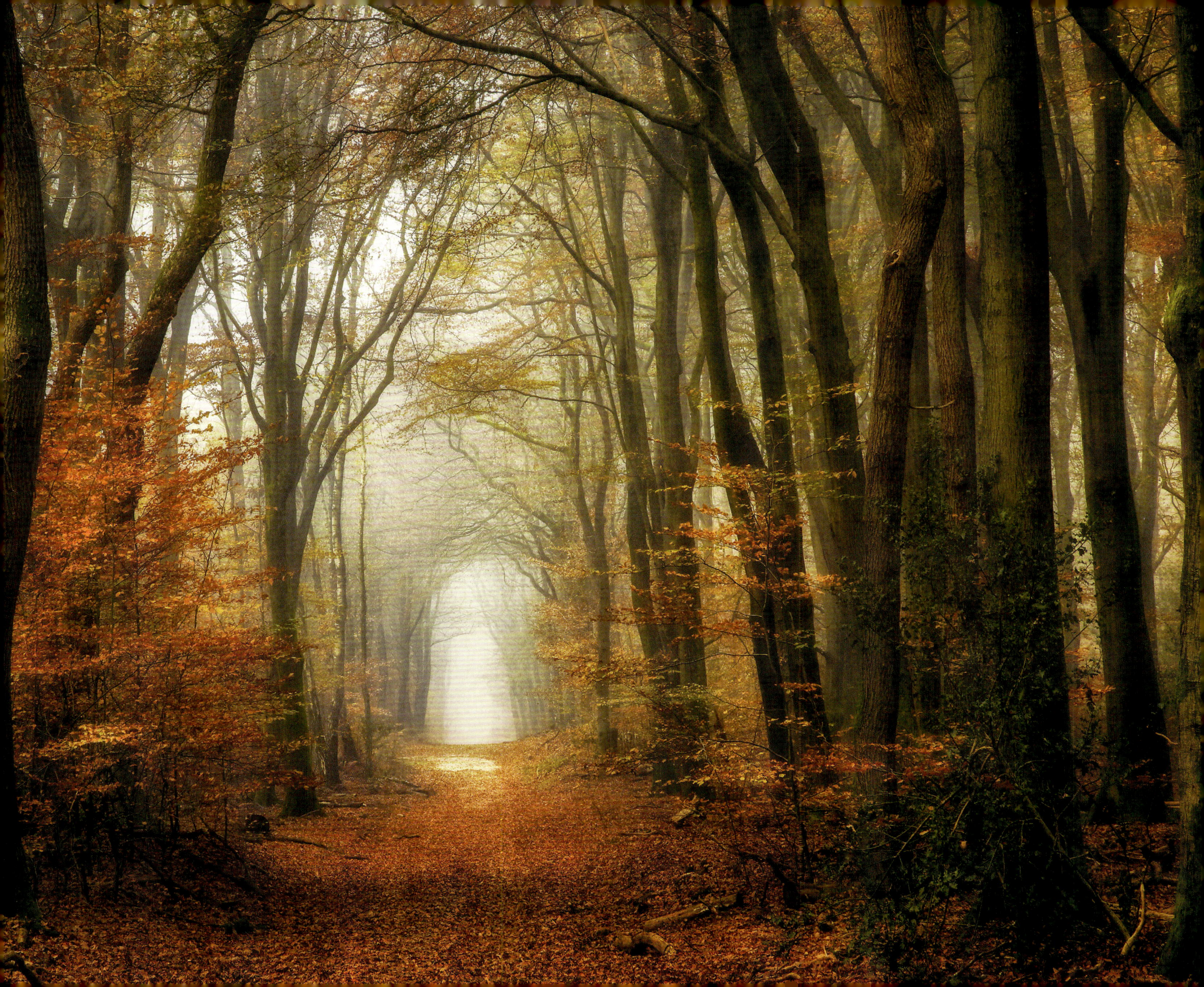

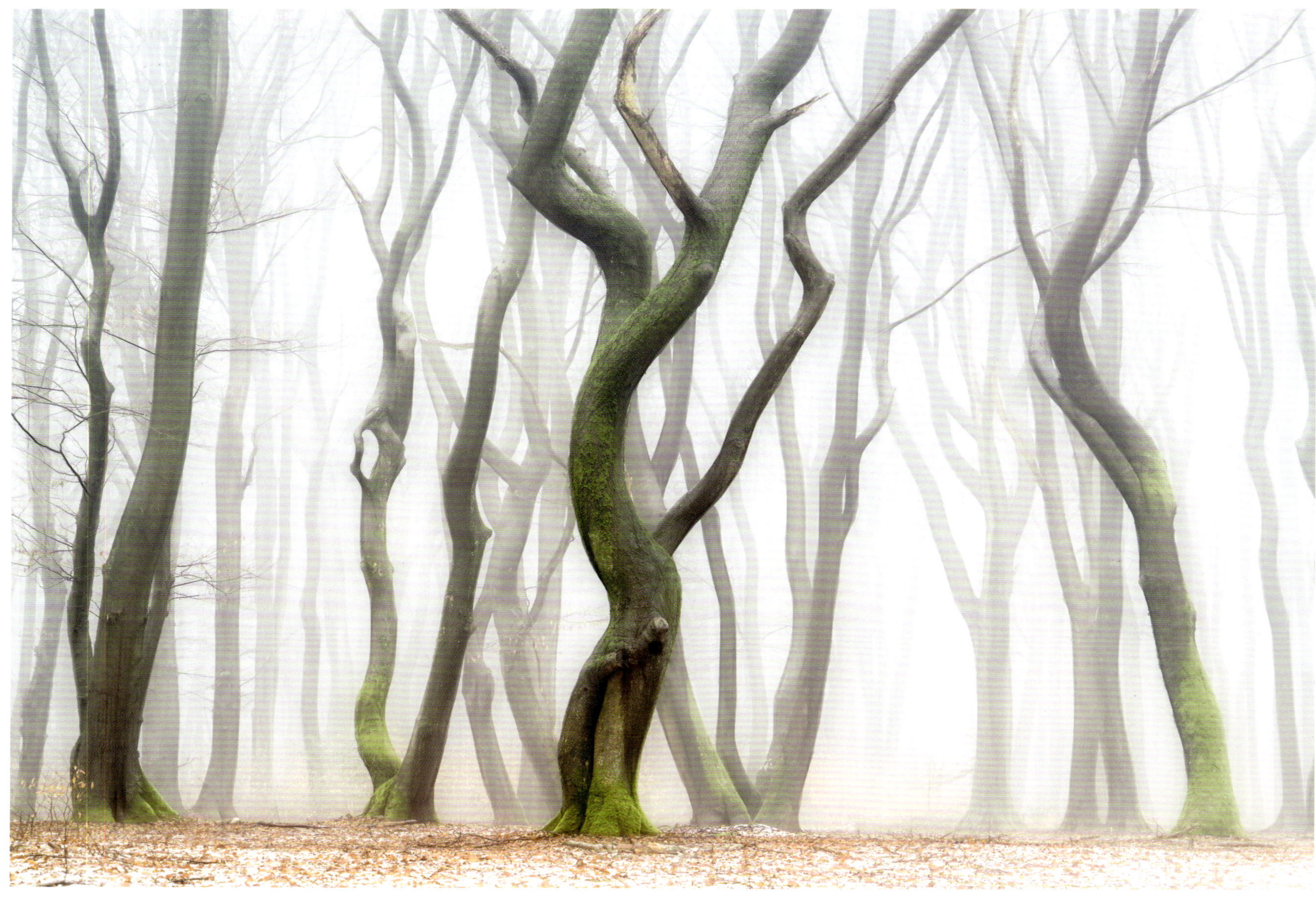

EARLY MORNING SHUFFLE

These are the dancing trees of Speulder Forest. The farmers used only the trees with a straight stem, so the curved strains were not touched because they were not usable. This process has lasted for years, resulting in a forest with curved trees. Generally, these curved trees are known as the "dancing trees." This particular image is in the less famous part of the forest. The trees that look like they are hugging is a favorite spot of mine, and I was unlucky many times, because there was no, or not enough, fog for a good image. But you have to be lucky only once!

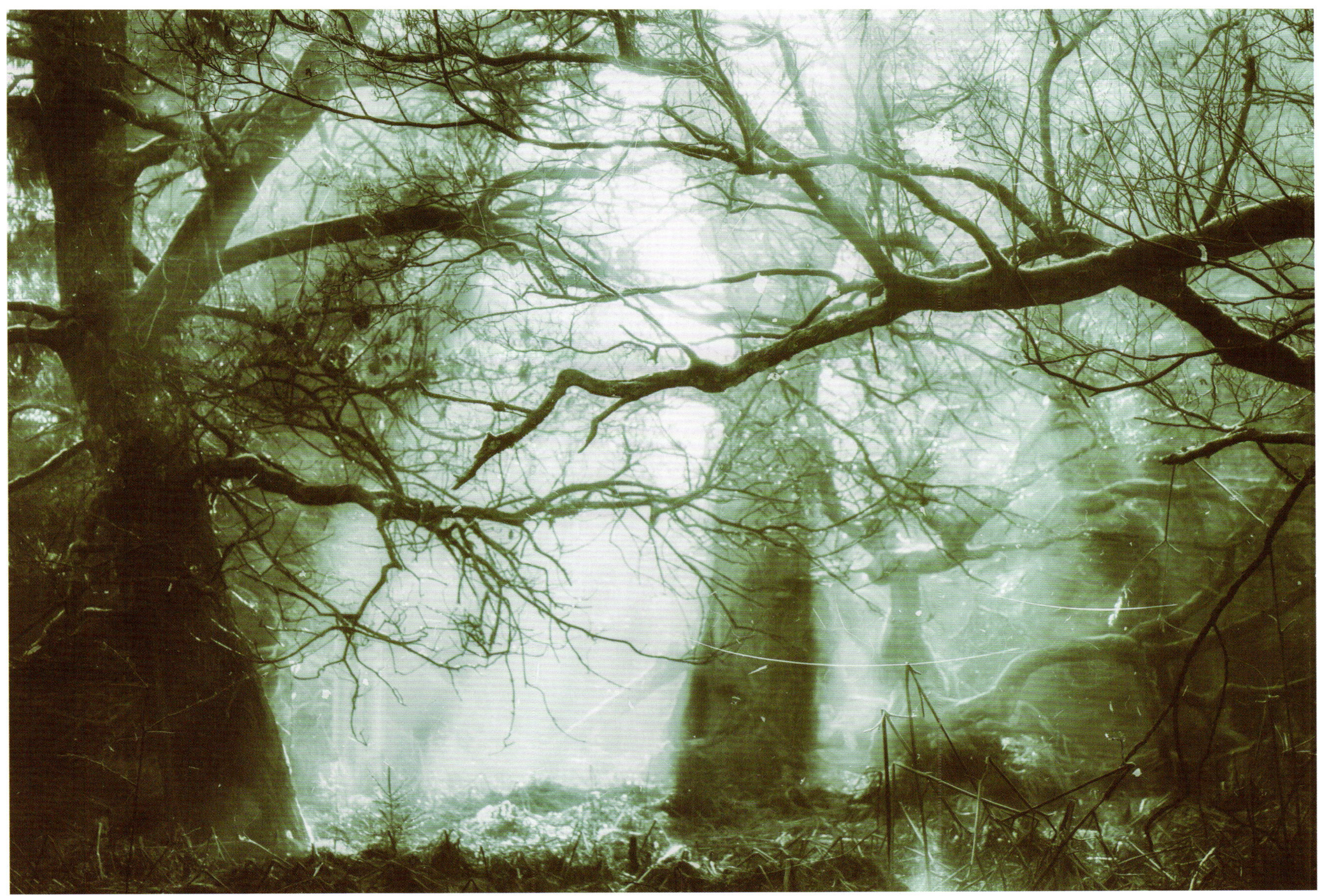

EYE OF THE FOREST

The woods of Sababurg in Germany are fascinating and filled with ancient trees. The wood is left totally untouched, which gives you a good idea how forests in the past must have looked. Such ancient and mysterious woods speak to the imagination, and fog or rays of light add even more mystery to them. On my way to this wood, I was driving in the thickest fog I had ever seen, however, two miles before I reached my destination all mist disappeared in seconds. I was feeling lucky, and thought that I might have at least some good light. I used a scratched texture for blending in post-processing to add to the atmosphere.

Q + A

You are a self-taught photographer—how important has "finding your own way" been in your work, technically and creatively?

Yes, I am self-taught. However, I wasn't looking for a particular style, or trying to find my own way, it just evolved playfully. I had no expectations and did what I wanted, not limited by any rules or knowledge, so that's why my own style arose. Of course, I had to catch up with the technical side of photography later on. When I started 10 years ago, I stepped right into the digital age of photography. Because of the quality of my first camera, and my lack of any technical knowledge of photography, I started very early on with editing my images to make them look better. Colors are of great importance to me. By changing the colors you can make a scene look very surreal, and yet it's familiar because it's a real picture. I always aim for an image that could be both a painting or a photograph.

What is the key ingredient in a successful landscape image composition?

The most important thing in any image is: is it appealing to the viewer? It is the same in landscape photography. Do we spot something we haven't seen before? Does the image stimulate the senses? If you look at any image of Patagonia for the first time, you will be in awe. If you have seen dozens of images of the same place, you will demand a more spectacular view to give yourself that same feeling you had with the first one. So ingredients other than composition or a particular editing style will determine how an image is experienced. When I started with photography, I had never heard of the "rule of thirds," so I composed my images the way I thought they looked best, and although using the rule of thirds works pretty well, I still do it the way I started. For me personally, I need the perfect light. I do a lot of scouting, and when the light is right, I know my spots. For woodland pictures, I prefer fog or early morning soft light. So the top ingredients are locations and light.

What do forests and woods offer a photographer creatively that can't be found elsewhere in the landscape?

I would say the magic. Forests, particularly covered in fog, do have a magical feel to them already. This inspires me to create fairy tale images. Mankind and forests go back a very long time. The connection we have with forests is still there. Old woods and forests do speak to our imaginations. From fairy tales to scary stories.

Woodland interiors are renowned for being chaotic environments— how do you find and achieve order and balance?

Woodland photography is a special discipline. For example, during my workshops, we drive to a beautiful forest location, and I ask the students to take a picture of it. Most of the time they all take out their wide-angle lenses. Indeed, woodlands are chaotic. First of all, you need to use your zoom or telephoto lens. By zooming in, you get rid of the useless information to the left and the right. Try to find some rhythm, harmony, a characteristic tree, or some balance, for instance. Keep the image as empty or as simple as possible, with not too much information. Also avoid the sky. You don't want to give the viewer too much information to look at. Lead their eye to what you think is the most interesting subject in the image.

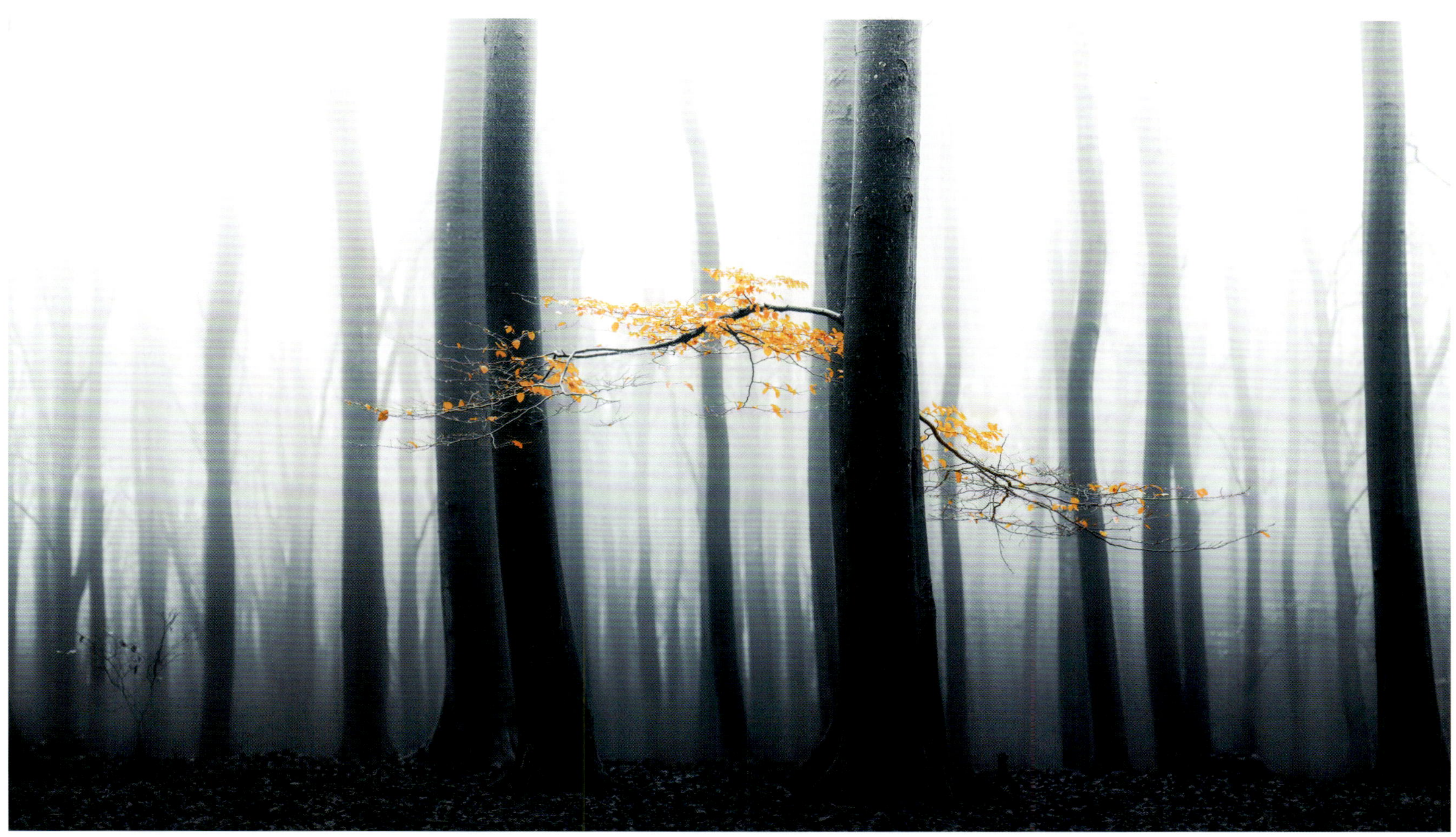

SPEULDER REVISITED

This was the winning image for the Hasselblad Masters Award in 2016. The stubborn last leaves of a beech form a perfect contrast with the fog in the background. Like with many of my images, if you just happened to pass by, you probably wouldn't have noticed it. The path was situated at a lower point which resulted in an interesting angle. Using an aperture set to f/2.8 made a beautiful shallow depth of field. I emphasized the blurry background in post-processing and made some color changes.

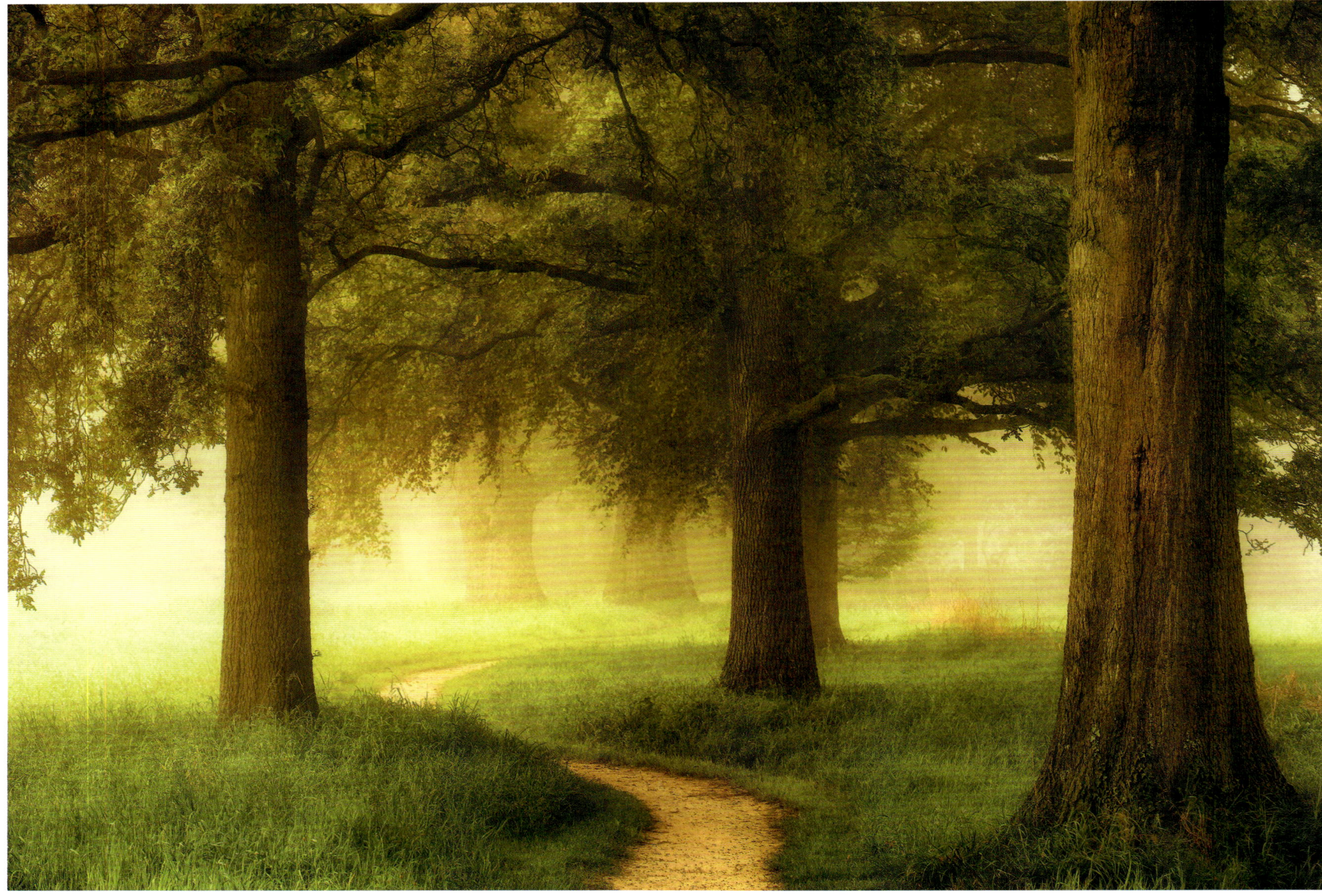

PATH OF AWAKENING

In the distance, there is a group of summer spikes of about 250 years old. These trees speak to the imagination.
It seems that this lane was formerly called the "Twelve Apostles," after twelve ancient oaks, nine of which are
still alive. You can find these majestic trees on the Ampsen estate near Lochem where I live. I must say it took me
a while to find the right composition for this image. Since the larger and more impressive trees are on the other
side, I started from there, but because of the light and better harmony, taking the photograph from this angle was
way better.

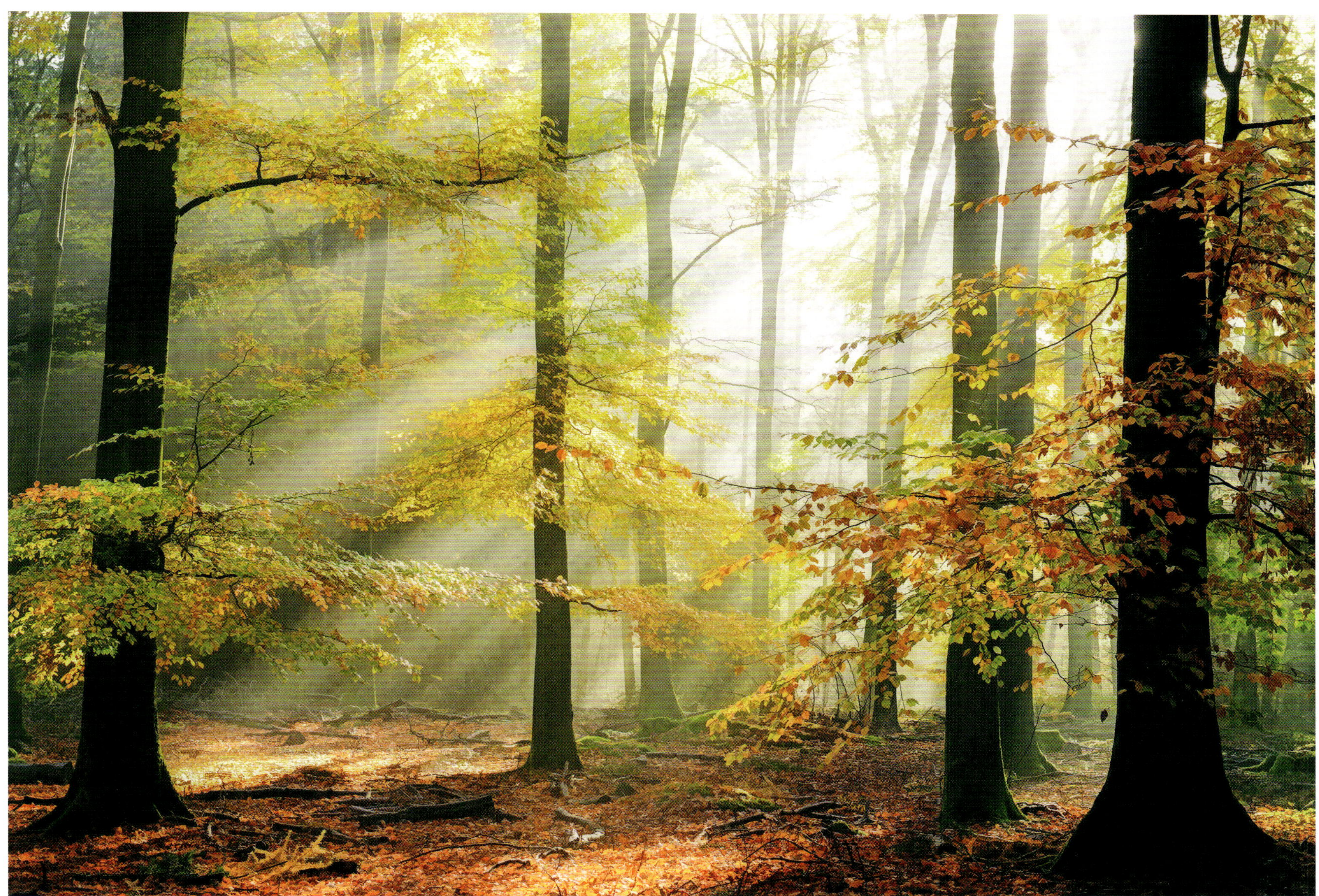

SINFONIA DELLA FORESTA

This was a blissful morning, with fall colors covered in rays of light. Of course, this is in the Netherlands, so one moment you have sunshine, and seconds later it's gone, never to return again that day. So you have to try to stay relaxed! Anyway, this was such a moment. I do not always have the patience to stick around one spot when I am in a magical forest. I could wait for hours for the perfect light, but then I feel too restless when I think about what else there is to be seen. So, often I just stroll around, and, when I am lucky, like with this image, where both composition and light are good, I feel gratitude.

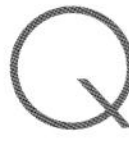 **Q**
+
 **A**

What are the particular technical problems of shooting in woodland environments?

Wind and the lack of light. While I don't mind a dark forest, when there is too much wind, a longer shutter speed is useless, and too much noise is often not an option. As I mentioned, I prefer a foggy forest. This is hard to predict, and I have found myself many, many times in dull and dark forests. So you need some luck, too. Some years have been great, others not. In some countries or regions you will have more changes, but be prepared to be unlucky.

What techniques do you use to achieve the "dreamy" look of some of your images?

You need some pleasant light to start with. Also, fog is a perfect ingredient for adding a dreamy feel to an image. Using a shallow depth of field is another way. By focusing on the first trees, for example, in a tree-lined alley, you will have that nice paint-like blur in the background.

What post-processing do you do to create the particular look you strive for in your work?

In post-processing, I often intensify the contrast between the sharp and blurred parts. I work very intuitively, besides some standard adjustments in RAW, I very much like to approach my images with fresh eyes. When editing, I would like to be surprised by what a certain filter will do. It must inspire me to go on. Sometimes, or most times, an image "dies" so to speak, in the process, and I cannot work on it any further. It doesn't mean the photograph is not good, but I can't improve it at that moment. Therefore, I almost never throw away my images. Years later, I might approach that image with whole new or improved skills.

As a master of landscape photography, what is your motivation to continue making photographs?

The same as when I started—walking around the corner and being amazed at what Mother Nature has to offer. It's the childlike wonder I am after, being surprised by nature's beauty, but also being surprised by whatever will arise during an editing process. My wife and I will soon be exchanging our house for a mobile home, and we will travel Europe for some years. It's important for me to discover new places and interesting situations.

TECHNICAL INFORMATION

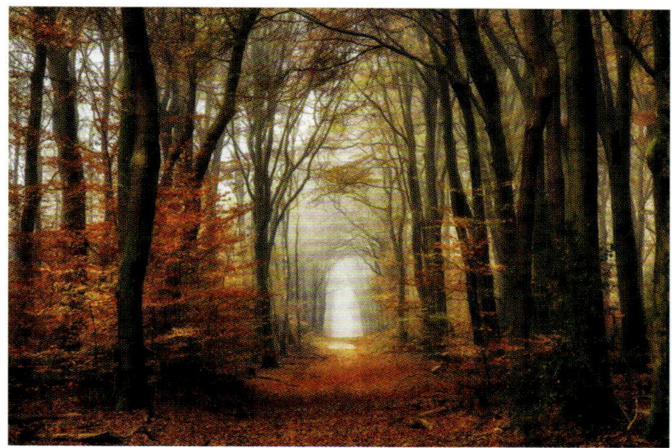

CLASSIC WOODS
SPEULDER FOREST, NETHERLANDS

Camera: Canon EOS 5D Mark II
Lens/Focal length: Canon 24–105mm f/4 at 105mm
Aperture: f/22
Shutter speed: 1/5 sec.
ISO: 250
Kit: Tripod

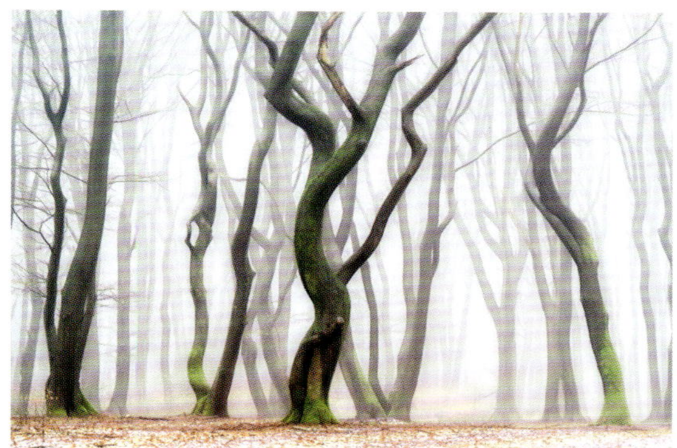

EARLY MORNING SHUFFLE
SPEULDER FOREST, NETHERLANDS

Camera: Sony a7R II
Lens/Focal length: Sony 24–240mm f/3.5-6.3 at 92mm
Aperture: f/8
Shutter speed: 1/10 sec.
ISO: 100
Kit: Tripod

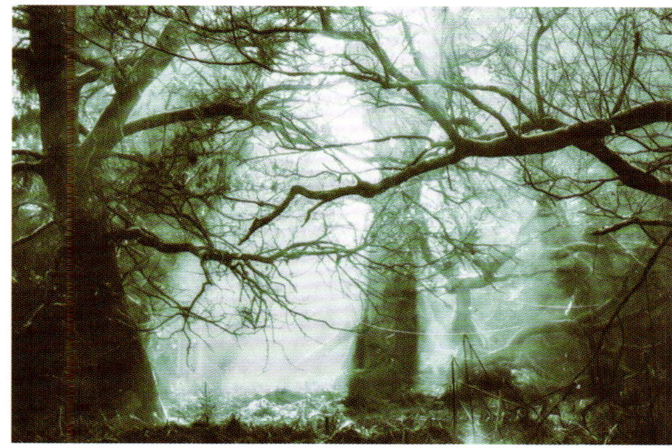

EYE OF THE FOREST
SABABURG, GERMANY

Camera: Sony a7R II
Lens/Focal length: Sony 24–240mm f/3.5-6.3 at 146mm
Aperture: f/16
Shutter speed: 1/10 sec.
ISO: 100
Kit: Tripod

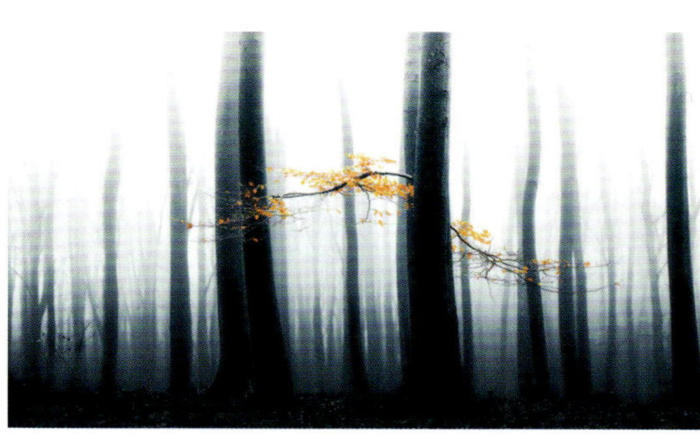

SPEULDER REVISITED
SPEULDER FOREST, NETHERLANDS

Camera: Nikon D800
Lens/Focal length: Nikkor 70–200mm f/2.8 at 100mm
Aperture: f/2.8
Shutter speed: 1/400 sec.
ISO: 800
Kit: Handheld

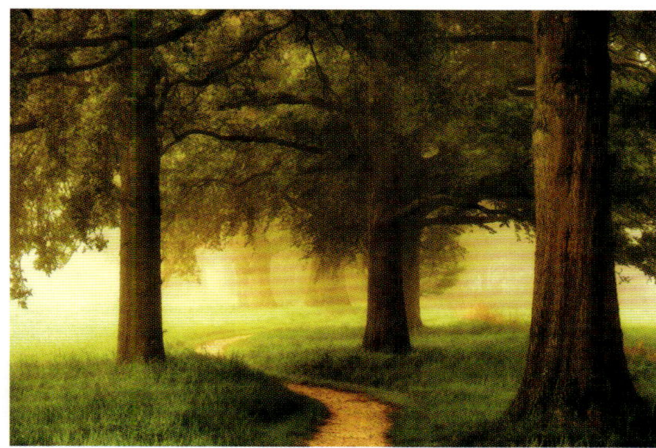

PATH OF AWAKENING
AMPEN ESTATE, LOCHEM, NETHERLANDS

Camera: Nikon D800
Lens/Focal length: Nikkor 70–200mm f/2.8 at 95mm
Aperture: f/6.3
Shutter speed: 1/100 sec.
ISO: 500
Kit: Handheld

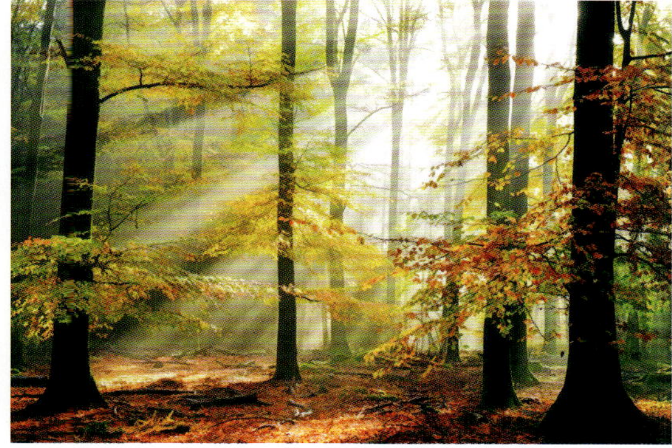

SINFONIA DELLA FORESTA
NETHERLANDS

Camera: Nikon D800
Lens/Focal length: Nikkor 24–70mm f/2.8 at 70mm
Aperture: f/9
Shutter speed: 1/80 sec.
ISO: 640
Kit: Handheld

MARC ADAMUS

Marc Adamus is based in the northwestern United States, and is often described as one of the most influential landscape professionals of his generation. A full-time professional photographer from 2005, Marc is today recognized as an original artist and a trendsetter in the modern age of landscape photography. The visual drama and artistry of his photographs are born of a keen eye for the many moods of nature and a lifelong passion for the wilderness.

Marc's style is unmistakable. He is able to capture the amazing light and fleeting atmosphere of great landscapes, creating a sense of the epic, majestic, and bold. His success derives from a patient, single-minded pursuit of all the unique moments that generate the magic and energy of the wilderness, often spending weeks or months immersing himself in the landscape he shoots, despite the rigors of season and weather. Marc's photographs have been published worldwide in a wide variety of media, including books, calendars, and advertising, and in publications including *National Geographic*, *Outdoor Photographer*, *Popular Photography*, and many more. Marc's clients have included Fortune-500 companies such as Apple, HP, Toshiba, and Blackberry.

FEARLESS

This image was a highlight in years of storm-chasing on the Colorado Plateau, and shows off the kind of great atmosphere that illustrates the layered landscape of the Grand Canyon. For me, the choice to include a lonely tree on a tiny ledge just below the rim was an obvious one once I realized the lonely perspective I could create, reaching into the scene. Thunderstorms are a near-daily occurrence in the Canyon in summer at times, but catching the lightning ahead of or behind the storm in the right spot can be tricky. I used a burst of frames to capture the frequent lightning where it occurred. It takes a little luck and a lot of time, and careful previsualization.

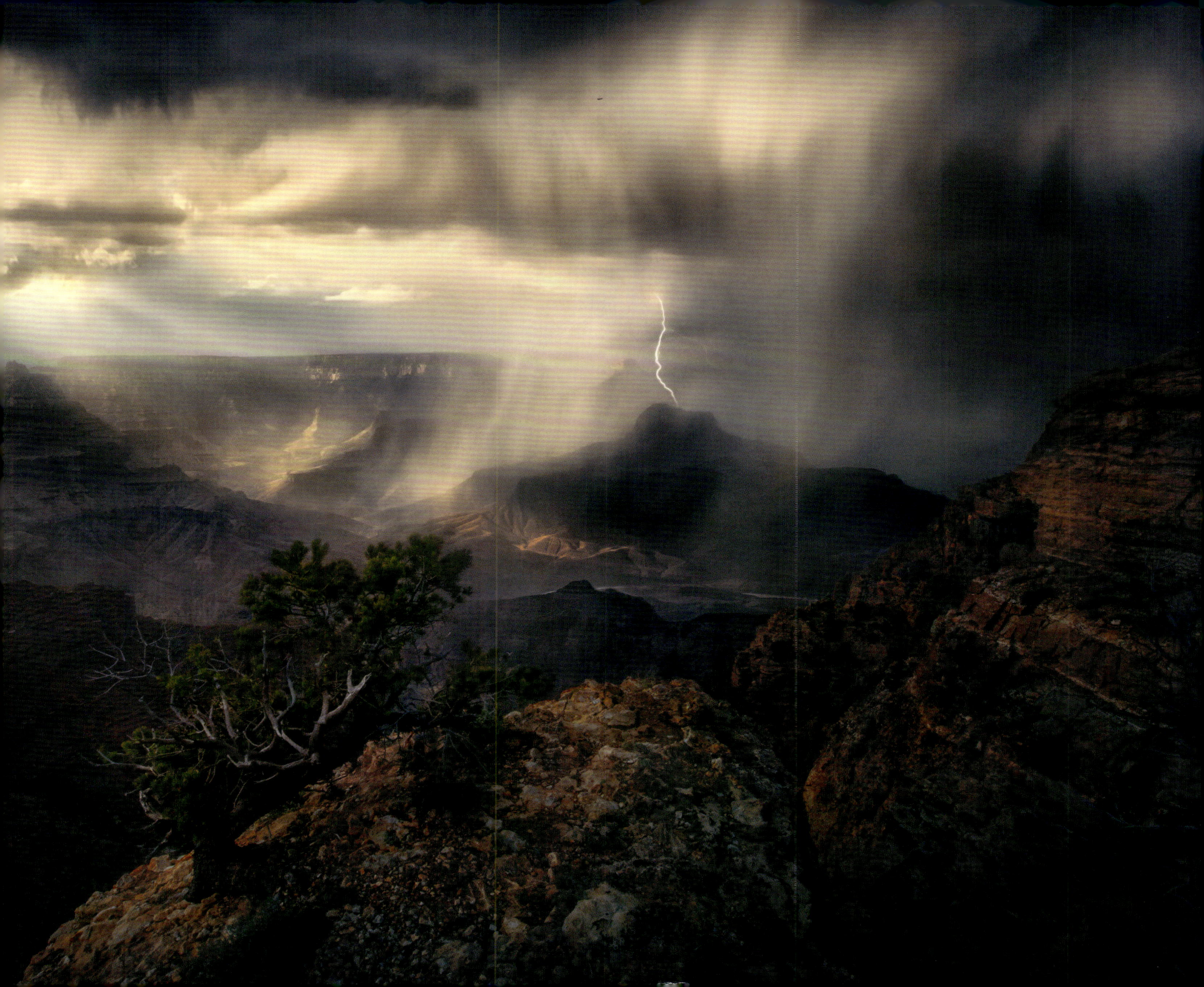

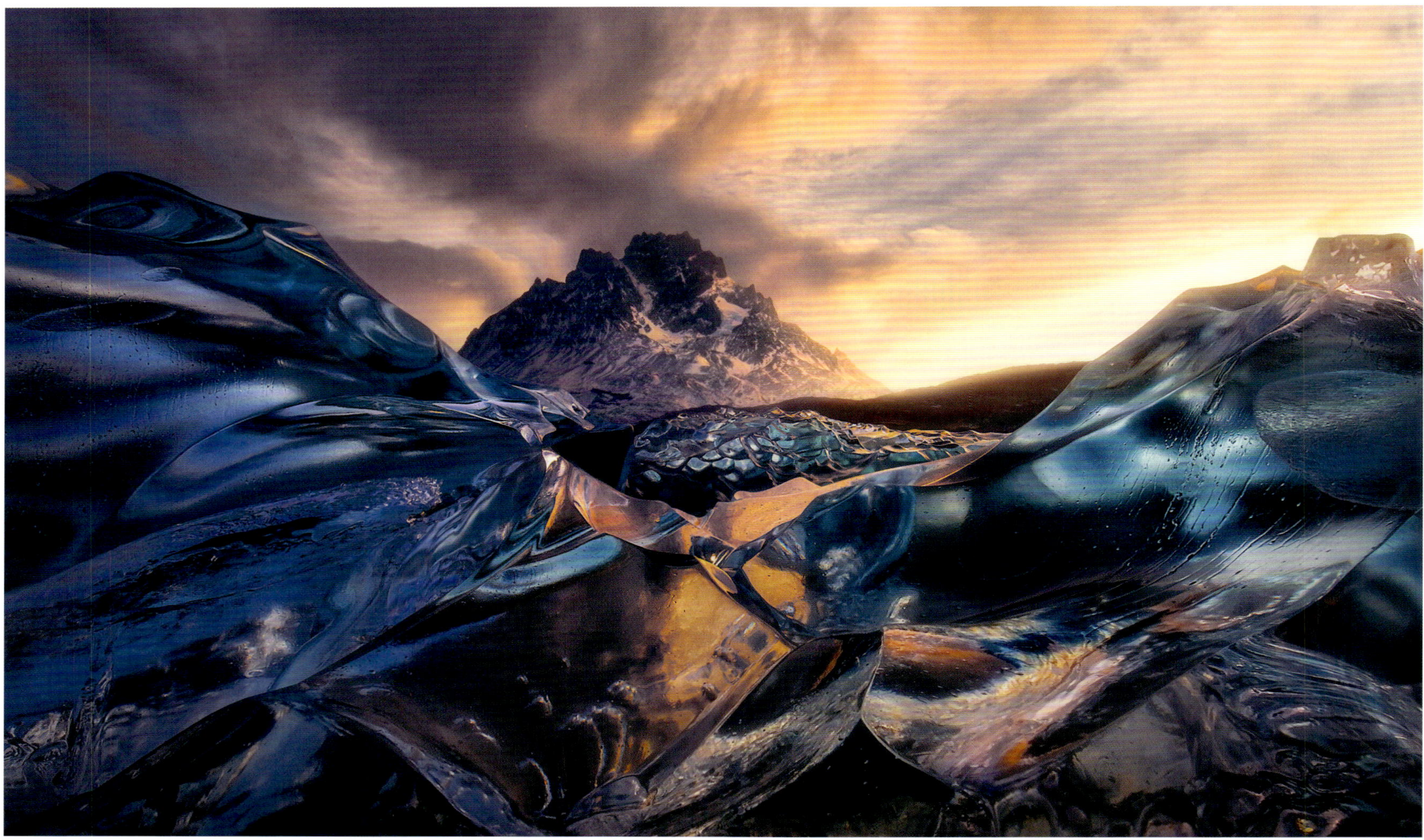

COOL THE FLAMES

After discovering that there were thousands of icebergs in Lago Grey in midwinter in 2014, my buddy Floris and I backpacked the 40-kilometer (25-mile) round trip to access the points of the lake we were interested in, carrying a small raft for shooting among the bergs. After waiting out a three-day windstorm and ocean-sized waves at a remote, off-trail location, we were eventually able to paddle our way to this spectacularly polished chunk of ice for shooting at sunrise. The shot lasted only a moment as the berg turned in the water, and we had to be very careful navigating the sea of larger ice in our tiny craft. All parts of the image are a single exposure.

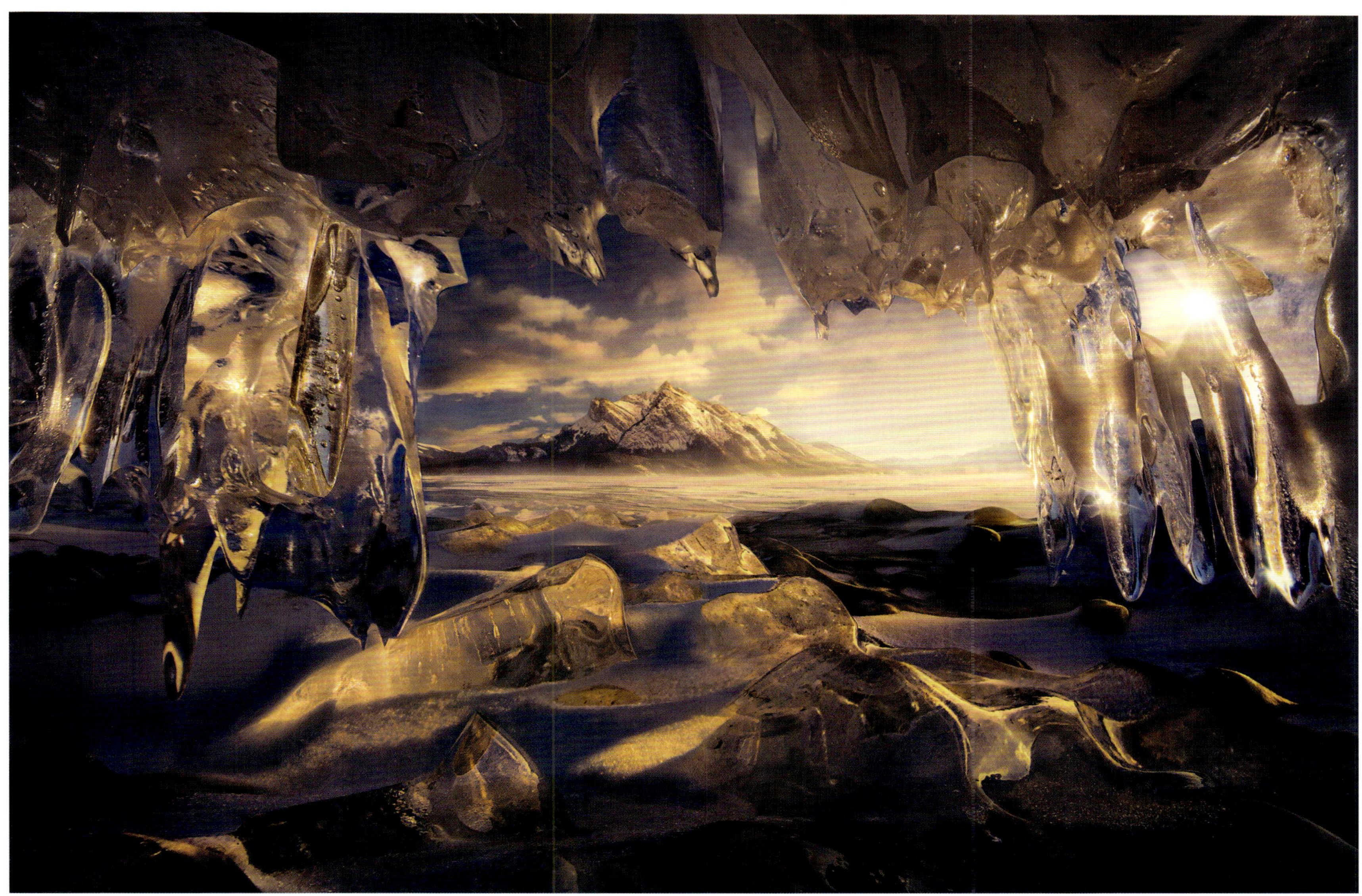

CRYSTAL WINDOW

Causing this crazy ice formation were 1.5m (5ft) high wooden trunks, which were stuck in the ground and had picked up some huge, freezing wave action earlier in the season when the water was exposed and higher on the receding shoreline. To get inside one of these tiny caves required some trickery, so this image comes from what were almost totally blind shots. I had to position the camera through a small hole in the base of one of the formations, and make my best guess on each frame to stitch, as well as the two focus points I needed for each foreground shot. After several tries over an hour or so, I got results that were good enough to work with. This was one of the hardest technical shots I've ever pulled off, especially considering the high winds and 14°F (-10°C) temperatures outside. I made a four-shot horizontal two-row stitch with the bottom two exposures being duplicated with a closer focus point. The camera was handheld but I positioned it on a rock and a chunk of ice.

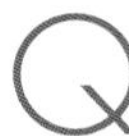

Q

+

A

What other artists or photographers influenced your work and how?

I was definitely influenced by the work of the late Galen Rowell, who was just outstanding. When I saw his photography, I thought he was really taking it to the next level. Galen was a great climber and photographer, and writer, workshop-leader extraordinaire of his day. I got the same equipment as him, and went out there, and gave it my best shot. It's been a time of great change in photography, and many influences have come and gone. I really strive to do my own work and present my own vision. One of the great painters that influenced me was Albert Bierstadt, because he was one of the first painters who painted the American West, which is where I'm from. He painted these fantastic, luminous, extraordinarily detailed landscapes of the places where we now do photography. So I like to look at his work, as a sort of benchmark for perfect lighting, unhindered by any weather or technical issues with the camera.

What first draws you to a location, and how do you begin to plan a trip?

Usually, the location will be one I want to explore personally because I really do have a passion for wilderness and adventure in these places. I am drawn to mountains and forests. The mountain realm has been the subject of my photography more than anything else, and for there the best tools to start with are topographical maps. Being a map aficionado my whole life means I'm able to apply topographical mapping, so I can determine—before I get to a location—what a peak is going to look like, how the light is going to hit it, how it's going to look through this lens, where I'm going to stand, in addition to route-finding. If I'm going to the coast, I might look at satellite pictures before I go, to look for sea stack formations, or offshore islands, for example. I also think about what lens I am going to use—is it going to be a big sky, wide-angle type of image, where I'm looking for framing and leading lines; or is it going to be a long-lens type, where I'm looking for layers or patterns; or an intimate, small-scale type of shot?

How much time do you spend exploring a location before you feel you're ready to capture its character and mood?

I find that my very best photography often comes in the very first 20 minutes of seeing a place. I find that it's a very sure and raw experience at that time—I haven't formulated any preconceived notions of how the light should work, for example—I'm not thinking in a formulaic manner, I'm just thinking in a reactionary way. When you open yourself up, and allow yourself to react, and allow the place to speak to you, often it's those first impressions that make the biggest impact, and I find myself very drawn to take the photograph at that time. I do believe that there are some advantages to getting to know a place over a very long period of time—understanding all the nuances of light, the weather, the foregrounds, the seasons, and such. But I'm an explorer, through and through, and I always like to see what's over the next mountain range, or around the next corner. I find that's when I'm most creative.

How do you create drama in a landscape image—how do you pull all the elements in a scene together?

When you're working with a two-dimensional medium—like photography, drawing, painting—the more you can create three-dimensionality, and bring the viewer into and through the scene, the more successful you're going to be. This is especially true of landscape photography, when you're dealing with a lot of different types of subject matter. You may have a waterfall, wildflowers, and then the mountain, then the sunset—and you've got to find a way to bring all those various subjects, which are all different colors, textures, lit in different ways, together; or, to pull the eye through them cohesively. I look for transitions through the entirety of the frame, either from everything that is not the focal point to the focal point, or from everything that's near to everything that's far away. And I look for ways to make those transitions, from out of focus to in focus, big to small, dark to light, cool to warm—one of my favorites is from high contrast to really no contrast, draining softer light in the background. So I really look for those things in the field, and when I get to post-processing, I'm able to use those elements to develop my theme, which gives the viewer a real sense of the place.

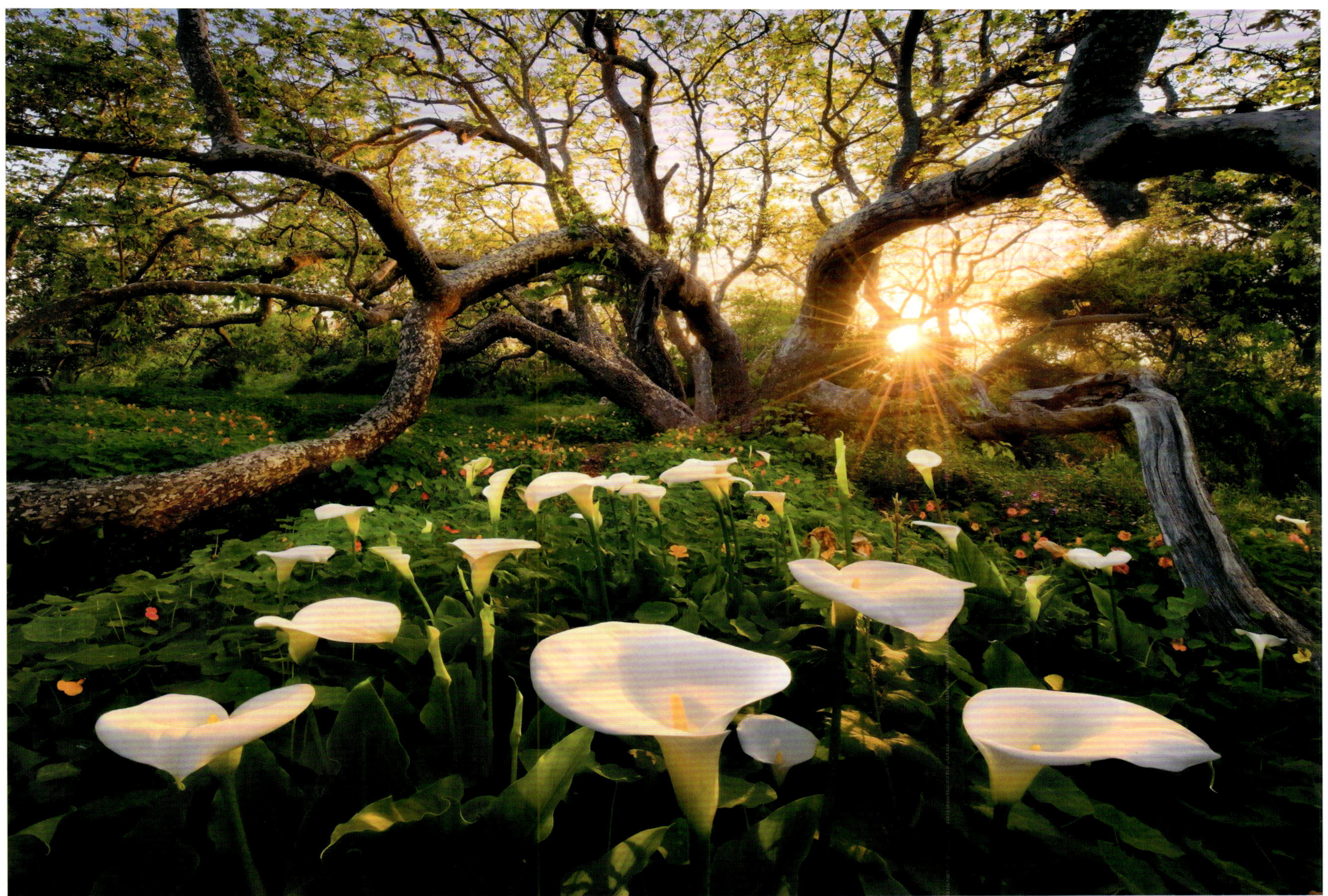

HEAVEN ON EARTH

On one amazing evening while taking a walk at the request of my four-year-old son, we stumbled upon this forest, and I beheld the most beautiful of all the landscapes I have ever photographed. You never know where or when nature will reveal to you its magic moments. This was one I will always remember. I went back later that week, and made the images that captured for me a place and time the like of which I would never see again. The image was focus-stacked from multiple exposures.

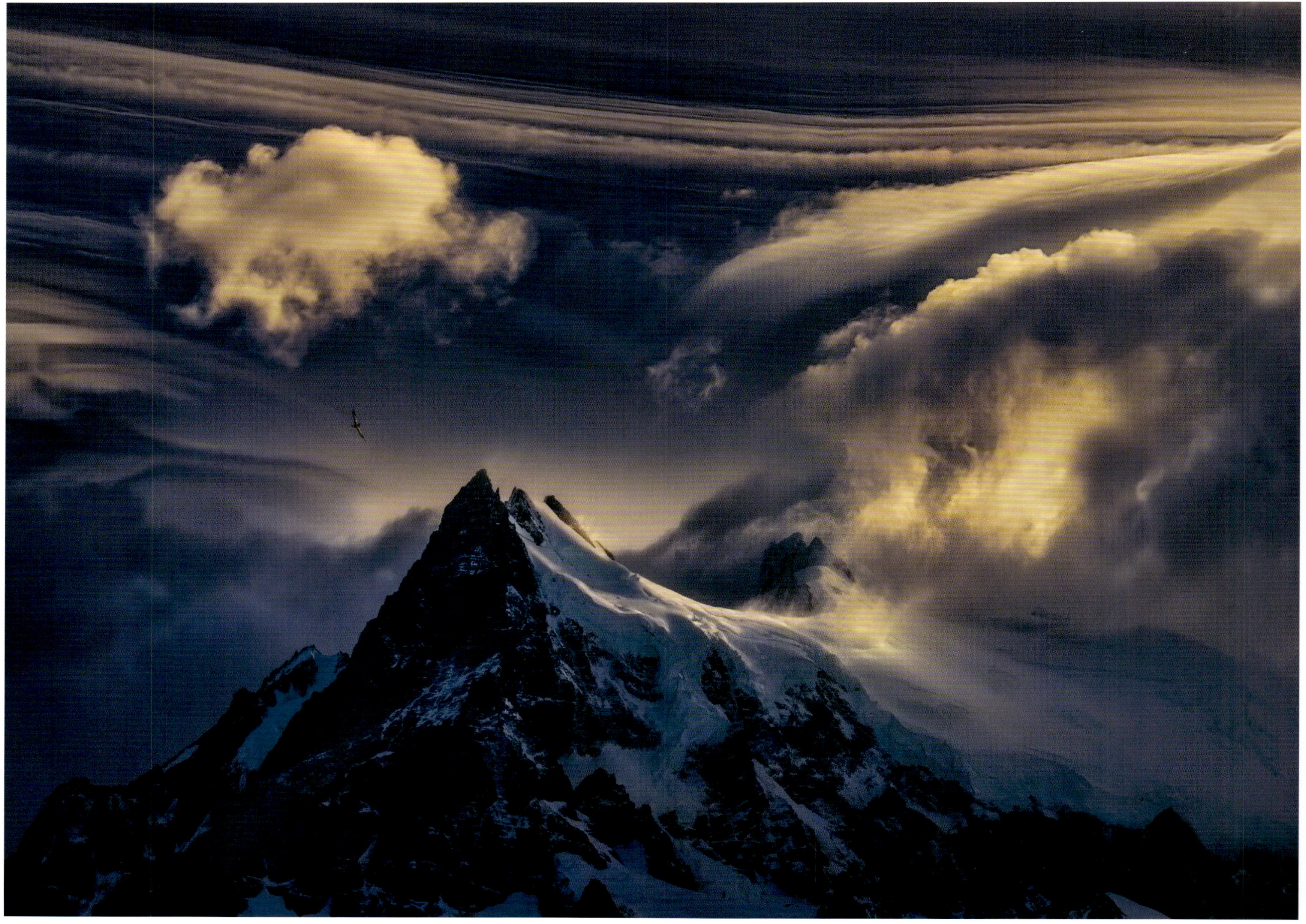

FOR ETERNITY

(Left) Photographers are artists. But art is not simply
about what is captured. Art is about what is spoken.
What is spoken comes from within. It evokes a
connection with an idea, or a subject, or even a mood.
And in that connection, somewhere there must be a
bond that runs deeper than simply what is before us
at that moment. It must be unique to us. I feel the best
images, this art, must speak from what is inside ourselves
first. This image is about finding clarity and strength in
times of turbulence and the unknown. This is the Cerro
Grande peak, with lenticular wave clouds and blowing
snow. A condor rides the wind, free from it all.

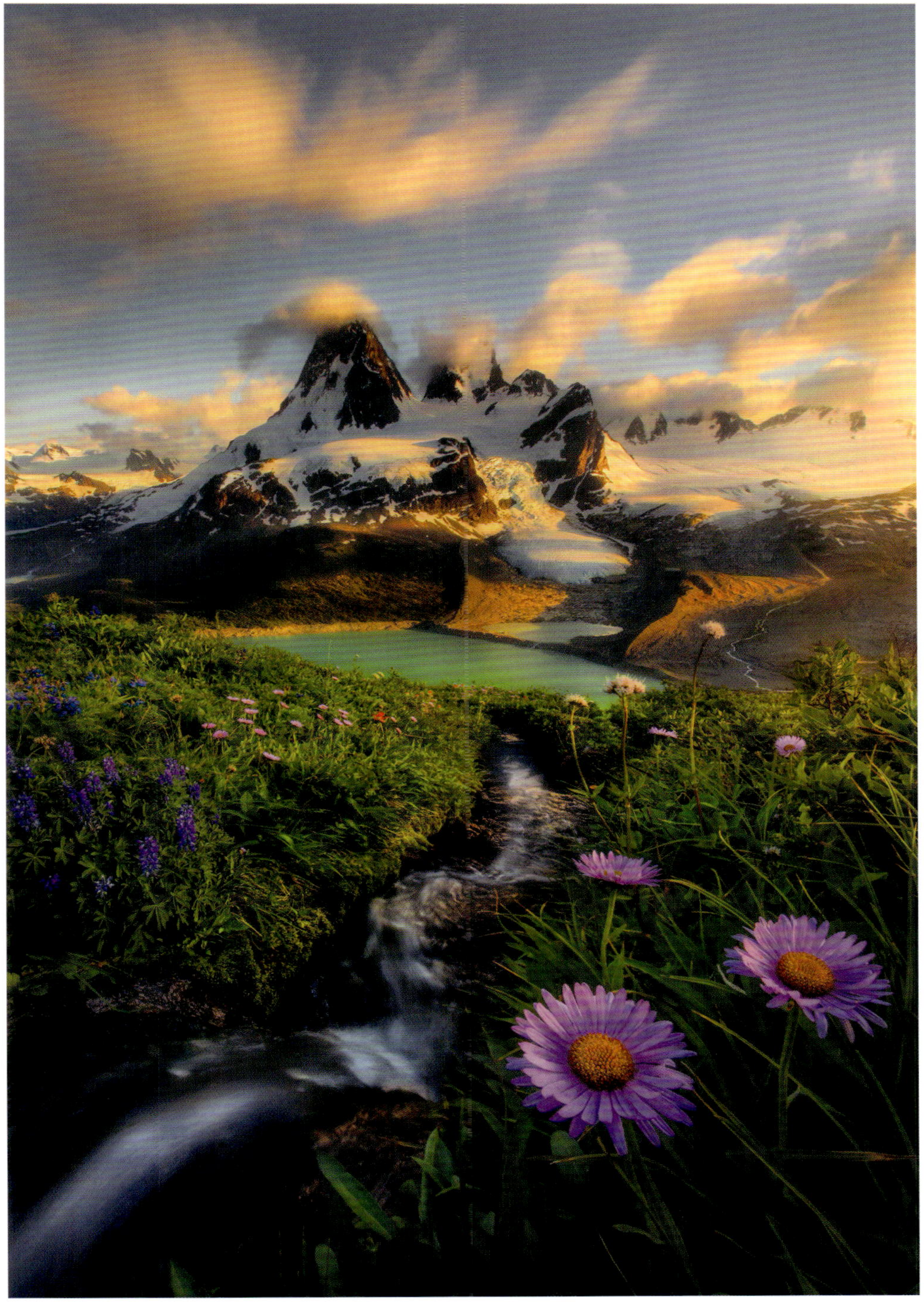

FIELD OF DREAMS

(Right) An incredible wilderness in summer colors awaits those
who venture into the coastal mountains of British Columbia and
Alaska. Here, in British Columbia's Tweedsmuir region, glaciers
pour from the flanks of high peaks above into turquoise waters
beyond. Up close, the fields of summer blooms are immense,
and a small cascade leads the way in. On this trip, I spent
eight days guiding a group of adventurous photographers off-
trail, backpacking through this awesome wild place, after we
were dropped off by helicopter. I focus-stacked the foremost
flowers with another exposure.

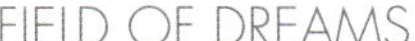

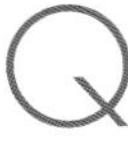
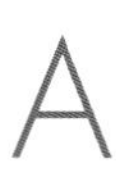

Q + A

Do you exposure-blend or use other key techniques in post-processing, to capture your vision of how a location should look?

Without getting into too much detail, because it would make another book, I created my own system for post-processing in Photoshop that allows me to just brush on the effect that I want. I paint very much like a painter, so if I want some more light, I paint it on with brushes. I do a whole lot of work with different brushes of my own design to optimize the light, luminosity, atmosphere, color, shading, depth—every part of the image is up for grabs in post-processing. There's a whole lot of other stuff I do, and exposure-blending is definitely one of them. But at the same time, I'm a guide who really does enjoy taking people to places and seeing those places myself, so the images must reflect the real places we see. So, I won't change the landscape itself, but everything else, from the color, to the light, to the atmosphere is very much worked on. I do make post-processing a high priority—to get a great-looking printable image, I spend an average of five hours per photograph. I can get the image 90 percent of the way there, in most circumstances, in 20 minutes, but the remaining time is spent doing refinements, small touch-ups here and there, until I get everything the way I want. There are also plenty of images with which I just spend 15 minutes in Lightroom and that's it, but then there are a few times when I've spent 20 hours in post-processing!

What is the hardest aspect of being a professional photographer today?

This is not so true for me so much, but if you want to get a foothold today, it's not enough to produce great work—unless it's truly unique and extraordinary—you need to spend time promoting yourself through social media. Today, 99 percent of people who become professional photographers are going to do so because they're capable in the business and marketing department, and they're able to get their work out in front of audiences. They'll also have the passion and the drive to develop that presence on social media. I'm just lucky to not really have needed to do that—I came along before social media really developed, and I have such a core base of clients who appreciate my work. That's a blessing, because I think it would be very difficult to keep on top of social media, promoting your work, writing about it, looking at your images, and at the same time also be inspired to create new photographs.

Why is wilderness so important to you, and what do you hope your images can communicate to the viewer?

For one, it's the sense of freedom, and another, it's the sense of truth. The wilderness is the way it is. You go out on a long wilderness trip, for day after day, and you don't see another person, you're alone, and there's no one to rescue you—you feel the power, you feel humbled by how incredibly intricate and beautiful nature is on so many levels, but also how harsh and unforgiving it can be. And all the details that fill up our lives, and may seem very important until you get out to explore the wilderness, and all of a sudden, it's "Wow!" This is how this place has been for so long, and here I am, just a visitor in it—it's humbling. I seek out places that people haven't seen or photographed, and I think very carefully about what kind of photograph I create to evoke the essence of that place, which is really a fusion of myself and the place, and my experience with it.

What single piece of kit is most useful in your work?

Other than the camera, I would say my truck. I've spent years of my life learning to customize these trucks that I drive everywhere, and help me get close to the trail heads. For these past 20 years, I've spent more nights sleeping out in my truck than I have in normal beds! It's very important to me to be minimalist, to occupy a small space, carry very little gear, and just throw everything in the vehicle and go.

TECHNICAL INFORMATION

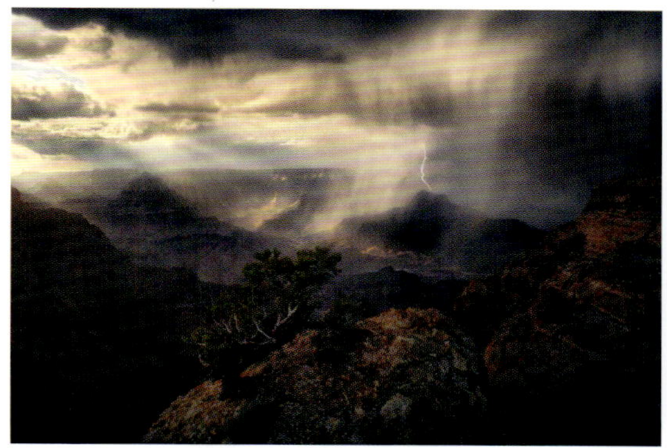

FEARLESS
GRAND CANYON, COLORADO,
USA

Camera: Nikon D800
Lens/Focal length: Nikkor 14–24mm f/2.8 at 18mm
Aperture: f/14
Shutter speed: 1/10 sec.
ISO: 32

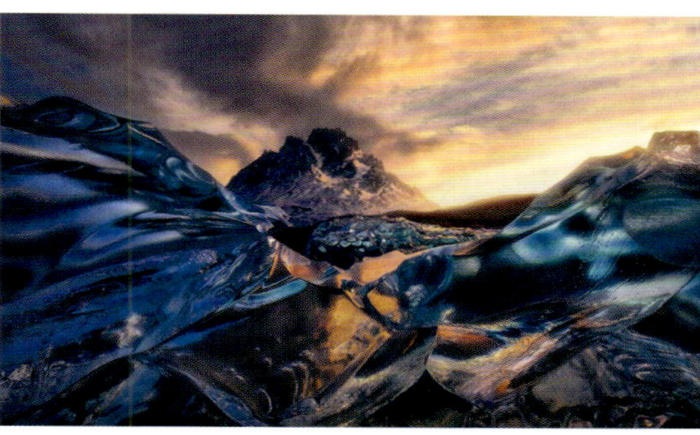

COOL THE FLAMES
LAGO GREY,
TORRES DEL PAINE NATIONAL PARK, CHILE

Camera: Nikon D800
Lens/Focal length: Nikkor 14–24mm f/2.8 at 22mm
Aperture: f/18
Shutter speed: 1/40 sec.
ISO: 400

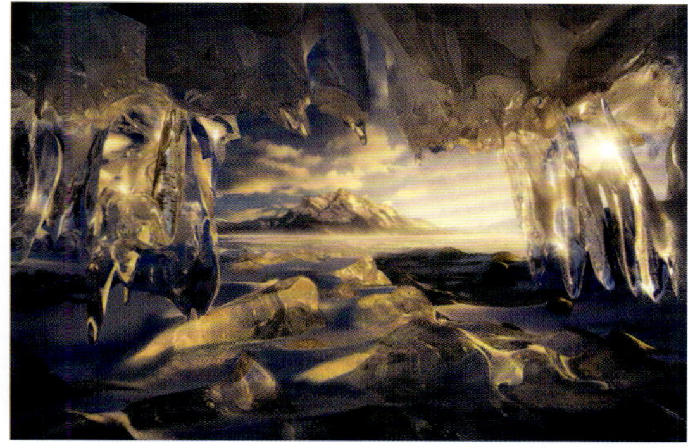

CRYSTAL WINDOW
ABRAHAM LAKE, BANFF, ALBERTA
CANADA

Camera: Nikon D810
Lens/Focal length: Nikkor 14–24mm f/2.8 at 15mm
Aperture: f/22
Shutter speed: 1/40 sec.
ISO: 200
Kit: Handheld, composite of six frames

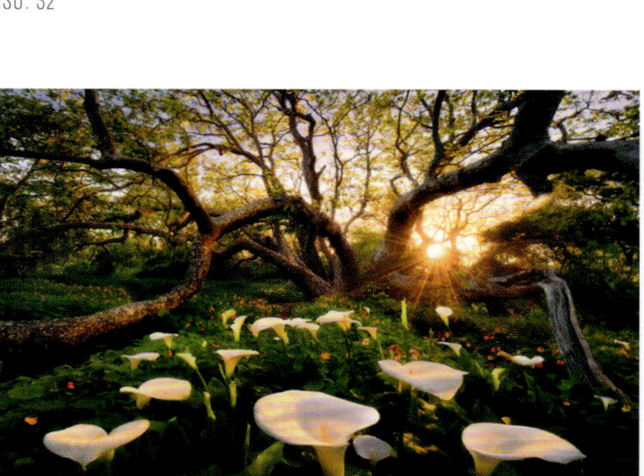

HEAVEN ON EARTH
EL CAPITAN STATE PARK, CALIFORNIA, USA

Camera: Nikon D800
Lens/Focal length: Nikkor 14–24mm f/2.8 at 14mm
Aperture: f/18
Shutter speed: 1/20 sec.
ISO: 100
Kit: Tripod, composite of several frames

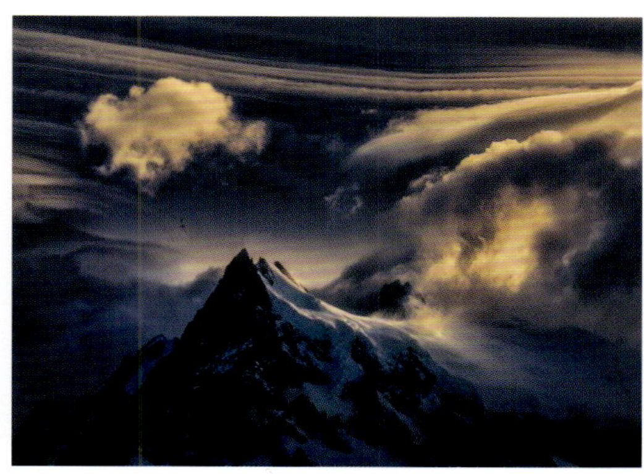

FOR ETERNITY
CERRO GRANDE, PATAGONIA, ARGENTINA

Camera: Nikon D800
Lens/Focal length: Nikkor 80–400mm f/4.5–5.6 at 200mm
Aperture: f/7.1
Shutter speed: 1/400 sec.
ISO: 200
Kit: Handheld

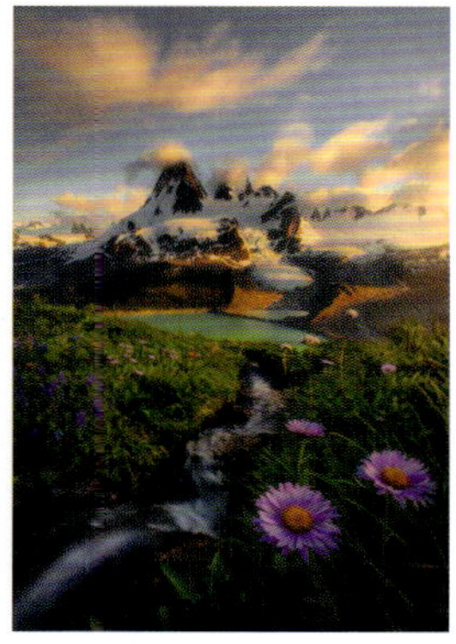

FIELD OF DREAMS
TWEEDSMUIR, BRITISH COLUMBIA, CANADA

Camera: Nikon D810
Lens/Focal length: Nikkor 14–24mm f/2.8 at 14mm
Aperture: f/18
Shutter speed: 1/5 sec.
ISO: 32
Kit: Composite of several frames

MASTER OF MOOD

MARK BAUER

Mark Bauer first became interested in photography while working in different countries in the early '90s, and has been a full-time professional landscape photographer since 2003, supplying images to stock agencies, corporate clients, magazines, and galleries—his images have been published worldwide. He has won awards in several major competitions, including the International Landscape Photographer of the Year, the Landscape Photographer of the Year, and the International Garden Photographer of the Year.

Mark is best known for his tranquil, atmospheric landscapes, shot in beautiful light. His aim is simply to showcase the natural beauty of his surroundings. Although he specializes in shooting the landscapes near his home in Dorset in the southwest of England—especially the famous Jurassic Coast—he has, in recent years, traveled to many other locations around the world in search of images. As well as being a regular contributor to the British photographic press, Mark is the author of five books, and is currently working on a sixth. His most recent book is the photography location guidebook *Photographing Dorset*.

CORFE CASTLE SILHOUETTED IN MIST

Corfe Castle has become a bit of a draw for photographers in recent years—it seems as if everyone wants to get a shot of the ruin rising above a low-lying mist at dawn. The reality is that these conditions don't happen too often, but as I'm lucky enough to live a couple of miles down the road, I've been able to shoot it many times. On this occasion, I decided to try for something different. Once the sun was up, I positioned myself so that the castle was backlit and silhouetted, with shadows being cast into the mist in front of it.

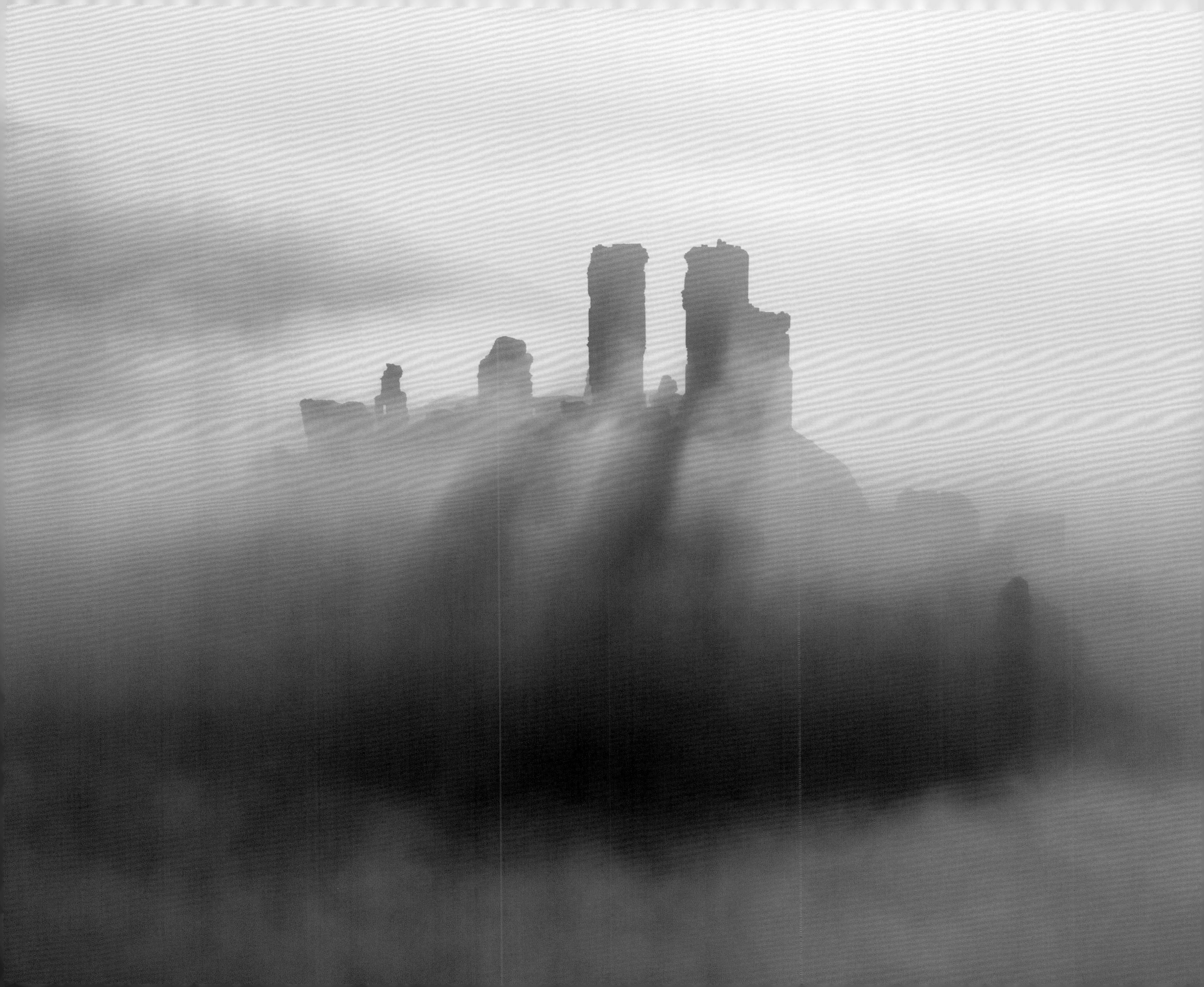

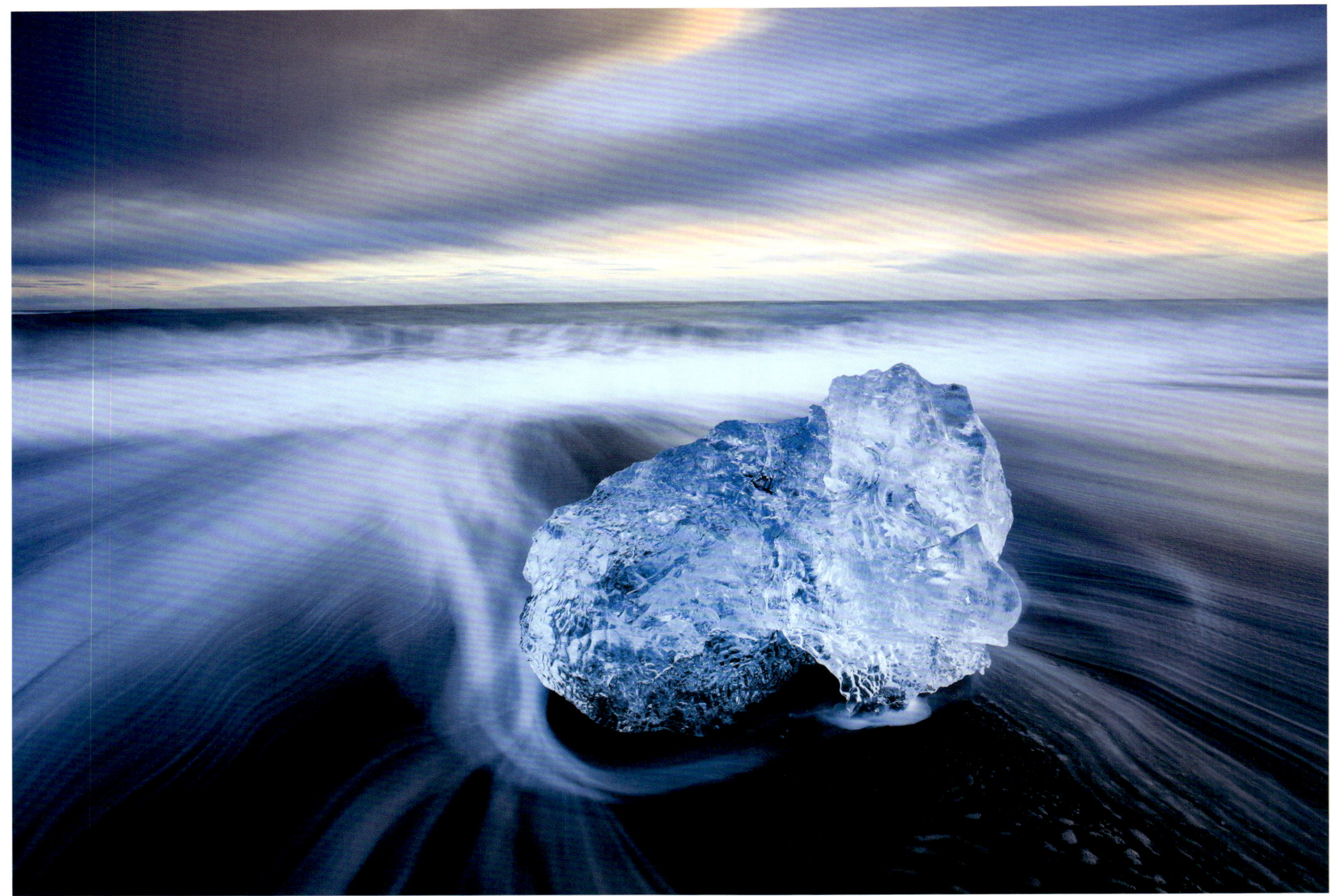

EVENING LIGHT, THE "ICE BEACH"

The "Ice Beach" (sometimes also known as "Diamond Beach") near Jökulsárlón in Iceland is one of my all-time favorite locations—I've shot there more times than I can remember, but I still get a buzz every time I arrive. For this shot, I got as close as I could to one of the icebergs, using a wide-angle lens, and shot an exposure of 4 seconds while a wave washed back around the ice. I've been here when there was more drama and color in the sky, but this image remains a favorite: the cool, subtle tones, with just a hint of color in the clouds, result in a far moodier image.

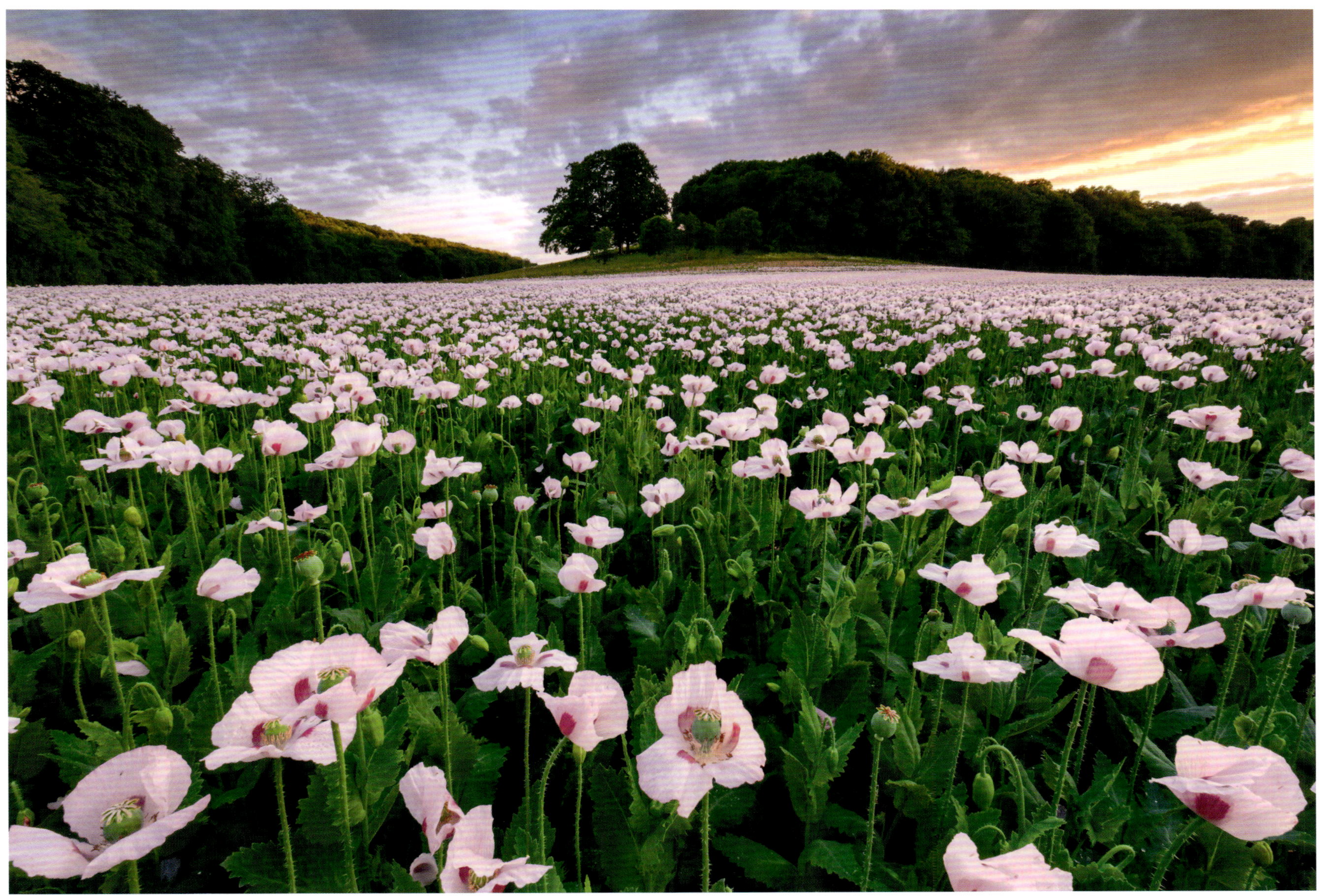

SUNSET OVER OPIUM POPPIES

Opium poppies are occasionally grown under license in mid- and north Dorset. They are beautiful flowers—a delicate pink in color, rather than a bold red. A photographer friend had kindly shared his knowledge of this fantastic field and I made a trip there one evening when there was the promise of a good sunset. However, I ended up shooting away from the color, as I felt there was a stronger composition with the shape of the hills and trees in this direction, and a stronger arrangement of poppies in the foreground.

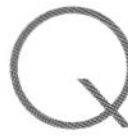

Q + A

Is it important for a photographer to find their own "style"?

Yes, I think it's really important. There are so many good photographers around these days that having a recognizable personal style is one of the ways someone can stand out from the crowd. There are formal styles, such as abstract or minimalist approaches, and these provide a good starting point, but a personal style goes a little bit beyond that and is defined by such things as choice of subject, preferred lighting and weather conditions, equipment choice (for instance, preferred focal length, filtration), post-processing techniques if you shoot digital, and so on. It's worth identifying what your preferences are and how these influence the "look" of your work, and then develop this into your own style. Having said all that, you also need to avoid the trap of just repeating the same formula and having all your pictures look the same—so it's definitely worth getting out of your comfort zone and trying something different every once in a while. All told, it's certainly a fine line we have to tread between being consistent and developing a personal style, while not becoming repetitive and getting stuck in a rut!

How important is it to have an intimate knowledge of your location?

It's rare for me to visit somewhere for the first time and come away with shots that I'm happy with. To get good shots of a location typically takes multiple visits—over a period of weeks, months, or, in some cases, even years. While there is clearly a lot of useful research that you can do—the internet and modern technology really help—there's absolutely no substitute for seeing somewhere in the flesh. The more time you spend in a location, the more you understand it—how the light falls at different times of day and year, and how different light, weather, and seasons affect the mood of the place. Generally speaking, you'll find the best shots of an area are taken by local photographers—partly because they're able to spend more time there, and partly because they can react quickly if conditions change favorably, but also because they have a deeper understanding of the area. I do a lot of my photography close to home; I'm lucky enough to live in a very beautiful and photogenic area, and I've developed a good understanding of the landscape around me over the years. It's an area I love and I never grow tired of shooting, but I do also make sure I get some balance in my work by traveling, not only to other parts of the UK, but also to other countries.

Do you ever think about how a photograph might sell when planning a shot?

Very rarely, to be honest. I just concentrate on the aesthetics and trying to compose a shot as best I can. Essentially, I shoot to please myself—the only exception to this is when I've been commissioned to shoot something and I'm following a specific brief. Otherwise, if I'm out taking "stock" shots, I'll just shoot what I want, how I want to shoot it. From a commercial point of view, this probably isn't the best way to go about things. I know there are lots of photographers who will, for example, make sure they leave space for text to be overlaid on an image, but I find this very hard to do if I think it will compromise the balance of a composition. If I have my commercial head on, I will remember to shoot both landscape and portrait format versions of a scene, but I won't always remember even that. I have to say, however, that, for whatever reason, I am lucky enough to take shots that people seem to want to buy—so perhaps it's best not to overthink things.

What creates mood in a landscape photograph?

There are many factors that influence mood and atmosphere. Perhaps the most obvious one is light. For example, the soft light and pastel colors predawn can suggest calm and tranquility, a silhouetted object against a colorful sky has a mood of high drama, low side-lighting is warm and inviting, and so on. The weather clearly has an influence, too—low-lying mist at sunrise can inject an atmosphere of mystery and romance, whereas dark, stormy clouds can lend a brooding feel to a scene. Color is also important— for example, blue suggests calm, freshness, and openness, and red signifies danger and excitement. The type of landscape is also important—it is difficult to suggest peace and tranquility when photographing a craggy mountain peak. Finally, how an image is composed has an influence on the mood we perceive—for example, if you shoot a lone object in a lot of negative space, then it will suggest isolation.

DAWN, SWANAGE OLD PIER

I'm very fortunate in that this wonderful location—the decaying remains of a wooden pier in Swanage—is literally on my doorstep. It's a fantastic subject for photography, especially for those who favor long-exposure minimalism. It's not normally accessible at dawn, as the new pier from where you photograph it is locked overnight. However, it was open early on this occasion, which happily coincided with a heavy sky and color on the horizon. I decided to simplify the scene by using a long exposure to smooth the water. In post-production, I cloned out one or two buoys to maintain the minimalist look.

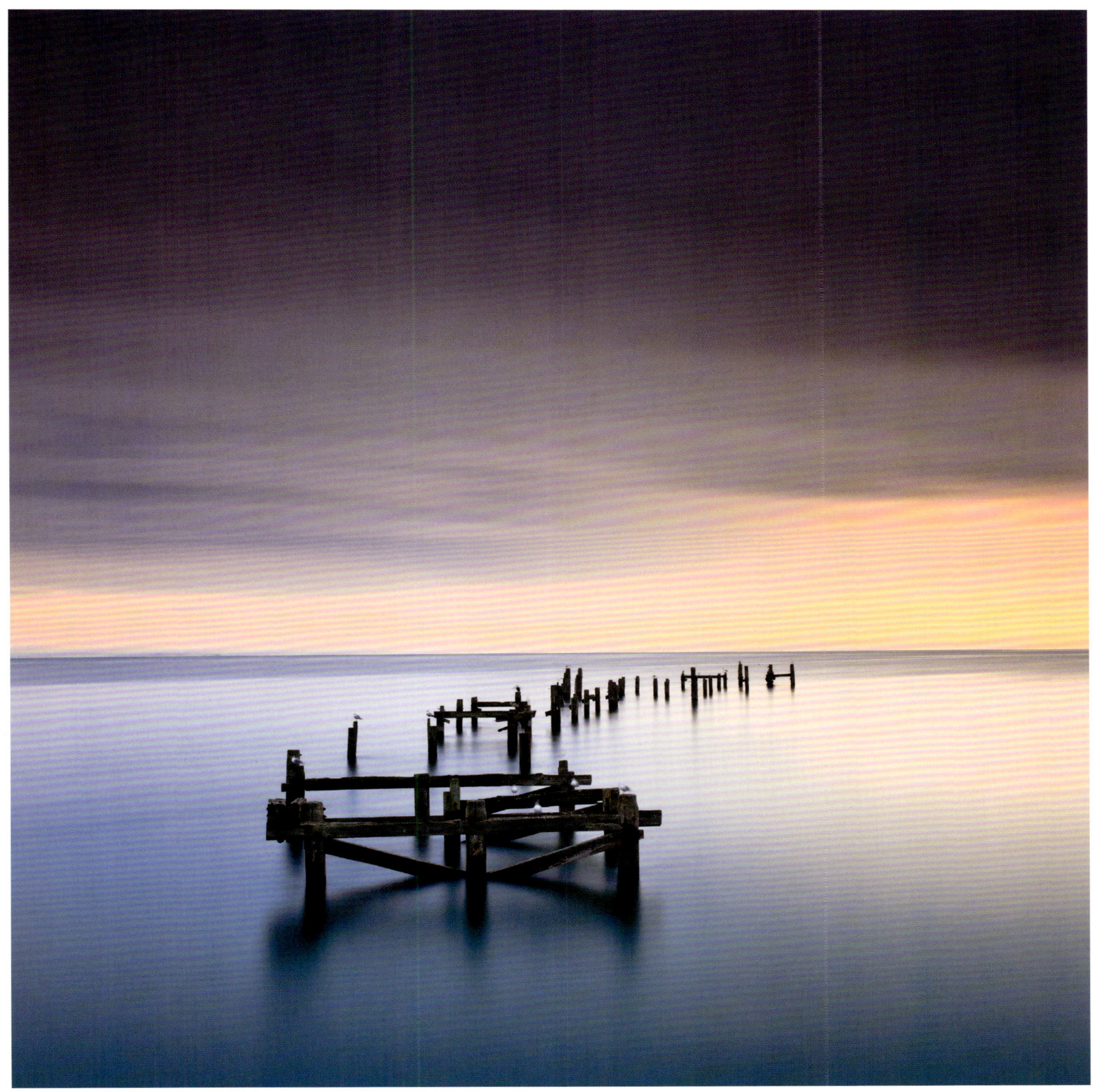

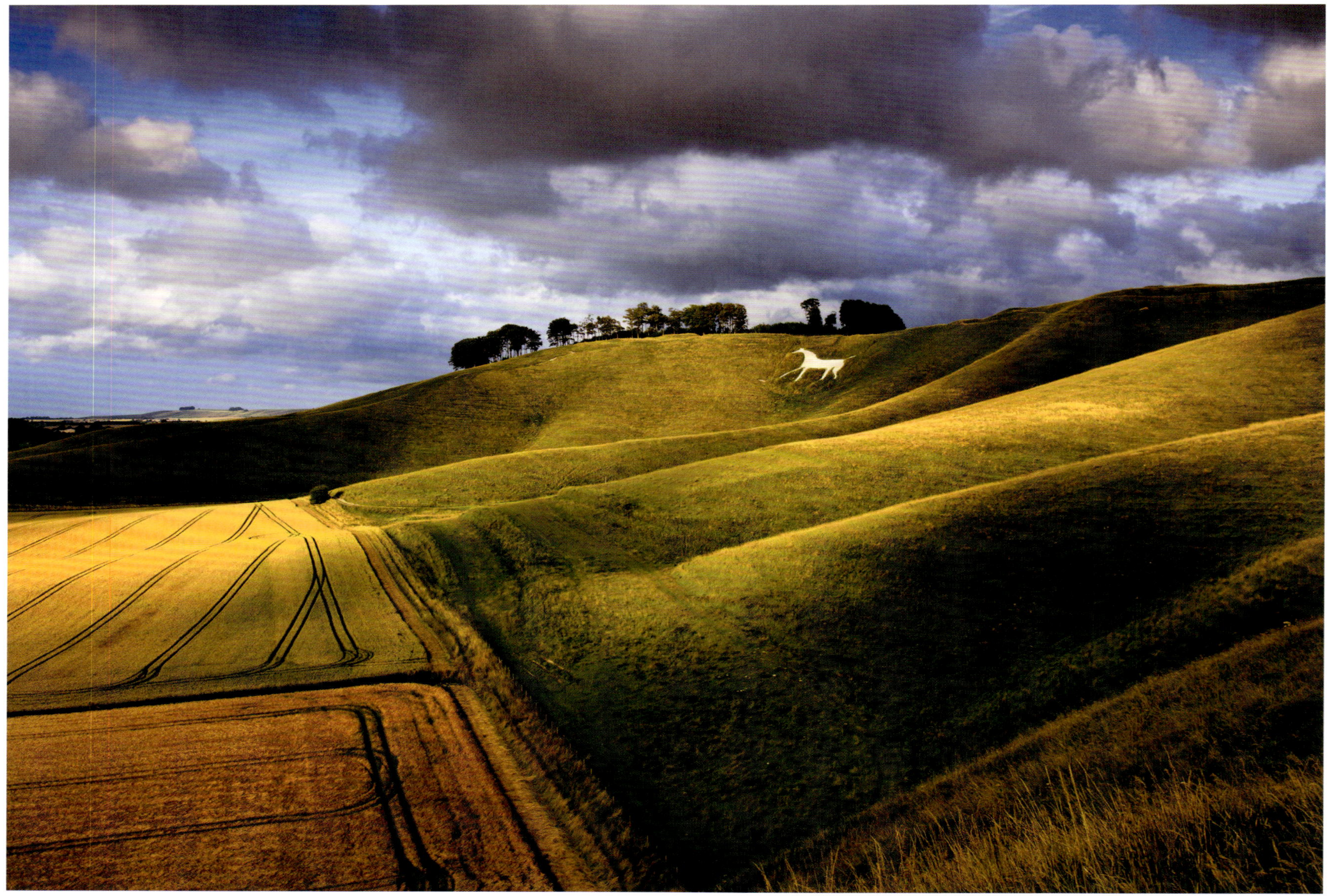

PASSING SHOWER, CHERHILL

I love changeable weather—as one weather front passes and another comes in, it is the time when you often get the most atmospheric conditions. Following a storm or shower, there can be wonderful clarity and a dramatic sky. I'd seen from the forecast that heavy rain was due to clear up in the early evening, so I climbed up the hill to my chosen viewpoint, set up, and waited for the rain to stop. When it did, the sun burst through a gap in the clouds, highlighting the ridges and spotlighting the chalk carving in the hill.

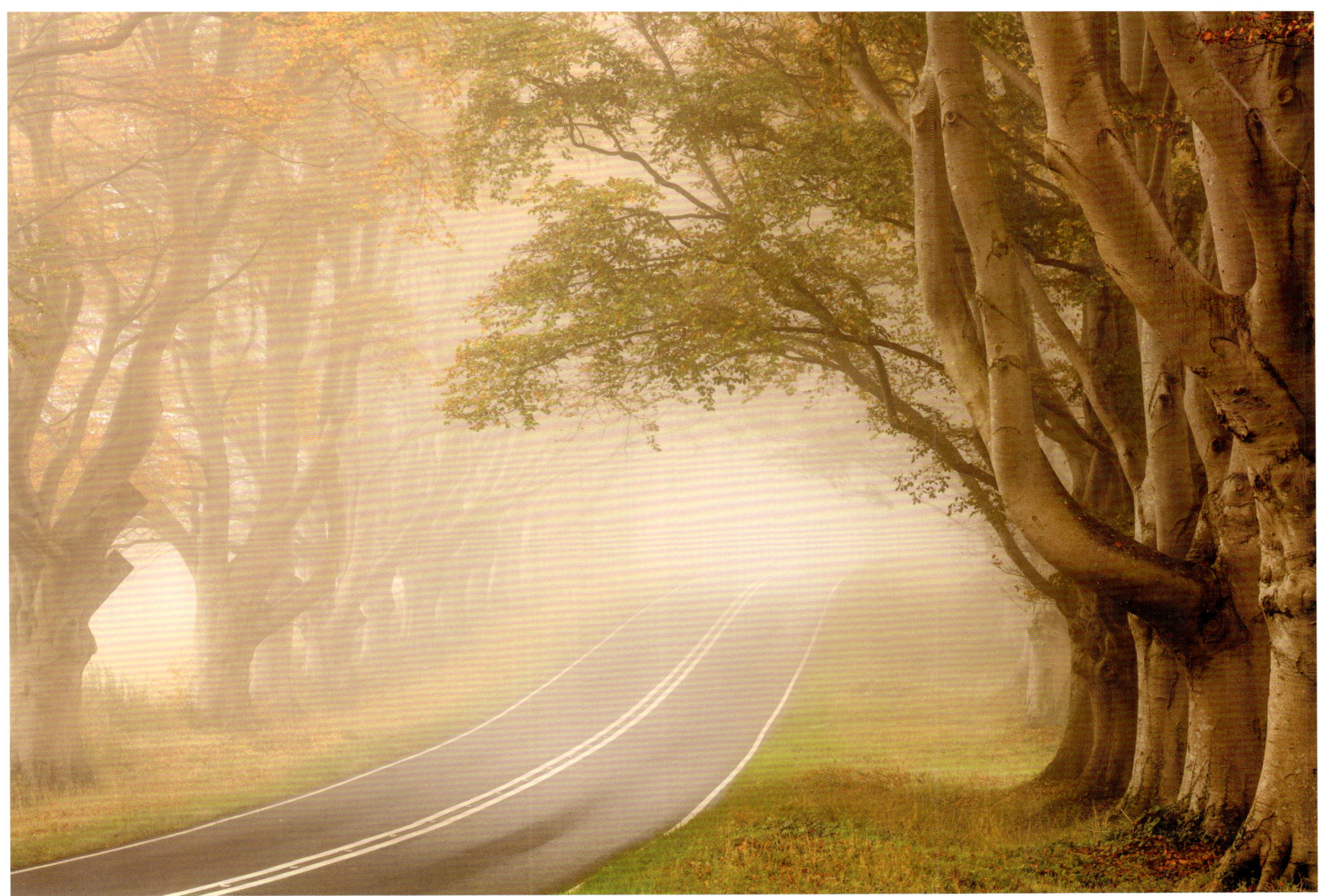

MISTY MORNING, BADBURY RINGS

This tree-lined avenue near Badbury Rings in Dorset is a magnificent sight, with over 600 beech trees lining the road as it rises and falls over small hills along its route—on foggy mornings, such as this, it looks particularly atmospheric. I chose a viewpoint where the road disappeared into the fog over the brow of a hill, and a longish focal length to compress perspective, making the trees appear almost on top of each other. Polarizers work especially well in these conditions, removing the sheen from foliage and saturating color, so I used one for this shot.

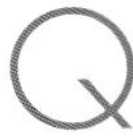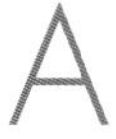

You have an affinity for the sea—how do you achieve the feeling of motion in an image?

How you photograph movement in water is a topic that causes intense debate among photographers! Do you deliberately blur the movement to create misty looking water, or do you use a fast shutter speed to freeze the motion, perhaps capturing the individual droplets of water as a wave crashes against the rocks? There is no "right" or "wrong" answer. Personally, I'm in the "blur it" camp. One of the things I love about photography is that you can capture subjects in a way the eye doesn't see them. Capturing the passage of time in a single frame is one way of doing that, and the results can be very ethereal. Of course, you don't have to blur water completely and reduce it to a misty texture with exposures of several minutes. Depending on the composition, it can often be more effective to use exposures of just a few seconds, which blurs the movement but retains some of the texture of the water—this can create a more "natural" look. Getting the effects I like is partly a matter of shooting in the right light—often at the beginning or end of the day—and partly a matter of using the right kit. Neutral-density filters are available in densities of up to 15 or more stops, and calculating exposure length with digital cameras is very straightforward compared to shooting film, as you don't have to account for reciprocity failure (when film becomes less sensitive in lower light levels).

How do landscape photographers hone their skills—would you recommend they study photography or perhaps attend a workshop?

As someone who runs workshops, I'm obviously going to recommend this option! Clearly, you can learn a lot from a good photographer and an experienced tutor, but also being in an environment where you are surrounded by like-minded people can be creatively stimulating. But I'd also recommend reading about the subject and looking at as many images as possible—not just photographs, but any visual imagery—and trying to identify why it does or doesn't appeal to you. This can help to "hardwire" the principles of composition and balance into your subconscious, which will certainly be of benefit when you're framing your own shots. Ultimately, though, the best thing you can do is just to get out and shoot as often as possible. This will help to improve both your technique (for example, exposure, focusing, filtration) and also your sense of composition. It will also have the benefit of improving your familiarity with your equipment. If you are able to operate your camera instinctively, without being distracted by having to think about how to change settings, you are then free to concentrate on what is the most important part of taking a photograph—composition.

What sort of set-up do you use for a long-exposure image at dawn or dusk?

A sturdy tripod and remote release are essential in order to reduce the chances of camera shake. At dawn and dusk, the contrast range can be greater than you'd think, as the sky is lit from below by the sun, but there is no direct light falling on the land. Therefore, a graduated neutral-density filter can be useful for preventing bright skies from overexposing. Depending on the light levels, I might also use neutral-density filters to manipulate shutter speed and obtain longer exposures. With most cameras, for exposures of longer than 30 seconds, you'll need to switch to Bulb mode and then lock the shutter open for the desired length of time. Some cameras, however, will allow you to manually set exposure times longer than that—for example, with my Fuji GFX, I can dial in exposure times of up to an hour, so Bulb mode is rather redundant. I also don't bother with Long Exposure Noise Reduction, as I find the Fuji (and the Canons that I used previously) produce very clean long exposures.

As a master of landscape photography, what is your motivation to continue making photographs?

It's partly the desire to keep improving and to become the best landscape photographer I can possibly be. It certainly helps that it's not possible to take the perfect photograph. When I review my shots, there's always something to criticize, something I'm not happy about, so I'll go back out and keep trying. But above all else, it's simply that I enjoy taking photographs. There's perhaps too much emphasis put on results and not enough on the process of photography. I enjoy the whole ritual of setting up, composing, metering, selecting filters, focusing, and releasing the shutter. It's a way of being in the moment and connecting fully with my environment. For me, it's as much about the journey as it is the destination, and I can't feel satisfied with the results if I've not enjoyed producing them. And the chances are, if you enjoy the process, you'll produce good results.

TECHNICAL INFORMATION

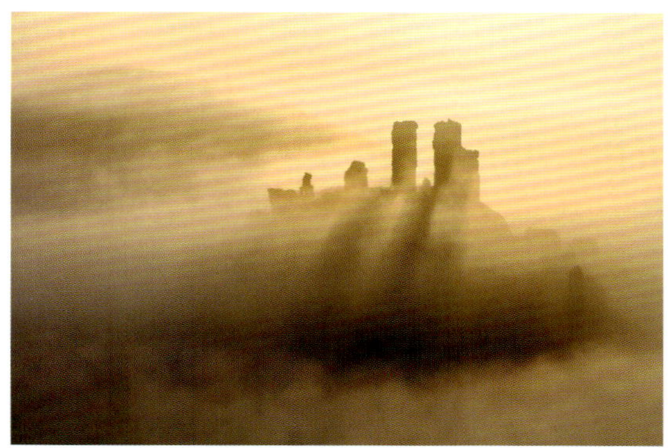

CORFE CASTLE SILHOUETTED IN MIST
DORSET, ENGLAND

Camera: Canon EOS 5DS
Lens/Focal length: Canon 70–300mm f/4-5.6 at 78mm
Aperture: f/8
Shutter speed: 1/800 sec.
ISO: 100
Kit: Tripod

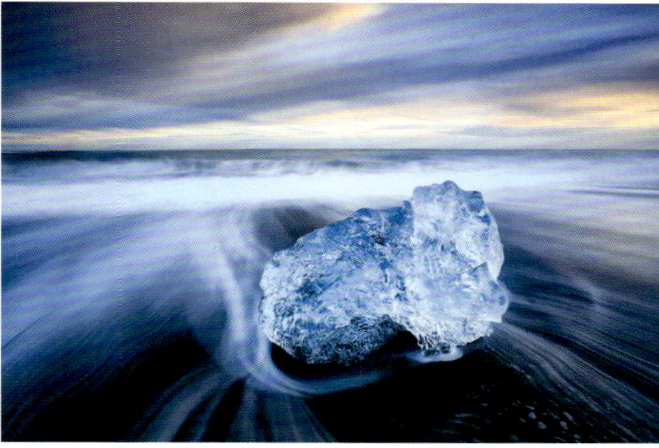

EVENING LIGHT, THE "ICE BEACH"
JÖKULSÁRLÓN, ICELAND

Camera: Canon EOS 5D Mark III
Lens/Focal length: Canon 16–35mm f/2.8 at 18mm
Aperture: f/16
Shutter speed: 4 sec.
ISO: 200
Kit: Tripod, polarizing and 0.6 hard ND grad filters

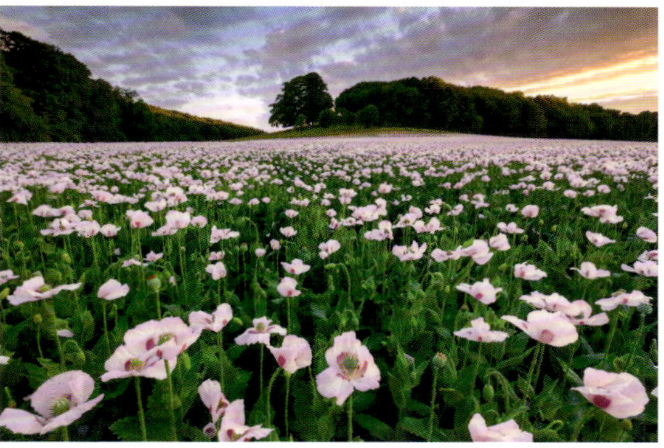

SUNSET OVER OPIUM POPPIES
DURWESTON, DORSET, ENGLAND

Camera: Fuji X-Pro2
Lens/Focal length: Fujinon 10–24mm f/4 at 10mm
Aperture: f/16
Shutter speed: 1/6 sec.
ISO: 200
Kit: Tripod, polarizing and 0.6 medium ND grad filters

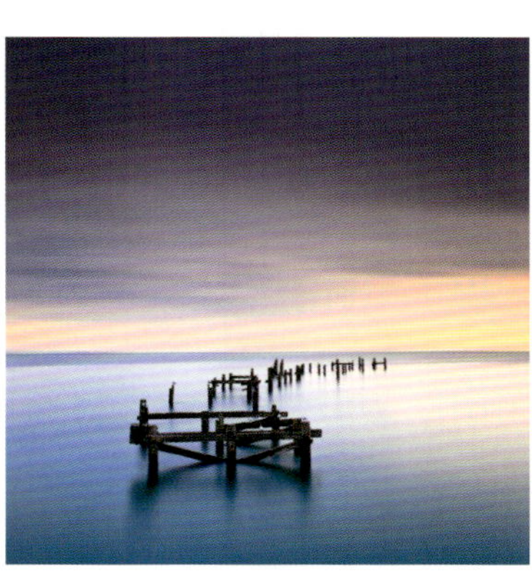

DAWN, SWANAGE OLD PIER
DORSET, ENGLAND

Camera: Canon EOS 5D Mark II
Lens/Focal length: Canon 24–105mm f/4 at 28mm
Aperture: f/11
Shutter speed: 311 sec.
ISO: 200
Kit: Tripod, hard ND grad and Big Stopper filters

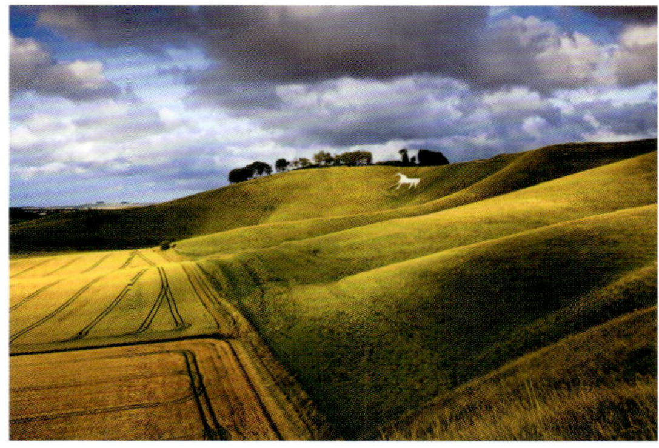

PASSING SHOWER, CHERHILL
WILTSHIRE, ENGLAND

Camera: Canon EOS 5D Mark II
Lens/Focal length: Canon 24–105mm f/4 at 35mm
Aperture: f/11
Shutter speed: 1/50 sec.
ISO: 100
Kit: Tripod, polarizing filter

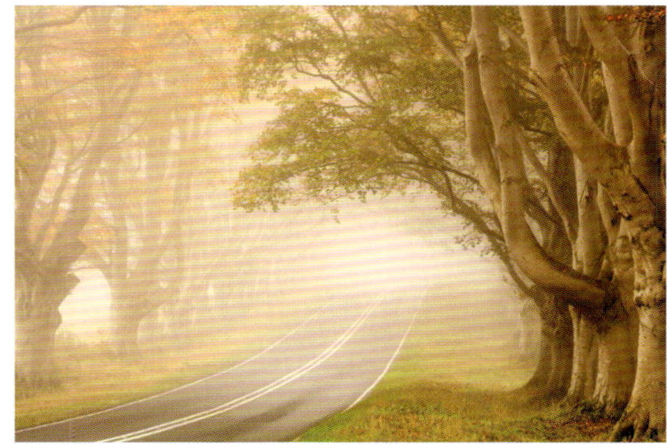

MISTY MORNING, BADBURY RINGS
DORSET, ENGLAND

Camera: Canon EOS 5DS
Lens/Focal length: Canon 70–300mm f/4-5.6 at 120mm
Aperture: f/16
Shutter speed: 1/2 sec.
ISO: 100
Kit: Tripod, polarizing filter

MIKKO LAGERSTEDT

Mikko Lagerstedt is a self-taught fine art photographer from Finland. He loves atmospheric photography, capturing the night sky, and, in particular, photographing simplistic or minimalist landscapes.

He remembers that the very first moment that inspired him to pursue photography was when he was driving on a summer's evening, on his way to stay at a relative's cabin. After a rainy day, the sun had started shining, and the mist was rising in the fields. Mikko just had to stop and watch, and then realized that he wanted to start to capture these kinds of beautiful moments.

His journey in photography began in December 2008, and from the first moments he fell in love with it. "I like to create visually and emotionally captivating pictures," he says, "and my goal is to capture the feeling I had when I took the photograph."

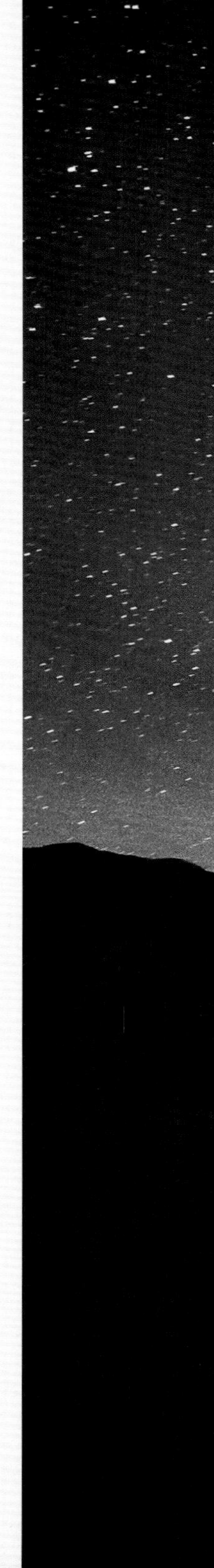

BURNED FOREST

One of my favorite trips was to Chilean Patagonia in December 2016, when we were shooting for a new TV series about photography. This capture was near all the popular locations in Torres Del Paine National Park. I was searching for a unique view of these burned trees. I shot for about two hours here, and, just as I was leaving, I shot one last long exposure, when a hint of light hit the burned trees from behind. It came from a car driving behind us and it looks more like a painting than a photograph. I added a slight blue color tint in Lightroom.

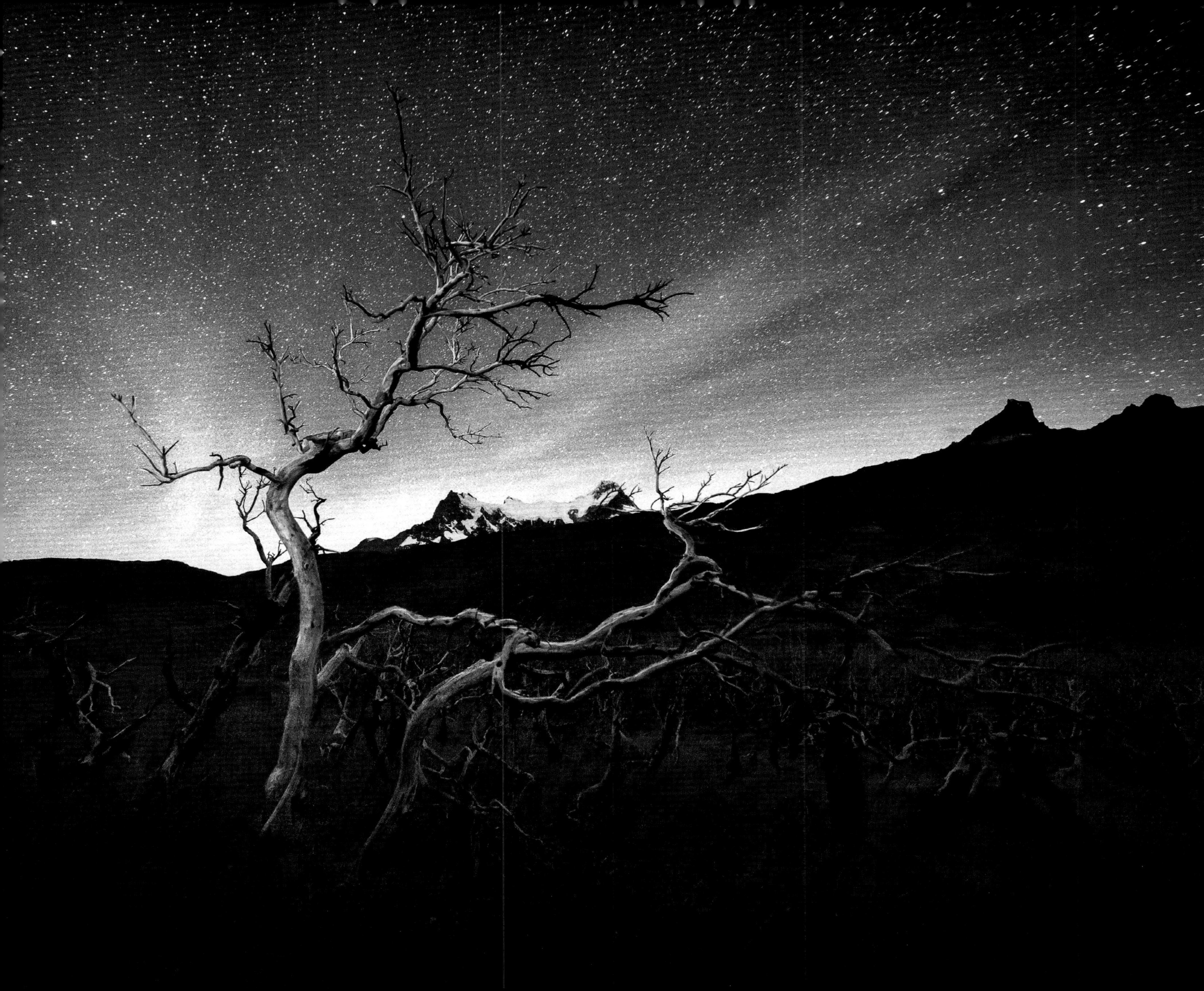

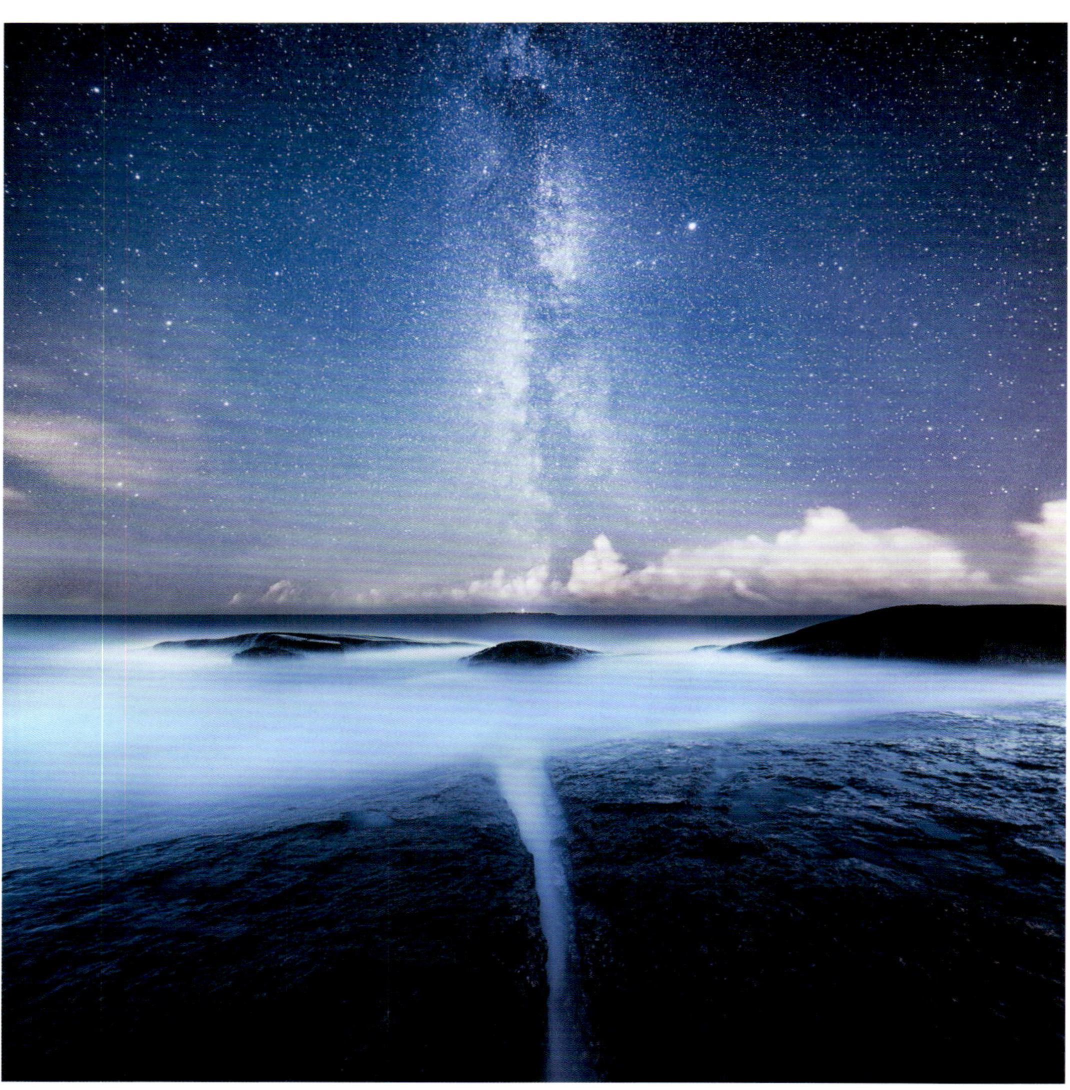

DIVIDED

(Left) After a long evening capturing the Milky Way on Yyteri beach, in Finland, I headed to Siikaranta, a nearby location, to see if I could capture an interesting foreground element with the Milky Way. After a couple of photographs, I found this small crack in the rocks, aligned with the sky beautifully. I placed my camera as low as the tripod would allow. I used two different settings to capture this scene with a sharp foreground.

THE LOST WORLD

(Right) Some of my favorite things to capture are abandoned places and objects. This shipwreck was in Emäsalo, Finland. Now the shipwreck has been fixed, and it's sitting in a nearby spot, upright, like all other boats. This image was created using multiple exposures. Due to heavy light pollution from a factory nearby, I had to use multiple images and a lot of luck to capture the scenery, with a mist all around the subject. I used Photoshop to create the final image, which included removing some distracting elements from the foreground and the heavy light pollution.

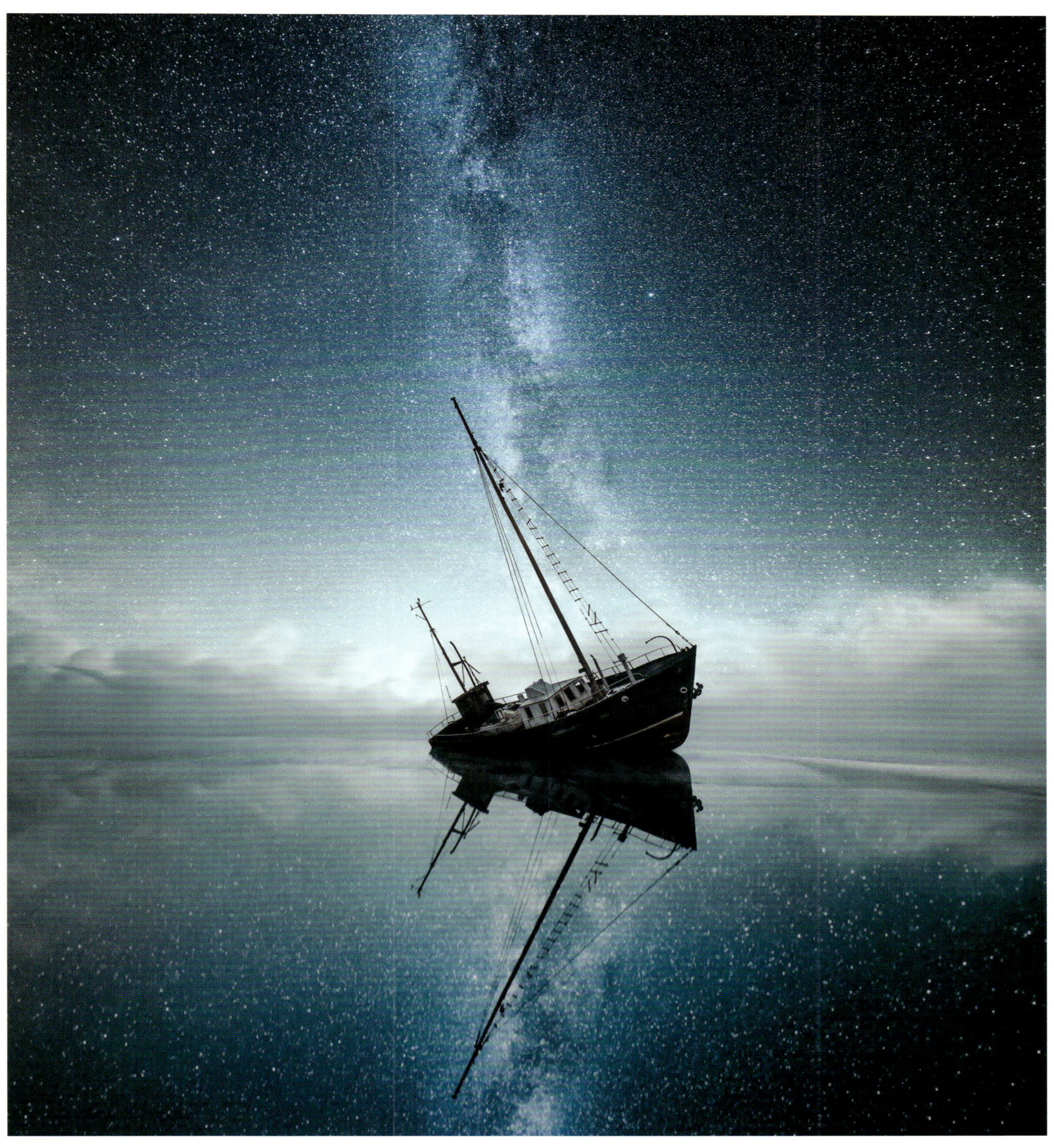

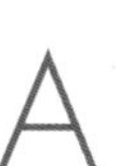

What attracts you to nighttime photography?

I love how the landscape changes in dim light. I enjoy the atmospheric look that low light gives to a place. I believe I get most of my visual view of the world when there is just enough light to see the scenery. When I'm out there photographing at night, I can focus on my work more easily than I can at any other time. Of course, there are times when you need to use the camera as your eye because it captures more light than your eyes can see. This is also the surprising aspect of nighttime photography, because you don't know what the final image will look like before you shoot it. I love the 20–30 second wait before you can view your photographs. Nighttime photography gives you time to appreciate the scenery while you wait—it's a type of meditation in nature for me. Nights are usually calm and quiet, when hearing just the sounds of nature can be inspiring.

How do you plan for one of your nighttime shoots?

Timing is everything. The first thing I check is the moon phase. Usually, I prefer not to capture moonlit scenes. If the moon phase is right for star photography, I find a place I would like to take a photograph—I prefer places away from light pollution—and I also check out beforehand where the Milky Way will be in the location. Depending on how I am taking the photographs, I try to go at least 40km (25 miles) from any big cities. I also scout to see if there are any particular spots I should try to capture at night. Then I check out weather forecasts, and head out when there is clear sky forecast. I might leave before sunset, so that I can get a decent view of a new place. In Finland, you can't capture the stars in the summer due to the midnight sun, so I need to travel south to see the stars. If I want to shoot something other than stars, I usually try to head out when there is a forecast that might imply a foggy night, and stay up until sunrise. I find it inspiring just to go out sometimes and enjoy nature without any plans. I get some of my favorite work with this approach, as well. Planning helps, but it doesn't mean you have to plan every shot.

How do you decide when and where to shoot for a particular astral subject, such as the Milky Way?

I use a couple of apps to see where the Milky Way will be at a given time. Also, a view outside a city is necessary because of light pollution. When I know the location, I will try to find an interesting subject matter or composition and capture the Milky Way. I love views near water and with reflections.

What does a typical nighttime-exposure set-up involve—is a little bit of trial and error needed before you capture the image?

I might do one test exposure to see what settings I should be using in the particular scenery. It has become easier to see what settings work, and mostly I use these settings with a 14–24mm Nikon or 20mm Sigma wide-angle lens: ISO 3200–6400, 20–30 seconds exposure, aperture at f/1.4–2.8, depending on the lens's capabilities. Also, when I try to have a subject near the camera, I need to capture multiple shots to ensure that each element is in focus. I might either use longer exposures, such as 5 minutes, with a smaller aperture, or focus-stack each exposure.

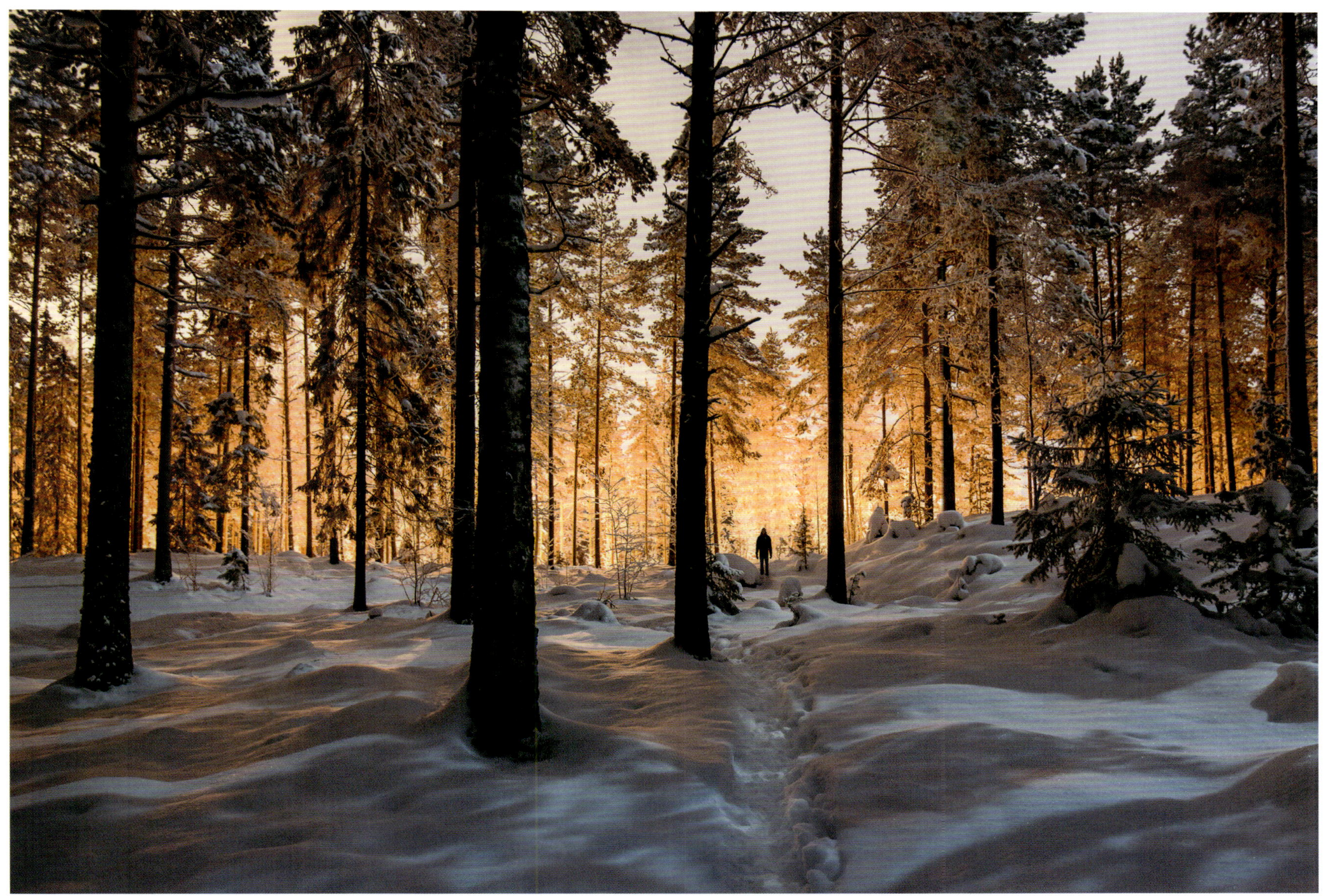

BETWEEN TWO WORLDS

One night before Christmas I went out to photograph the sunset and frosty trees in Nokia, in Finland. I shot the sunset and waited for the moonlight to take over the landscape. I had my camera on a tripod and captured myself in the scenery to give it some scale. The trees were covered with snow and frost, which gave this place a surreal vibe. The background light comes from a skiing track, and the moonlight illuminates the foreground snow. I did minimal editing to this image, only boosting the background color just a little.

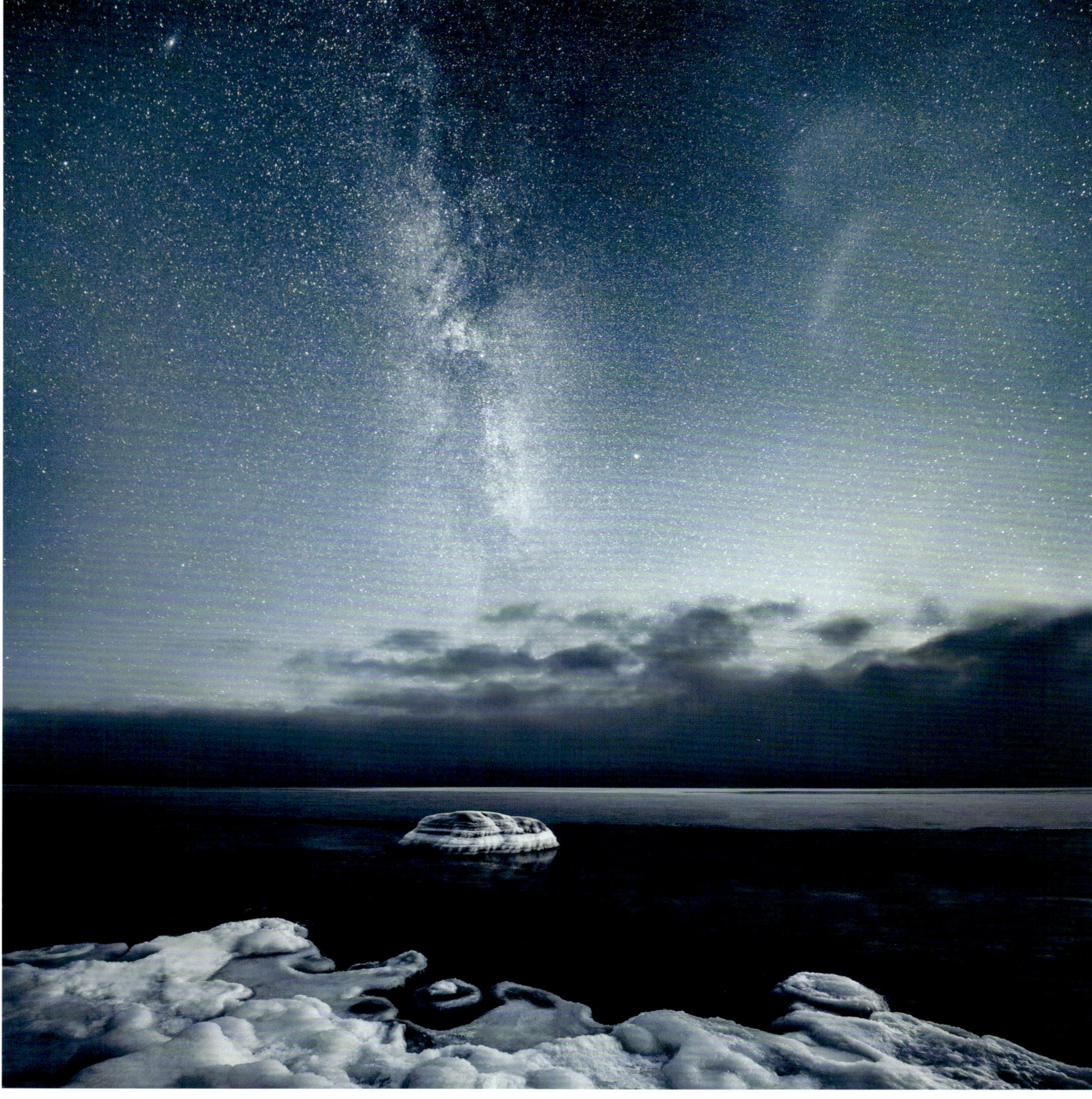

FROZEN ECHO

(Left) After a cloudy winter day, I headed to the south coast of Finland, hoping to capture the night sky as the sky was starting to clear. The temperature started dropping, and by the time I shot this photograph it was -13°F (-25°C). After the shot, a thin layer of ice started to pile up on the ground, and I remember just standing there and being in awe of nature. I captured this view with two horizontal images, which I then combined manually in Photoshop.

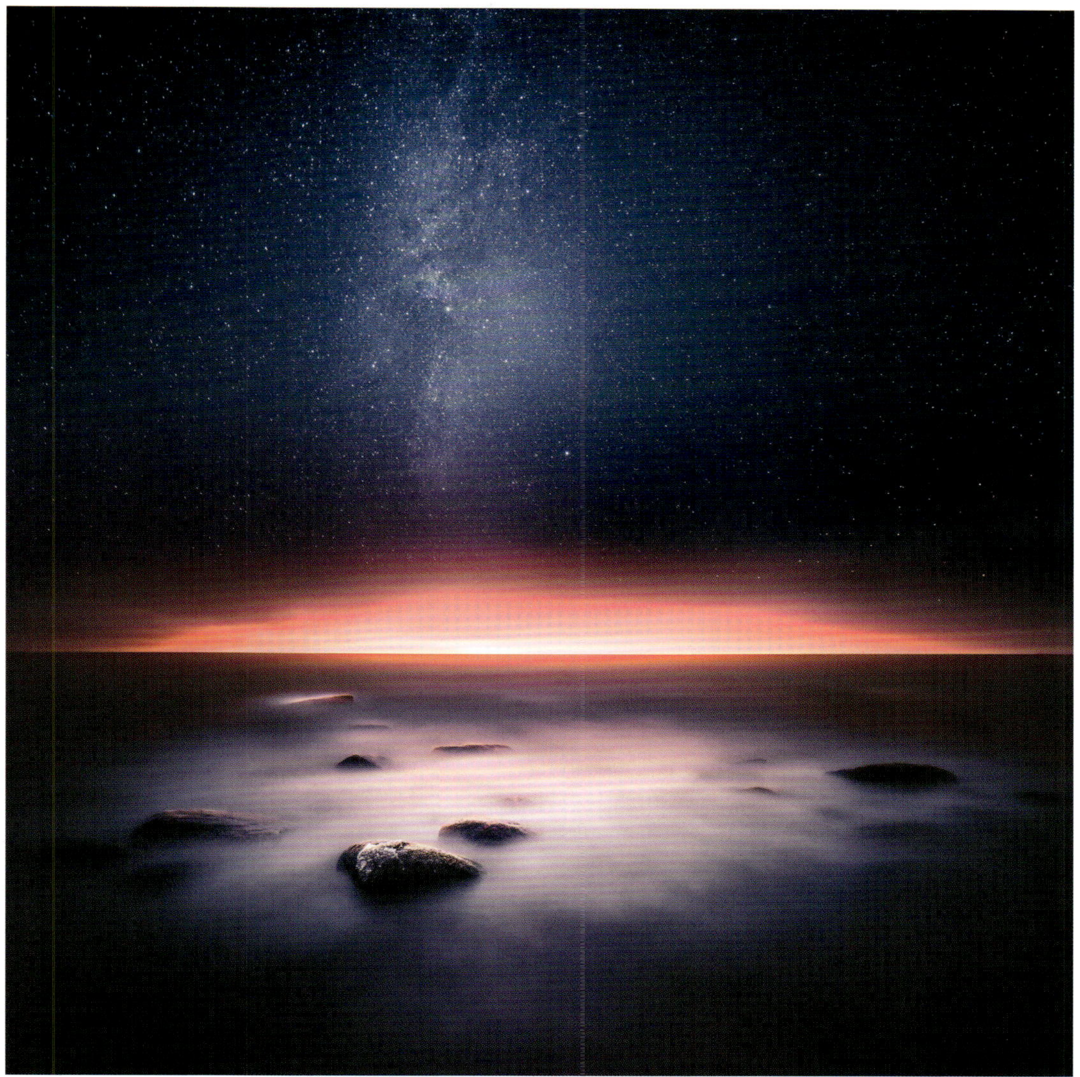

THE WHOLE UNIVERSE SURRENDERS

(Right) This image is more of an experimental view of the world. I was photographing on the coast of Finland at a beautiful sunset when I got the idea to capture the same place at sunset and again when the stars are starting to appear on the horizon. I waited five hours to capture both shots and headed home to combine the images in post-processing.

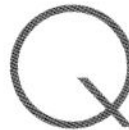
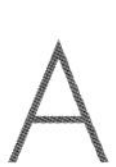

What practical challenges does shooting at nighttime involve?

In Finland, weather is the most challenging aspect of nighttime photography. There might only be a couple of clear nights during fall when you can see the Milky Way at its brightest, with most of the center of the galaxy. Finding interesting subjects is hard as well, because you can't capture near cities with light pollution. You might need to drive around a lot during the night to find interesting places and subjects. Staying up through the night is also a huge challenge at times when you want to balance your sleeping rhythm. I might stay up three nights in a row and then try to restore my sleeping pattern after that. You can feel quite tired during the daytime.

How have the low-light and high-ISO capabilities of the latest digital bodies changed the way you work?

You can push your camera further to capture low-light sceneries today. My first camera had a maximum ISO of 1600, and it wasn't that great, but now I can use ISO 6400 with decent quality on my Nikon D810. This gives you the flexibility to capture more detail of the Milky Way and stars. Before these new ISO capabilities, you had to use stacking to get most detail out of the night sky, but it's something I have not done recently. It's crazy how much more a camera can capture than your eyes can see.

What post-processing steps do you take to create one of your nighttime images?

It all depends on the picture. I start my editing in Lightroom. I use basic settings such as exposure, contrast, and clarity. I make adjustments in parts of the images with the adjustment brush, graduated filters, and radial filters, depending on the photograph. With these tools, I usually add detail with clarity and contrast. For 80 percent of the time I only edit with Lightroom, but sometimes I use multiple exposures to capture the scenery how I want. In those cases, I need to put them together manually in Photoshop, because you can't rely on automatic blending when you use nighttime photographs. After Photoshop, I open up the image in Lightroom and finish it with sharpening and final color edits.

As a master of landscape photography, what is your motivation to continue making photographs?

I love to share the beautiful moments I capture in nature with people all around the world. My key vision is to motivate people to go out and enjoy nature. I also like to challenge myself to create work that inspires me and others.

TECHNICAL INFORMATION

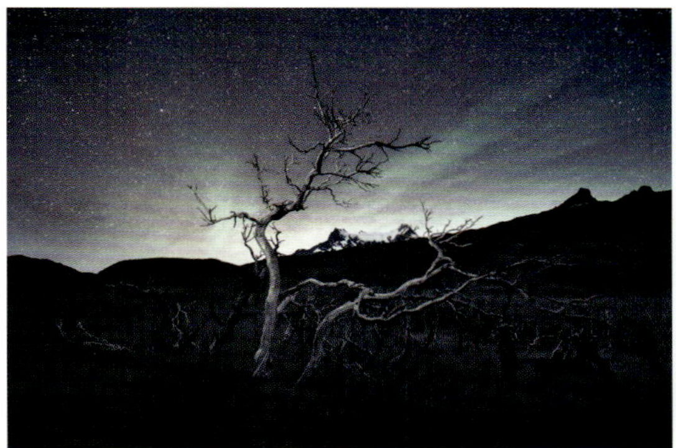

BURNED FOREST
PATAGONIA, CHILE

Camera: Nikon D810
Lens/Focal length: Nikkor 14–24mm f/2.8 at 14mm
Aperture: f/2.8
Shutter speed: 30 sec.
ISO: 6400
Kit: Tripod

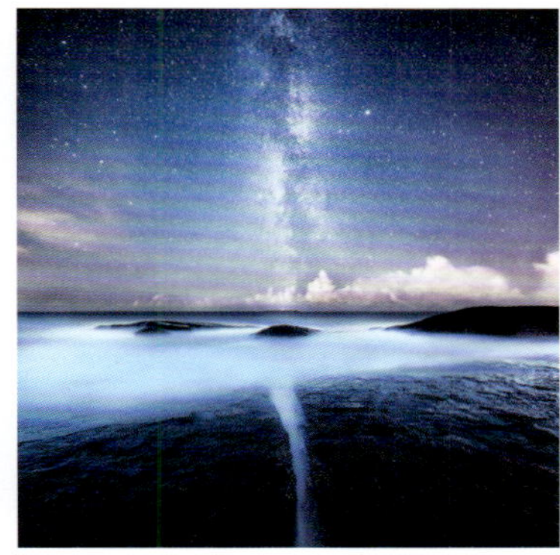

DIVIDED
MERI-PORI, FINLAND

Camera: Nikon D800
Lens/Focal length: Samyang 14mm f/2.8
A composite of two frames:
  Sky: f/2.8, 30 sec., ISO 6400
  Foreground: f/8, 669 sec., ISO 800
Kit: Tripod

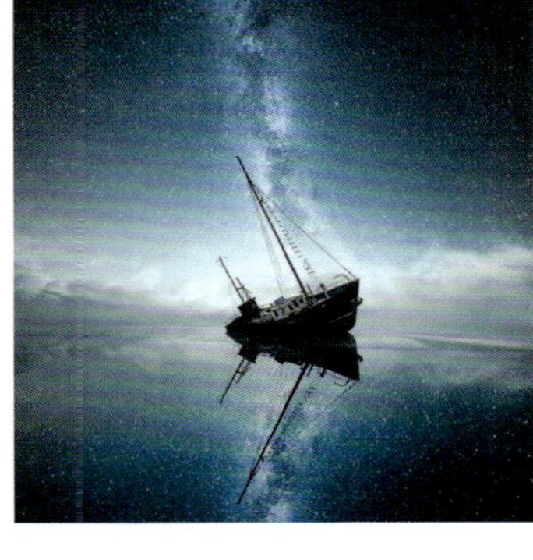

THE LOST WORLD
EMÄSALO, FINLAND

Camera: Nikon D810
Lens/Focal length: Nikkor 14–24mm f/2.8
A composite of three frames:
  Sky: f/2.8, 30 sec., ISO 6400
  Shipwreck: f/4, 30 sec., ISO 800
  Foreground: f/2.8, 30 sec., ISO 6400
Kit: Tripod

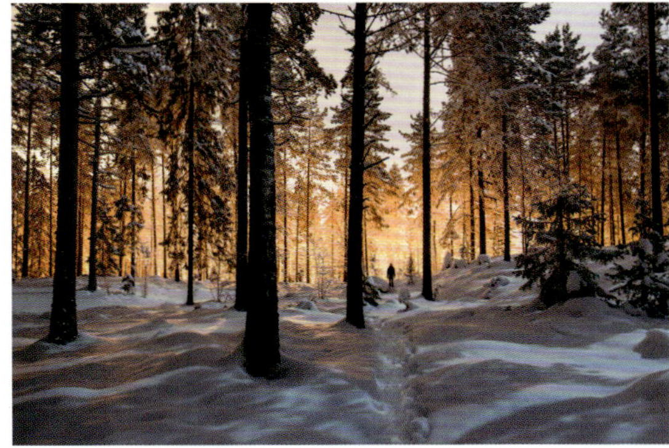

BETWEEN TWO WORLDS
NOKIA, FINLAND

Camera: Nikon D800
Lens/Focal length: Nikkor 16–35mm f/4 at 24mm
Aperture: f/4
Shutter speed: 15 sec.
ISO: 800
Kit: Tripod

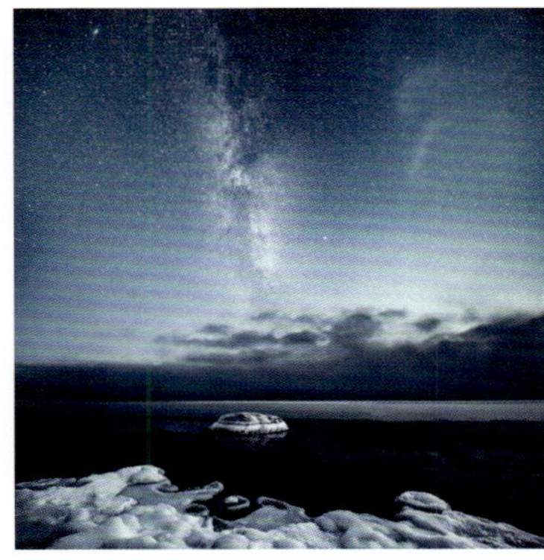

FROZEN ECHO
EMÄSALO, FINLAND

Camera: Nikon D800
Lens/Focal length: Nikkor 16–35mm f/4.0 at 16mm
Aperture: f/4
Shutter speed: 25 sec.
ISO: 3200
Kit: Tripod
Other: Composite of two horizontal frames

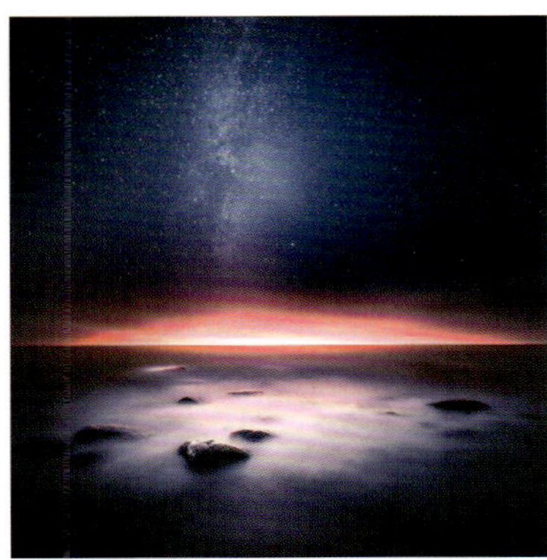

THE WHOLE UNIVERSE SURRENDERS
EMÄSALO, FINLAND

Camera: Nikon D800
Lens/Focal length: Nikkor 16–35mm f/4 at 16mm
A composite of two frames:
  Sunset: f/9, 449 sec., ISO 100, B/W 10-stop ND filter
  Milky Way: f/4, 25 sec., ISO 3200
Kit: Tripod

ROSS HODDINOTT

Ross Hoddinott is one of the UK's best-known outdoor photographers. Based close to the rugged northern Cornish coast in southwest England, Ross is a multi-award winning photographer and author of several photography books. He is best known for his intimate close-ups of nature and his simple and evocative portrayals of the landscape, particularly the stunning countryside and coastline near his home. This region and its natural history are a constant inspiration, and Ross hopes that his images will help to highlight the beauty and importance of the environment on which we depend.

From a young age, Ross developed a passion for the natural world. His parents introduced him to photography when he was 10, and a year later in 1990 he won BBC Countryfile's junior flora and fauna category. He subsequently triumphed in the Young Wildlife Photographer of the Year competition. Ross turned professional aged just 17, and has now been supplying imagery to a wide variety of clients and magazines worldwide for over two decades.

Ross has enjoyed multiple successes in the international Wildlife Photographer of the Year competition, and in 2008 was on the judging panel. In 2009, Ross won British Wildlife Photographer of the Year, and he has had images commended in Take-a-View and International Garden Photographer of the Year. He is an Ambassador for Nikon UK (2013–15), Manfrotto, Paramo, and F-stop Gear. He is also a member of 2020VISION, the largest, most ambitious multimedia conservation project ever staged in the UK.

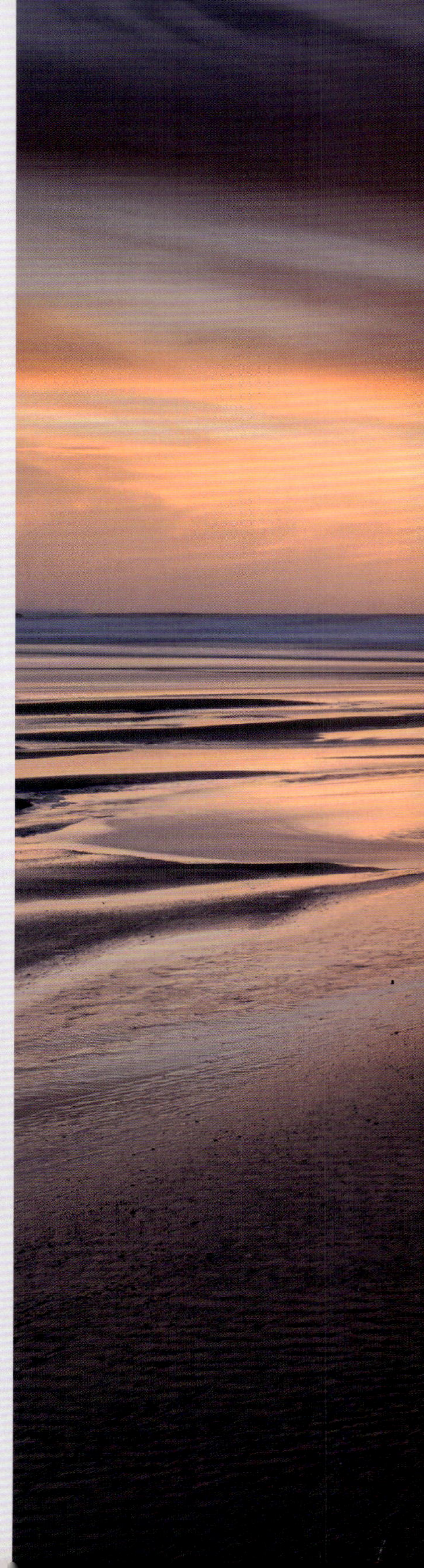

HOLYWELL BAY

Do all photographs need to have a meaning, or have to tell a story? I don't think so. Sometimes a photograph is simply recording nature's ability to wow—nothing more, nothing less. This shot is just a sandy beach, an impressive sky, and a lonely, silhouetted island. It might tell a story, but hopefully it invites the viewer to experience scenes like this for themselves.

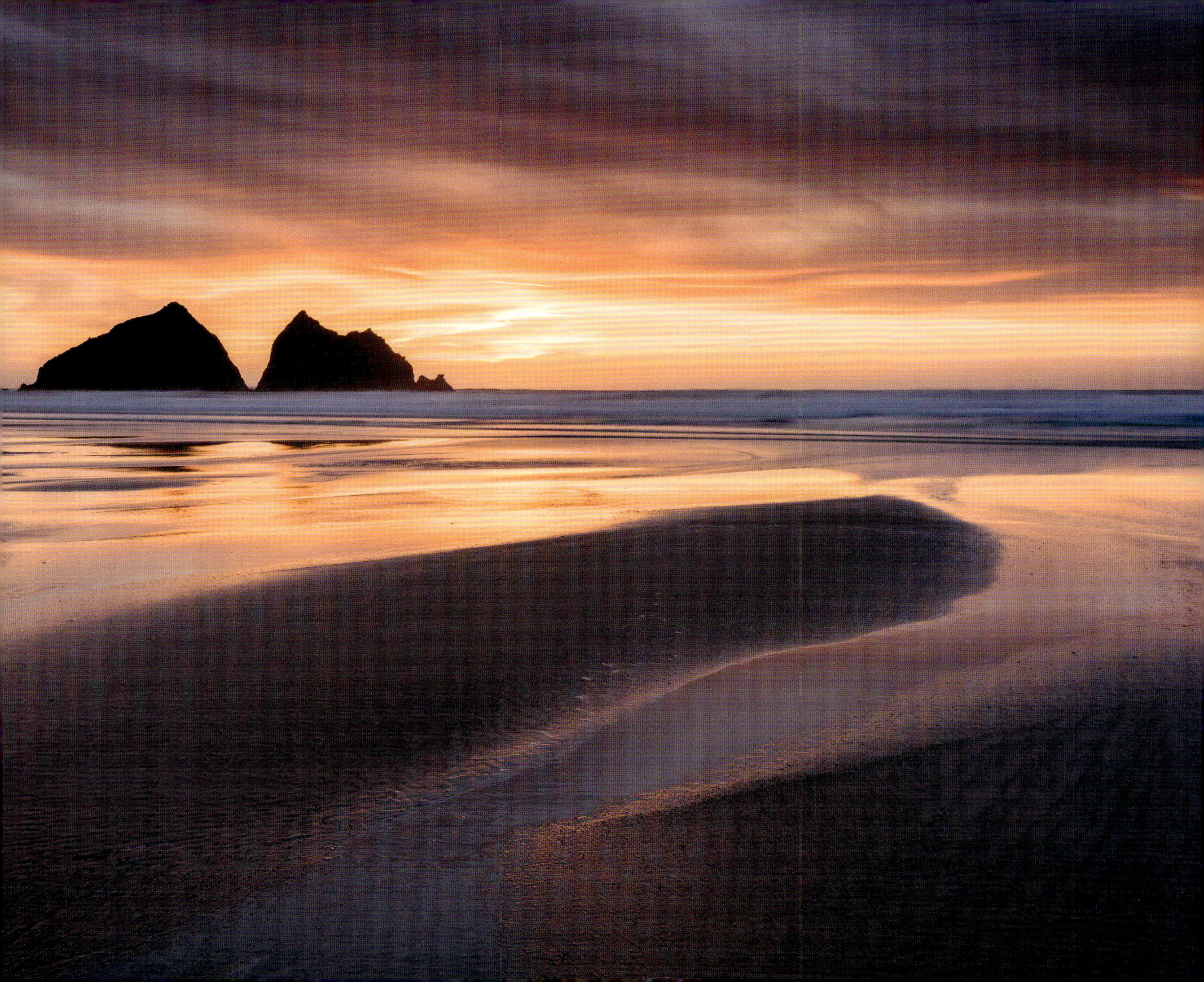

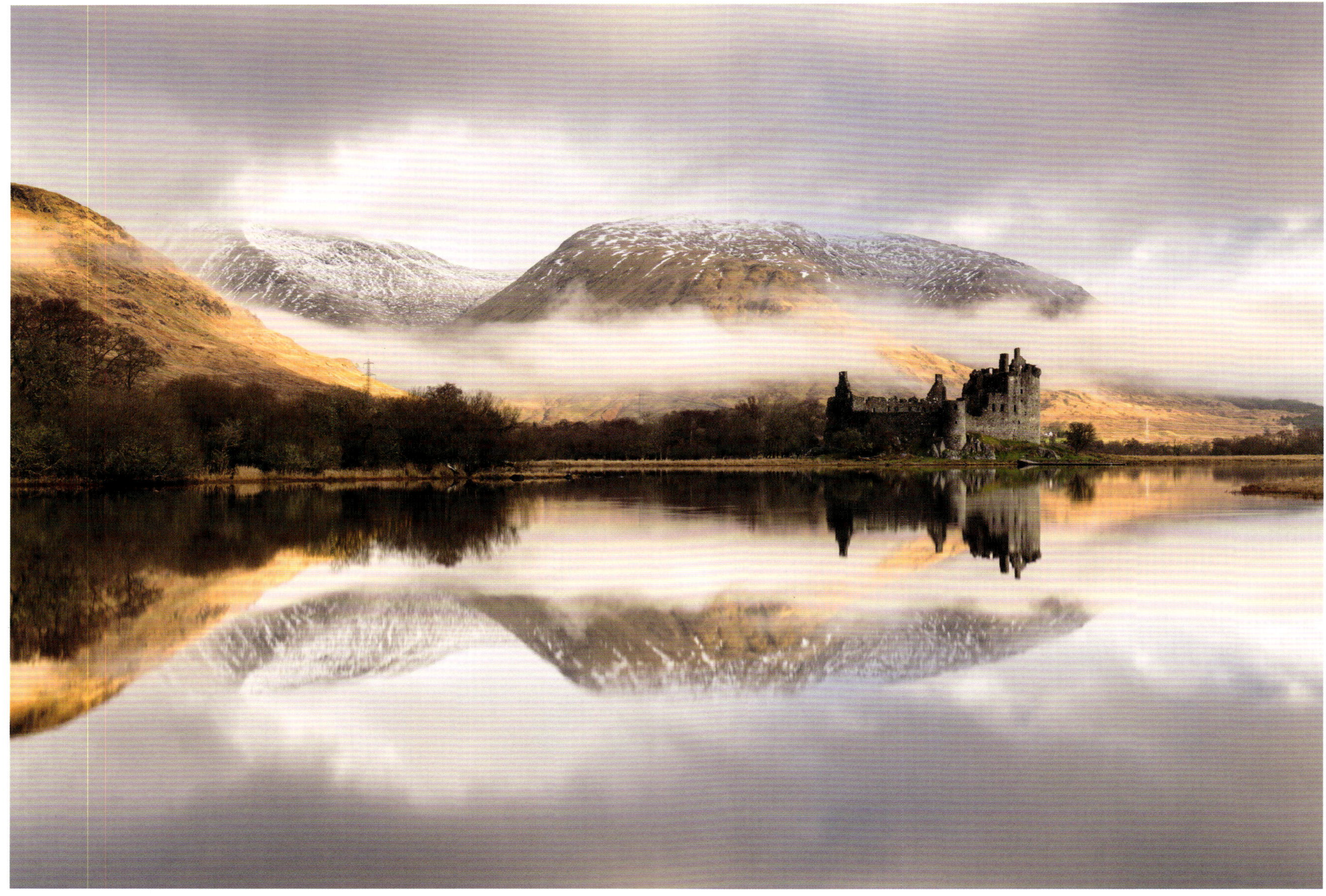

KILCHURN CASTLE

They say good things come to those that wait. An early alarm call and long drive were necessary to get to the
water's edge prior to sunrise, but I had to wait for the mist to clear, the castle ruins to appear, and sunlight to kiss
the mountains before I could take this image of one of Scotland's most iconic castles.

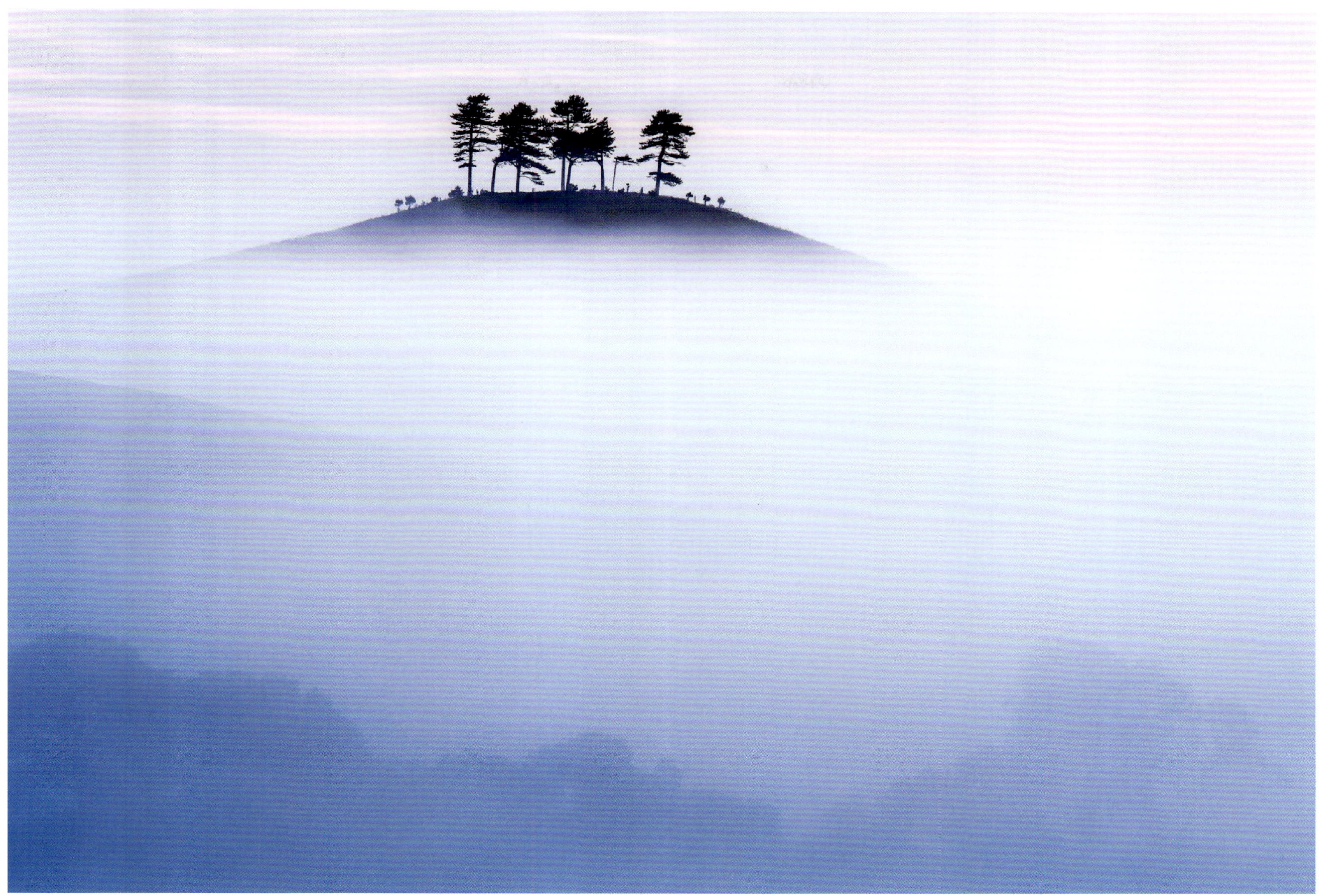

COLMER'S HILL

Mist simplifies the landscape—obscuring detail and reducing it to a series of layers. This little group of conifers, growing atop Colmer's Hill, is an obvious hotspot for photography. The conditions were just lovely on the morning I took this, with the trees just poking up above the sea of mist. The tones prior to sunrise are naturally cool—and the muted hues appealed to my aesthetic instincts.

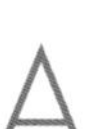

Q + A

You started out young, in wildlife photography initially, and then pursued a successful career as a professional photographer from your teens—what were the key events or steps in your growth as a photographer?

Yes, I had a slightly unconventional upbringing! I hated school, so my parents took the self-sacrificing decision to educate me at home. I inherited their passion and respect for nature, and when I discovered photography, aged 9 or 10, I instinctively wanted to photograph wildlife. I won a couple of photography competitions and began selling my photographs to magazines in my early teens. Rather than continue my studies, I effectively turned professional aged just 17. Looking back, it was a reckless, arrogant decision, but I was consumed with the idea of taking photographs for a living. My parent's ongoing encouragement was key to the decision being (ultimately) a success. Winning Young Wildlife Photographer of the Year was an important springboard and other competition successes helped raise my profile as a young, aspiring professional. Then, in my early twenties, I discovered landscapes—a genre that has given me a far greater understanding of light, depth, and balance.

How exactly does a photographer find their "niche" or "style"?

By being instinctive and selfish. Only take the images that you want to take—the subjects you like to shoot. Whether you wish to be conventional or unconventional, it is up to you—it is your journey, your path, your style. Don't let others influence you unduly. Listen, learn, develop, and be inspired by others, but ultimately don't feel you have to conform to a certain philosophy or outlook. Photography should be fun, a creative outlet, and a method of communication. You can't force creativity, but you will soon discover your niche and individual style.

Why do you think less is often more in landscape photography?

Personally, I've always been drawn to simple, uncluttered compositions. I look for simplicity—regardless of subject matter. Why? Well, I guess I'm a fairly simple soul, and I've always known my own mind. It is easy to overcomplicate an image—to be greedy and cram too much into the frame. I think landscape photographers can be guilty of growing over-reliant on super-wide-angle lenses today, and this can lead to the inclusion of more space or confusion than is necessary or useful. Less is so often more, in my opinion. Thoughtful framing, or the selection of a longer focal length, can help exclude elements within the landscape that aren't actually enhancing the scene. What we decide to remove from the image space can prove just as influential to the look of the final image as the elements we decide to feature. I don't want things to conflict with one another in my shots, but to create balance and harmony instead.

Other than camera handling skills, what other abilities do outdoor photographers require—for example, understanding how light or weather influences atmosphere?

An understanding of light, weather, tides, seasonal changes, and what exactly creates mood and atmosphere are all key skills for outdoor photographers to possess. However, possibly the most important thing is motivation. Regardless of how good your camera skills are, or how meticulously you plan a shoot, photographers are reliant on something completely out of their control—nature. Whenever you head out with your camera, there is no guarantee you will return home with a good shot— you need to get lucky too. It can be frustrating and demoralizing when the light, sky, or conditions disappoint, as they regularly do. However, as the saying goes, "the harder you work, the luckier you will get." It is important to retain the motivation to get up early, stay out late, and walk long distances laden with camera kit if you wish to witness and capture those special and unique moments. Lose your motivation and work ethic, and you lose everything.

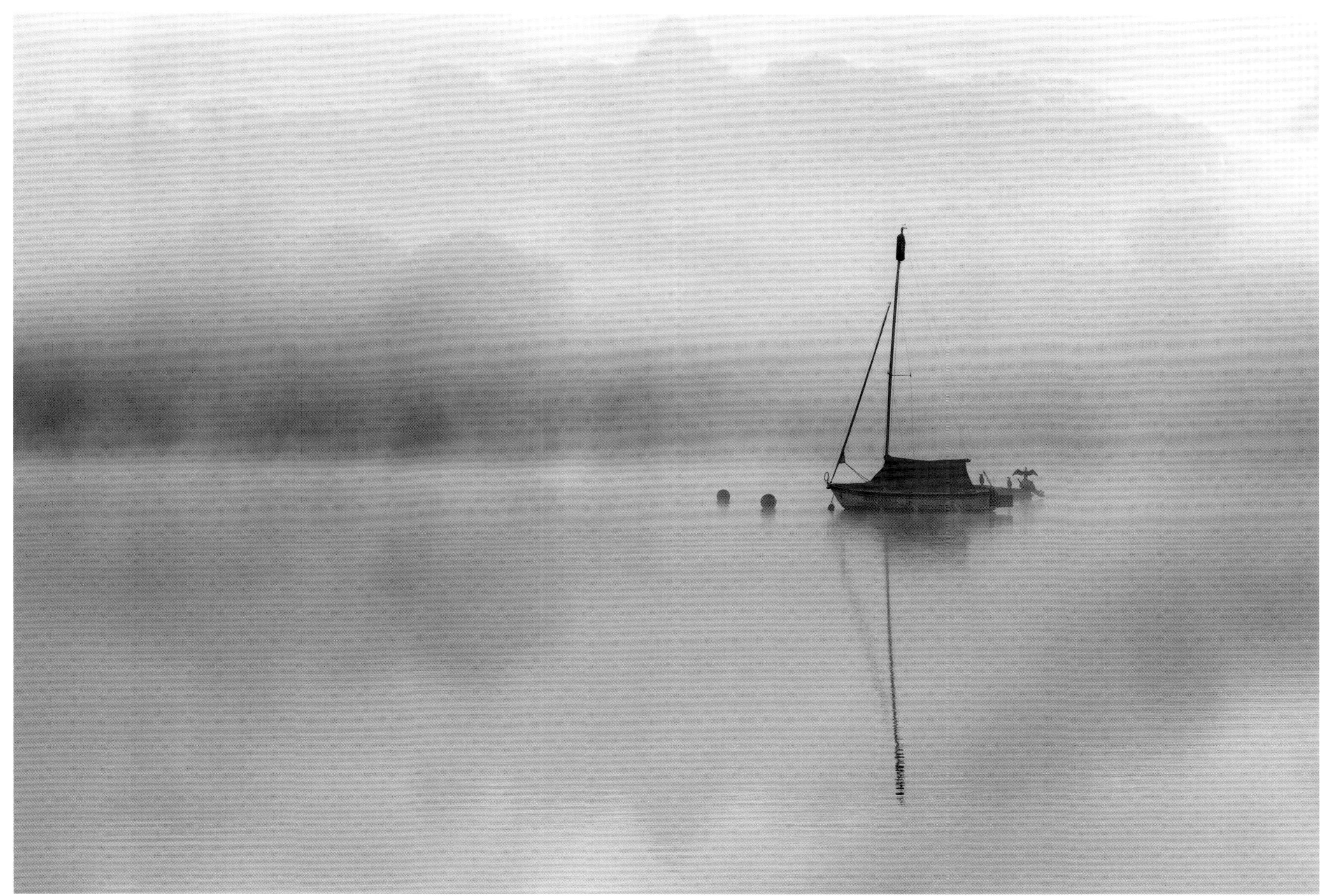

SAILING BOAT

I try to avoid overcomplicated compositions. It is tempting to be clever for the sake of it—including unnecessary or inappropriate foreground interest, or maybe cramming more into the frame than is needed. Sometimes it is better to simply trust your instincts—don't overthink things. I waited for the mist to begin to clear, and the cormorant to stretch out its wings, before triggering the shutter.

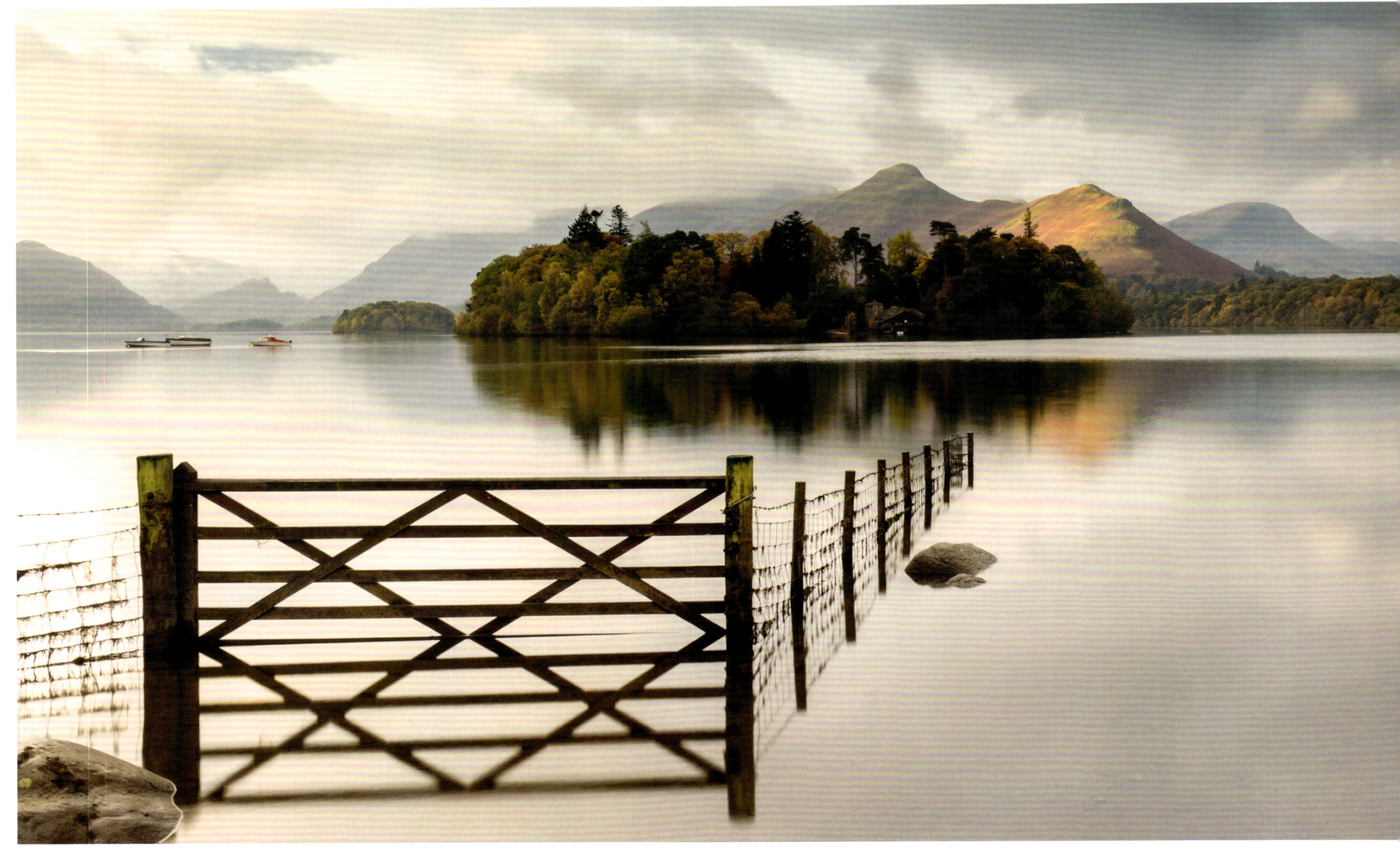

DERWENTWATER

An early alarm call and a still October morning at Derwentwater resulted in me taking this image. I rarely shoot panoramics, but this scene suited the format perfectly. A few gaps in the cloud created some lovely light play on Cat Bells, while the flooded gate helped to provide depth and interest.

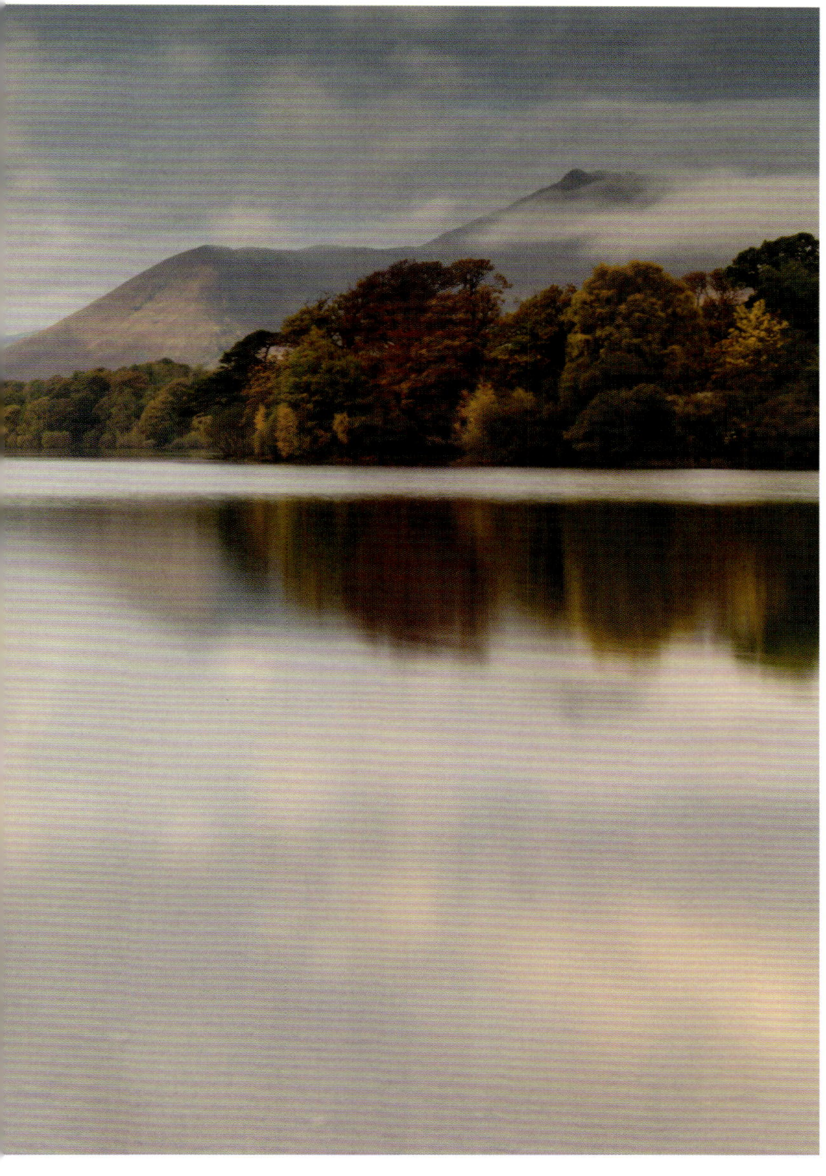

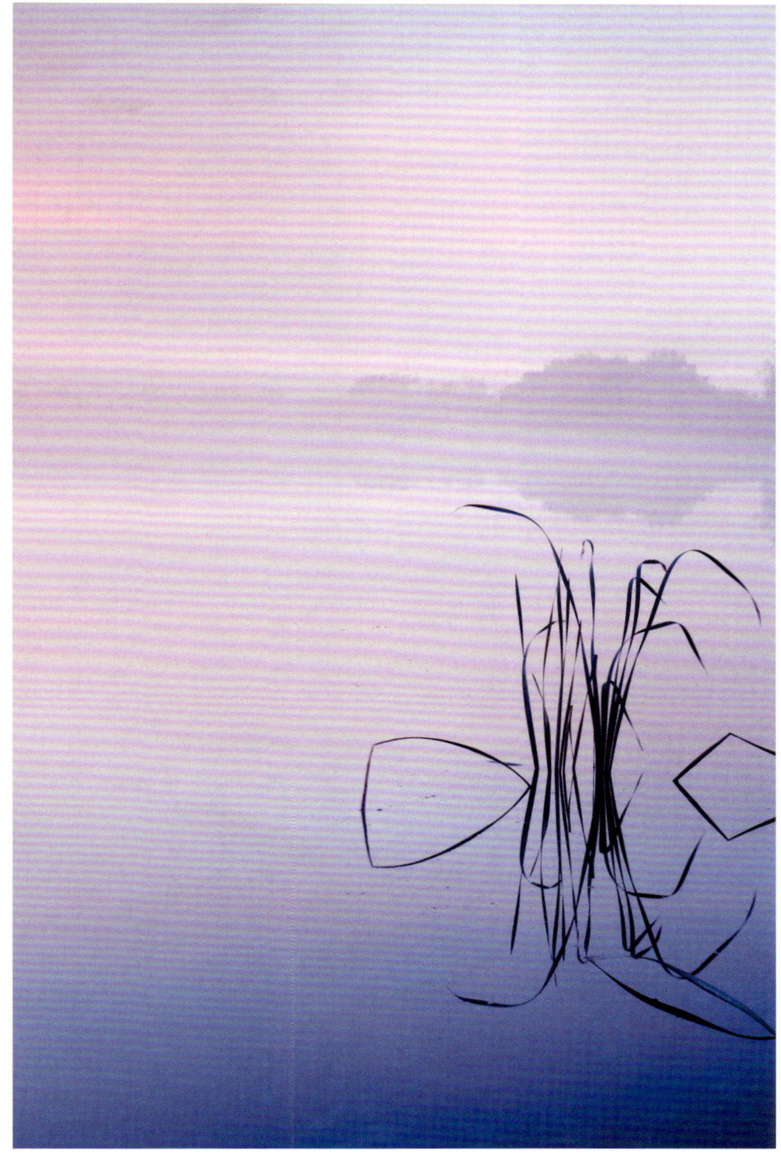

SILHOUETTED REEDS

I love shooting close to home. In an age when photographers can travel widely and easily, I still prefer to work near to where I live in Cornwall. What are the benefits? You get to know the landscape intimately—its qualities, its character. This was taken at a little reservoir just a few miles from where I live. The shape of the reeds, contrasted against the diffused, misty backdrop, helped to create a simple, yet graphic frame.

Q
+
A

Over the years, you've won a number of awards. Would you advise aspiring photographers to enter competitions—what are the potential benefits and pitfalls?

At a young age, I found photography competitions provided me with a platform to showcase my work and establish a name. Due to my past experiences of entering competitions, I often recommend aspiring photographers do the same as a way to help showcase their talents. A word of warning, though—they are fickle beasts. Obviously, photography is massively subjective—what I like, you may not, and vice versa. In reality, no judging panel can ever say one photo is irrefutably better than another, and there can be a very fine line between winning and being placed nowhere. Therefore, if you enter a competition, don't take it personally if you are unsuccessful—it isn't necessarily a reflection of the quality of your work. I always say that being successful in a photography competition doesn't make you a better photographer, but neither does being unsuccessful make you a worse one.

What is more important, a high level of technical ability or a creative eye?

I'm really not a very technical photographer. I discovered photography young, and when you are just 10 or 11 years old, your only focus is taking nice pictures, not f-stops and ISOs. Ultimately, sound technique is essential in order to consistently capture the images you previsualize. However, I still don't obsess about technique, the gear I use, or spend long processing my images. For me, the creative aspects of photography are most important—vision, use of light, composition, creative interpretation, for instance. These are the things that will define your images and make them stand out. Being technically adept alone will not get you very far in a creative industry such as photography.

What are the most important areas to focus on as a professional photographer other than the photography itself?

Making a living from photography is getting increasingly difficult. Being a good photographer doesn't guarantee success and selling photographs alone is rarely enough today to produce a stable, reliable income. To be a professional, you have to be multifaceted—for example, I write and run photography workshops. There are far better photographers than me, but I've always worked hard, not only to develop my skills as a cameraman, but to market my images, build relationships, and align myself with other brands. Self-publicity doesn't generally come easy to creative types, but in order to make a living from taking photos (of such an accessible and popular subject as landscapes) it is essential to be able to run a small business and develop a brand.

As a master of landscape photography, what is your motivation to continue making photographs?

Photography is an addiction, maybe even an obsession for me personally. It's all I've ever done; it is an integral part of my life. It offers the perfect excuse to be outdoors, to be lost in big spaces, and to be immersed by nature—what more motivation do you need? I also want to improve, though, to overcome my failings as a photographer, develop, and to inspire, and be inspired. Taking pictures is what I do—I can't envisage that ever changing.

TECHNICAL INFORMATION

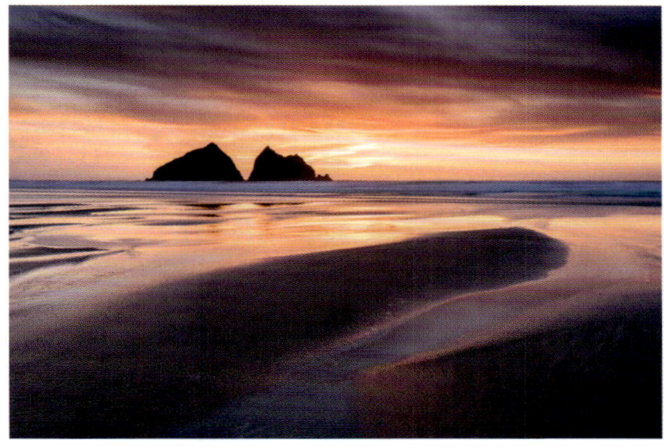

HOLYWELL BAY
CORNWALL, ENGLAND

Caamera: Nikon D810
Lens/Focal length: Nikkor 17–35mm f/2.8 at 32mm
Aperture: f/11
Shutter speed: 5 sec.
ISO: 64
Kit: Tripod, 0.6 ND grad filter

KILCHURN CASTLE
SCOTLAND

Camera: Nikon D810
Lens/Focal length: Nikkor 24–70mm f/2.8 at 38mm
Aperture: f/13
Shutter speed: 2 sec.
ISO: 64
Kit: Tripod, 0.6 ND grad filter

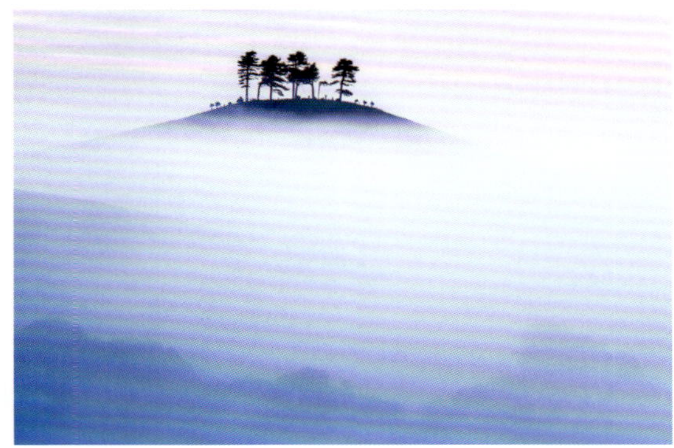

COLMER'S HILL
DORSET, ENGLAND

Camera: Nikon D800
Lens/Focal length: Nikkor 70–200mm f/2.8 at 125mm
Aperture: f/11
Shutter speed: 5 sec.
ISO: 100
Kit: Tripod

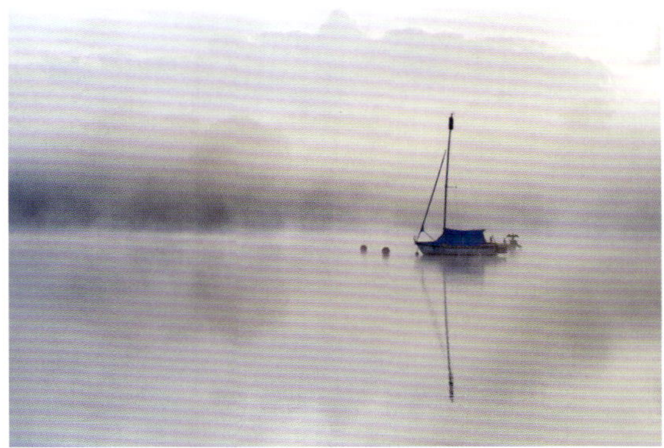

SAILING BOAT
SOMERSET, ENGLAND

Camera: Nikon D810
Lens/Focal length: Nikkor 70–200mm f/2.8 at 102mm
Aperture: f/8
Shutter speed: 1/80 sec.
ISO: 100
Kit: Tripod

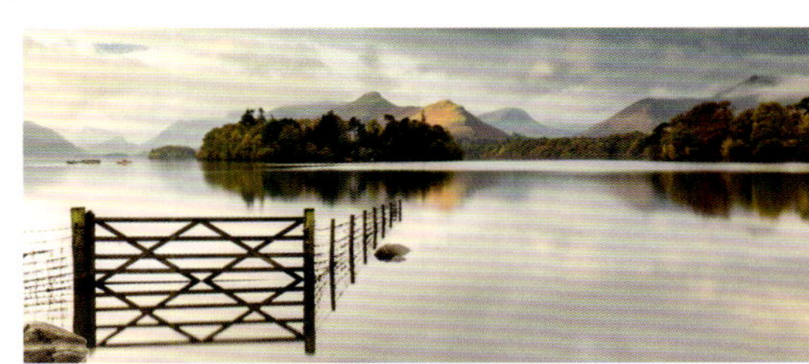

DERWENTWATER
CUMBRIA, ENGLAND

Camera: Nikon D800
Lens/Focal length: Nikkor 24–70mm f/2.8 at 27mm
Aperture: f/16
Shutter speed: 5 sec.
ISO: 100
Kit: Tripod, 0.6 ND grad filter

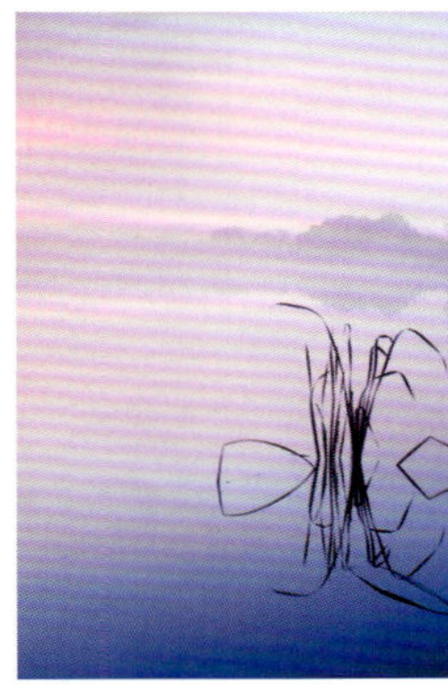

SILHOUETTED REEDS
CORNWALL, ENGLAND

Camera: Nikon D300
Lens/Focal length: Nikkor 17–55mm f/2.8 at 50mm
Aperture: f/14
Shutter speed: 13 sec.
ISO: 100
Kit: Tripod

MASTER OF CREATIVITY
SANDRA BARTOCHA

Sandra Bartocha is a German freelance photographer, artist, and author, who specializes in natural landscapes, forests, and plants, as well as abstract work, with the specific aim of creating images that evoke an emotional response. The beauty of nature and natural light are a great source of inspiration to Sandra. She tries to photograph nature in an artistic way rather than trying to document it, focusing on details, light, colors, and moods, and using creative camera techniques to capture the beauty of a scene.

Sandra is vice president of the Society of German Nature Photographers (GDT), and is chief editor of the magazine *GDT Forum Naturfotografie*. Her pictures have been published in European magazines, several coffee-table and teaching books, as well as calendars. She has been traveling all over Europe to give her audiovisual presentations "Rhythm of Nature" and "LYS," and has shown her artistic work at numerous exhibitions. Her images have won awards in many international competitions—including the International Photography Awards, European Wildlife Photographer of the Year, Asferico, BioPhoto, and the Wildlife Photographer of the Year competition in 2010, 2011, 2012, 2014, and 2016.

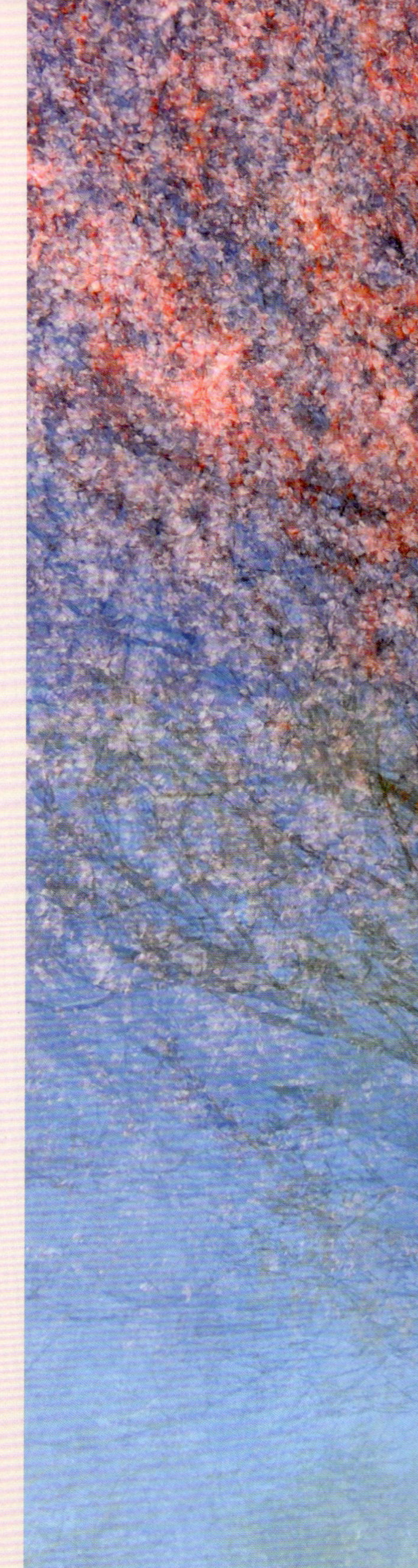

TREE VISIONS

This image was the first one of a whole series of tree images that I took across all seasons. I wanted to capture the beauty of the flowering trees. When a single exposure didn't do justice to the overall scene, I started creating multi-exposure images in order to add depth. Finally, I decided to take 10 exposures, done in-camera, changing my position slightly with every exposure. Doing that, I managed to create an overlay of the blossoms, providing a more impressionistic image.

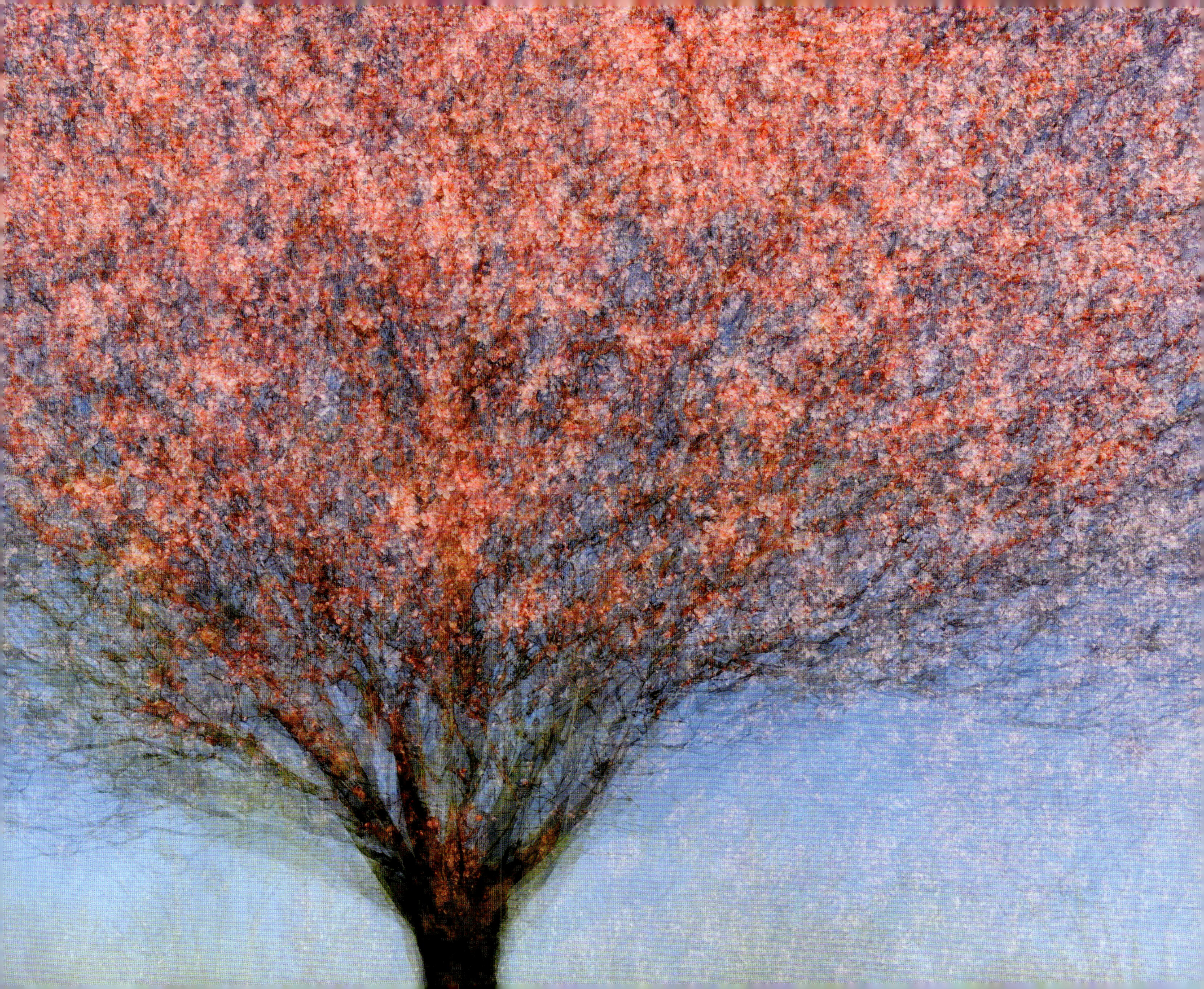

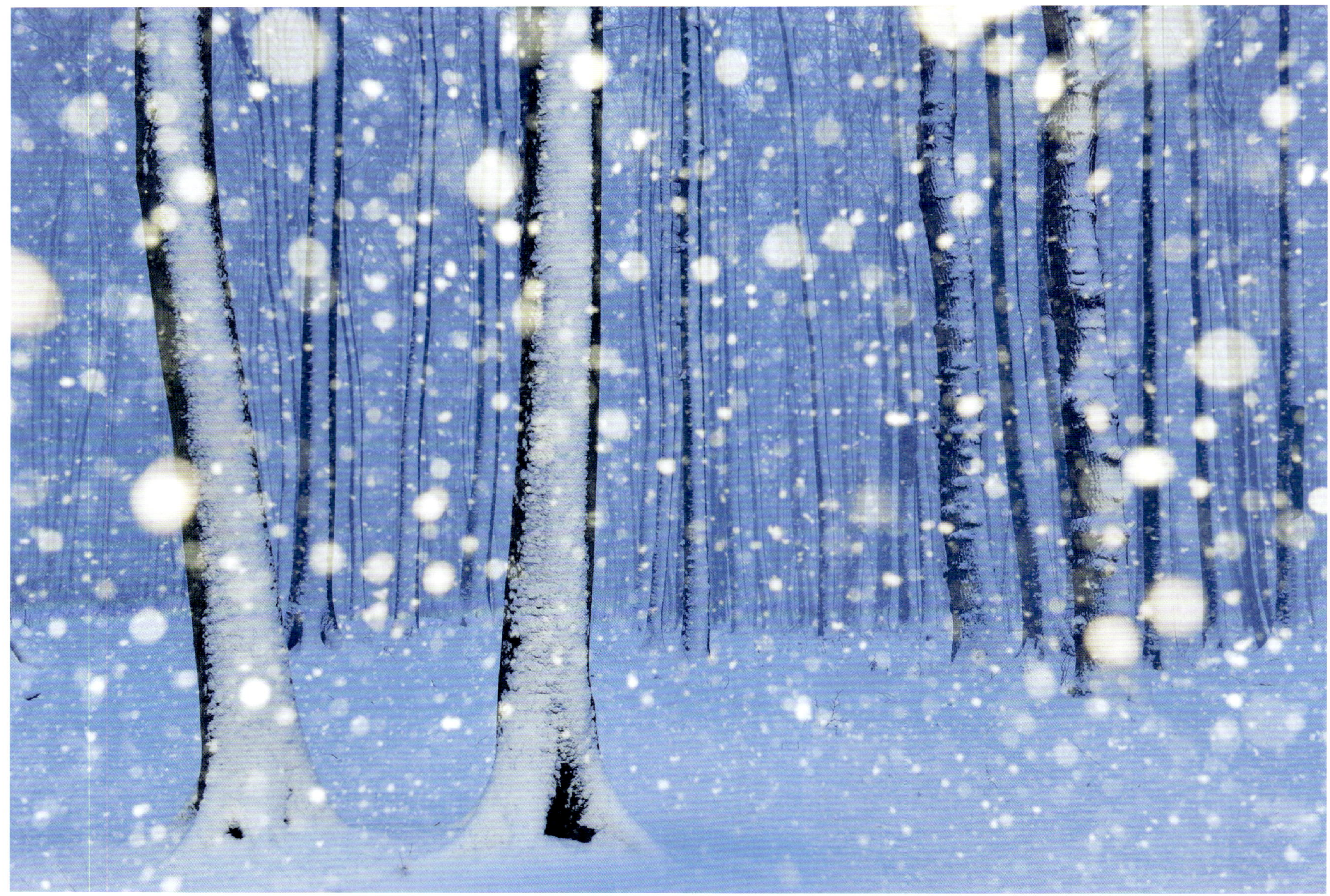

SPOOKY FOREST

The "Gespensterwald" is a coastal beech forest in northern Germany. The winds from the Baltic Sea have contributed to the lack of ground cover and the forest's reputation as a spooky place. After a heavy snowfall in January, I spent the whole day in the forest, waiting for the perfect conditions. Only after the night fell, it started to snow again with heavy snowflakes. I used the internal flash of the camera in order to make them visible, as well as to create a magical and surreal mood.

THIN LINE

It was a cold September morning at the Kitka river in northern Finland, and my aim was to photograph the beautiful slender spruce trees of the taiga for our book project *LYS*. Fog was covering the whole landscape. As the sun was rising, small parts of the landscape appeared shortly and disappeared again. Instead of capturing the complete scene that was enfolding in front of me, I used a telephoto lens to isolate small patches for a minimalist approach.

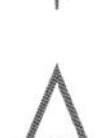

How did your passion for photography become your profession?

I always knew I wanted to be a photographer, so it was a natural evolution after university, where I read media and film studies, for me to move into being a professional photographer. Luckily two big projects, right at the beginning of my career, helped me find my path and boosted my profile as well—one of them being a regional three-year commission for an audiovisual presentation by the Müritz National Park in Germany, and the other one was being part of the "Wild Wonders of Europe" project.
The intensity of the first assignments for WWE in southern Italy, where I was commissioned to photograph orchids and forest landscapes in a new and interesting way, have had a huge influence on how I shoot plants and trees until this day. Going from being a student to a professional nature photographer wasn't such a big difference in the beginning. I kept my financial overhead as low as possible, and worked in the field as much as I could. At that time, I never cared about what would be selling well—I only cared about expressing myself with my camera.

How heavily do other forms of art influence your style?

Inspiration is everywhere. Wherever I go, whatever I see, whatever I listen to on a daily basis—the world around me acts as a huge melting pot of ideas for my photography. Although I am a deeply rooted nature lover, I never intended to just document the beauty of the world around me. I always wanted to show something more, convey my emotions, capture easily overlooked beauty, celebrate nature, and photograph the perfect evocation of a scene. It always helps to be open-minded, and my interest for all kinds of art, from historic and contemporary paintings to video installations, has definitely influenced the way I see and portray nature.

You capture the natural world in a beautifully intimate way—just how do you stay creative in your work?

It is very difficult these days to always be creative and to constantly innovate—especially with an audience that never tires of seeing the same old work, over and over. The key to new work is probably staying completely unimpressed by the feedback of the crowd and the demands of the market. Being guided directly by your own heart and soul, focusing solely on self-expression, never really growing up, and keeping a child's approach to seeing are surely the other important parts of staying creative. I get bored with my own and others' work easily, which can be daunting on the one hand . . . but it always helps me to search for new forms of photographic representation.

What techniques do you use to create your fresh and innovative images?

I am not an advocate of using techniques for the sole purpose of creating something "new" and "innovative," as in the end this is very often just an overlay on top of the intended content of the image. Techniques should always be used to underline and support the idea and message behind a photograph. I always try to stay true to the subject and try to capture the essence of a place, or characterize what I believe is special about it with the help of a certain technique. And yes, of course, I'm using quite a few different photographic approaches in order to convey the ideas I have in the field. I love working with long exposures, and have been using double and multiple exposures very intensively in several ways over the past few years. Finding and adapting old lenses with interesting bokeh is also great fun and helps to capture the magic of certain landscapes.

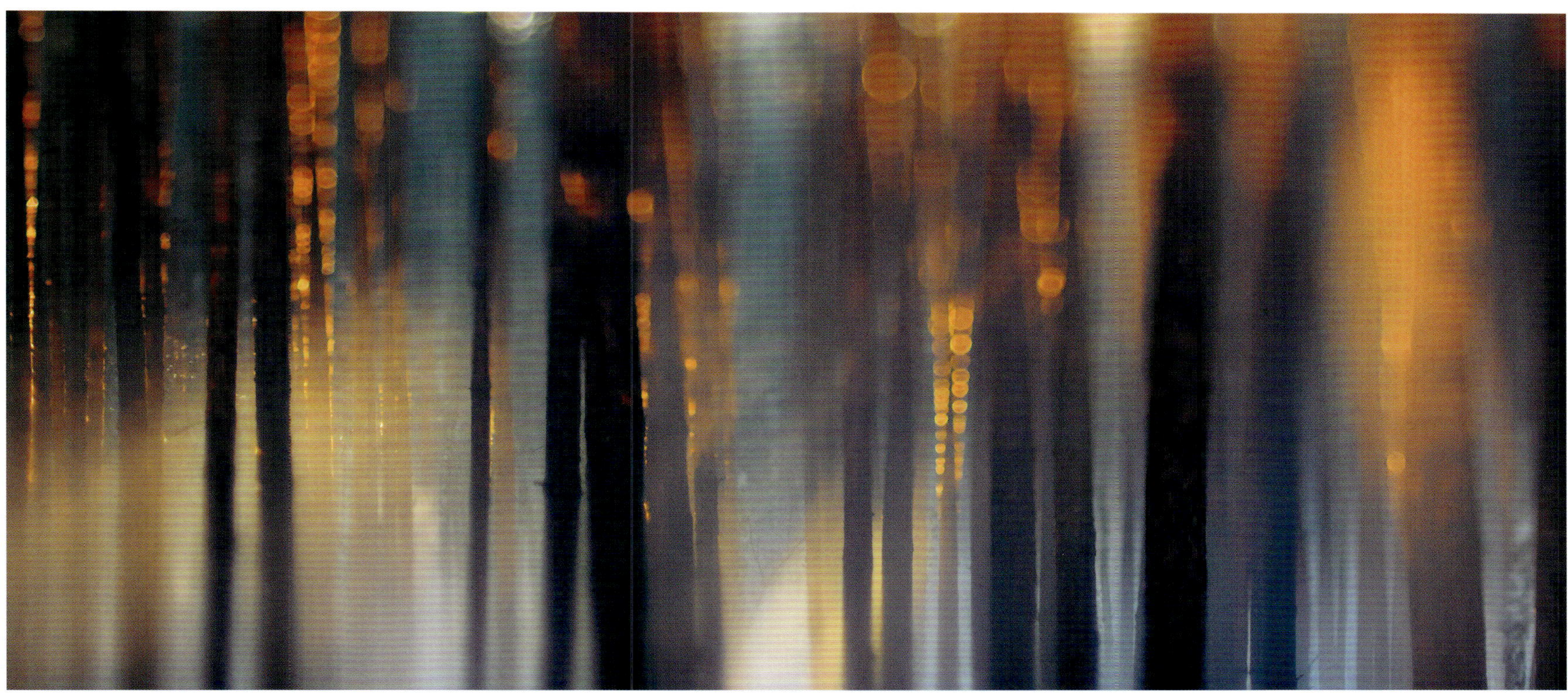

LIGHT SHOW

A warm winter day. As the snow started to melt, a thick fog began to wrap itself around the forest near my home. I immediately saw the photographic potential of the situation, grabbed my camera, and went straight to the forest. The evening sun created a glow around the tall, wet trunks of the Scots pines. It was breathtaking. Carrying only my small mirrorless camera with a tilt-lens combination allowed me to change the layers of sharpness from parallel to horizontal. I started experimenting with several different focal planes and an open aperture, which resulted in an unexpected interpretation of the image.

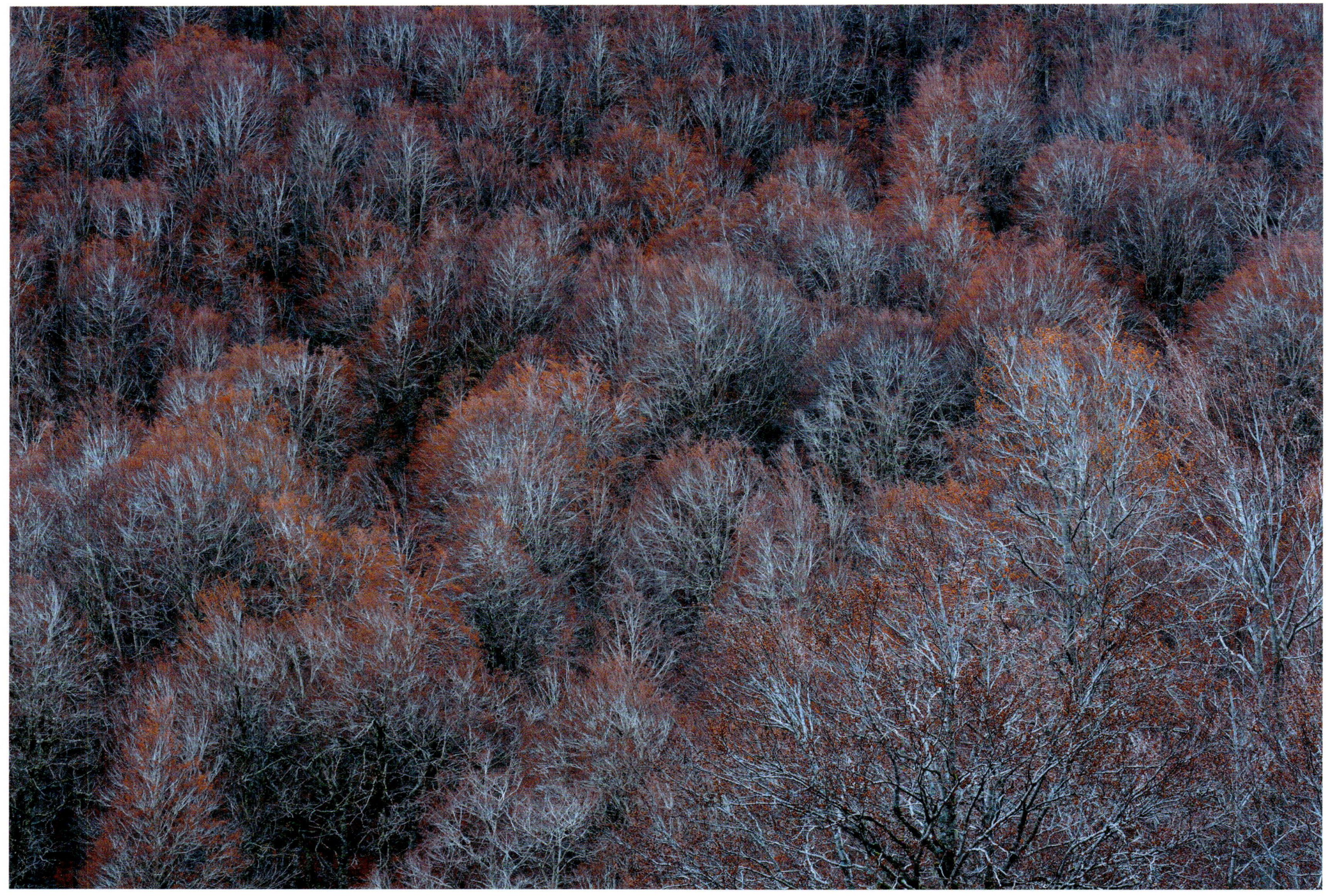

BEECHNUT RHYTHM

The forests in the Abruzzo National Park are among the oldest and most pristine in Europe. A heavy storm had taken all the fall leaves very early in the year, leaving only the beechnuts at the tip of the branches of the European beech trees. Taken from a higher viewpoint on an opposite mountain, the trees formed a perfectly regular rhythm. The image was taken in twilight, which creates the bluish color of the trunks in contrast to the glowing red-brown of the beechnuts.

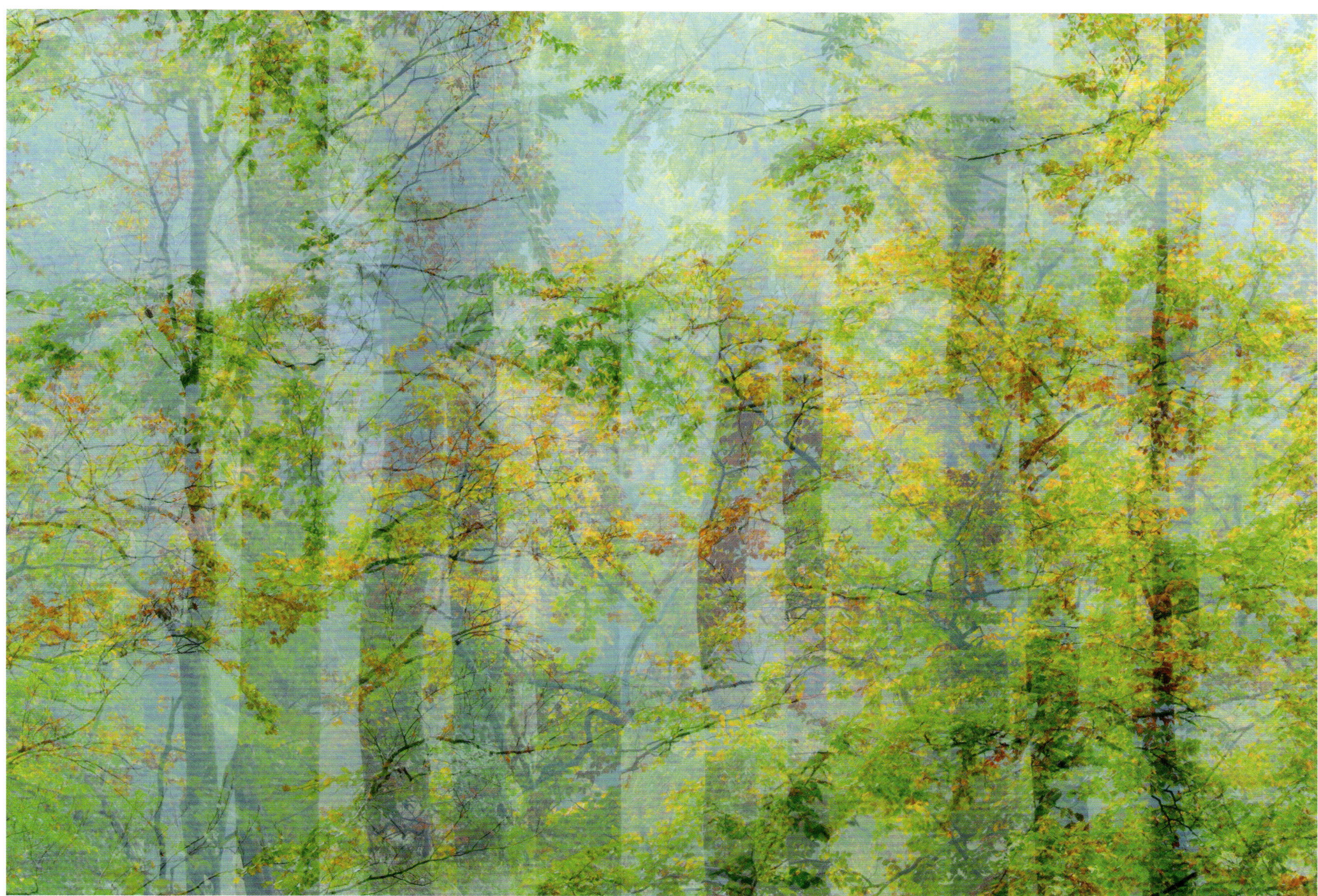

AUTUMN MURAL

It had been raining all day, and the colors of the beech trees in the UNESCO World Heritage Site in Serrahn had not yet changed completely as it was still two weeks until peak season. But some of the leaves were already yellow and reddish, creating a beautiful pattern of mixed colors. I used a strong zoom lens to achieve a tight framing, and applied a triple exposure to create a translucent impression of branches, foliage, and background merging into each other. The overall atmosphere and the pastel mood was enhanced by the still, humid, and moist air.

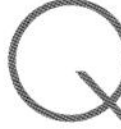
Q + A

How important is experimentation in your work?

It does play a very important role. I am constantly trying out new ways of representation by exceeding the limit of what is expected in classic photography. It starts with being brave with composition and exposure, and ends with constantly being on the lookout for interesting lenses or techniques. Many of my most popular images are the result of combining cameras and lenses that originally don't belong to each other, or experimenting with exposures and intentional camera movement (ICM). In the end, though, it will always be the trained eye and the focused mind of the photographer that are responsible for great and timeless imagery.

Do you have a favorite subject or approach?

I guess my heart is lost in the forest and by the sea. Like so many other photographers, I am deeply rooted within the landscapes I grew up in as a child, and I repeatedly visit these areas. They have a special power and offer solitude for me as a person, and opportunities for me as a photographer. The variation of the beauty of trees never ceases to amaze me. I love to follow the seasons in the woodlands—I enjoy capturing the graphic quality of the tree trunks and the changing colors of the foliage. My approach to taking pictures differs depending on the day. Sometimes I just go out and see what is waiting there for me, and, at other times, I have a clear concept and vision in mind, and try to find the perfect location and subject in order to photograph what is in my head. Both ways can be very rewarding and can lead to interesting results. The conceptual approach helps to create a more coherent body of work, though.

Does being a leading female photographer in a field still dominated by men present any special challenges?

I find it can be both a help and a hindrance. Sometimes it is an advantage, as there are so few women in the field that this leads to opportunities that might not have happened in such a highly competitive field—such as being invited as a speaker or onto competition juries to fulfill a female quota. On the other hand, that leads to the question of whether I'm invited because I'm a woman or because of the quality of my work! However, I do believe that the female mindset and taste, as well as our approach in the field, are a bit different to those of male photographers, and at times it isn't easy to stand tall, and be confident because of your own work . . . and I do have to work hard to not be reduced to being known as a "flower photographer"! In the field, there is not much difference—you either cope with the challenges that come with being out and photographing nature in sometimes harsh conditions, and carrying a heavy backpack or you don't. One advantage here is that we tend to be less impressed by equipment and camera gear, and are able to concentrate more on the subject.

What single piece of equipment is most useful in your work?

I'm a real low-tech photographer. It is very often just me, my camera, and my lens. If I have to decide which piece of kit is the most important to me, then I would probably say my Nikon D810 and the Nikkor 80–400mm lens. That combination gives me a huge range of opportunities to capture the landscape and details in an intimate way.

TECHNICAL INFORMATION

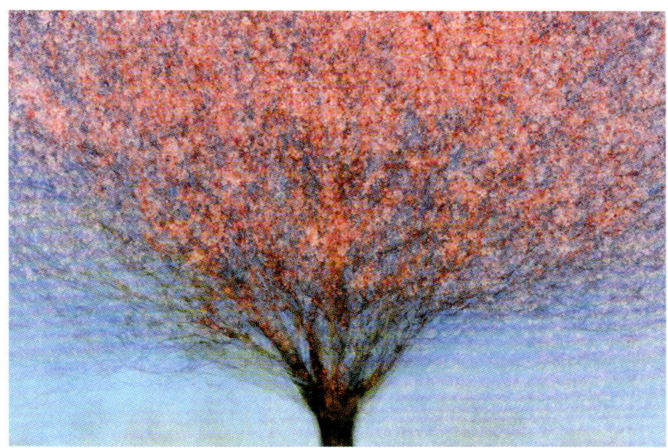

TREE VISIONS
NEUBRANDENBURG, GERMANY

Camera: Nikon D700
Lens/Focal length: Nikkor 24–70mm f/2.8 at 55mm
Aperture: f/16
Shutter speed: 1/20 sec.
ISO: 200
Kit: Tripod, composite of 10 frames

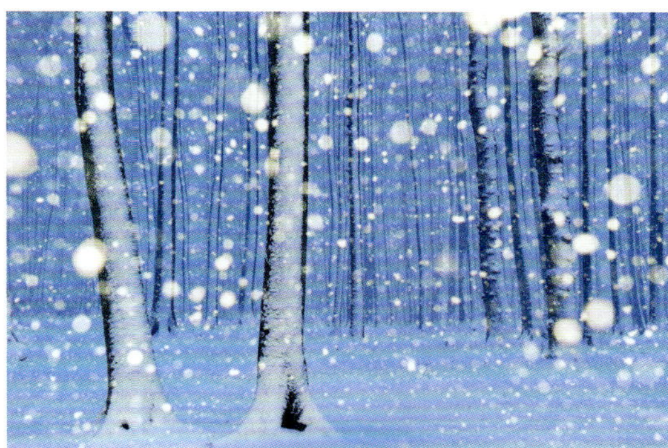

SPOOKY FOREST
NIENHAGEN, GERMANY

Camera: Nikon D700
Lens/Focal length: Nikkor 24–70mm f/2.8 at 50mm
Aperture: f/5.6
Shutter speed: 0.8 sec.
ISO: 200
Kit: Internal flash, tripod

THIN LINE
OULANKA, FINLAND

Camera: Nikon D800E
Lens/Focal length: Nikkor 80–400mm f/4.5–5.6 at 155mm
Aperture: f/18
Shutter speed: 1/100 sec.
ISO: 100
Kit: Tripod

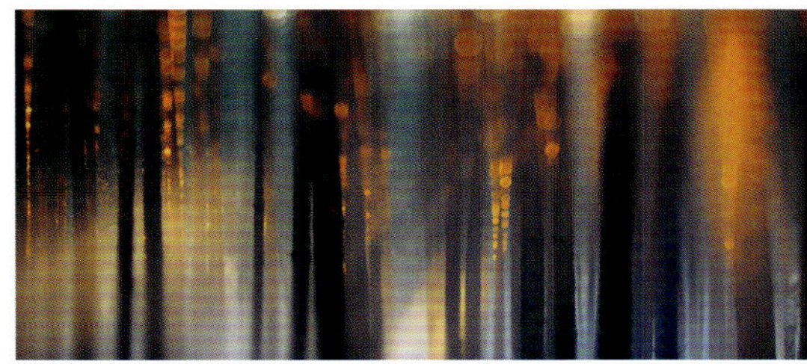

LIGHT SHOW
POTSDAM, GERMANY

Camera: Sony NEX-5
Lens/Focal length: Nikkor 50mm f/1.4, adapted with
Lensbaby Tilt Transformer
Aperture: f/1.4
Shutter speed: 1/640 sec.
ISO: 200
Kit: Handheld

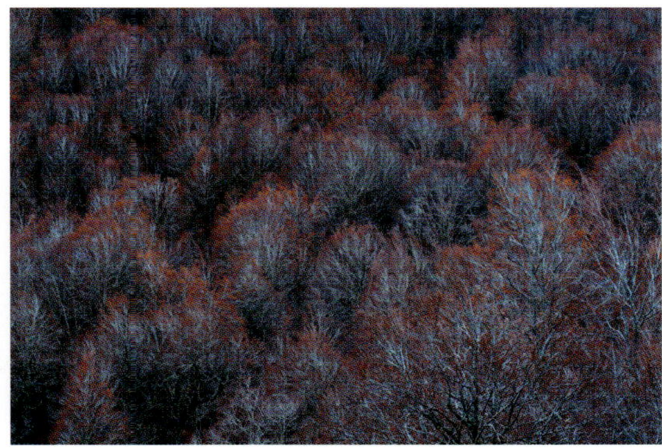

BEECHNUT RHYTHM
PESCASSEROLI, ABRUZZO NATIONAL PARK,
ITALY

Camera: Nikon D800E
Lens/Focal length: Nikkor 80–400mm f/4.5–5.6 at 95mm
Aperture: f/16
Shutter speed: 5 sec.
ISO: 100
Kit: Tripod, polarizing filter

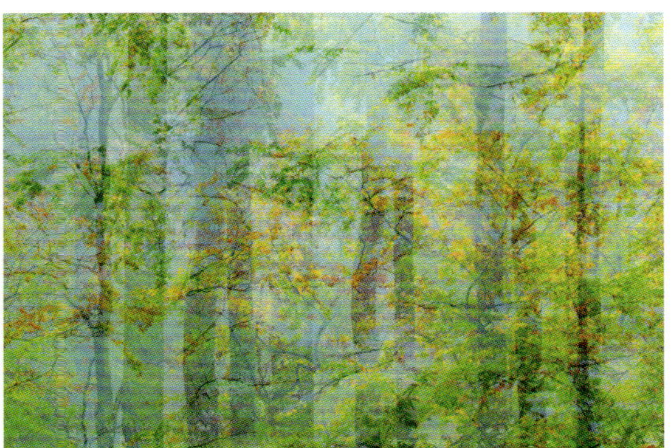

AUTUMN MURAL
SERRAHN, CARPIN,
GERMANY

Camera: Nikon D810
Lens/Focal length: Nikkor 80–400mm f/4.5–5.6 at 220mm
Aperture: f/16
Shutter speed: 6 sec.
ISO: 64
Kit: Tripod, polarizing filter, composite of three frames

THIERRY BORNIER

Thierry Bornier is a French photographer who started his working life as a chief financial officer in an international fashion company in New York. Finding that numbers were not enough to satisfy his creative vision, he has, since 2008, pursued his passion for photography, and his desire to capture moments of truth and beauty in both fashion and the landscape.

After a time spent traveling, Thierry found southwest China offered the most beautiful landscapes and made his home in Yunnan. He is entirely self-taught, and used the internet to study lighting techniques, and strives continually to improve. For him, lighting is like cooking: after learning the basics, the ability to create new tastes and moods is unlimited. Thierry also draws inspiration from the world of art, and in particular the works of Leonardo da Vinci and Rembrandt as masters of chiaroscuro, and Monet and Van Gogh for their exploration of the landscape.

Every scene provides a unique challenge and Thierry finds love in experimentation. His approach to photography is to constantly push himself, be curious, and learn from others. Thierry has discovered and photographed some of the world's most striking landscapes, focusing on capturing the beauty in nature, as he believes that one day these will only live in memories due to the destructive action of climate change.

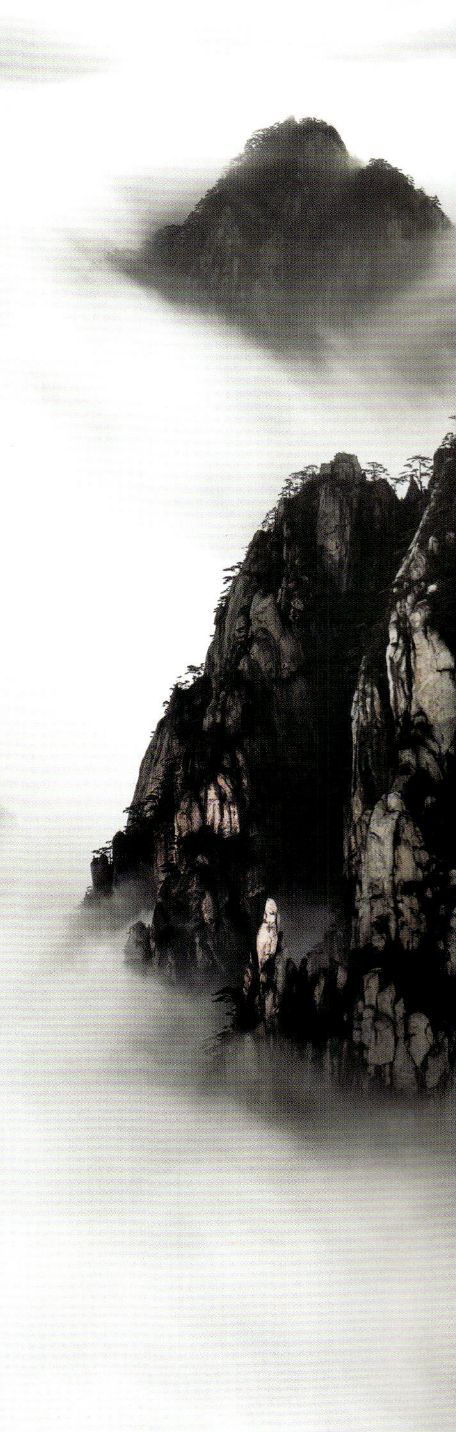

CLOUDLAND

Mount Huangshan (Yellow Mountain), with its uniquely shaped pine trees and majestic peaks rising from the mist, has featured in Chinese art and literature for over 1,000 years. To photograph this view, I had to climb steps carved in the mountain for over an hour, in total darkness. At the summit, the temperature was recorded as 19°F (−7°C), and it was a further three hours before the conditions were perfect to capture this shot. With landscape photography, there is one element you cannot control and that is the weather. The local photographers told me that they had never seen this phenomenon, and that it could be another 100 years before it might happen again.

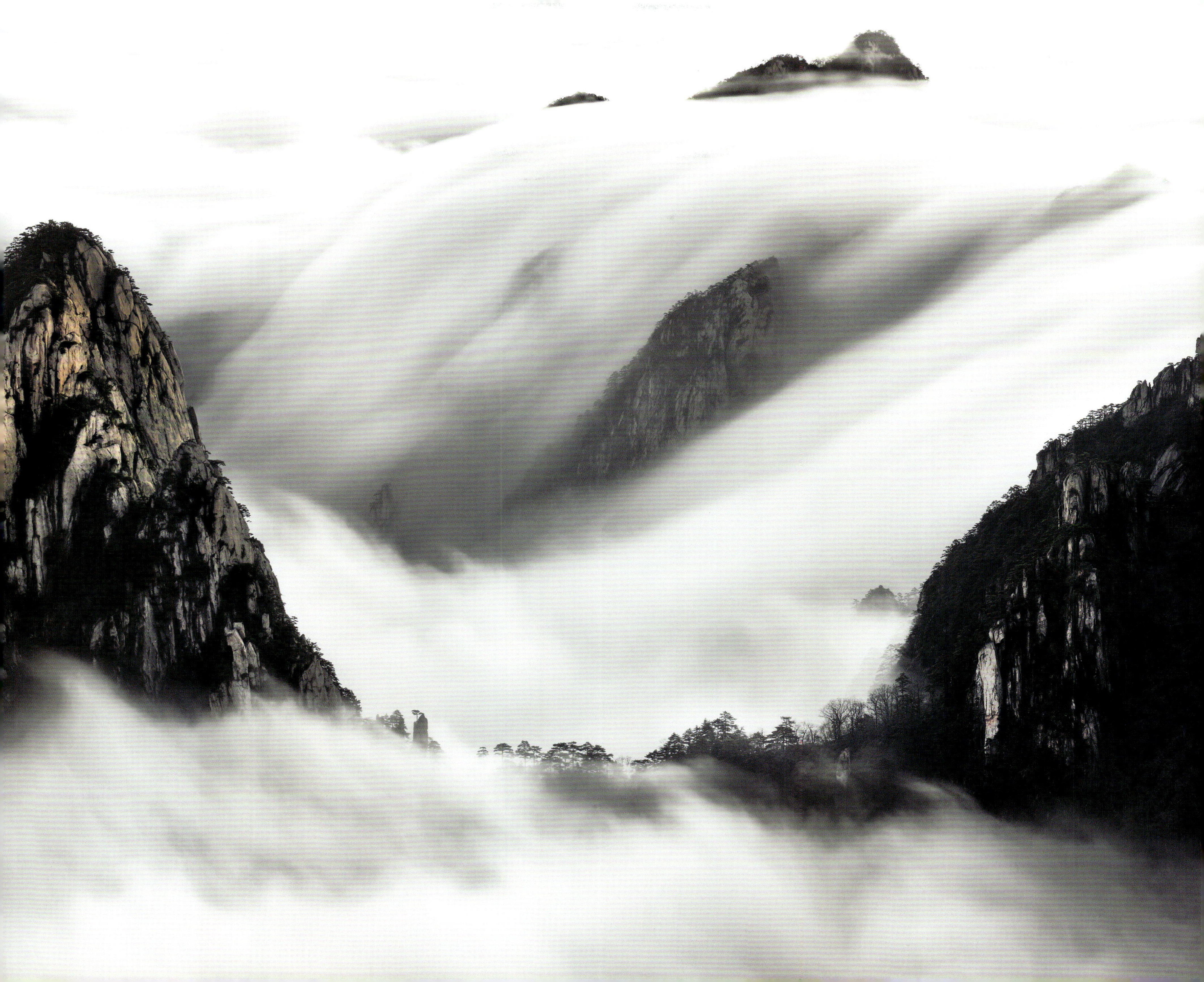

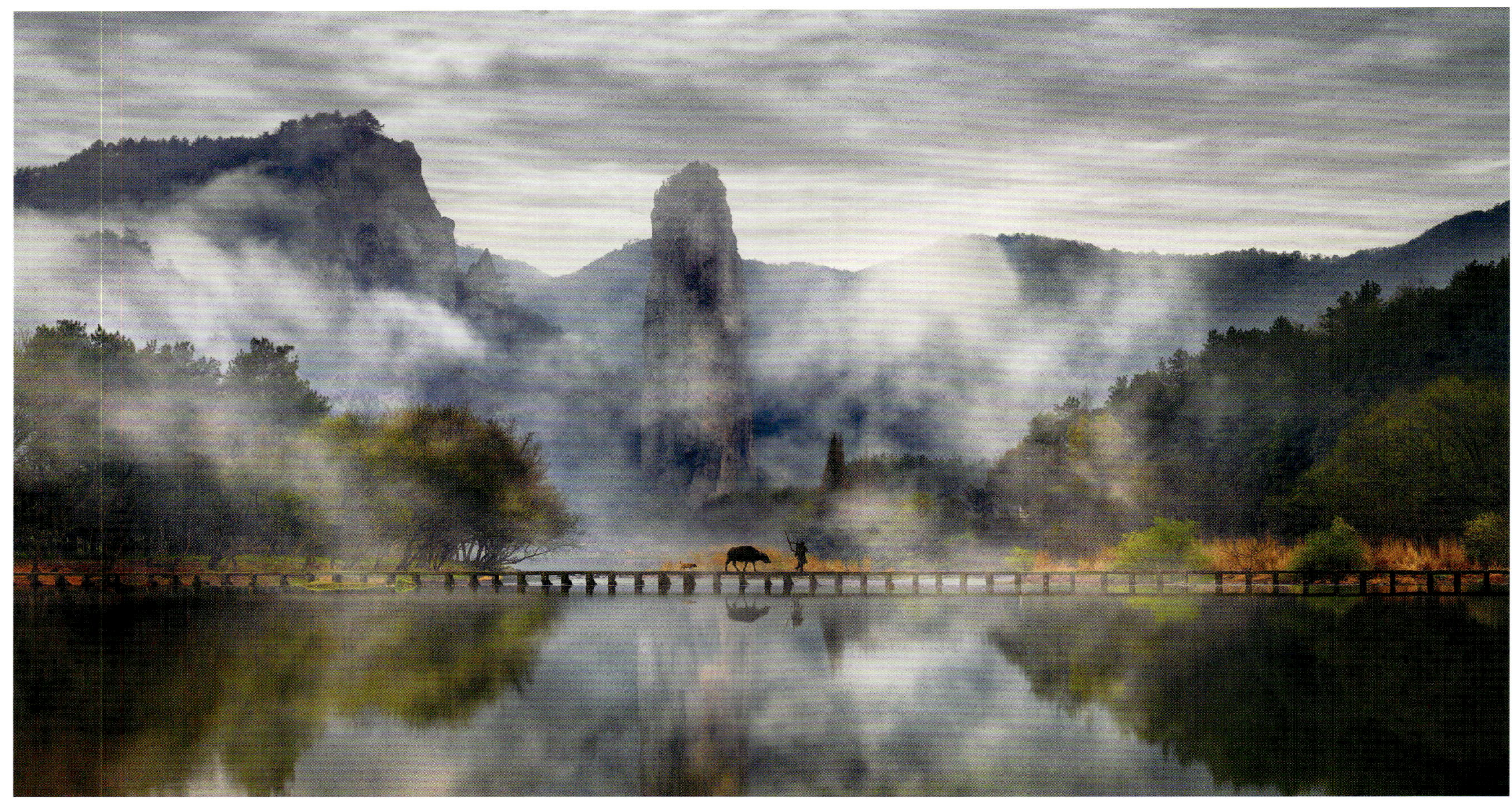

FAIRY LAND OF ZHEJIANG

This is an image of patience. It took me three years to capture this photograph. In landscape photography, you are so reliant on the light and the weather conditions. I visited this location numerous times, but was frustrated to find there was either no fog or too much fog. When I finally found the right conditions, I managed to photograph this image of daily life—a farmer, with his cow and dog, heading to work, as he had done every morning for the previous 10 years. I took three images and stitched them together to make this panoramic shot. Looking at this image now reminds me that photography is about being patient and to persevere if you want to get results.

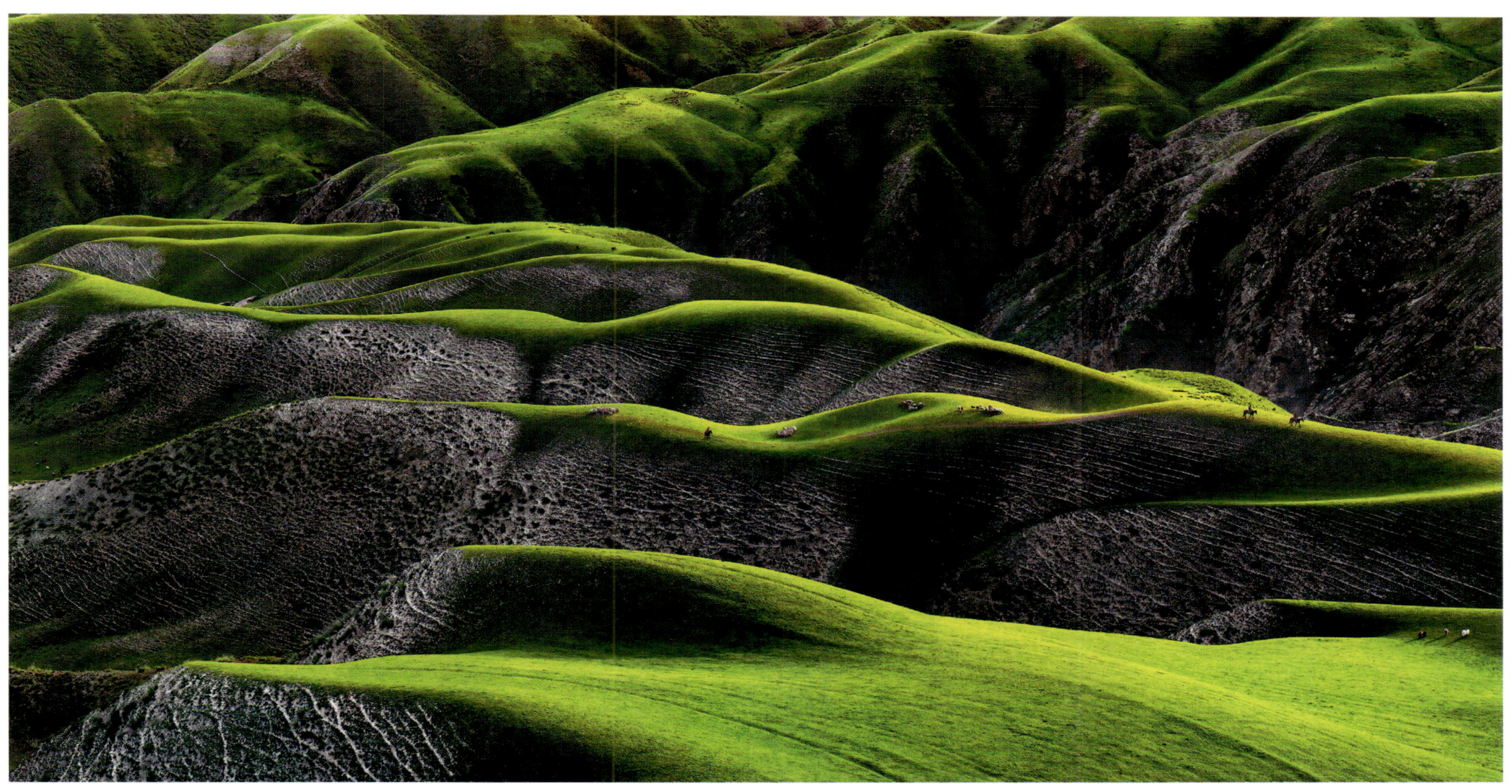

GRASSLAND OF HUMAN BODY CURVES

China is famous for its grasslands and Xinjiang has the most spectacular patterns I have ever seen. To capture this photograph, I had to fly five hours from Kunming in Yunnan province to Xinjiang province. I then rented a car and drove over 1,200 kilometers (745 miles), slept in a Mongolian tent, and waited until the light was just right. The life of a professional landscape photographer involves spending a lot of time on the road and making sacrifices to accomplish your dreams. When people look at a photograph, they just see the image, they have no idea of the journey and how complicated it can be to take a beautiful photograph. This image was made by stitching two photographs together.

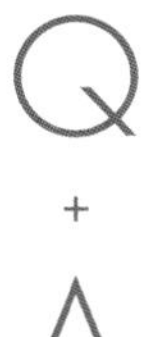

Q + A

Although you are a successful fashion and portrait photographer, you also spend much of your time shooting the landscapes of China—what is it about landscape photography that appeals to you so much?

I've lived in China for 10 years, and I come from a finance background—I was not originally a photographer. I left my job for one year to travel around China, and I bought a small camera, having never studied photography before, and one of my pictures was selected for *National Geographic*. I was thinking about making a change in my life, and trying photography for a couple of years, and I'm still here—I didn't go back to finance! When I started out, I did mainly portrait and fashion photography in studios—to understand lighting—and when my lighting skills were more or less what I needed, I branched out to landscape photography. Lighting in landscape is more challenging, because of the weather—you cannot control it. I love nature and landscape photography, but I'm very picky about what I shoot. When I started landscape photography, I had no idea, but step by step I built my portfolio. Landscape photography is always fascinating because it's always challenging, not just in terms of the photography, but also challenging in your life—you're always on the road and you're forced to make sacrifices. It's a completely different approach to working in a studio, but both have one thing in common—you need good lighting.

What fascinates you about the landscapes of China?

If you look at my portfolio, you'll understand! China is a huge country and the diversity of the landscape is so great. I now know China better than many Chinese, because I am always traveling. China is a very beautiful place, and so very different from everywhere else—I recently photographed a grassland landscape and it was very beautiful, and I'd never seen anywhere like this in the rest of the world. I have a lot of Chinese followers of my work now, and they contact me every day to tell me how they love their country more now because of my pictures. Until about three years ago, Chinese people never traveled in China—so this is very new for the Chinese. Now they see my pictures, they really want to go and see these places, so my work is helping people to see how beautiful the country is.

How do you create images with such dramatic mood and lighting?

I am very picky about some places, such as the rice fields—I'm a specialist in the rice fields, and I know the rice pickers well—I go there many, many times. Every place has different light and mood, and I will spend all the time I need there to capture exactly what I'm looking for in my image. I don't go there just for two or three days. When I go there I need to wait until I get exactly the image I'm thinking about. So sometimes I need to stay there a very long time until I get these images, and I have to go a lot of times. For some of my images, I kept going there for two years until I got the image I wanted. I always say that you always need three very important things for a good image: the first is a story in the picture, the second is the lighting or the mood, and the third is the composition, of course. There is also a fourth thing—and this is one you can never control—and that is luck. Luck for the landscape photographer is very important. I'm not always successful. It's like fishing— sometimes you come back and you have no fish!

What type of lighting do you tend to prefer when photographing landscapes?

I like mostly to have the light behind me, but I never like the light in front of me because of the flare, and many other issues. The nature is there, in front of you, it never changes. The only thing that changes every time you go is the mood, because the light is not the same. The mood is affected by the lighting, the sky, cloud, for example— every time is so different—so every time you need a different approach for your mental image, and you have to be very lucky. I imagine the photograph I want to create—there are so many different possible scenarios for the lighting—but I know what kind of mood I want for a place. I will stay there as long as I need to get this mood. Sometimes, unfortunately, I don't get it and I need to go back, but I will go back, and go back again, because one day, for sure, it will happen.

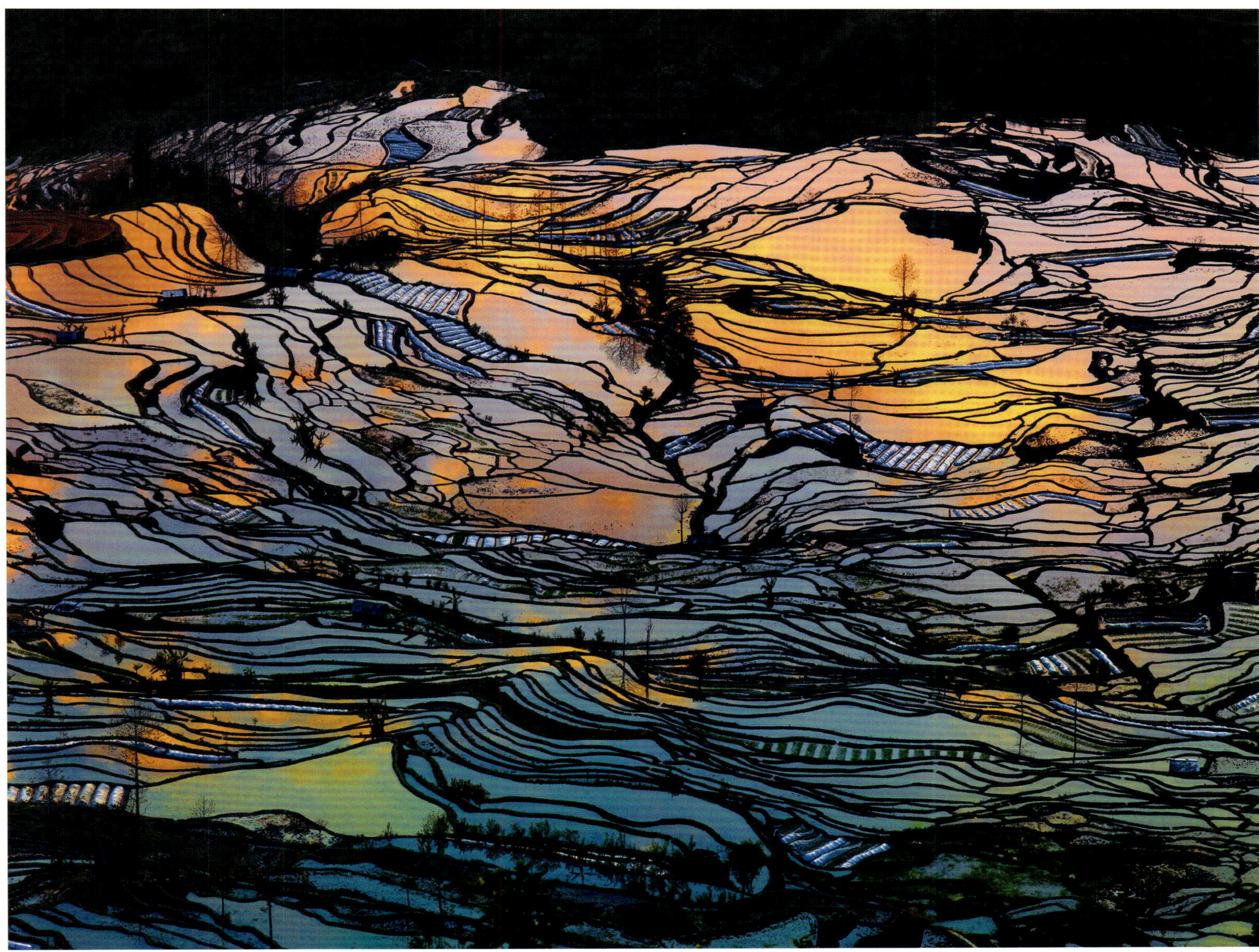

GOD'S PALETTE

The Yuanyang rice terraces in the Ailao Mountains of the Yunnan province are some of the largest in the whole of China. I took this photograph at the end of the day, just before sunset. The sky was full of clouds and the reflections on the water created the most amazing patterns and sense of warmth. This area is important to me as I live in Yunnan province and hold a photography workshop at the fields each year. Some of my earliest photographs of these terraces were published by *National Geographic* in 2010, and it inspired me to become a landscape photographer. This image won numerous awards and is one of my most iconic images of the landscape of China.

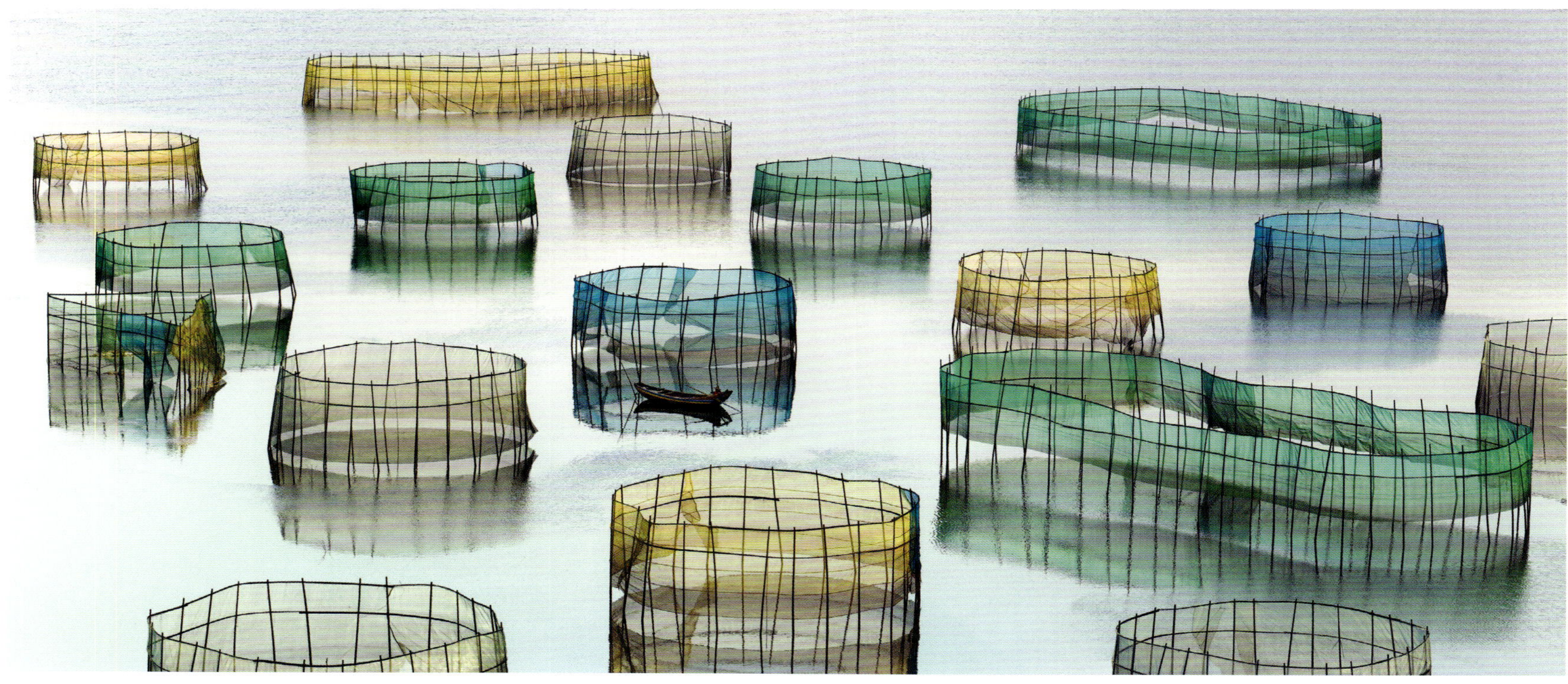

PASTEL FLOATING DREAM

Xiapu is a small fishing village in the Fujian province. These nets are used for farming crabs and lobsters. I took this photograph at the end of the afternoon, while a local fisherman was resting inside his boat. The reflection of the blue net almost makes it look like the boat is caught in its own net. I decided to create this panoramic photograph by stitching three images together to retain definition and ensure a quality final image. I am not keen on using a wide-angle lens for this type of shot as it can create distortion.

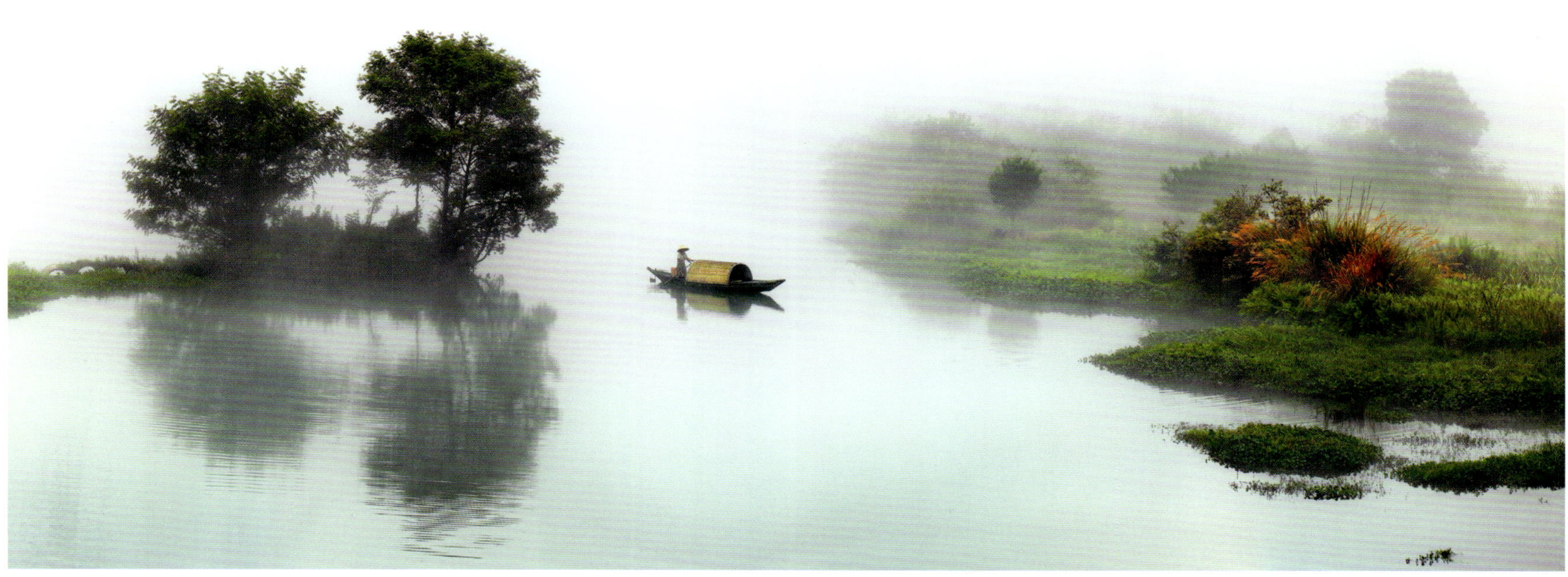

PASTORALE SCENERY

This photograph is full of atmosphere and has the feeling of a traditional Chinese painting. After climbing to the roof of a nearby house to see what the view was like from higher up, I saw this small patch of water that I wanted to shoot. At the time, there was no-one on the river, but always confident, I was hoping for something and prepared my camera. Then, as I was waiting, a boat quietly appeared from the mist. Moving from left to right, the boat stopped at the bank by the tree, and then, while smoking a cigarette, the fisherman guided the boat into the middle of the water. I captured the shot the way it is and I was happy to have achieved the image I was expecting in my mind. Some days you are just lucky.

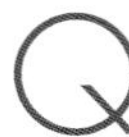

Q + A

How do you tell a story through your photography?

First of all, I go to check the best angle for my shot, so I think about what kind of story I want to tell. For example, when you see the rice fields, they're so big, so that's one story I want to tell about those places. Or an image can be of nature by itself, or maybe there are some people walking in the landscape—for instance, if someone is walking with his cow across the rice field, with a beautiful sunrise behind, that tells a story. Different parts of your landscape tell a different story, so you have to choose which story you wish to tell, and what your image is going to mean to people. It's not just about the light—it's also the meaning. For example, with one image I took, there's a large landscape, but if you look very carefully, you can see people with their horses walking across it. So there's the big landscape, the people, and the light, and there's your story.

Do you have a preferred lens for landscape photography?

I never really use wide-angle lenses for many reasons, such as distortion. My way of working is usually to take a long lens and take several pictures, and stitch them together to produce the same field of view as a wide angle, but with much better definition of the scene. I shoot with a medium-format Phase One camera and my favorite lens is a 150mm Phase One lens.

How important is post-processing in your work?

Post-processing is very important for this reason—a camera cannot see contrast, color, or three dimensions. All camera meters are set up to see 18 percent gray, which means you need to do some post-processing to readjust the contrast and color. I never do high-dynamic-range (HDR) photography, because I don't like it—I never try to make the pictures look surreal in Photoshop. I prefer to use ND filters when I shoot. Some people ask me why, because you can use Photoshop, but the most important thing for me is to try to capture the image in the most correct way from the outset. I will use a polarizer, sometimes a Big Stopper filter, or natural ND, to be sure I can capture the picture in-camera in the right way. I will just use Capture One and Photoshop to adjust the contrast and color, and maybe to clean up the image a little. But I don't like to do any special effects, adding elements that weren't there. It's very important to me to make sure that what I saw and the picture are the same. I just use post-processing to correct the imperfections of the camera.

What single piece of equipment is most useful in your work?

My tripod is the most important thing. It's like if you don't have legs, you cannot walk! I'm very, very picky with my tripod—mine is from Really Right Stuff, with an Arca Swiss C1 head—because my camera needs a very steady platform. I pay attention to every detail to make sure my picture is very sharp, and not affected by the wind. A tiny breeze can make a big difference to my image. But a picture is not made with a camera—it's made with your story, your past, your personality, and the camera is five percent of an image, the rest is inside me.

TECHNICAL INFORMATION

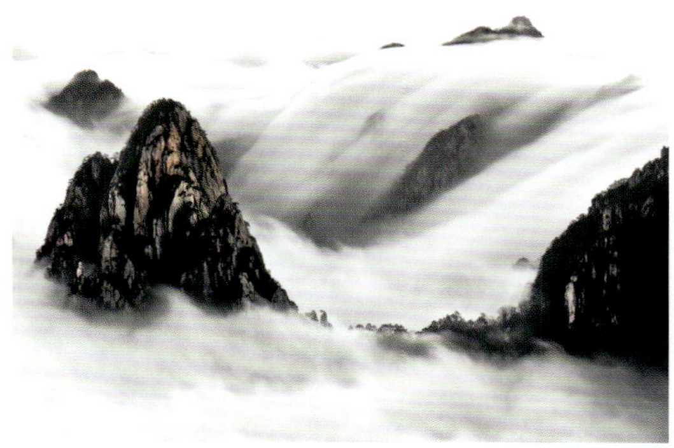

CLOUDLAND
MOUNT HUANGSHAN, ANHUI, CHINA

Camera: Phase One IQ280
Lens/Focal length: Schneider Kreuznach 80mm f/2.8
Aperture: f/14
Shutter speed: 3 sec.
ISO: 50

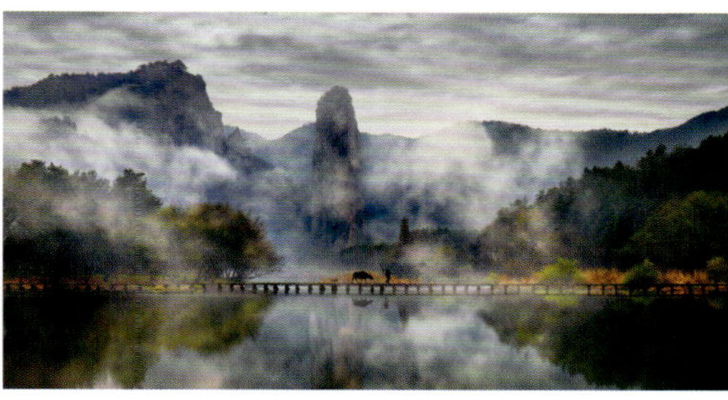

FAIRY LAND OF ZHEJIANG
ZHEJIANG, CHINA

Camera: Phase One IQ280
Lens/Focal length: Schneider Kreuznach 110mm f/2.8
Aperture: f/11
Shutter speed: 0.5 sec.
ISO: 100

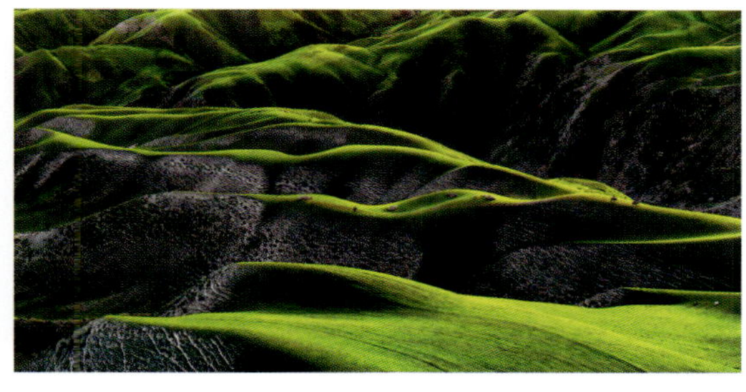

GRASSLAND OF HUMAN BODY CURVES
XINJIANG, CHINA

Camera: Phase One IQ280
Lens/Focal length: Schneider Kreuznach 150mm f/2.8
Aperture: f/11
Shutter speed: 1/60 sec.
ISO: 100
Kit: Polarizing filter

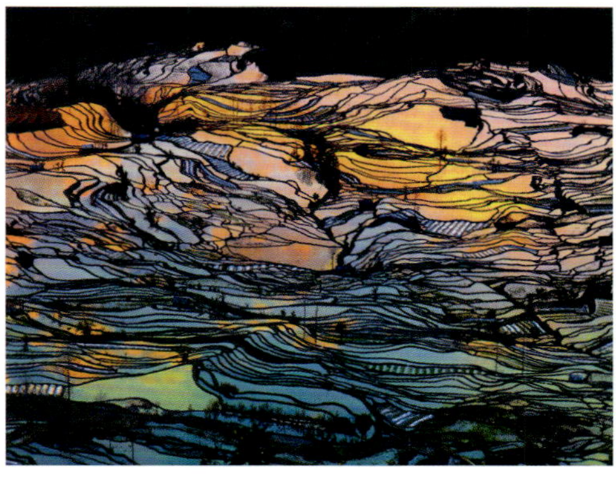

GOD'S PALETTE
YUANYANG, YUNNAN, CHINA

Camera: Phase One IQ280
Lens/Focal length: Schneider Kreuznach 240mm f/4.5
Aperture: f/12
Shutter speed: 1/6 sec.
ISO: 35
Kit: Polarizing filter

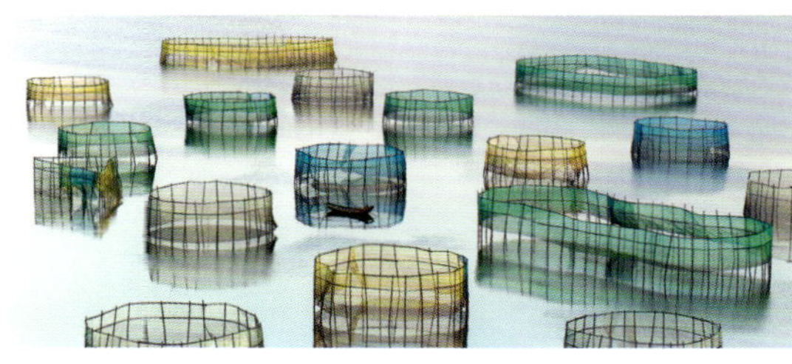

PASTEL FLOATING DREAM
XIAPU, FJJIAN, CHINA

Camera: Phase One IQ280
Lens/Focal length: Schneider Kreuznach 55mm f/2.8
Aperture: f/11
Shutter speed: 1/50 sec.
ISO: 50
Kit: Polarizing filter

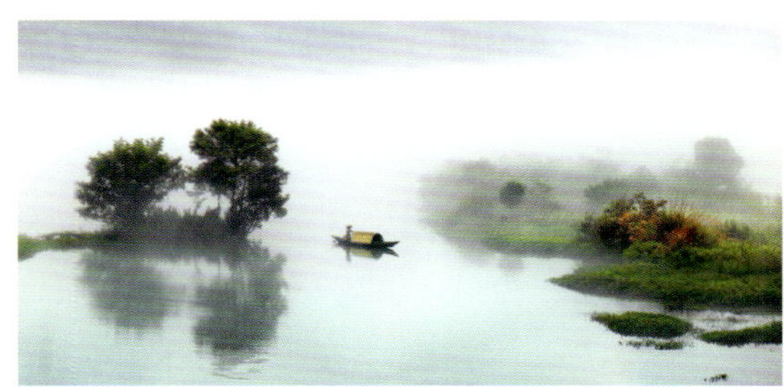

PASTORALE SCENERY
CHINA

Camera: Phase One IQ280
Lens/Focal length: Schneider Kreuznach 240mm f/4.5
Aperture: f/11
Shutter speed: 1/20 sec.
ISO: 100
Kit: Polarizing filter

TOM MACKIE

Tom Mackie is recognized as one of the world's finest landscape photographers, with his affinity for light, perspective, and color being the hallmark that has established his name internationally. A photographer all his working life, Tom began his career with a five-year stint as an industrial and architectural photographer in Los Angeles, fresh from gaining his degree in commercial photography. Traveling extensively through the vast, cinemascope terrain of the western states in America during this period ignited a lifelong passion for landscapes, and he realized the confines of a commercial studio were no longer going to be enough.

In 1985 he moved from his native US to the UK to pursue a full-time career as a landscape photographer, and rapidly made his name with calendars, books, and magazine work for a wide range of clients. Architectural and travel commissions added to his repertoire, with accolades from The British Institute of Professional Photographers, the Ilford Awards, and the Business Calendar Awards, and inclusion in *The World's Top Photographers: Landscape,* published by RotoVision.

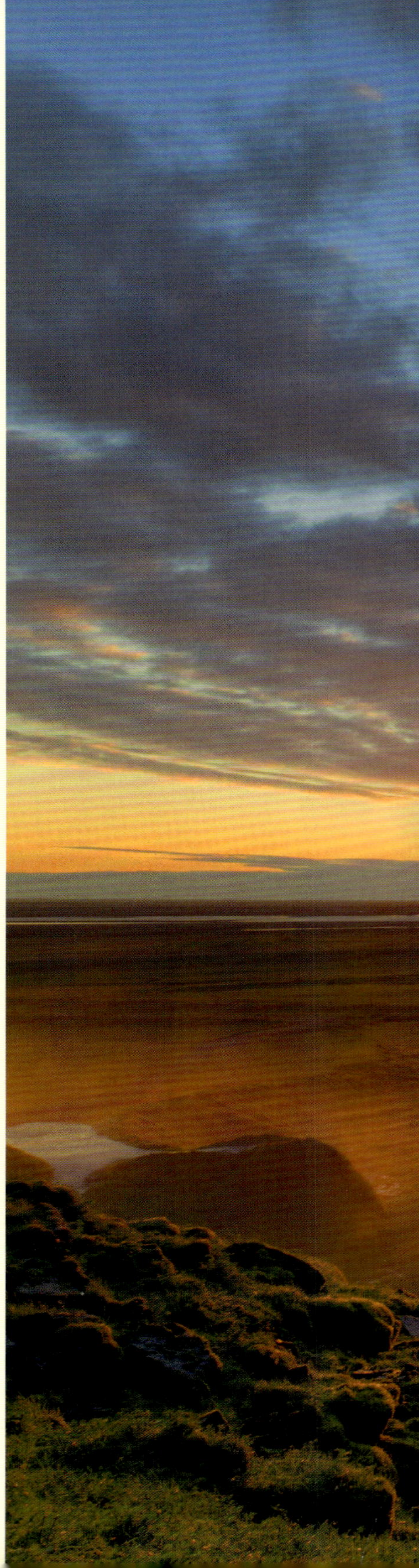

SELJALANDSFOSS WATERFALL AT SUNSET

In the winter of 2010, I visited Iceland for the first time. It was so amazing that I went back that summer to capture the midnight sun. Seljalandsfoss waterfall is an ideal location, as the position of the sun sets behind the falls at this time of year. The exposure range was too great, so I made six exposures with 1-stop increments. I combined the exposures in Photomatix Pro HDR software.

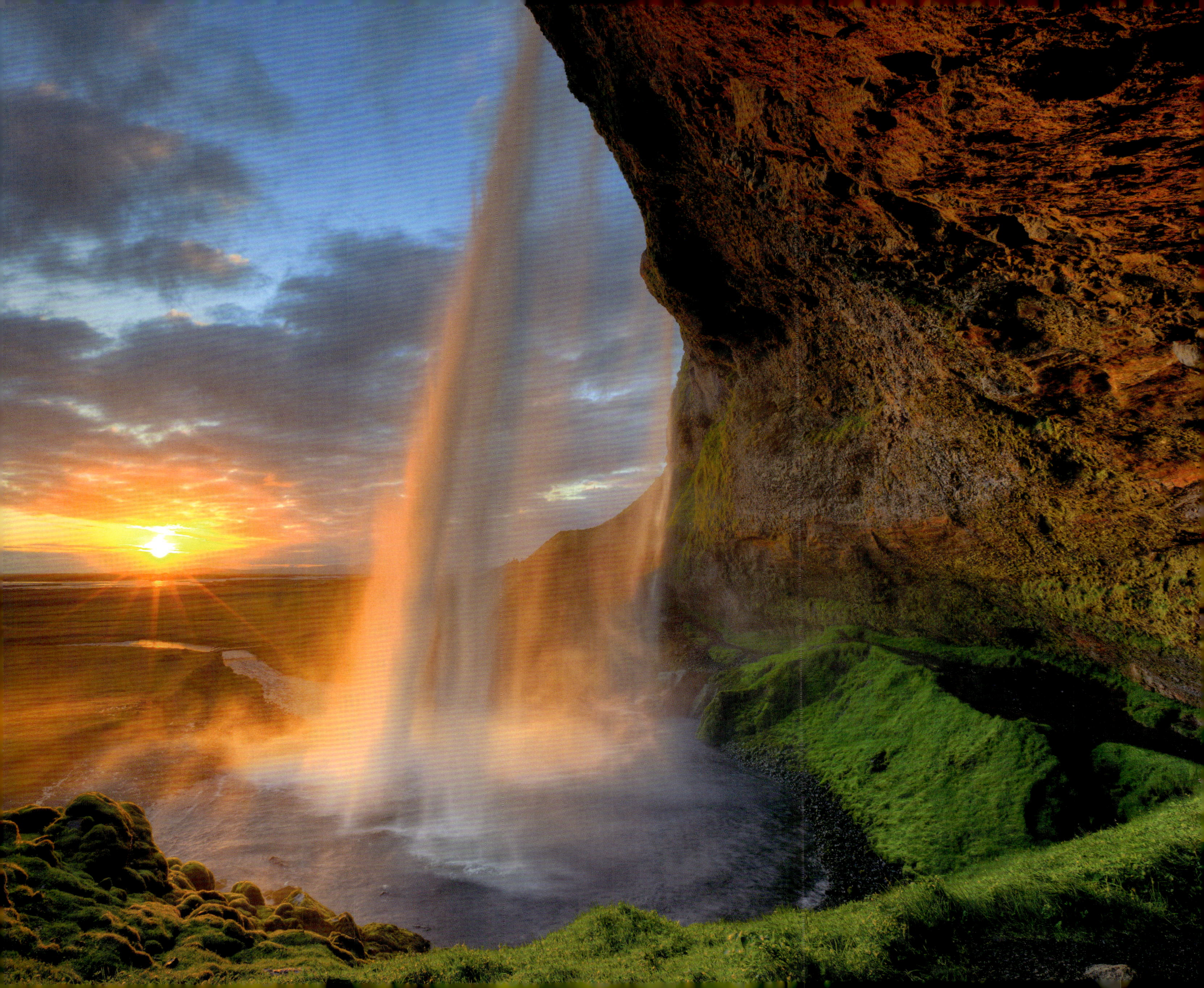

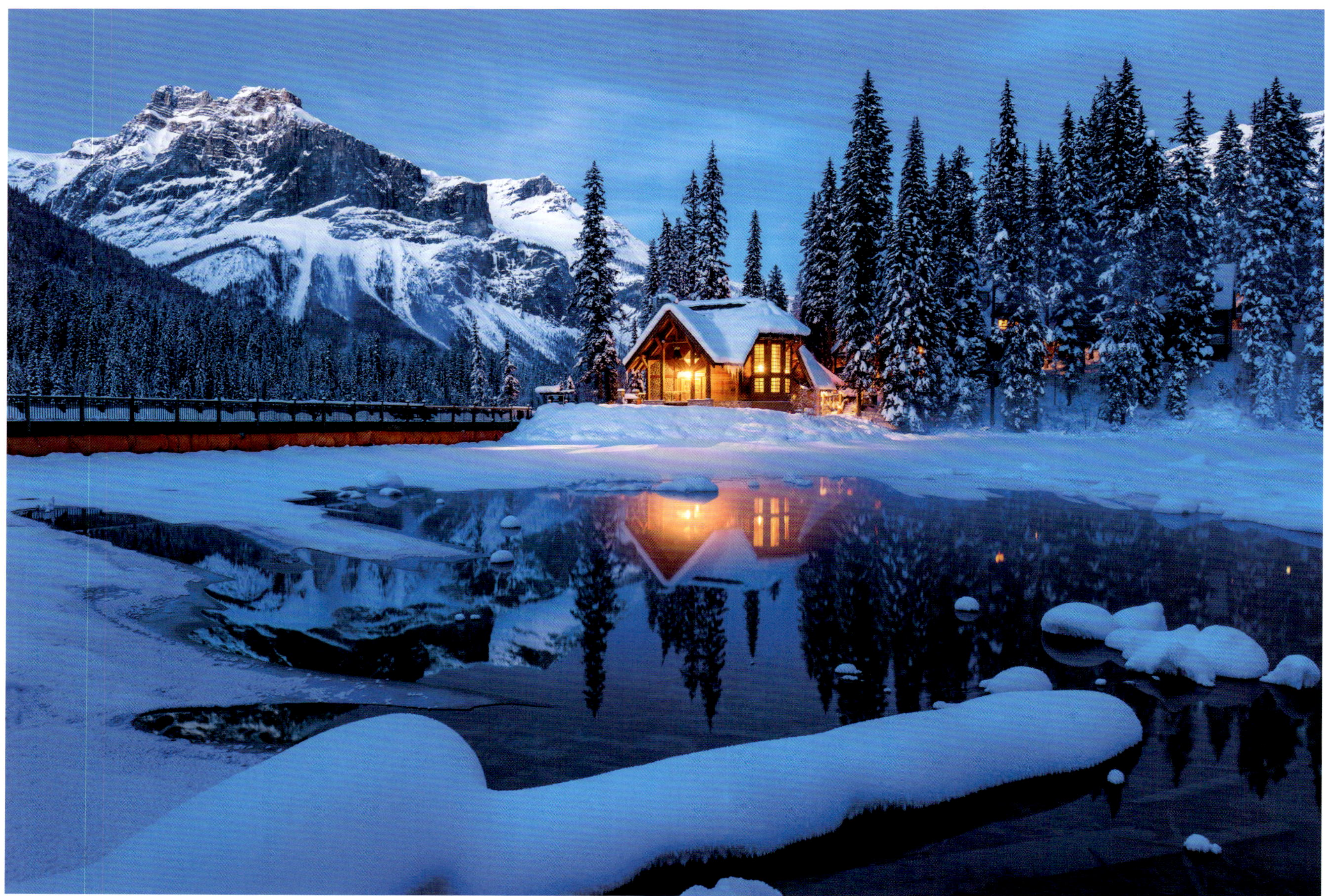

CHALET REFLECTIONS AT TWILIGHT

The "blue hour" is a perfect time to create a color contrast between the cool blue tones of twilight and any illuminations within the scene. I broke the traditional rules of composition by placing the chalet in the center of the frame, because the combination of the snow-covered log in the foreground as a leading line, the sweeping lines of partially frozen ice, the mountain, and vertical lines of trees all help to create a circular composition around the chalet. It conveys the feeling of warmth and security against −31°F (−35°C) outside. It's very reminiscent of the American artist, Thomas Kinkade.

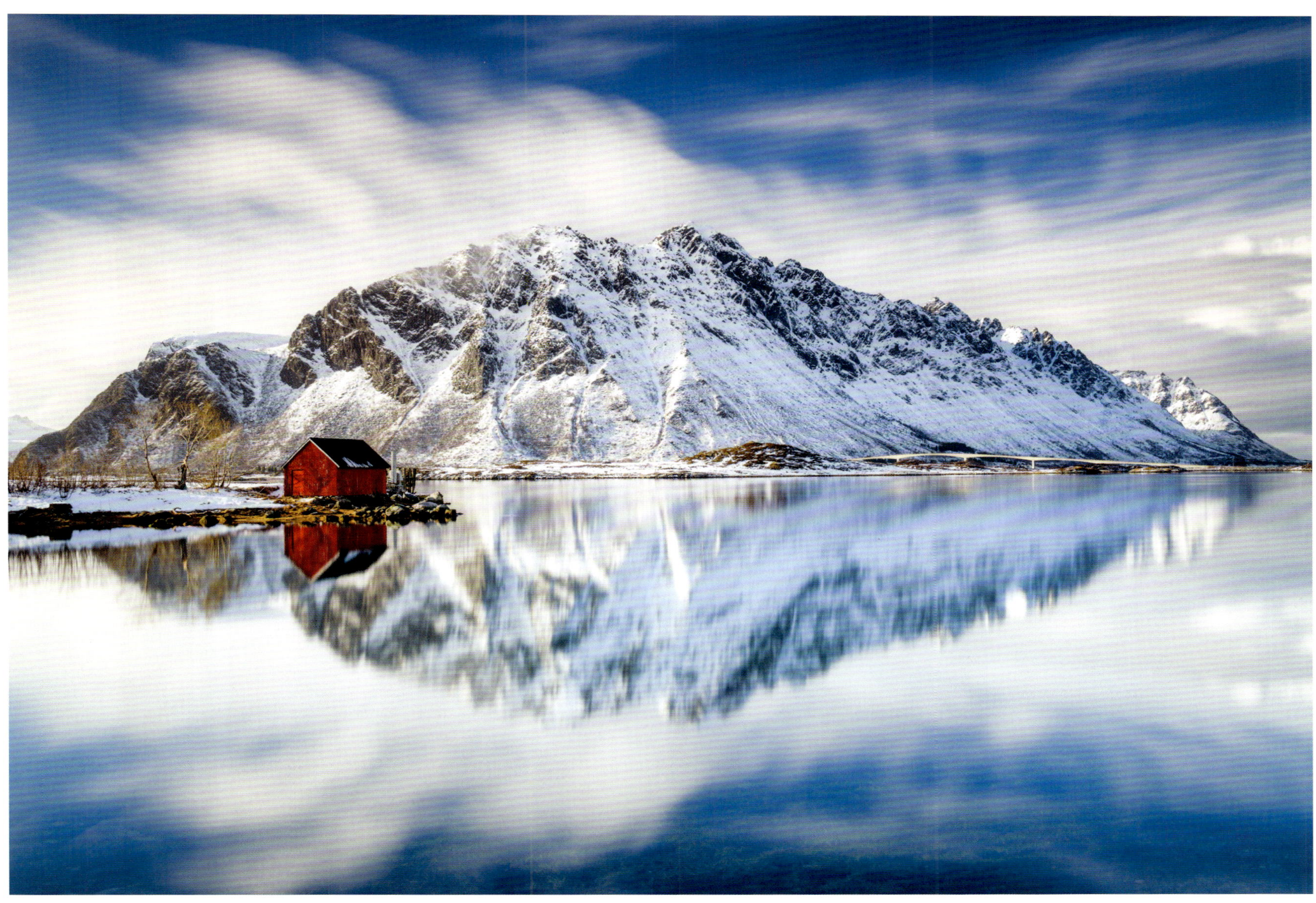

SVARTTINDEN MOUNTAIN REFLECTIONS

I've been going to the Lofoten Islands for the past five years to lead workshops. It's an amazing location that always produces new images as a result of the changing weather patterns. Winter landscapes, in general, tend to have a limited range of color, with white snow and blue skies, so the inclusion of this red boathouse provides spot color. I used a Lee Big Stopper 10-stop ND filter to smooth out the water, improving the reflections and getting some movement in the clouds.

Q

+

A

Do you often make multiple visits before a successful shoot?

I usually try to visit a location before I intend to photograph it, in order to better understand the layout of the landscape and determine the best time for the light. Even though I use various apps and devices to provide location information, there might be an obstacle that would block the light or create distracting shadows. I will also look for potential compositions at that time, so I don't waste time when the light is at its best. There is a lot of planning that goes into a shoot, so I have a good understanding of the location before I arrive, but, ultimately, I'm still reliant on Mother Nature, so it often takes several visits before I get the right conditions. There are times when I've done my homework, read the weather conditions, and turned up for the first time to capture some incredible images. It's great when a plan comes together, but usually I make several visits.

How do you create an image with impact—what do you look for?

I prefer images that are straightforward and uncluttered. I always find myself searching for strong graphic elements that I can focus on within a scene. Too many elements within the picture frame confuse the viewer as to the photographer's intention, and dilute the overall impact of the image. What I look for are elements that constitute essential character and mood. Line and color are the two basic components that make up a picture. Lines are the building blocks of an image, but it's color that sets the mood. Together, these are the elements that I look for in recognizing potential compositions. Whether it's repetitive patterns, striking colors, or exciting forms and graphic shapes that attract me to make photographs, I usually won't stop with the first image, but continue refining it, either by changing the angle slightly or coming in even closer. Finally, timing often plays an important part in creating an image that has impact. It can be a matter of a split second when the elements in the frame come together, such as a leading line of a wave on a sandy beach, waiting for the right clouds to drift into the right position, or getting that sunburst as the sun breaks the horizon.

What attention do you give to color choices in a scene—for instance, do some color combinations have particular impact?

Color is a factor of major creative importance in my work. As well as delighting the eye, color can define form, set a mood, and evoke emotion. Whereas black-and-white photography has to rely on tonality and composition to get a message across, color introduces a more direct response. If you have a good understanding of the color wheel, it will enable you to choose colors that work together to create either contrasting or harmonious color combinations. I recently photographed the super bloom in the deserts of California, which happens every 10 years, on average. There were a variety of color combinations that I was working with, but the orange California poppies against a deep blue saturated sky had the most impact. Colors that are opposite on the color wheel will work the best in creating strong color impact, and there are three color combinations that often occur in landscapes—red/blue, red/green, and blue/orange. By using colors consciously, you can change how the perspective appears in an image. Warm shades of red, yellow, and orange advance in the picture frame, for example, while cool shades of blue, green, and cyan recede. Using saturated warm and cold colors together gives bold contrast in an image.

Are there some directions or angles of light that work better for enhancing color within the landscape?

Most definitely—side lighting is my particular favorite, because of its capacity to emphasize contours, textures, and shapes. As the light is at a right angle to the subject, it allows for maximum polarization as well, which increases color saturation and makes the image "pop." It helps to add dimension to the subject by making it stand out from the background, as in the image of the Wanaka tree. If this same scene were lit from the front, it would appear flat and the colors would be much more muted. Backlighting is used to emphasize shape but can also be used to enhance the color of a subject, such as golden fall leaves against a blue sky. It will make the color of any translucent subject stand out, especially if the subject is situated against a dark background. The difficulty with backlit subjects is controlling flare if the sun shines into the lens. I try to place the sun directly behind the subject or shield the lens with my hand if a lens hood doesn't cope with the angle. The other issue is achieving a correct exposure. With the subject illuminated by the bright light source, the meter will underexpose the image. I use the exposure compensation dial, starting with plus 1 stop to bring the exposure back to where the colors look vibrant.

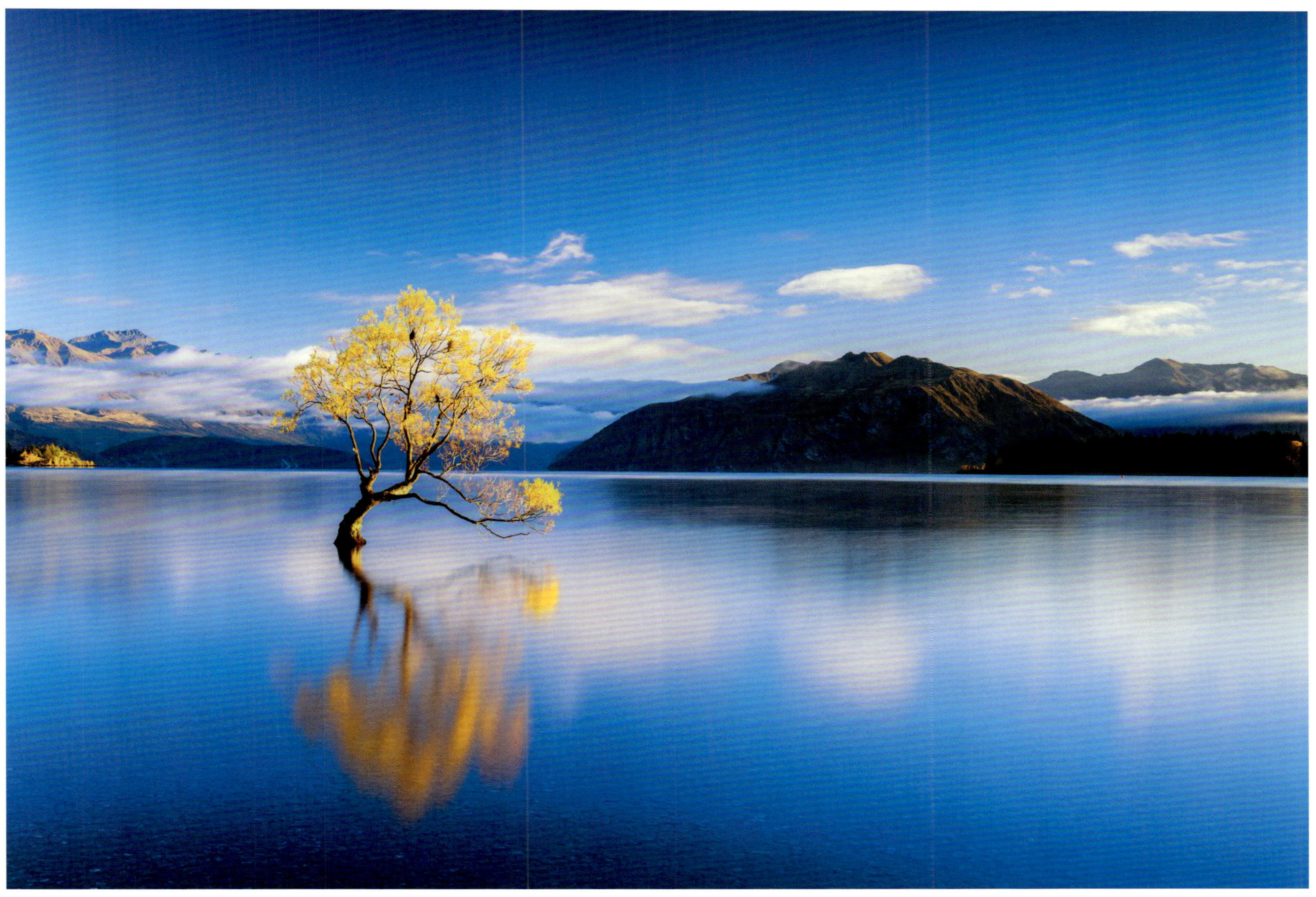

WANAKA TREE IN AUTUMN

During my first trip to New Zealand, I went to Wanaka to see "that tree" to find out what all the fuss was about. The clearing storm gave way to a pink sky at sunset, but I felt this type of light didn't accomplish the full potential of the golden fall leaves of the tree. I calculated the sun would rise 90 degrees to the tree, providing beautiful side lighting that would enhance the yellow leaves against the blue sky. I used a polarizing filter to complete the image by increasing the saturation and emphasizing the color contrast between the blue and yellow, along with a Lee Big Stopper ND filter to smooth out the surface of the water.

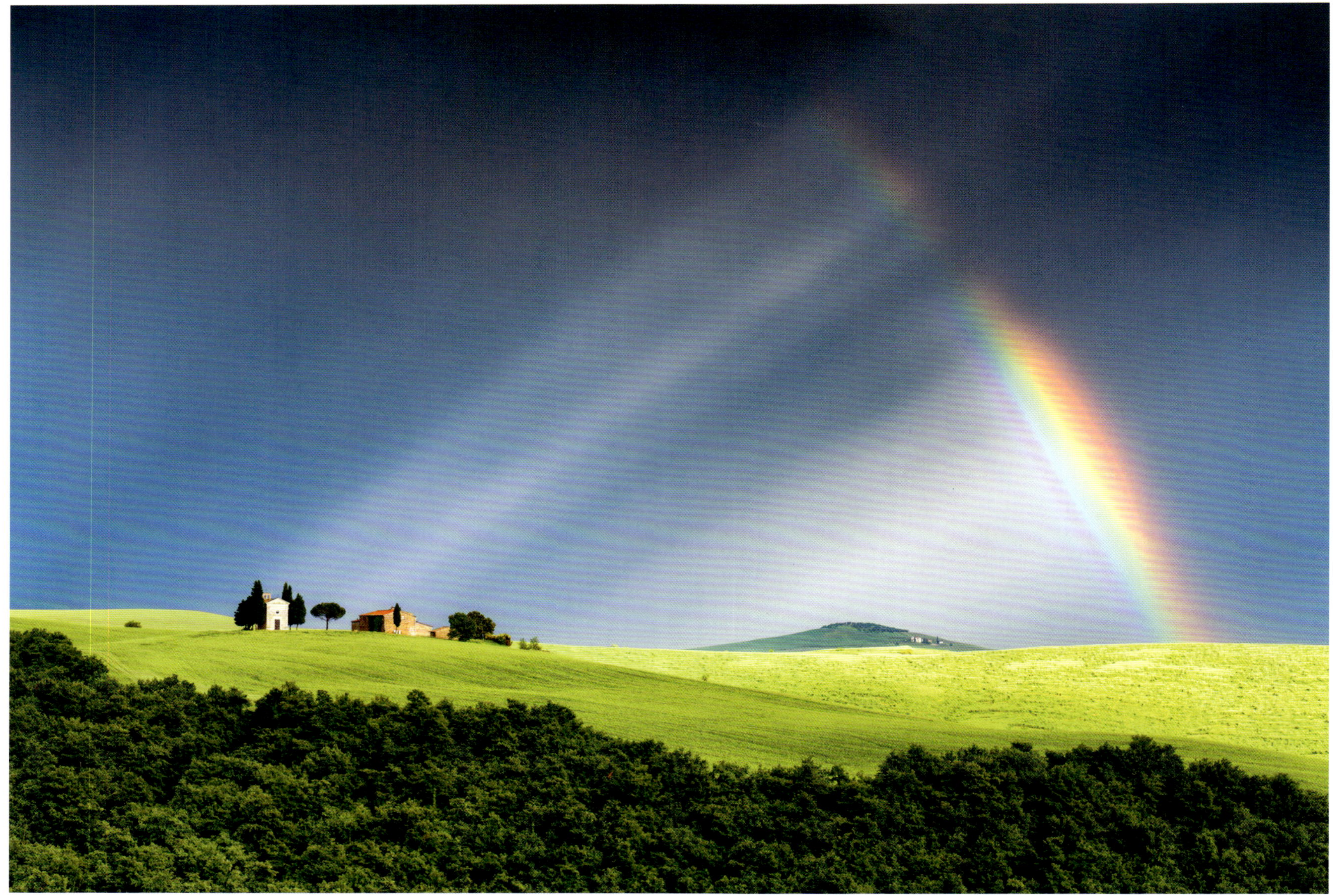

FRAGMENTED RAINBOW AND LIGHT RAYS OVER CHAPEL MADONNA DI VITALETA

We had rainbows two consecutive days during my Tuscany workshop, and, on the third day, the conditions were also favorable, with dark, gray skies. We decided to wait across from the chapel on the hill to see if it would happen again. After waiting for half an hour, I could see cumulus clouds forming in the west, which is a sign of changing weather patterns. We set up our cameras on the tripods and within minutes a double rainbow appeared. I composed the chapel on the third of the frame with a section of the rainbow on the left. Then something I'd never seen before happened—the rainbow fractured into sections with light rays tracking across the landscape toward the chapel.

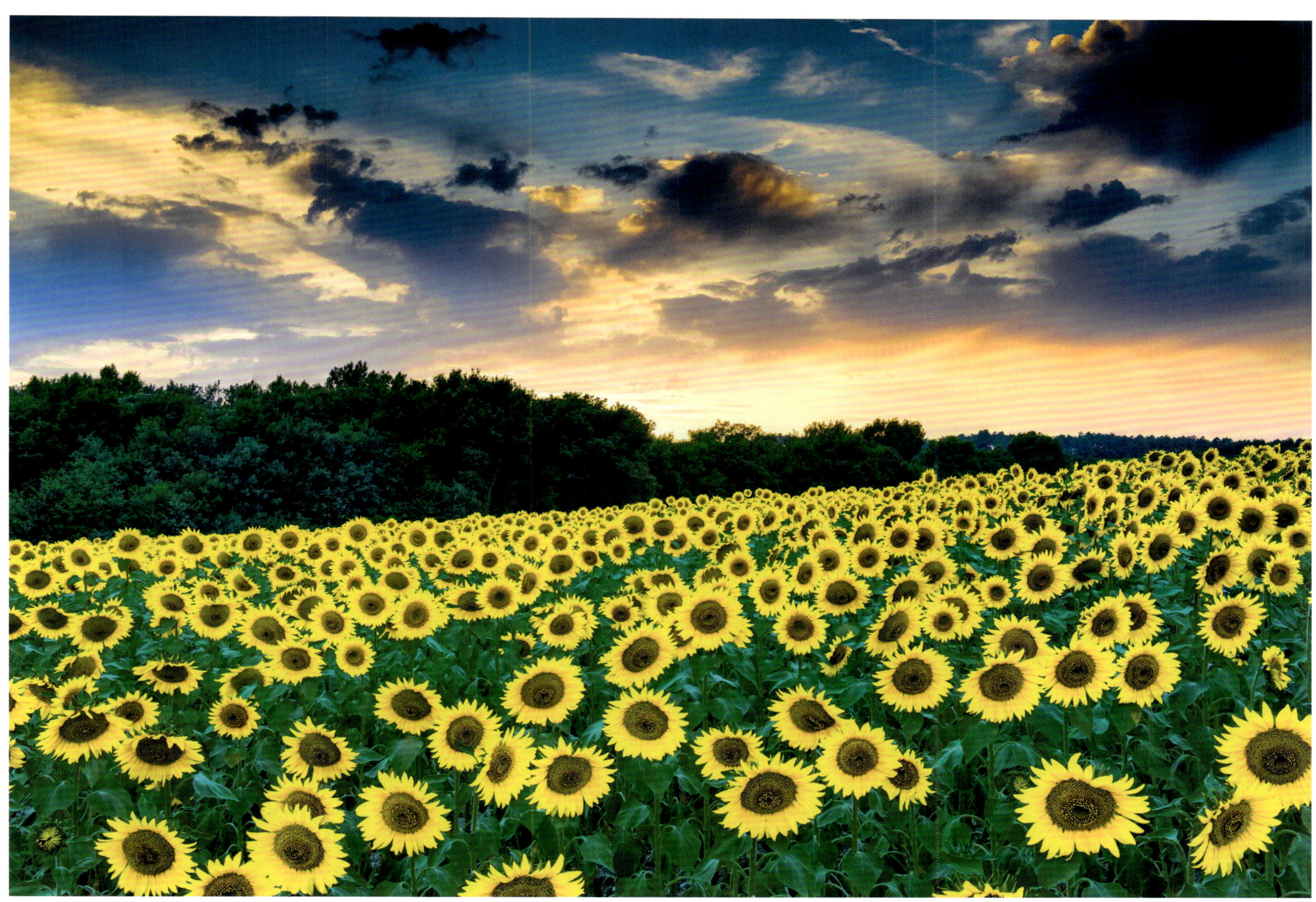

FIELD OF SUNFLOWERS AT SUNSET

During my annual workshop in Provence in France, I was showing the group how to use ND grad filters to balance the exposure between the sky and foreground. I used a Lee 1.2 ND hard grad filter over the sky to maintain the bright sunset and correctly expose the tone of the foreground. For an added challenge, I used the optimal exposure of f/8 for critical sharpness, making six exposures at different focus points.I combined the exposures using Zerene Stacker software, which has a great tool to correct moving objects such as the slight movement of the sunflowers.

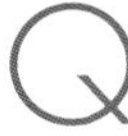 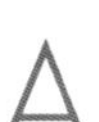

Q + A

You've now been a leading landscape photographer for a couple of decades—how important is it to master a range of skills other than photography itself, in order to be successful?

It's not enough to be a good photographer, especially with technology today—there are so many good photographers out there. To be successful, you have to build a brand by every means possible. Marketing is essential to make people aware of your work, and I do this by writing books, writing articles for magazines, having a good e-commerce website, running workshops, giving talks, using social media, and making sure that my published work is always credited. I often get new clients where they have seen my work published in magazines, calendars, and posters. I'm affiliated with equipment manufacturers, such as Lee Filters, Lowepro camera bags, and Gitzo tripods, which helps to make their client bases aware of my work. Like any other creative profession, it's easy to forget that it's also a business and has a value. There are so many photographers willing to give their work away for free in hope of getting published or further paid work. Do you think a client will want to pay a photographer that gives his or her work away for free? I've always been willing to walk away from a sale if the fee is too low. You have to have a bottom line that you don't go under.

Do you still use physical filters, such as a polarizer or neutral-density (ND) filters, in your photography?

As I mentioned, I'm affiliated with Lee Filters and use the ND grads, landscape polarizer, and ND filters all the time in my work. I don't like to spend a lot of time behind the computer, working up images, so I try to get the image the way I want it at the time of capture, if possible. If I had to use only one filter, it would be a polarizer as it really helps to remove reflections from foliage, increase color saturation, and make clouds pop out against a deep blue sky. I love the effect that the ND filters, Little Stopper, Big Stopper, and Super Stopper can achieve with moving clouds, smoothing out water to improve reflections, and creating motion blur in moving subjects such as flowers.

What enhancement, if any, do you do in post-processing?

When I shot film, I loved the color saturation of Fuji Velvia. I try to re-create the same look in my digital work, but with the advantage of a wider exposure range. I've created a preset that comes close to the look of Velvia, though some colors are still not as vibrant. I have a workflow that works for me, doing my RAW conversions in Lightroom, applying my preset, and then making adjustments as needed. Oddly enough, I don't overdo the saturation slider, setting it at no more than 7. I can be more liberal with the vibrance slider, setting it at about 30, as it only affects the unsaturated pixels. Then I do any major retouching work in Photoshop, finishing off the image using the Nik collection. In Color Efex Pro, I mainly use the Pro Contrast and Skylight filters. I'm amazed at how the Pro Contrast filter can give an image that extra lift to make it stand out. To achieve images that have a strong color presence, the primary method, first and foremost, is to have a good understanding of light and how it affects the color in the subject. If you don't capture the colors correctly, it will look too obvious. Remember the saying, "garbage in, garbage out." Getting it right in the field makes it easier to enhance the image in post-processing.

What piece of equipment, software, or skill is most useful in your work?

The ability to see images—without this, I wouldn't have a career. As photographers, we all see things differently. Put a dozen photographers in the same location and, chances are, it will result in 12 different images. It's something that we tend to take for granted, but it defines each of us as photographers. During one of my workshops, I was photographing next to one of my participants. We were on a narrow footpath overlooking a river in fall, so there wasn't much room for moving our camera positions. Our compositions were completely different. When we compared the two, he could see why I placed elements where I did, making it a stronger composition. I'm probably a bit liable to obsessive-compulsive disorder, as I'm always looking and organizing scenes in my eye. If something feels out of place to me, I'll move it or change my position so the composition works the way I want it to. But if I have to choose a piece of kit, it would be Adobe Lightroom. I don't consider myself to be an equipment junkie, and I certainly don't like using complex software, but since using Adobe Lightroom for my workflow it has made RAW conversion and organizing my images so much easier. It's very intuitive and has to be the best photographic software for photographers.

TECHNICAL INFORMATION

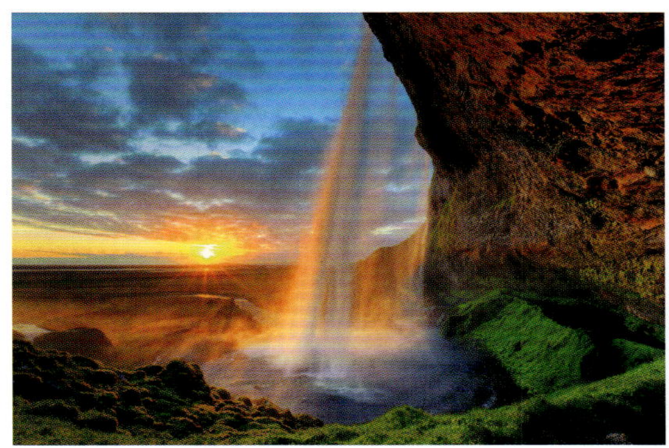

SELJALANDSFOSS WATERFALL AT SUNSET
ICELAND

Camera: Canon EOS 5D Mark II
Lens/Focal length: Canon 16–35mm f/2.8 at 16mm
Aperture: f/13
Shutter speed: High-dynamic-range composite of six exposures
ISO: 100
Kit: Tripod

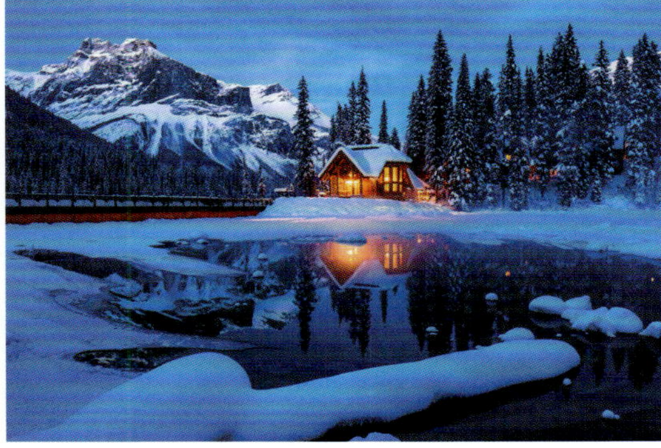

CHALET REFLECTIONS AT TWILIGHT
EMERALD LAKE, YOHO NATIONAL PARK,
BRITISH COLUMBIA, CANADA

Camera: Nikon D810
Lens/Focal length: Nikkor 24–70mm f/2.8 at 24mm
Aperture: f/8
Shutter speed: 20 sec.
ISO: 400
Kit: Tripod

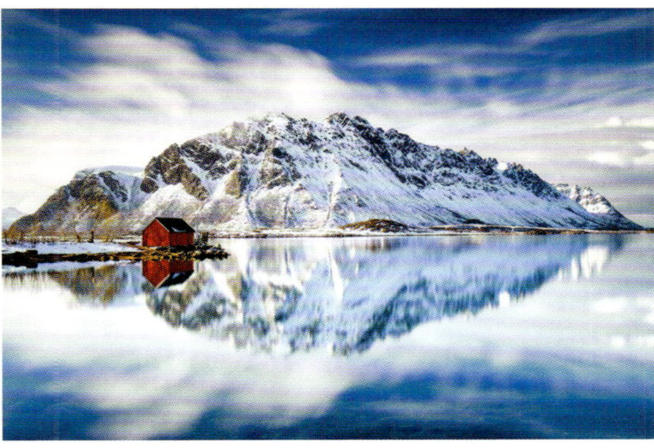

SVARTTINDEN MOUNTAIN REFLECTIONS
LOFOTEN ISLANDS,
NORWAY

Camera: Nikon D810
Lens/Focal length: Nikkor 24–70mm f/2.8 at 35mm
Aperture: f/8
Shutter speed: 45 sec.
ISO: 100
Kit: Tripod, Big Stopper ND filter

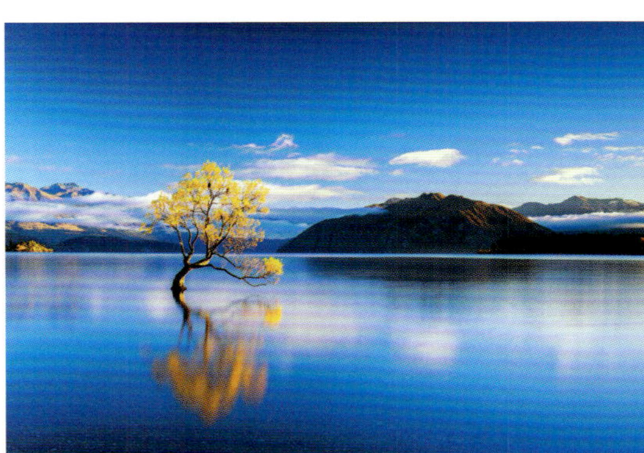

WANAKA TREE IN AUTUMN
WANAKA,
NEW ZEALAND

Camera: Nikon D810
Lens/Focal length: Nikon 24–70mm f/2.8 at 40mm
Aperture: f/8
Shutter speed: 45 sec.
ISO: 100
Kit: Tripod, polarizing and Big Stopper ND filters

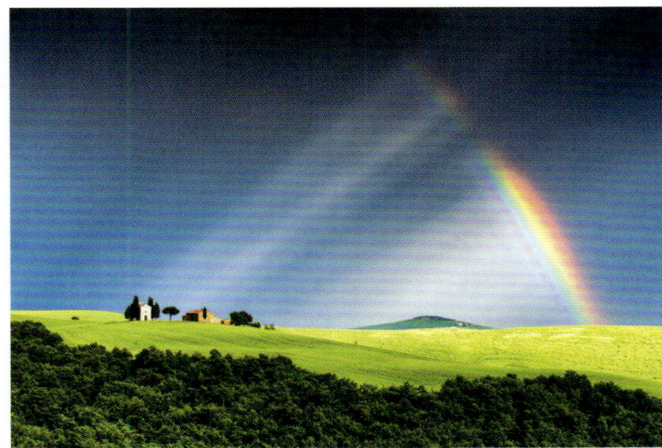

FRAGMENTED RAINBOW AND LIGHT RAYS
OVER CHAPEL MADONNA DI VITALETA
TUSCANY, ITALY

Camera: Nikon D810
Lens/Focal length: Nikon 24–70mm f/2.8 at 70mm
Aperture: f/8
Shutter speed: 1/15 sec.
ISO: 100
Kit: Tripod, polarizing filter

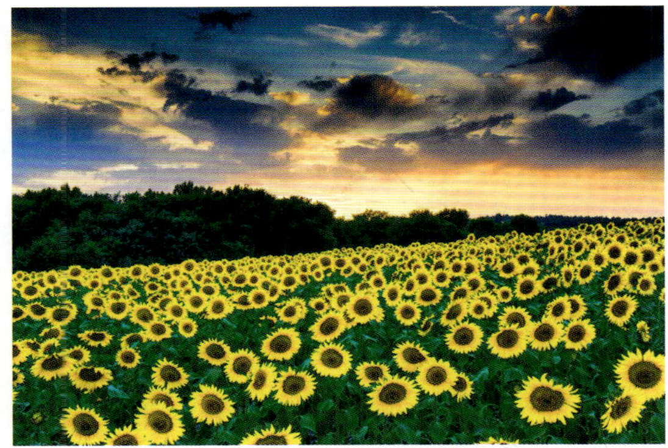

FIELD OF SUNFLOWERS AT SUNSET
PROVENCE,
FRANCE

Camera: Nikon D810
Lens/Focal length: Nikon 24–70mm f/2.8 at 38mm
Aperture: f/8
Shutter speed: 1/3 sec.
ISO: 100
Kit: Tripod, 1.2 ND hard grad filter, composite of six focus-stacked images

VALDA BAILEY

Valda Bailey is a freelance photographer living in Sussex and first became passionate about photography when she was 14. Valda's approach to photography is greatly informed by her background in art—she came back to photography after years of painting, and never quite being able to make the marks on the canvas that she saw in her head. Valda explains that her influences come as much from artists as photographers. She is largely motivated by color and form, and the tension and dynamism that these components can bring to an image.

Valda's objective is to portray an interpretation of a scene rather than a literal representation. She makes her images using camera movement and multiple exposures—two techniques that help to create abstract shapes and blur extraneous detail. Although this approach is controllable to a certain degree, there remains a great element of chance and Valda finds that this delights and frustrates in equal measure. She explains that it is certainly not prescriptive in the way conventional landscape photography is with regard to f-stops and shutter speeds, and so on, and so it's a way of making images that is certainly not for everyone. But Valda finds it rewards a curiosity and a willingness to "play" with the camera.

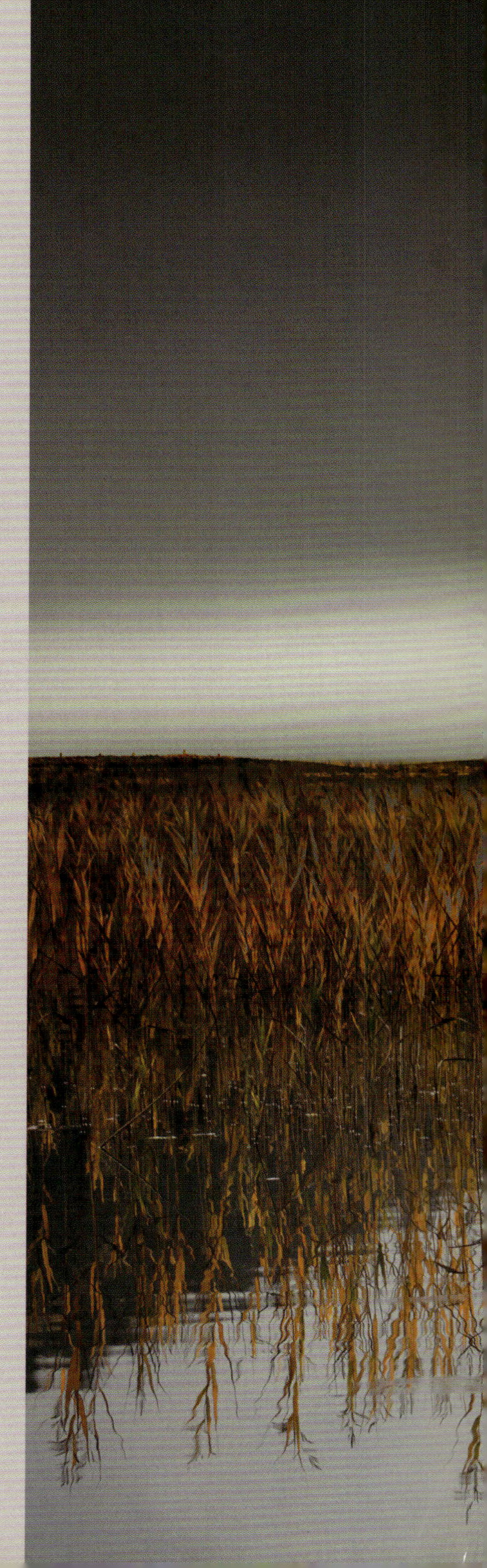

APPROACHING LINDISFARNE

I love the castle and Northumberland skyline, and it's a view I have photographed many times. I was mainly interested in the incoming weather front and the strong lines present in the landscape. The blend modes in my camera allowed me to create shapes and abstract detail. The sky has cut into the castle and distorted the form and solidity. The foreground was cluttered, so I turned my camera around and overlaid some grasses on top of the distracting detritus at the edge of the water.

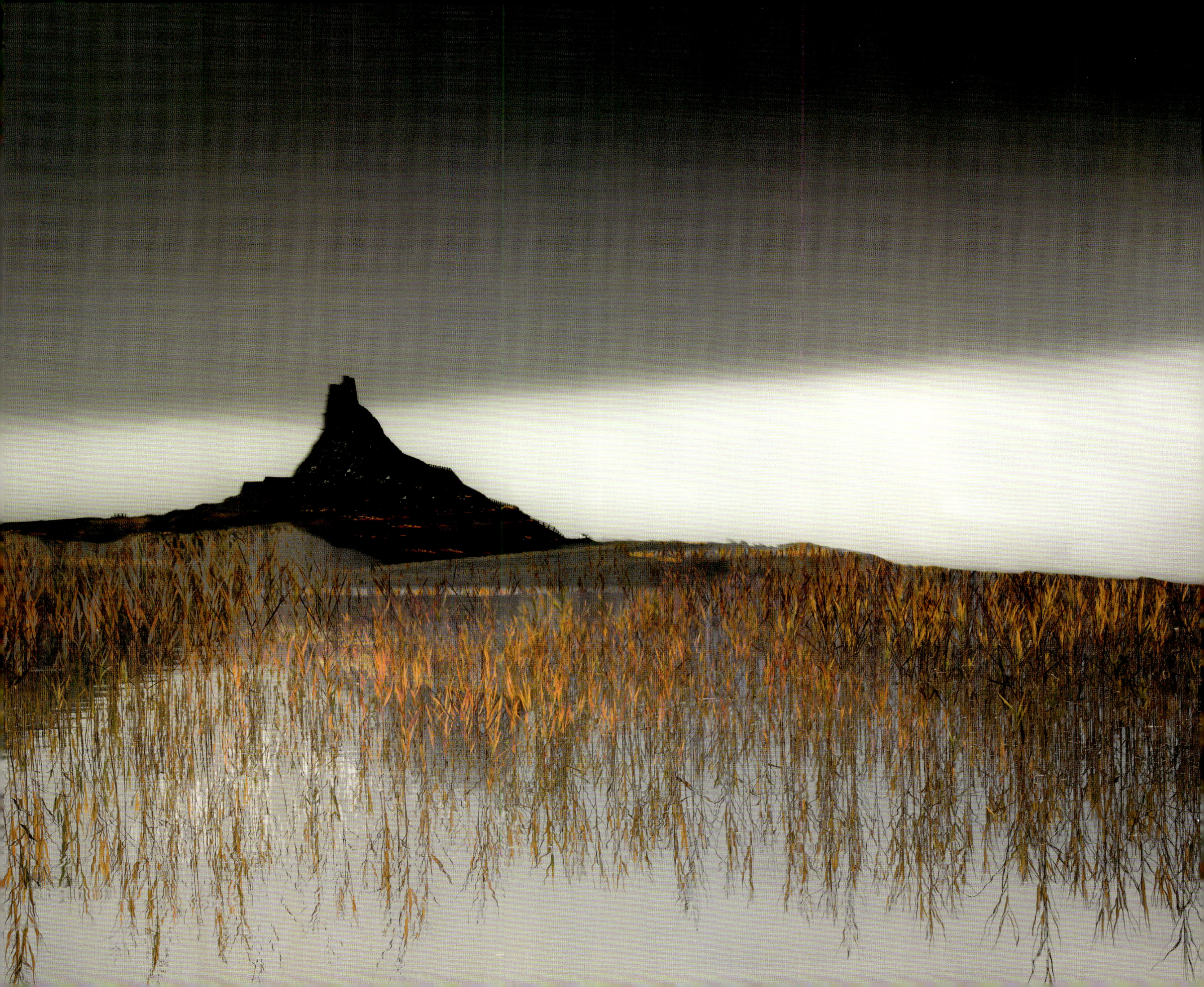

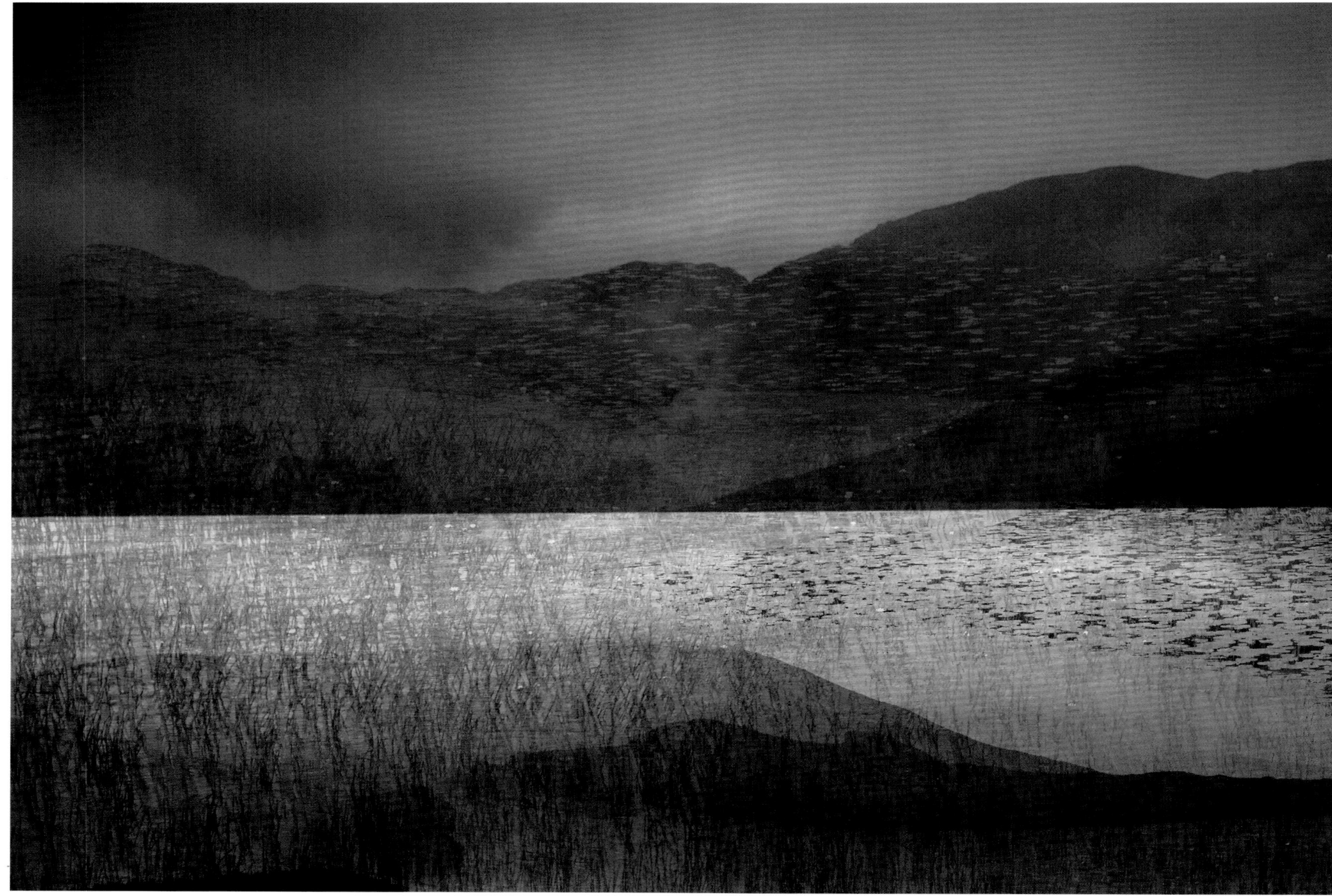

RAINDANCE

This was taken in the Outer Hebrides in a downpour. Unusually for me, it's a black-and-white image. I wanted to show the unrelenting gloom and the bottomless skies, and so I layered about three images together. To create a little blur, I used some intentional camera movement on one of those images. Although I almost invariably work in color, I decided that black and white best conveyed the atmosphere I was seeking.

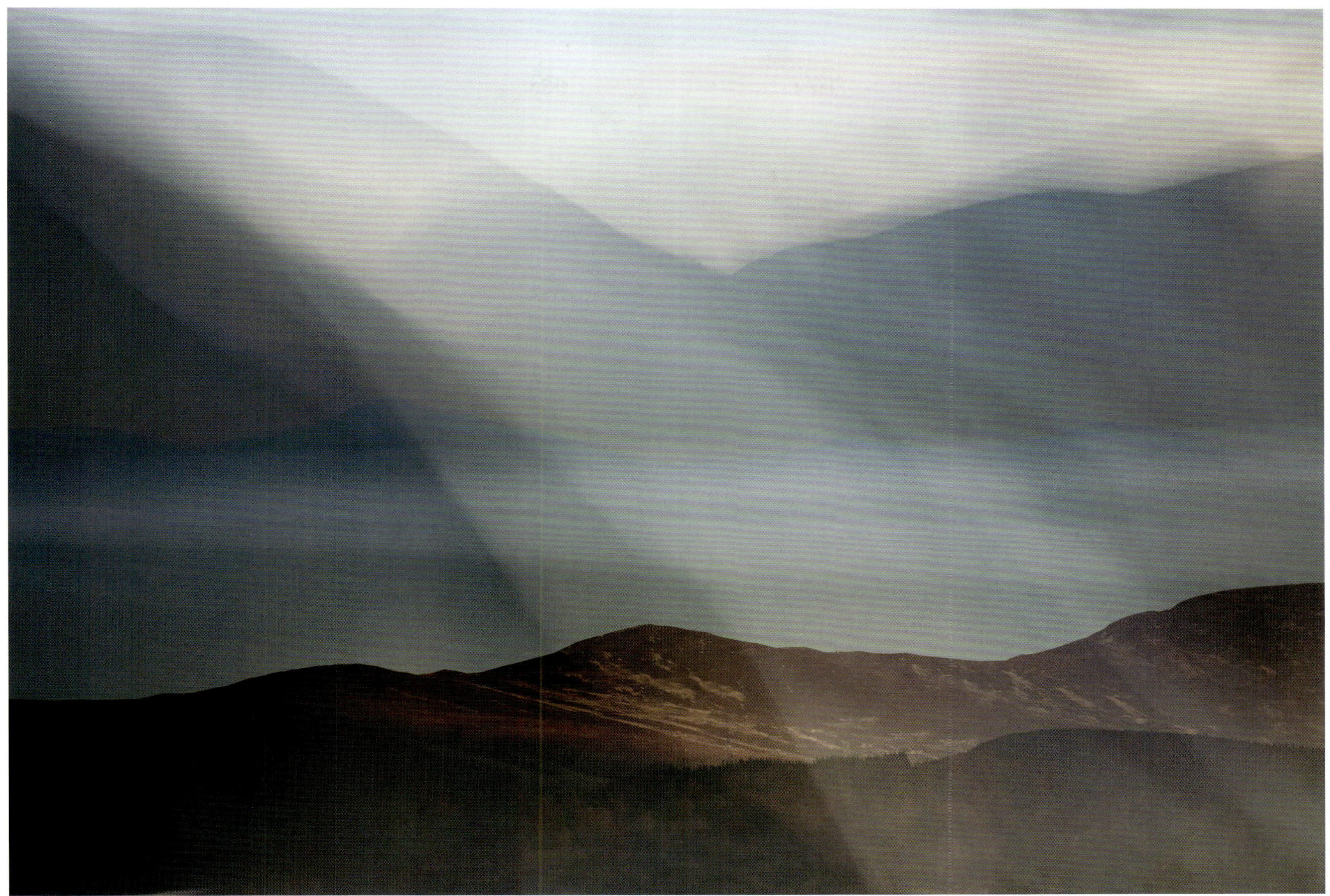

WHISPERING HILLS

This is an image made while leading a workshop in the Cairngorms. The weather fronts move quickly in Scotland and patience is usually rewarded. On this fall afternoon, the sun was disappearing rapidly and low cloud advancing. It was bitterly cold on the beach, but the unfolding drama was too good to miss. I layered several images on top of each other in an attempt to show the rapidly disappearing mountains and the advancing mist.

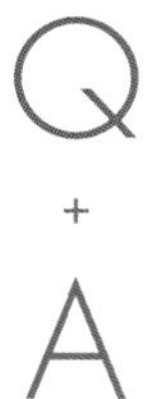

Q
+
A

You specialize in abstract, impressionistic images of the landscape, more closely resembling paintings than photographs—why did you decide to use a camera as a creative tool rather than, say, brushes and paints?

It was less of a calculated decision, more a case of things evolving unconsciously. I came back to photography after years of painting and never quite being able to make the marks on the canvas that I saw in my head. I didn't initially realize that it was possible to take photographs in such an impressionistic way. I started out as a street photographer as I believed (incorrectly, I now understand) that it was the only way of producing work that was unique and largely unrepeatable. However, after discovering intentional camera movement (ICM), I then went on to explore different techniques and ways of expressing myself in a style similar to what I had tried to achieve with a paintbrush. Little did I realize how fiendishly difficult this approach is.

What has been the biggest creative influence on your work?

That is very difficult to answer, and I would have to say it is a "who" rather than a "what." Chris Friel was the person responsible for setting me on the path I follow today and, after coming across his extraordinary images, I spent a long time—far too long—trying to emulate them. The celebrated street photographer Jay Maisel has also been an enormous influence—I have been fascinated by color and form for a long time, and Jay uses both with great artistry. He studied painting with Josef Albers whose book *Interaction of Color* remains an illuminating commentary into the art of seeing and the magic of color. Influences come from many sources—often subliminally. A book, a film, a poem, a piece of music— snippets of interest get mentally filed away and bubble up at the most unexpected moments. The most all- encompassing influence, however, would have to be the internet. We are utterly blessed to be living in an age where information is ours at the touch of a button—all manner of visual stimulation can be instantly accessed.

What features within the landscape inspire you when envisaging an image—what are looking for?

I look for contrasts first and foremost. The reasons for this are two-fold. From a technical point of view, it seems to me that multiple exposure or ICM photography works best when contrasting elements are present within the frame. With multiple exposure this is because blend modes prioritize certain tonal values and, to exploit this fully, I like to seek out areas of light and shade. Artistically, I also look for contrasts and conflicting elements to bring together within the frame. When I was working on my book *Fragile*, I was initially attracted to very obviously frail and vulnerable elements within the landscape. However, as I continued with the project in greater depth, I started to notice, and be fascinated by, conflicting elements and contrasts— specifically, the way the most delicate characteristics of my chosen subject matter were magnified when contrasted against their more sturdy surroundings. With regard to subject matter, I have an ongoing fascination with the ocean. I was brought up in Jersey in the Channel Islands, and I took easy access to the beach for granted. Now I live in East Sussex and the nearest coast is 45 minutes away— not a enormous trek, but far enough away for me to have to plan a visit. There is something utterly captivating about the sea; it speaks to me in so many ways. Having said that, trees and woodlands come a very close second and are, for me, much more accessible.

How do you piece together a composite picture—is it a step-by- step process and do you plan the whole process before you begin?

I have been shooting this way for several years now, so I do have a reasonable idea of how the camera is going to combine the frames before I begin. However, as mentioned before, it is a way of working that rewards play and experimentation and an enormous amount of thought. I find it quite difficult, if not impossible, to shoot images for myself when I am teaching, because it needs such a degree of concentration and complete absorption in the process. My camera allows me to review my progress as I shoot through a sequence and I slowly work away, making minor adjustments as I go. The number of variables that can be employed within a given sequence are virtually limitless—shutter speed, focal length, white balance, number of exposures—all these elements can be modified. And, obviously, one can point the camera in any direction one chooses throughout the sequence— really, there is an infinite number of permutations. And for people wanting to learn about this way of shooting, it is crucial to appreciate this. Beyond the initial instruction about how and why the camera blends images the way it does, it really is down to the photographer to go off and explore, preferably with the inquisitive mindset of a five-year-old. So, in a word, no; there is usually little planning, other than an innate understanding of what my camera will produce in a given set of circumstances.

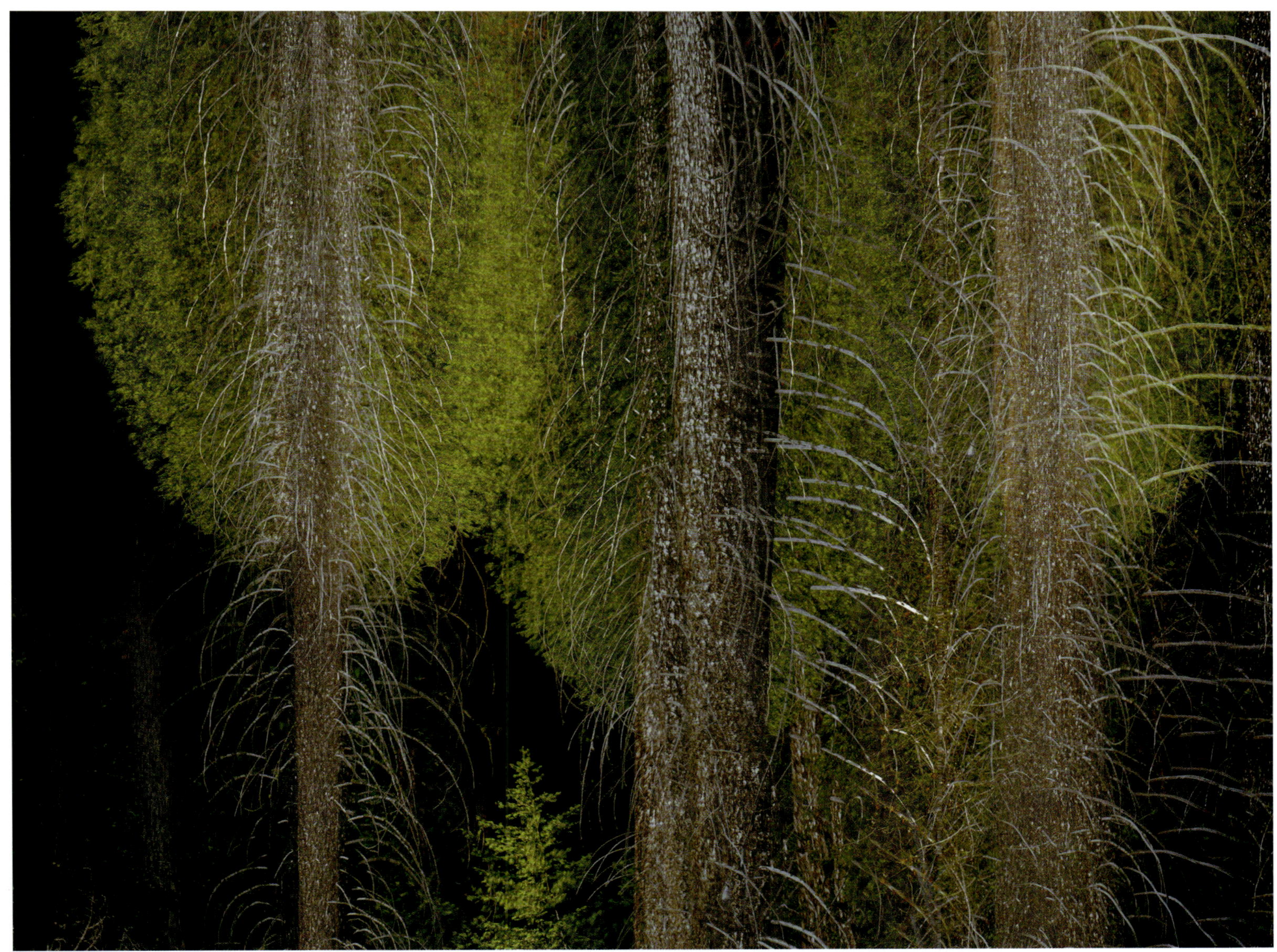

THE WOODS CALL WITH A HUNDRED VOICES

This image is one of an ongoing series about the different aspects of woodlands the world over. Taken in a pine forest in Wyoming, I was interested in the juxtaposition of the bare trunks of the pine trees and the highlighted foliage behind. I was trying to replicate the naive, lollipop shape of a child's drawing. By selecting a bright blend mode, I was able to overlay the silvery branches on top of the darker background.

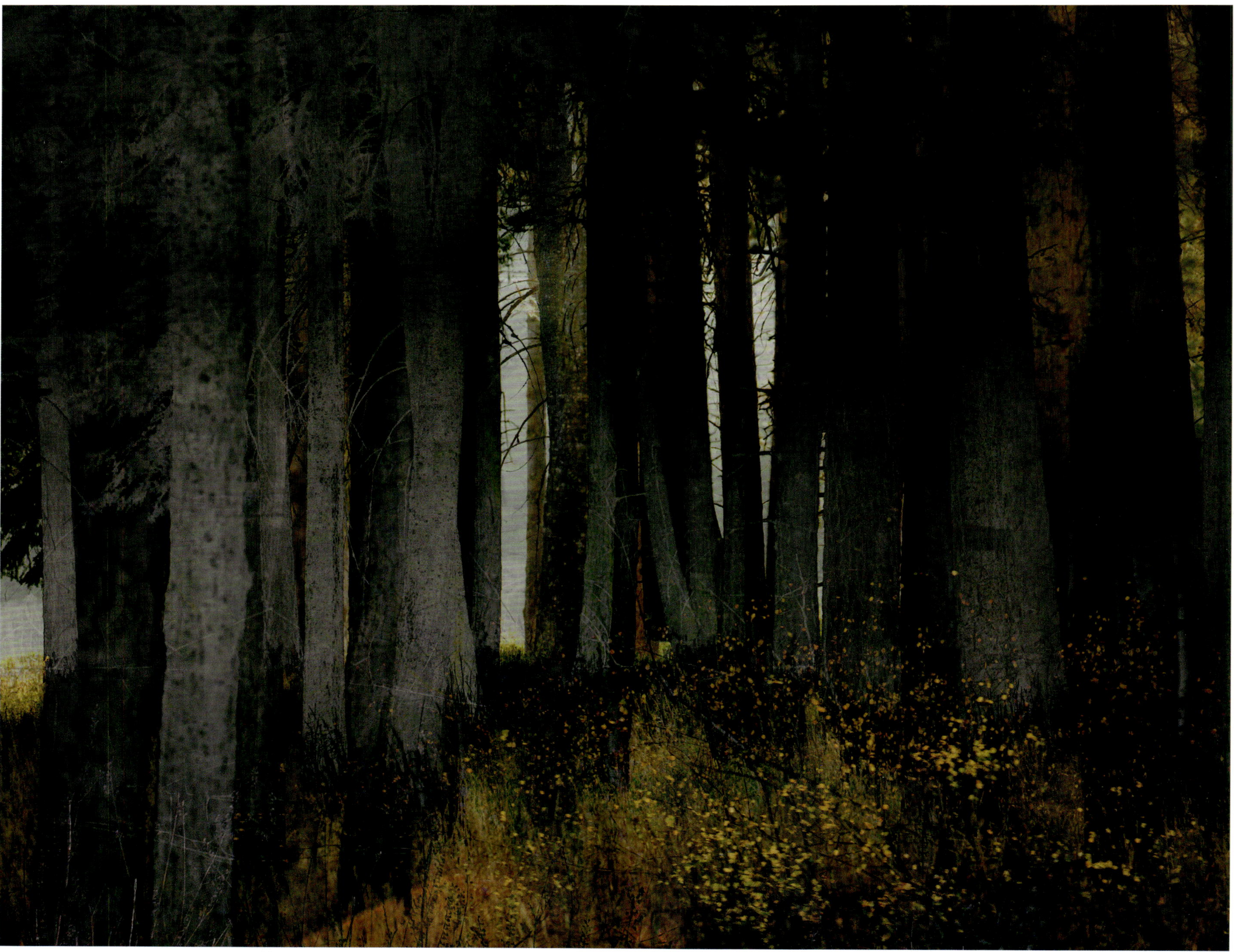

GOLD DUST

(Left) Another woodland fascination. This time I was taken by the shapes of the silhouetted trees and the sprinkling of golden foliage in the foreground. I took a long time and a lot of experimenting with the almost infinite number of variables I have at my disposal when combining images in camera. I sat in the same place for close to an hour to get the image as close to how I wanted it. I was trying to highlight the strong solidity of the trees and contrast it with the light delicacy of the fallen leaves.

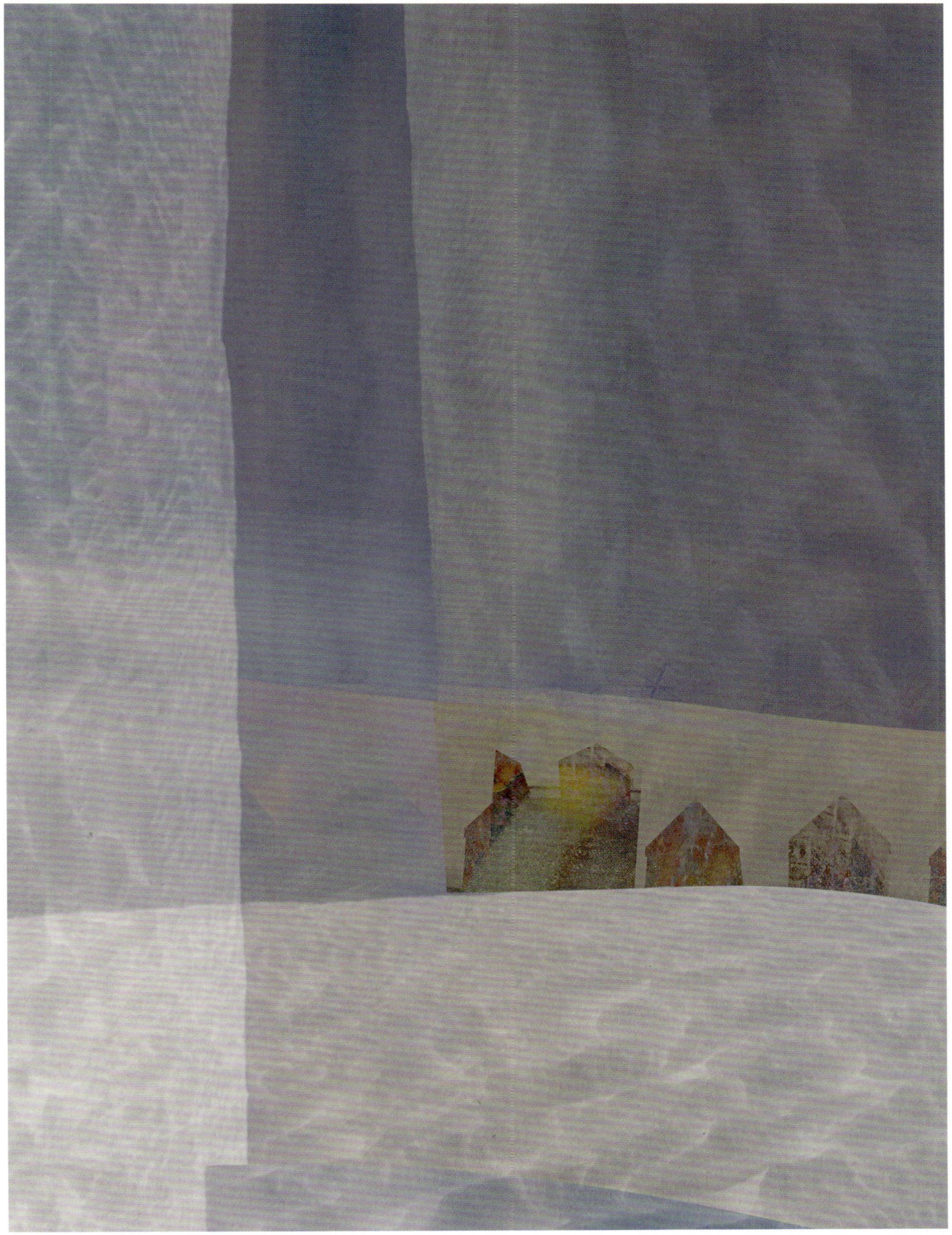

ALL AT SEA

(Right) My camera allows me to take an image that exists on my card and use it as a base to layer another sequence over the top. This allows me to mix locations and blend modes. This image is a fusion of shots taken at the White Sands National Monument in New Mexico and some beach huts at West Wittering. Similar techniques can obviously be employed in post-processing, and although I do use Photoshop, I prefer to get as much done in my camera as possible.

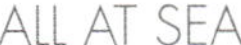

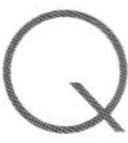

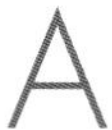

What are the key post-processing techniques you employ when creating one of your images?

Just as the shooting techniques mentioned before aren't prescriptive, so it is with post-processing. I have no interest in a beautifully arranged histogram—my exposure values are an artistic decision that I make, dependent on what it is I am trying to convey. Likewise, the color palette I use. As mentioned before, I am fascinated by color, so I spend an inordinate amount of time abusing the hue, saturation, and luminance sliders in Lightroom, in order to try to create tension or harmony in the image. It is during such endeavors that I realize how lucky I am to shoot the way I do—I have no constraints about the accuracy of the hue or tonal values. If I say the grass is going to be red, then so be it. Obviously, this approach is largely informed by my background in painting, but once you cast aside the shackles of conventional shooting and editing techniques there is an enormous amount of fun to be had playing around with colors and tones.

How do you set up your camera for intentional camera movement? Do you overlay multiple exposures in camera or in processing?

Intentional camera movement can be achieved with any camera, as long as one has a way of limiting the amount of light reaching the sensor (or film). One of the reasons this way of shooting suits my personality is because it requires very little in the way of accessories. Accessories—which I have a tendency to lose, or break, smear, or sit on—are largely best avoided. I do have a variable ND filter, which I use when absolutely necessary, but my 70–300mm lens will stop down to f/45 and this is enough to give me a two- or three-second shutter speed most of the time. I rarely shoot in the middle of the day, and am often ensconced in darkish woodlands, so I can usually get away with not using a filter. My camera can overlay up to nine exposures and produce a composite image utilizing an assortment of blend modes. I do some post-processing work but I would rather get as much right in camera as I can, simply because I already spend far too much time in front of my computer and it's much more relaxing being out in the landscape.

You're a great advocate of printing images—why do you think a physical print of a picture is so important?

I think it's important for a number of reasons. It's enormously satisfying to produce something tangible at the end of one's endeavors. The process itself—while often quite frustrating and reasonably complex to master—is fascinating. It's lovely to be able to experiment with different papers, print sizes, mounts, and frames, for instance, to best show off a piece of work. And they are lovely things to own and put on one's wall. My studio walls are adorned with work from photographers I admire, and I feel lucky to be able to gaze up at them whenever I need a break from the screen. Back in the day, we would send our films off to be processed, collect them a week later, then probably put them in a shoe box under the bed to gather dust. But at least they were there for us and subsequent generations to enjoy. I find it hard to imagine people crowding around a backlit screen for a good old dose of nostalgia. The chances are the files wouldn't be readable anyway. Or the hard drive would be corrupted. The USB ports would almost certainly be outdated if my spidery collection of wires and adaptors is anything to go by.

As a master of landscape photography, what is your motivation to continue making photographs?

Because I love it. It's what I like doing more than anything else in the world. It's a source of huge frustration that, as my work has gained more exposure, and as the teaching, the exhibitions, the interviews, and so on, have presented themselves, the time I get for my own work has been drastically curtailed. I suppose its ego that has me agreeing to all these opportunities that come along—not a particularly edifying admission, I'm sure you'll agree. It aggrieves me that there is so much I want to learn, so many ideas to pursue, so many things to master, and time is so short. The old adage, "the more you know, the more you know you don't know," has never been more true. And that, I suppose, is the motivation—the hunger for knowledge and improvement. I console myself with the thought that the day I think I've got it nailed is the day I might as well give up.

TECHNICAL INFORMATION

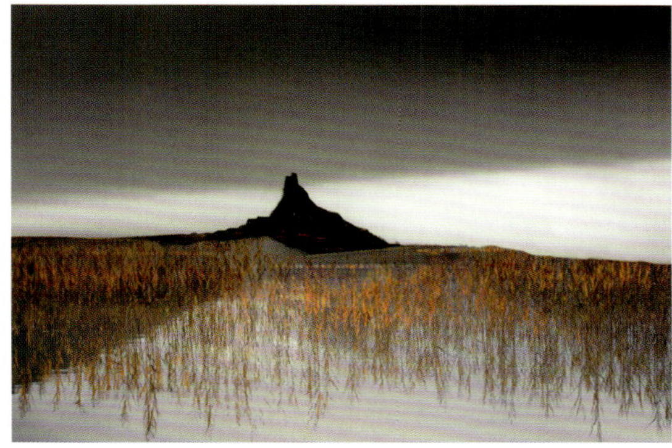

APPROACHING LINDISFARNE
LINDISFARNE, NORTHUMBERLAND,
ENGLAND

Camera: Canon EOS 5DS R
Lens/Focal length: Canon 70-300mm f/4.5-5.6
Process: Multiple exposure of about five images, varied aperture, shutter speed, white balance, ISO

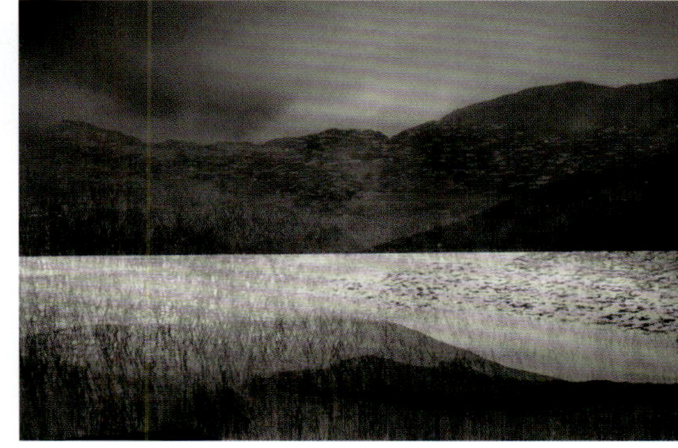

RAINDANCE
OUTER HEBRIDES,
SCOTLAND

Camera: Canon EOS 5D Mark III
Lens/Focal length: Canon 70-300mm f/4.5-5.6
Process: Multiple exposure of about three images, varied aperture, shutter speed, white balance, ISO

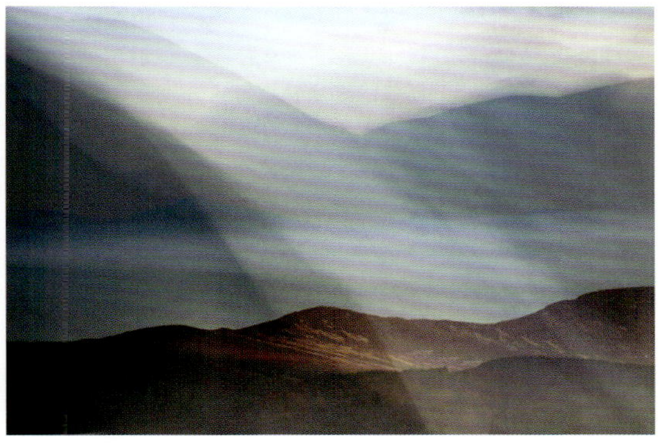

WHISPERING HILLS
LOCH MORLICH, CAIRNGORMS NATIONAL PARK,
SCOTLAND

Camera: Canon EOS 5DS R
Lens/Focal length: Canon 70-300mm f/4.5-5.6
Process: Multiple exposure of about seven images, varied aperture, shutter speed, white balance ISO

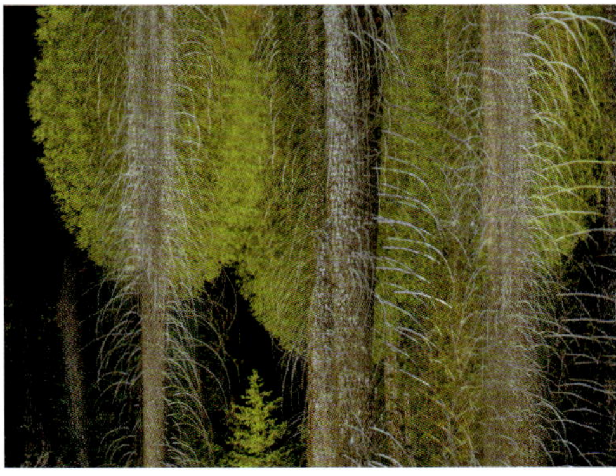

THE WOODS CALL WITH A HUNDRED VOICES
WYOMING, USA

Camera: Canon EOS 5D Mark III
Lens/Focal length: Canon 70-300mm f/4.5-5.6
Process: Multiple exposure of about five images, varied aperture, shutter speed, white balance, ISO

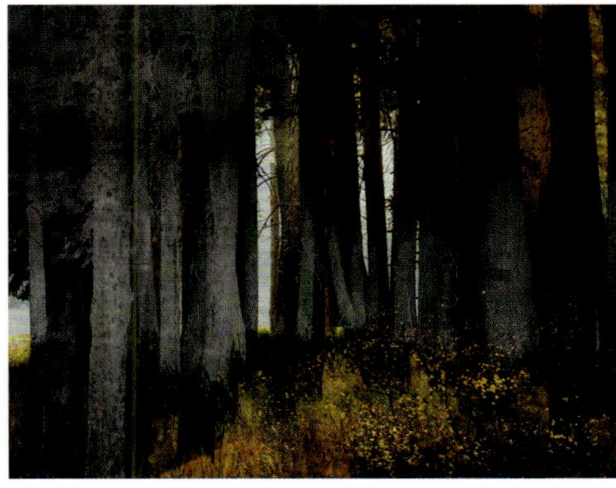

GOLD DUST

Camera: Canon EOS 5DS R
Lens/Focal length: Canon 70-300mm f/4.5-5.6
Process: Multiple exposure of about five images, varied aperture, shutter speed, white balance, ISO

ALL AT SEA
WHITE SANDS NATIONAL
MONUMENT, NEW MEXICO, USA,
AND WEST WITTERING, ENGLAND

Camera: Canon EOS 5D Mark III
Lens/Focal length: Canon 70-300mm f/4.5-5.6
Process: Multiple exposure of about seven images, varied aperture, shutter speed, white balance, ISO

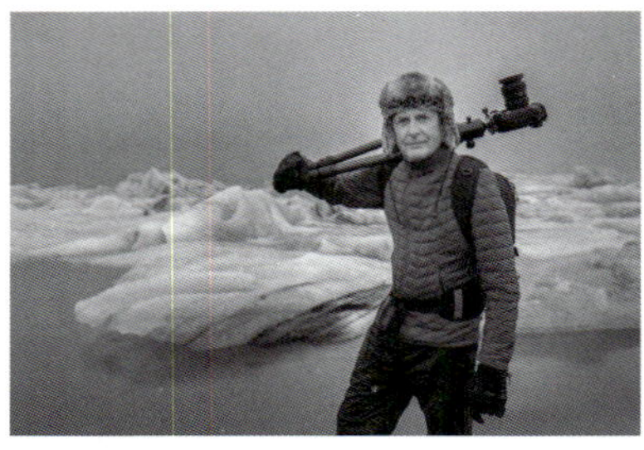

ART WOLFE
MASTER OF CONSERVATION

www.artwolfe.com

Art runs a wide range of events, seminars, and workshops all around the world. For more information, and to purchase prints, books, cards, calendars, and DVDs, visit Art's website.

Facebook: art.wolfe.photography
Instagram: @artwolfe
Google+: +artwolfe
Twitter: @artwolfe

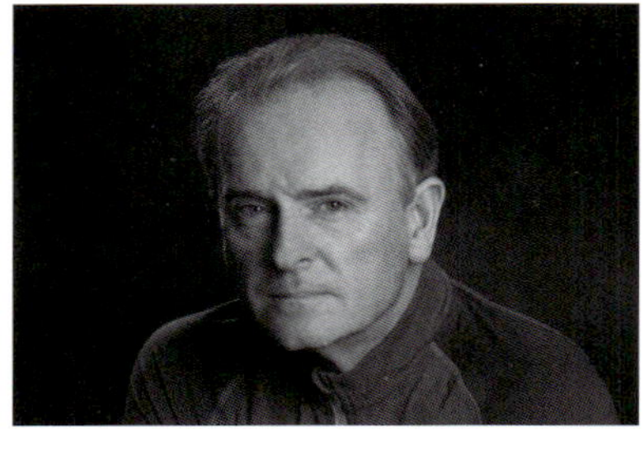

COLIN PRIOR
MASTER OF MOUNTAINS

www.colinprior.co.uk

Colin's current project, *Fragile*, explores the habitats of wild birds and their vulnerability to change, and he was recently the subject of two BBC documentaries entitled *Mountain Man*.

Facebook: colinpriorphotographer
Instagram: @colinprior
Twitter: @colinprior

Publications:
Scotland's Finest Landscapes, 2014
High Light, 2010
The World's Wild Places, 2006
Highland Wilderness, 2004
Living Tribes, 2003
Scotland—The Wild Places, 2001
Highland Wilderness, 1993

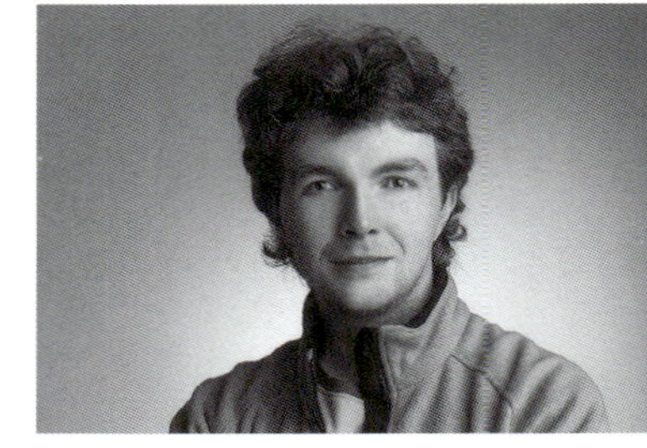

DANIEL KORDAN
MASTER OF ADVENTURE

www.danielkordan.com

Daniel runs photographic workshops, tours, and expeditions throughout the year. For more information, visit his website.

Facebook: dk.scape
Instagram: @danielkordan

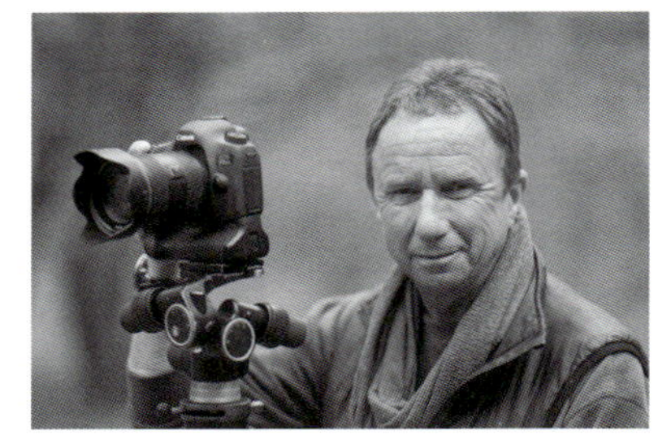

DAVID NOTON
MASTER OF LIGHT

www.davidnoton.com

David enjoys a loyal following from photographers and travelers across the globe and he communicates directly to them with his *f11 Photography Magazine*, monthly email updates, and social media posts—many of which are sent from the field.

www.f11photographymagazine.com
Facebook: davidnotonphotography
Instagram: @notonphoto
Twitter @davidnoton

Publications:
Full Frame, 2010
The Vision, 2013
Waiting for the Light, 2008

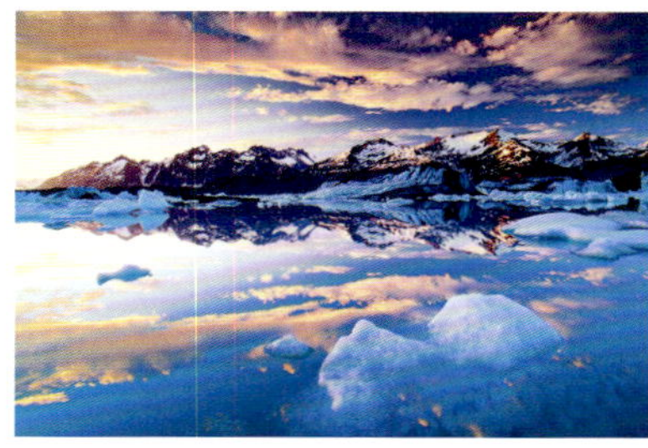

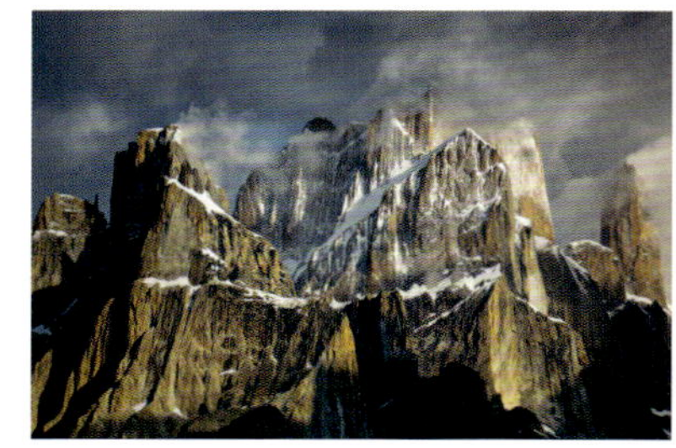

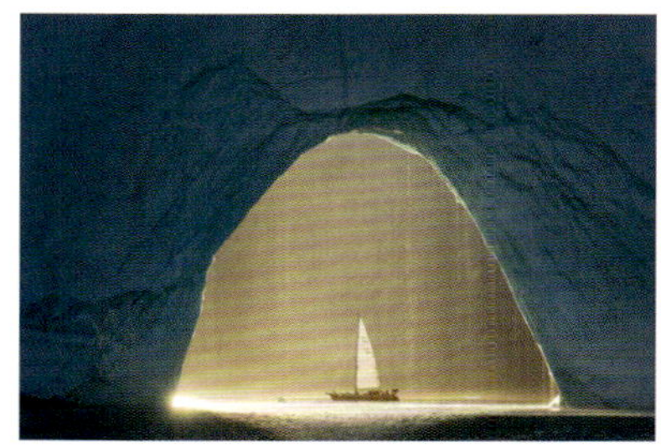

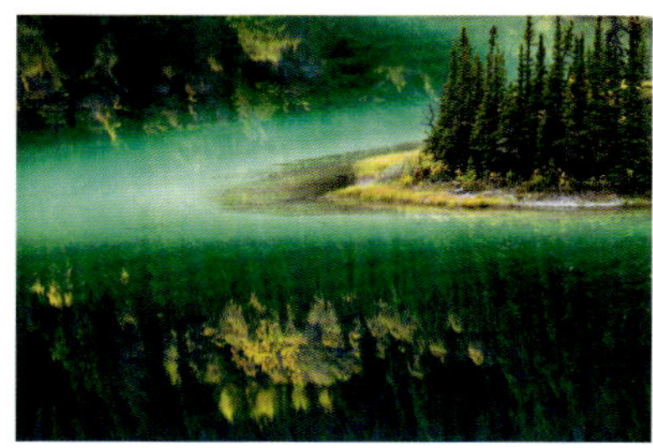

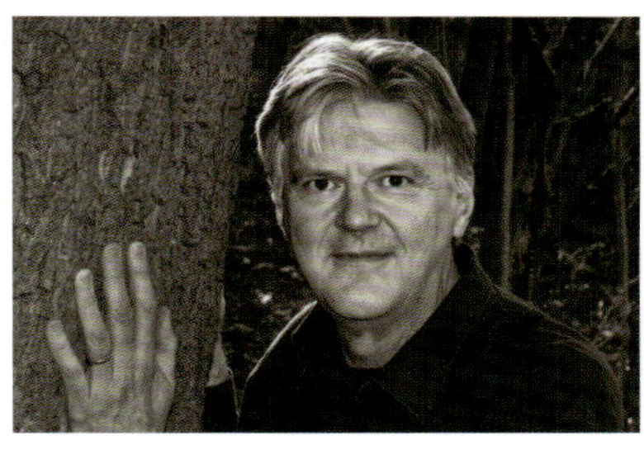

HANS STRAND
MASTER OF INTIMATE LANDSCAPES

www.hansstrand.com

Hans has displayed his work in numerous exhibitions and publishes in many international magazines. He has published seven books featuring his landscape photography.

Publications:
Intimate I, 2015
Iceland, Above & Below, 2014

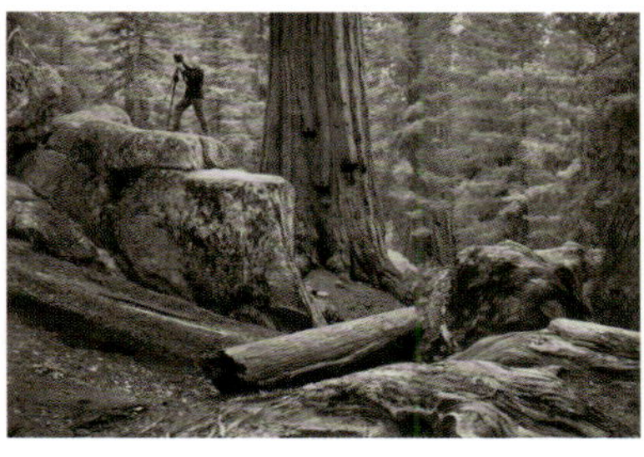

JOE CORNISH
MASTER OF BALANCE

www.joecornishgallery.co.uk

The Joe Cornish Gallery in Northallerton, North Yorkshire, in the United Kingdom, is a welcoming space for all photographers and art lovers alike. There is a great café, reading spaces, and books, the work of many outstanding photographers on show, and regular events. A workshop space is available for hire, as well as printing facilities.

Facebook: jcornishgallery
Twitter: @jcornishgallery

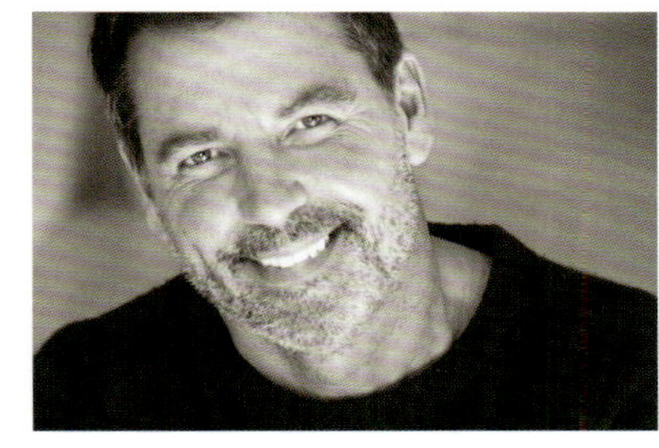

JONATHAN CHRITCHLEY
MASTER OF MINIMALISM

www.jonathanchritchley.com

Jonathan was named one of the "Top 100 Photographers of All Time" by *The Sunday Times*. His first book, *Silver*, a 136-page fine art edition, was published in 2013, and in 2016 he was made a Fellow of the Royal Geographical Society (FRGS). An active supporter of ocean conservation, Jonathan currently resides in the South of France, close to Biarritz, with his wife and young family.

www.captureearth.com
www.oceancapture.com

Publication:
Silver, 2013

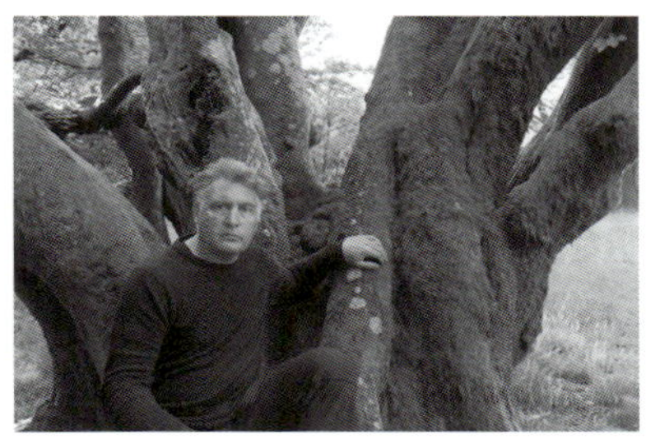

LARS VAN DE GOOR
MASTER OF WOODLAND

www.larsvandegoor.com

In September 2017, Lars and his wife exchanged their house for a mobile home to traveling Europe. You can follow their experiences and see Lars' images on his blog.

Facebook: larsvandegoor
Instagram: @larsvandegoor
Twitter: @larsvandegoor

Publication:
Seebook
www.larsvandegoor.com/seebook

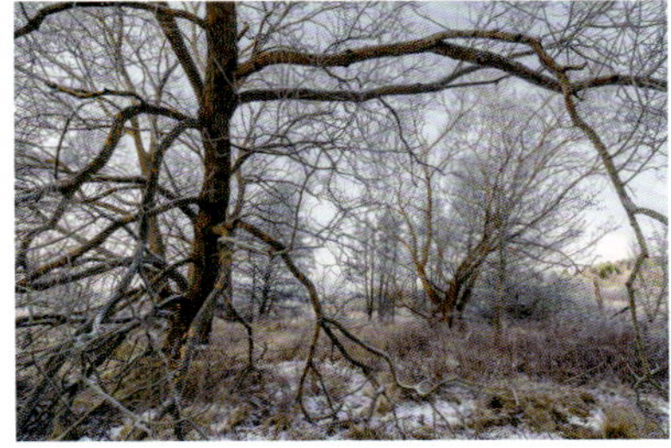

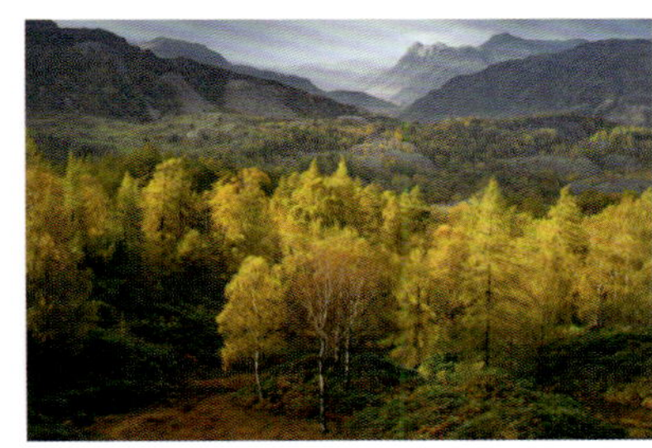

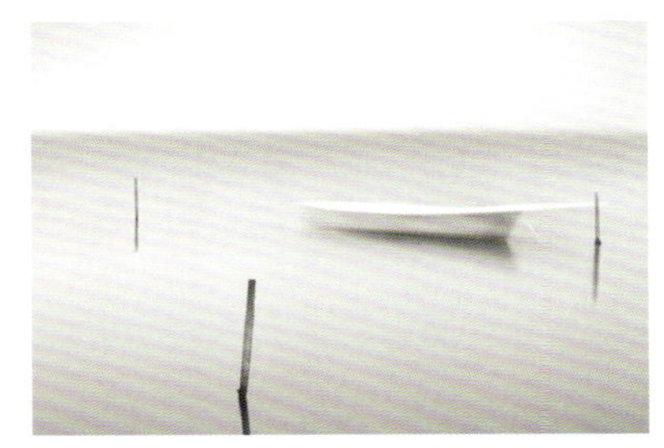

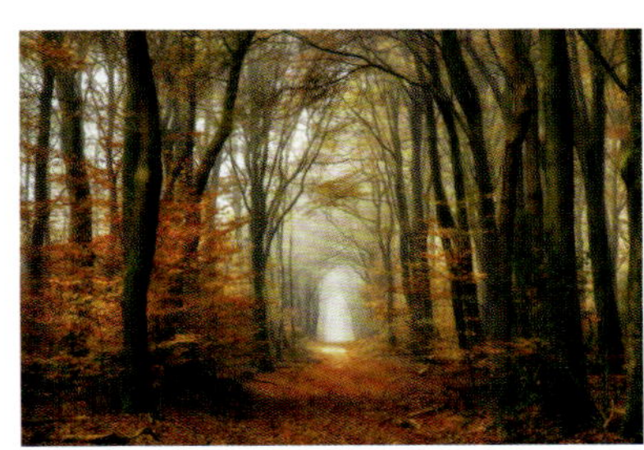

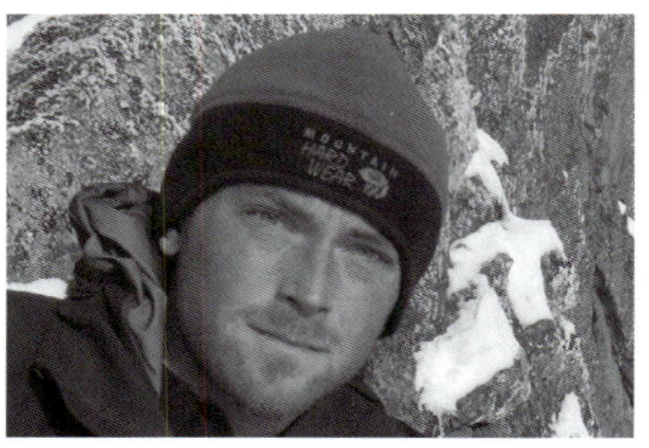

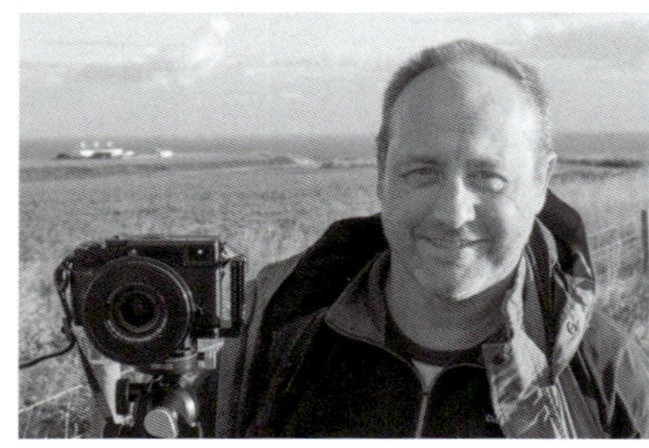

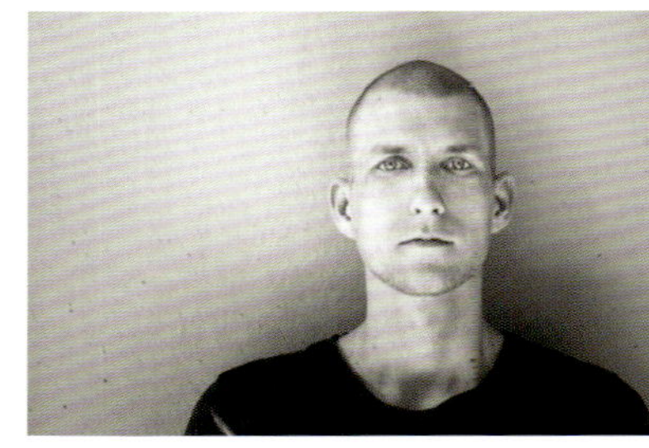

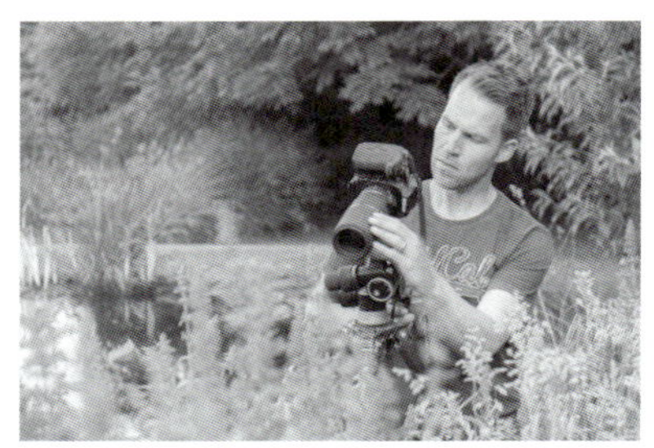

MARC ADAMUS
MASTER OF WILDERNESS

www.marcadamus.com

Details of Marc's photographic "adventure" tours, along with his publications and fine art prints, can be found on his website.

MARK BAUER
MASTER OF MOOD

www.markbauerphotography.com

Details of Mark's photography workshops can be found on his website, along with fine art prints for sale and a list of publications.

Facebook: markbauerphotography
Instagram: @markbauerphotography
Twitter: @markbauerphoto

Publications:
Photographing Dorset, 2016
The Art of Landscape Photography
   (with Ross Hoddinott), 2014
The Landscape Photography Workshop
   (with Ross Hoddinott), 2012

MIKKO LAGERSTEDT
MASTER OF NIGHTTIME

www.mikkolagerstedt.com

Prints of Mikko's work are available from his website, which also features a blog and technical information.

Contact: info@mikkolagerstect.com
Facebook: mikkolagerstedt
Instagram: @mikkolagerstedt

ROSS HODDINOTT
MASTER OF SIMPLICITY

www.rosshoddinott.co.uk

Ross is an Ambassador for Nikon UK, Manfrotto and a Global Icon for F-stop Gear. He is the author of several photography books and co-runs Dawn 2 Dusk Photography—who specialize in running workshops throughout the UK.

Contact: info@rosshoddinott.co.uk
Workshops:
www.dawn2duskphotography.co.uk

Publications:
The Art of Landscape Photography
   (with Mark Bauer), 2014
Wildlife Photography Workshop
   (with Ben Hall), 2013
The Landscape Photography Workshop
   (with Mark Bauer), 2012

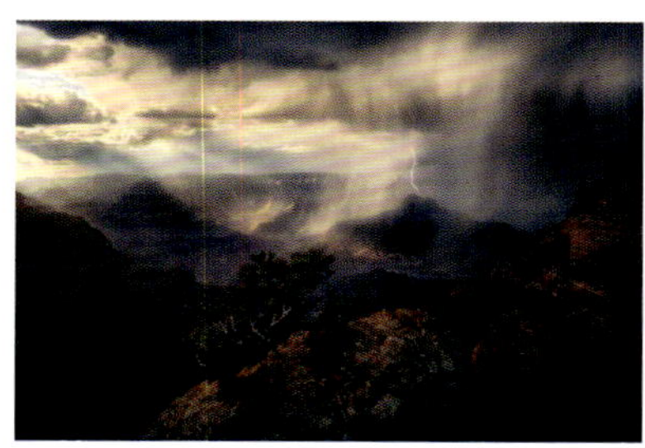

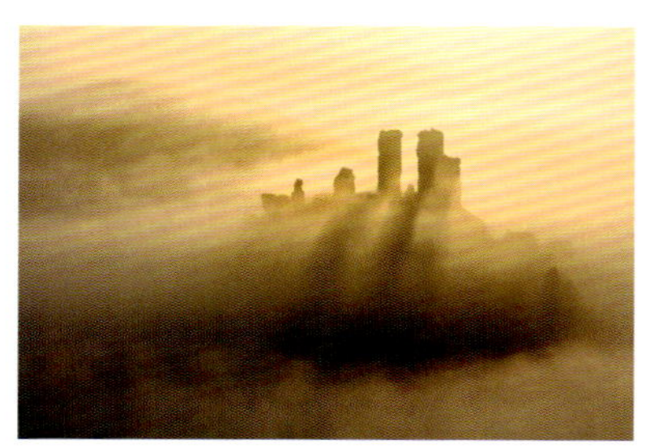

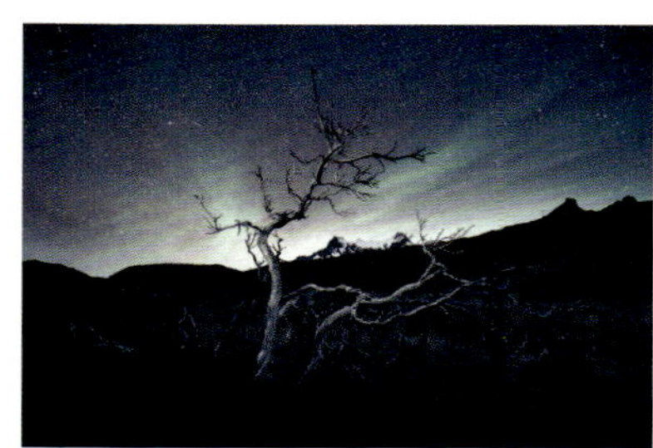

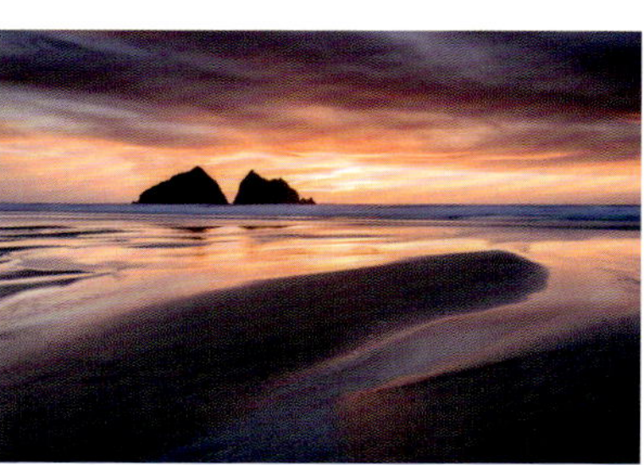

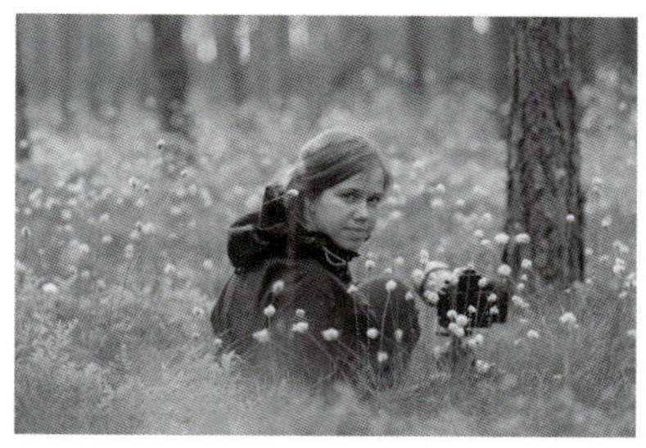

SANDRA BARTOCHA
MASTER OF CREATIVITY

www.bartocha-photography.com

Sandra was part of the photographic team on the pan-European Wild Wonders of Europe initiative and has been working on a long-term project about the north of Europe—LYS. As a result, Sandra has produced a 45-minute audiovisual show, as well as a large coffee-table book: *LYS—An Intimate Journey to the North*. Recent projects include regional work in northern Germany, as well as a new long-term project about tree species.

Facebook: bartocha.photography

Publications:
LYS—An Intimate Journey to the North, 2016

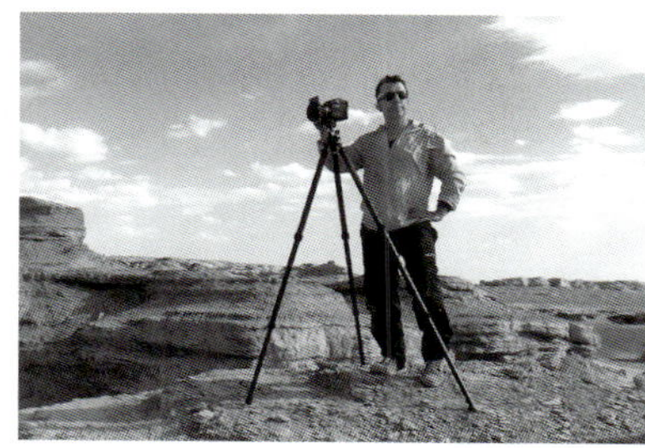

THIERRY BORNIER
MASTER OF WEATHER

www.thierrybornier.com

Thierry has had his work published in *National Geographic*, and is the winner of many photography competitions, such as the One Eyeland and EPSON International Pano Awards. Thierry encourages all people who enjoy landscape photography to travel to China to experience the beautiful places that he has discovered. He loves to share his passion for landscape photography in China, and runs workshops to inspire and help other photographers to capture these amazing natural and historic scenes.

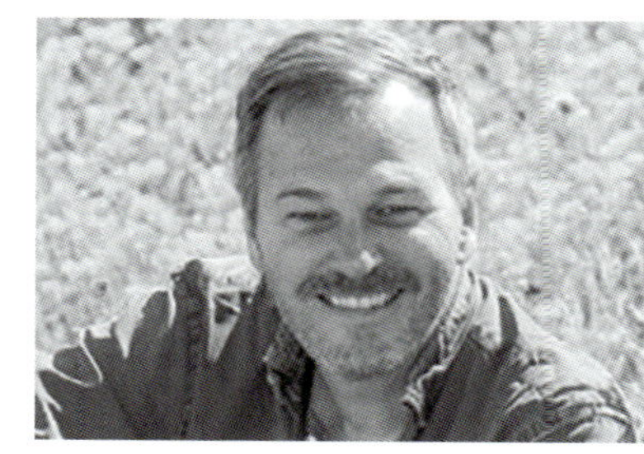

TOM MACKIE
MASTER OF COLOR

www.tommackie.com

Tom Mackie has written several books, most notably *Photos With Impact* and *Tom Mackie's Landscape Photography Secrets*, as well as numerous articles for photography magazines in the United Kingdom and abroad. He lectures to other professionals on the art of landscape photography, and runs a series of acclaimed photography workshops in spectacular locations around the world.

Publications:
Tom Mackie's Landscape Photography Secrets, 2008
Photos With Impact, 2006

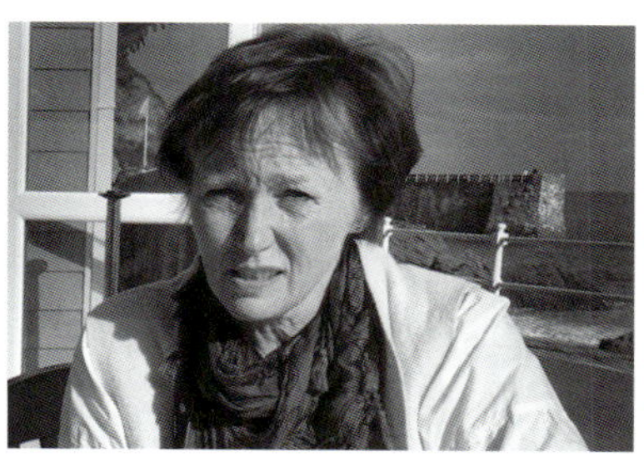

VALDA BAILEY
MASTER OF IMPRESSIONISM

www.valdabailey.com

Details of Valda's work, workshops, galleries and publications can be found on her website along with her blog.

Workshops: www.lightandland.co.uk
Print sales: boshamgallery.com
Facebook: valdabaileyphoto
Twitter: @tanyards

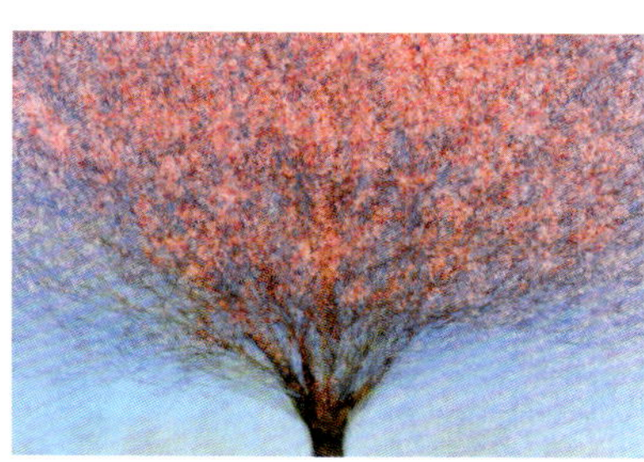

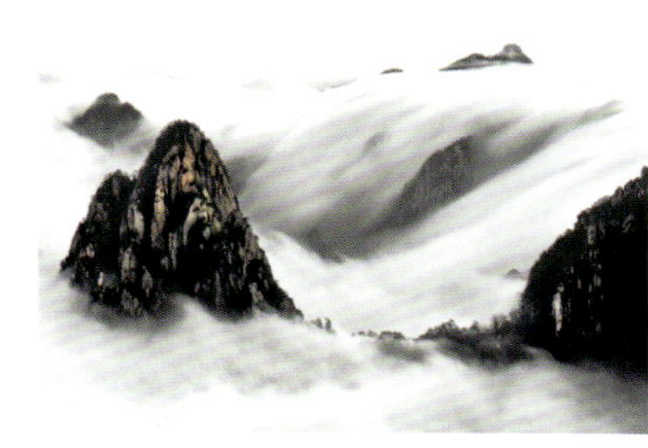

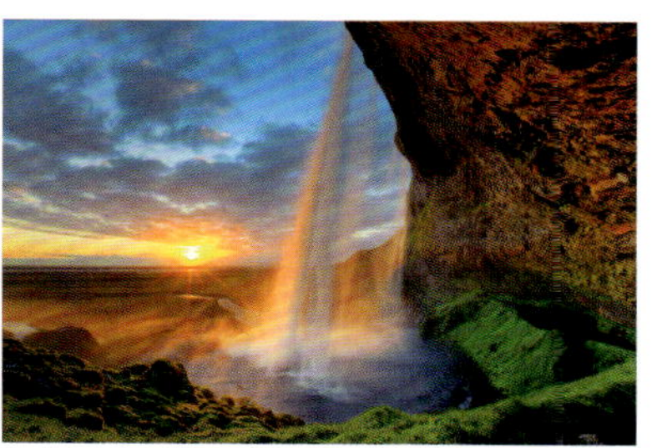

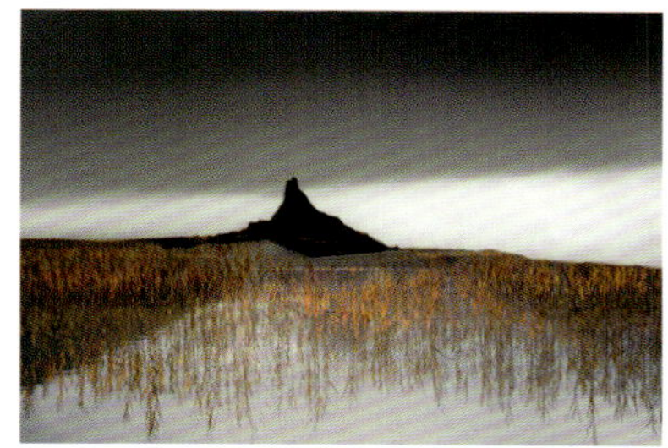

ACKNOWLEDGMENTS

The publishers and editors would like to thank the photographers for all their hard work and assistance, and for their kind permission to reproduce the images in this book:

Cover, p.8–11, p.122–131 images copyright © Ross Hoddinott/rosshoddinott.co.uk
Title page, p.142–151 images copyright © Thierry Bornier/thier-ybornier.com
p.12–21 images copyright © Art Wolfe/artwolfe.com
p.22–31 images copyright © Colin Prior/colinprior.co.uk
p.32–41 images copyright © Daniel Kordan/danielkordan.com
p.42–51 images copyright © David Noton/davidnoton.com
p.52–61 images copyright © Hans Strand/hansstrand.com
p.62–71 images copyright © Joe Cornish/joecornish.co.uk
p.72–81 images copyright © Jonathan Chritchley/jonathanchritchley.com
p.82–91 images copyright © Lars van de Goor/larsvandegoor.com
p.92–101 images copyright © Marc Adamus/marcadamus.com
p.102–111 images copyright © Mark Bauer/marcbauerphotography.com
p.112–121 images copyright © Mikko Lagerstedt/mikkolagerstedt.com
p.132–141 images copyright © Sandra Bartocha/bartocha-photography.com
p.152–161 images copyright © Tom Mackie/tommackie.com
p.162–171 images copyright © Valda Bailey/valdabailey.com
p.172–175 images copyright © individual photographers, as above
p.173 Joe Cornish portrait photograph copyright © David Ward

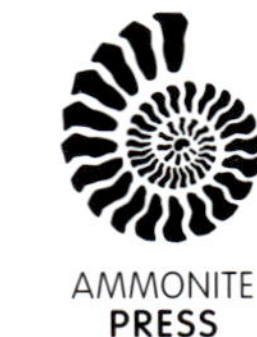

AMMONITE
PRESS

www.ammonitepress.com